Dedicated to Glenn Davidson

Glenn:

I sincerely enjoyed our brief
debate the other day.
; I hope this book gives you
fuel to come back for more
so we can go and discuss
these things with a beer!

Warm regards

Macca

BUSINESS SERVICES ORCHESTRATION

BUSINESS SERVICES ORCHESTRATION

THE HYPERTIER OF INFORMATION TECHNOLOGY

WAQAR SADIQ
Electronic Data Systems

FELIX RACCA
Fuego Inc.

CAMBRIDGE
UNIVERSITY PRESS

PUBLISHED BY THE PRESS SYNDICATE OF THE UNIVERSITY OF CAMBRIDGE
The Pitt Building, Trumpington Street, Cambridge, United Kingdom

CAMBRIDGE UNIVERSITY PRESS
The Edinburgh Building, Cambridge CB2 2RU, UK
40 West 20th Street, New York, NY 10011-4211, USA
477 Williamstown Road, Port Melbourne, VIC 3207, Australia
Ruiz de Alarcón 13, 28014 Madrid, Spain
Dock House, The Waterfront, Cape Town 8001, South Africa

http://www.cambridge.org

First published 2003

Printed in the United States of America

Typefaces Berkeley Oldstyle 10.75/13 pt and Franklin Gothic   *System* LATEX 2$_\varepsilon$ [TB]

A catalog record for this book is available from the British Library.

Library of Congress Cataloging in Publication Data
Sadiq, Waqar.
    Business services orchestration : the hypertier of information technology / Waqar
Sadiq, Felix Racca.
       p.   cm.
    Includes bibliographical references and index.
       ISBN 0-521-81981-4
    1. Business – Computer network resources.   2. Business information services.   I. Racca,
Felix, 1955-   II. Title.
    HF54.56 .S23   2002
    658.4′038 – dc21   2002074198

ISBN 0 521 81981 4 hardback

This book is dedicated to my wife, Talat, and to my children, Zan and Marium, for their continuing support and understanding while I was writing this book.

Waqar Sadiq

I dedicate this book to my wife, Marta, who has had infinite patience during the writing of the book, and to my children, Marina, Santiago, and Mariano, who were deprived of their usual weekend outings with their Dad.

Felix Racca

About the Authors

Waqar Sadiq has more than 16 years of experience in software development. He currently leads EDS's Web services strategy as head of several proof-of-concept teams for building future service offerings. Prior to that, he developed application server technology before EJB specifications came to market. Mr. Sadiq has also worked in key technical roles at Vitria Technologies, maker of business process automation software, helping clients solve real problems by automating business processes. He is the author of *Developing Business Systems Using CORBA*.

Felix Racca has more than two decades of experience developing and delivering the right software at the right time. Alongside fellow developer Emilio Lopez-Gabeiras, Mr. Racca co-founded InterSoft S.A. in 1983. By 1989, InterSoft took a majority share of the enterprise resource planning software market in Latin America. In 1996, Mr. Racca co-founded Fuego Technology Corporation, which focused on the Business Process Management tool that today has become Fuegotech. Mr. Racca is a frequent speaker and contributor to the enterprise infrastructure software community. He has appeared in numerous magazines, including cover stories in *Information Week*.

Contents

Foreword

Does technology encourage or inhibit business innovation? At first blush, the question seems naïve and the answer obvious: It is clear that information technology is an enormous spur to innovation. New technological capabilities enable companies to perform activities of which they had previously only dreamed. Modern data management facilities, for example, allow organizations to conduct customer analyses that they always had desired but previously had been unable to do and thereby develop customized offerings and marketing messages. In some cases, new technology even allows companies to solve problems of which they had previously been unaware. A classic example is the invention of the xerographic copier. Prior to its arrival in the marketplace, people did not have an expressed need for such a device. They used carbon paper and similar technologies to make extra copies of a document while it was being produced and resigned themselves to living in a world where one could not make copies thereafter. Indeed, early market research studies showed no demand for a convenience copier. Only later, as people started to appreciate the capability that the new technology offered them did they recognize the opportunity that it represented.

At times, however, technology can have the opposite effect and inhibit business innovation. In particular, investments in expensive technology platforms represent a "sunk cost" for most organizations, a cost that they are reluctant to reincur. Even when they recognize that new technology might have important applications, the prospect of abandoning existing technology and the investment in it prevents many companies from acquiring and exploiting the new technology. The costs that discourage innovation go beyond the money needed to purchase the new technology; they also include the expense and travail of converting databases, retraining personnel, and so on. This helps account for the peculiar phenomenon where developing countries often are equipped with more advanced communications infrastructures than are highly industrialized countries. Countries with massive investments in facilities find it difficult to abandon those investments to move to the next generation of technology.

Nowhere is this inhibiting behavior more evident than in the sphere of so-called legacy systems. In effect, a legacy system is any application system that a company regrets having installed in the first place, usually because it lacks the capability to support new requirements. Clearly, no one sets out to create such a system. All large system investments must clear such hurdles as extensibility, compatibility, upgradability, and so on. Yet if the history of information systems teaches us anything, it is that organizations inevitably create systems that turn into legacies. The underlying reason is, of course, that one doesn't know what one doesn't know. When installing a major system, managers can validate that it satisfies all the criteria currently on the company's radar screen. The nature of business, however, is such that new business goals and systems criteria inevitably arise, and only by the rarest happenstance is an existing system compatible with these new goals and criteria. For example, when systems were built in the 1960s and 1970s, few people saw the need to ensure Y2K compatibility; this issue came to light only in the late 1990s and led, of course, to massive remediation and system replacement efforts.

In the absence of catastrophic consequences, such as those associated with Y2K, companies cannot afford to replace their legacy systems simply to meet a new business need. The number of times that managers have been told by systems personnel that "The system won't let us do that" and that replacing the system with one that could do that is far too costly is beyond counting. Systems installed by well-meaning people to meet immediate business needs inevitably turn out to be inadequate for meeting future needs and opportunities not anticipated at the time the systems were installed. As a result, these needs and opportunities remain unaddressed for long periods, while aggressive new competitors, unburdened with legacies of the past, are able to respond to these opportunities and harvest enormous benefits from them.

Today, this phenomenon is being felt keenly in the arena of business processes. "Process" is a term widely misused and misunderstood. The sense in which it is used here has nothing to do with bureaucracy and formal procedure; rather, "process" means end-to-end work – holistic work that spans an organization to create a result of value to customers. The work of most companies is encompassed by a relatively small number of major business processes (such as order fulfillment, order acquisition, product development, post-sales support, and the like). These in turn can be decomposed into a relatively small number of subprocesses. Processes represent a novel way of looking at work and business – novel at least since the Industrial Revolution. For the past 200 years, work has been broken down into constituent tasks as part of the doctrine of division and specialization of labor, first articulated by Adam Smith and later championed by Henry Ford and Frederick

Taylor. The task-oriented, functional approach to work had its advantages. It enabled mass production by dramatically increasing task productivity and it allowed organizations to grow rapidly in the face of escalating customer demand.

Unfortunately, it also had significant disadvantages. Fragmenting work across an organization creates an enormous amount of non-value-adding work, overhead needed to "glue" the pieces of work back together. This non-value-adding work in turn leads to costs, errors, delay, and inflexibility. These consequences have been with us since the beginning of the industrial era, but until recently, the customers who had to suffer them had little recourse. No longer. Today's economy is characterized by extravagant customer power as a result of overcapacity in virtually all industries, global competition, the commoditization of products and services, and increased information availability. Customers now are in a position to demand unprecedented levels of performance that cannot be delivered by work that is decomposed into piecemeal tasks and fragmented across an organization. The non-value-adding overhead associated with conventional work design can no longer be borne. Yet while the business environment for which the task approach to work was relevant died in the 1970s, organizations have persisted in adhering to it.

Forced by their customers, companies are now embracing the process concept. By looking at their work holistically and managing and designing it on an end-to-end basis, they are achieving startling improvements in performance. Reductions in cycle time of 80 percent to 90 percent and cost reductions of 50 percent to 75 percent are very common when work is seen through the process rather than the task lens. Process has come out of the shadows and has entered the business spotlight.

Converting a traditional organization into one focused on its processes is not an easy undertaking. It entails massive organizational change, as virtually all aspects of the enterprise, from metrics through career paths, need to be realigned around processes. Technology, in the form of a company's legacy information systems, is also a significant barrier to harnessing the power of processes. For most of the past five decades, companies built systems that matched their organizational structures and corresponded to individual functional departments. Procurement, manufacturing, marketing, sales, and customer service each had its own system with its own database, tailored to optimize the performance of that department and its activities. Lost in the shuffle was the larger context, the end-to-end processes of which each of these activities was just a part. As companies began to focus on and address their processes, they discovered that their existing systems only supported pieces of them. One system might handle credit checking, another inventory allocation, yet another production planning, and another billing. The process, however, crossed all these areas and systems, and to support, measure, and manage it, a system that similarly spanned all of them was required.

Neither of the two traditional solutions to this challenge is viable. The first, of course, is to undertake a massive system replacement to substitute a new process-oriented system for the portfolio of legacy systems. Rare indeed is the company that is willing to accept the level of cost and investment this would entail. The other solution is to retrofit the legacy functional systems together into a process system by using various application integration tools. Whereas this is superficially promising, it is also not practical. The result of such an effort is, in fact, just another legacy system, inflexible and wired to a particular way of doing business. Should the business need to redesign the process – and it will – then it must "rewire" these constituent systems, now joined in a fixed and even incomprehensible fashion. Moreover, systems are part – an important part, but still just a part – of a complete process. Some process steps are performed by systems, some by people using systems, and some just by people. Leaving people out of the process framework prevents the organization from tracking work through the process as a whole and measuring its overall performance.

History teaches us another important lesson: Whenever we install a system that purports to support an end-to-end business process, we discover before long that this process is, in fact, only part of a larger process that crosses even more organizational boundaries. For example, some ERP systems support a process that begins with order entry and ends with receipt of payment. However, many companies have decided that the "real" process begins earlier and ends later than this, extending from initial customer contact through follow-on sales. This process is not circumscribed by an ERP system, but rather requires the integration of ERP with CRM and possibly other systems. Nor does this phenomenon end there. The latest development in the process arena is the growing importance of inter-enterprise processes, processes that cross corporate as well as functional boundaries. For example, "supply chain" is not a euphemism for procurement but is a process that begins with the provider of raw materials and ends with the final customer. Supporting this process on an end-to-end basis requires integrating systems from separate companies. Trying to create an "ultimate" process system through application integration is akin to pursuing the Holy Grail: An unachievable goal.

For these reasons, companies have been unable to develop systems to support new processes as quickly as they can develop and install the processes themselves. In other words, the difficulty of creating end-to-end process systems acts as a significant brake on companies' ability to address their business processes and to reap the benefits of doing so.

Where technology inhibits, however, technology also liberates. Enter the Business Service Orchestration (BSO) described in this book. BSO encompasses a philosophy, a methodology, and a system architecture; it is a new way of thinking about how to support processes with information systems. BSO recognizes that legacy systems will always be with us and that the road to process management has twists and turns that cannot be anticipated – indeed, that it may never end. Accordingly, BSO argues that processes must be supported through a hyper-layer of software that focuses directly on the process itself, independent of the underlying systems or other mechanisms used to implement it. This layer enables companies to define and document their processes, measure and manage them, and specify which parts will be performed by what system. The methodology directs how to address a business process, model it in the hyper-layer, and connect it to tangible systems and other service providers. The system architecture relates these concepts to the current mechanisms, from J2EE to XML and SOAP, that are emerging as ways of connecting disparate systems into a coherent whole.

Winston Churchill is reputed to have said, "America can be counted on to do the right thing, once it has exhausted all the alternatives." Something similar might be said about large enterprises and their information systems organizations. Having tried a wide range of mechanisms for supporting their processes, the enthusiasm for an application software-independent approach is growing. This book, the first to articulate an entire approach based on this philosophy, should accelerate business's progress toward this goal.

Michael Hammer
President, Hammer and Company, Inc.

Acknowledgments

Like any large project, this book was a team effort. A lot of people from our respective companies and circles of friends helped write this book. Although all of them cannot be named here, we do want to specially recognize some who went out of their way in their support.

Scott Beaudreau, Fred Cummins, Robert Standefer, Emilio Lopez Gabeiras, John W. White, Dan Atwood, Mark Theilken, John Stasick, Gordon Sellers, and Brandon Dean provided reviews of various chapters and we benefited greatly from their collective experience and thank them for their valuable ideas and critiques. Sherry Jaco, Larhonda Jefferson, and Rob Brown provided administrative support and helped throughout the book.

Our special thanks to Shahzad Sadiq, Adriana Racca, Pila Racca, Santiago Racca, Javier Racca, Marta San Julian, Adolfo Critto, Ron Brittian, Tom Hill, Lekha Rao, and Sadiq Mohammad Khan for providing constant support and encouragement.

Many thanks to Marco Antonio Silvestre da Souza as well as to Jorge Rava for their courage in trying out the new ideas when they were still raw.

Finally, for having created the spark that brought the two authors together, we would like to thank Ed Bednar.

Felix would like to acknowledge Waqar for his continuous pestering to get the book finished and his wonderful family for their amiable hospitality at their home for the final long nights to complete it.

Introduction

To start, we would like to set the stage. Please read slowly, and use your imagination. Remember the scene in *2001: A Space Odyssey* where the *Blue Danube* waltz is sounding. The space shuttle is rotating on its axis trying to match the rotation of the space station. Perfect synchronization. Harmony. Striking beauty. A fantastic Orchestration.

For these first paragraphs only, we will use *Star Trek* as an allegory while the finely orchestrated waltz of *2001: A Space Odyssey* sounds in the background. We will say that the Federation (as in *Star Trek*) is the modern enterprise, the president of the Federation its CEO. The *USS Enterprise* is one of the many starships that are capable of performing a mission according to a predefined plan (implementing an Orchestration): an orchestration vehicle. Captain Kirk is the mission owner (Orchestration owner) for this orchestration vehicle. He is ultimately responsible for the different possible missions (deliverables) and maintains the captain's log. He is also responsible for overseeing the execution of the process (Orchestration) that fulfills the mission. He is not an expert in managing the engine; that's Scotty. He's not an expert in connectivity; that's Ohura. He's not an expert in dealing with the crew's ailments; that's Dr. McCoy.

The *USS Enterprise* needs to be able to use its own internal services (engine, molecular transporter, computer, view screen, navigation equipment, communication equipment, energy sources, crew services, etc.) at different points in the space-time continuum to complete the mission. The *USS Enterprise* also needs to be able to utilize services from external sources as well as respond to external stimuli such as attacks from the Klingons. The Klingons are the Federation's competitors. They too have starships, with different capabilities in terms of their internal services and ability to respond to external stimuli. The *Enterprise* needs to have security features such as electromagnetic shields that protect against Klingon attacks. Our *USS Enterprise* has many smaller fighter ships that also constitute orchestration vehicles. And the *USS Enterprise* is subject to Earth as the master orchestration vehicle.

So, an orchestration vehicle is a self-propelling system that can manage internal and external services according to a plan to fulfill a mission.

Hear the lazy loops of the *Blue Danube* as you imagine the Earth orbiting the Sun, spawning starships that embark on their elliptic trajectories, which spawn fighter ships that have their own missions and trajectories. If you have been able to see the fireworks while you hear the waltz, you are one of the visionaries who have the ability to orchestrate images and music in four dimensions in your mind, that fourth dimension being time. You can be an Orchestrator; you're a natural, you can play three-dimensional chess, you would be Spock in *Star Trek*. A complete Vulcan could not be an Orchestrator, but, as Spock, who is at least half human, you would be motivated to make an impression on the audience. If you immediately identified with Captain Kirk, you are a Process owner. You are to build the requirements for the Orchestrator to create a flight plan that will allow you to accomplish your mission. If you would rather deal with the health of the crew, or the engine room, or communications, you are a member of the functional staff that participates in the mission in your preferred role.

For Spocks and Kirks, this book is a must read; it's the reference for implementing orchestrations that accomplish missions. In the smaller fighter ships, the orchestrator and the captain are one and the same. Must read. In the Federation we have the Admiral, the Master Orchestrator (CIO). Must read. The Presidents of the Federation may want to read the first two chapters, just to know what the half-Vulcans are talking about. The McCoys need to read the first third of the book, the Ohuras the middle. All of the above may benefit from a careful read of the last third.

The Orchestration engine is the source of energy for the Orchestration vehicle; it's what makes it self-propelling, it's what puts the crew and the automated services in different points of space-time so that they can perform the appropriate activity within the necessary series to accomplish the mission. The Scottys are in charge of keeping that engine up and running. They need to know everything about the enabling technologies for that engine and how to discover and manage the services it will use. The Scottys needs to read this book; they need to master the middle third and read the last third.

We all know that without the Dilithium crystal-powered orchestration engine, the modern *Enterprise* would not fly. Its predecessors, based on fission reactors (work-flow engines), could never attain warp speed. This is why, initially, there was this idea that warp speeds could only be attained by ships without their own propulsion systems, ships that "sailed" on the legacy photon streams and slingshot trajectories of gravitational pull (messages on a universal messaging bus – EAI) from solar system bodies (the legacy applications). Scientists called this "loosely coupled" navigation. However, building the huge phaser belts (adapters or connectors) needed to create the photon streams around each star had proven to be too expensive and complicated and there had been a number of accidents due to the inability to foresee exceptions such as asteroids or worlds passing through the streams. On top of it all, there was the discovery of various parallel universes, whose photon streams were incompatible with ours.

Many visionaries had been telling us about the need for self-propelled orchestrations for a couple of decades. We didn't want to listen. Self-propelling spaceships are like off-road vehicles. They are perceived as risky because they leave the main spaceways. This means navigating uncharted space, having to build charts of your own and being able to change them on the fly. We thought we were incapable of doing it. We thought that our legal counsel would never approve of it – too much risk. We thought this approach was for savage Klingons who wanted to reinvent the wheel and didn't care to die. We wanted to follow the charts of our legacy and thought that just piecing them together would give us a chart of the Universe; we would be navigating the Perfect Economy! We were wrong. There was much more white space than charted space; furthermore, the Universe is in continuous expansion but charts are not. The Klingons were taking over the ever-growing white space. It took the bursting of the supernova bubble that took most of the phaser-belt adapter companies along with it for us to come back to our senses. We needed to go back to the principles of the Free Enterprise and pioneering that made our Federation great.

We finally reacted. Now, let's get on with the principles of Business Services Orchestration (BSO) and then . . . let the waltz begin!

NAVIGATING THROUGH THE GALAXY

Let's be honest. The galaxy is large and complex. So we will divide it into two virtual sectors. Sector 1 comprises Chapters 1 through 4 and Sector 2 comprises Chapters 5 through 9.

Sector 1 was designed so that the Kirks, McCoys, Spocks, and Scottys could all feel reasonably comfortable in them. Although BSOs have the primary goal of increasing business performance, the orchestration of business services ends up weighing more heavily on the Spocks and Scottys than on the Kirks and McCoys. Therefore, Sector 2 is a place where only the Spocks and Scottys would feel comfortable.

In Sector 1, we have Chapters 1 through 3, which introduce the main concepts of BSO. All of those chapters have parts that are definitely in the Kirks' domain of expertise, but few that are in McCoys' domain. They are primarily oriented toward the Spocks. The Scottys will probably get impatient and want to move on quickly through Chapters 1 and 2, but we recommend that they look closely at the definitions.

Chapter 3 is where the desired architecture for the *USS Enterprise* is discussed. The Spocks and Scottys must master this chapter because it's the basis for understanding Sector 2; the Kirks may want to read it to understand the lingo.

Chapter 4 delves into the methodology framework for planning services that the enterprise will provide to the Federation. This chapter is a must-read for Kirks and Spocks. A crucial part of any stellar mission is the planning. The Scottys will probably fall asleep here and the McCoys will protest that they have real work to do. So please, Scottys and McCoys, read this chapter as a curiosity. The Kirks and Spocks should pay special attention to phase 2 of this chapter because it provides an end-to-end example that may prove to be very important for lucrative missions.

Sector 2 comprises Chapters 5 through 9 and is mostly for the Spocks and Scottys. This sector describes the technologies that enable development of BSOs.

Chapter 5 gives an overview of the important capabilities required from any platform used to build business services. The Scottys will find useful reference material in this chapter; the Spocks will find a good overview of the necessary capabilities. Even Kirk and McCoy may pick up some knowledge about the technologies, enough to be dangerous.

Chapter 6 starts talking about the technologies implemented on top of platforms and starts putting into perspective some guiding principles behind different integration approaches. Spocks among the readers will find this chapter most useful. The Scottys will find discussion of the technologies related to Web services interesting, but the Kirks and McCoys may just want to gloss over the chapter.

Chapter 7 is mostly for the Spocks. This chapter introduces metadata concepts related to the BSO reference model introduced earlier in the book. The Scottys may find it useful as well because the metadata are managed by the underlying infrastructure.

Chapter 8 discusses in detail the capabilities required to form a BSO system. This chapter talks about the basic and advanced concepts involved in process automation. These concepts are discussed through examples of an XML-based language, describing the data items that need to be captured for them. This chapter borrows the concepts and features available in many of the available orchestration languages that exist today.

Fundamental to BSO is its ability to integrate human services. It accomplishes that through work portals. Chapter 9 discusses involvement of human participants in the orchestration through the portal interface. This chapter will be of interest to Kirks, McCoys, Spocks, and Scottys alike.

CHAPTER 1

A Holistic View of Enterprise Systems

1.1 INTRODUCTION

The first part of this introduction is for the Kirks, Spocks, McCoys, and Scottys. As it gets more technical, the Kirks may want to skip directly to Section 1.3, from which point the content is more business oriented.

To Orchestrate is to organize the harmony and tempo of various instruments into a single impressive musical delivery, such as in Strauss's *Blue Danube* waltz. If the result is anything but impressive, the orchestration is not worthy of such a name. An Orchestrator differs from an Architect in that the latter designs something static, such as a house, a bridge, or a landscape, that is, something that doesn't vary in time. The Architect designs only the deliverable, not the process used to deliver it. An Orchestrator designs a delivery of music rendered in time, in the harmony and tempo needed to achieve a desired effect.

Orchestration is nothing but a modern metaphor that describes a well-known, but not very well understood, discipline: the automation of business process management. Traditionally, business processes were managed by people. Managers drove the steps that employees – with or without instruments or tools – needed to complete or fulfill a business process. This is analogous to an orchestration being managed by a maestro by keeping tempo, cueing in the different players, managing the intensity of what is being played, and conveying a style to the performance.

The same way MIDI tools manage the automation of musical execution, Business Services Orchestration (BSO) tools manage the automatic execution of business services to fulfill an enterprisewide or interenterprise business process.

The problem with this concept is that, since the advent of the computer era, there have been many waves of automation, all of which could be confused with BSO. The key to understanding the difference between BSO and other types of automation is precisely that BSO automates those cumbersome, iterative, and mechanical things that management was forced to do to run a business, not the highly specialized functions of any specific discipline such as accounting, engineering, law, sales, or procurement. Examples of these generic tasks include prompting people to do their specialized work; prompting systems to do their specialized work; measuring what people and systems do; interpreting, translating, and routing information; time management; resource allocation; and many others. These activities don't require creativity, specialization, or great amounts of intelligence – just a huge amount of attention to detail, patience, and a preestablished plan that rules the execution.

At this point, the technical reader will say: "That's nothing new, that's work flow!" But it isn't. Or at least it isn't work flow as it has been understood by industry analysts and by software providers to date. There has been close to unanimity of opinion in the technical community that work flow (and its more modern successor, business process management [BPM]) are a feature set of enterprise applications (departmental work flow) or a feature set of integration suites (BPM), or in the most generic case, a document management facility. Most industry analysts believe that there is no chance for an overarching orchestration strategy – one that automates the management of processes across people, applications, departments, divisions, and enterprises – to succeed as a product category.

It is the belief of the authors that this type of solution that is *specialized* in being generic, automating generic recurring tasks and automating the management of services from inside and outside an organization, is precisely what is needed to fix the problems of the modern enterprise. What are these problems?

- Geographic dispersion makes it difficult to coordinate work.
- Language, time zones, and cultures need to be managed.
- Platforms, computer languages, runtime environments, and disparate, specialized applications need to be made to work the way the business requires them to work.
- Time that could be put to better use is spent by people interpreting data from one application and putting it into another.
- Activities that are recurrent and mechanical are still being performed by people.

The list could go on, but let's get to the most important problem of them all: *Although most companies have plans, these plans are at a high level and do not constitute **actionable plans** that are understood and agreed upon by all of the management*

team as well as those who will execute or supervise the work required by them. There-
fore, companies have trouble understanding and communicating, at a detailed level,
which services from specialized people and systems they really need in order to succeed
in their objectives.

These actionable plans can be called company execution contracts. They are understood by everybody involved and they rule that involvement. What generic language is there to express these contracts or actionable plans?

The best language invented to date is the graphical representation of process models that explain what people, systems, and other organizations need to do for the business to fulfill its objectives. Process models are to business people and workers as librettos are to the maestro and the musicians.

Now, let's suppose that we can feed those process models *exactly as they have* *been designed and understood* to a software engine and this engine prompts people to do their job, presents them with interfaces that are adequate, receives communication from people as they complete tasks, invokes functions in underlying applications, uses the return arguments as data for function invocations in other applications or to present new data to people, manages due dates, presets times to launch work from people or systems, and creates information on everything that was done, by who, how long it took, what tools were used, etc.

What we have just described is a business services orchestration engine (BSOE). The key here to distinguish BSO from prior technologies is that the process models that are executed by the BSOE need to be exactly what the management team agreed upon. The process models deal with generic management and supervisory issues. Activities undertaken by specialized people, systems, or organizations are business services that the BSOE invokes, coordinates, manages, and measures according to the process models it has been fed.

Therefore, we can say that we are in the presence of a BSO project only when:

- Management agrees among themselves and with appropriate workers on actionable plans across departmental silos and partner companies.
- These plans are represented as process models.
- These same process models can be fed into a BSOE that automates their management and execution.
- These same process models constitute the contract between senior management, supervisors, workers, and information technology (IT) staff on the scope of what services people and systems need to provide the business.

We are in the presence of BSO tools only when:

- There is a process designer that allows the graphical creation of orchestrations by management-level users, and a capability to automatically generate connectors to applications and presentations for human participants by IT-level users.

- The orchestrations are the implementation framework for everything that IT has to do thereon.
- The exact orchestrations that were designed are what runs in the BSOE.
- The orchestrations can be changed without modifying IT infrastructure or having to retrain users.
- The BSOE creates process execution information that is easily exploited by management to continuously improve the processes.

As can be seen, this is clearly a top-down approach toward automating cross-enterprise processes. Traditionally, we have taken a bottom-up approach: we have created specialized automations that do sophisticated calculations and organizations of data. We have attacked the problem correctly; we have solved the greater pains first. However, in today's world the greater pain has become that these specialized systems don't work together, nor are they coordinated with work from employees and business partners.

We dedicate the rest of the introduction to a more technical overview of what has been done to date to support businesses through IT.

Let's investigate what companies have done in the past to orchestrate their business functions using IT. Initially, companies developed internal software to facilitate the work of specific working groups. IBM's business machines provided specific language compilers for different types of applications. Programmers specialized in languages. For example, there were COBOL programmers, dedicated initially to creating administrative applications, and FORTRAN programmers dedicated initially to creating engineering applications. As time went by, programmers started creating applications for Human Resources, Manufacturing, Logistics, Cost Analysis, Procurement, Delivery, and many other functional areas of the enterprise.

Initially, these systems were built in-house. IBM and others were marketing a "General Purpose Machine" capable of running virtually any program, and they trained their customers to build internally developed programs that accelerated business functions.

As programmers left those companies, the programs they created became unmanageable black boxes that were difficult to use and costly to update. In response, a new generation of software vendors introduced department-specific applications that were supported by cost-effective maintenance contracts. Those initial software vendors were domain experts in one or more functional silos, and they specialized in systems that helped the workers in those specific silos to improve their work.

Companies soon realized that they needed to share work with other departments, and that this sharing required that transactions or reports be sent between various departmental systems. Some smart software vendors started to sell "integrated modules" that would later be known as enterprise resource planning (ERP) suites. ERP was described as the end-all, cover-all, integrated system that would allow companies to conduct business with a minimum of paperwork. The rationale was that by running everything under one system and one database, the company would have access to all the functionality and information it could ever need.

That sounded great, but new times bring new challenges and, as companies realized a growing need to manage their supply chains and customer relationships, supply chain management (SCM) and customer relationship management (CRM) software entered the marketplace. Those systems ran on their own database structures, which had nothing to do with either the ERP or with the customer or supplier databases. The dream of a common, centralized database had been seriously compromised.

Not having been designed as a part of ERP, these new SCM and CRM applications, by nature, have data that are redundant between them and with ERP, and have overlapping processes (i.e., purchase order data and the order fulfillment process). When companies do business in different markets, they usually have at least one or two systems that are not included in any of the "integrated suites." For example, telecommunications firms use billing and OSS systems, insurance companies use policy and claims management, and financial services need case management and branch office automation software.

So, the modern enterprise has deployed ERP, CRM, SCM, and two or more industry-specific applications, their Intranet, Extranet, Internet servers, and content, plus e-mail, plus personal productivity and collaboration tools. This is the scenario in today's market. What do all of these applications have in common? They were built to provide functionality to the intended user according to the *user's* perception of what is needed to do his/her job. People within the companies that use them are in charge of taking these fragmented processes and data representations and producing a real (as opposed to virtual) business process that satisfies their customers.

It's no wonder that, having all of these islands of integrated software, companies are struggling to integrate their business.

The simple truth is that some employees spend a tremendous amount of time swivel chairing from one application to another trying to maintain their data in synchronization. It's easy to see that this is a very cumbersome and error-prone task. Therefore, at first blush, it would seem that companies want to integrate applications to eliminate the swivel-chair operators. However, that improvement alone will not convince management to buy a multimillion-dollar license for integration software, and spend five to seven times that in professional services. No. There must be another reason.

In our experience, the reason companies integrate applications is to improve the performance of their critical processes so that they can better serve their customers and/or be more efficient.

They wish to do this in a way that will produce measurable returns on their investment, if possible within the budgetary year. The challenge is made greater because various parts of these critical processes are embedded and redundant in their CRM, SCM, and ERP applications, industry-specific suites, Web applications, personal productivity and collaboration tools, and the capacities of their employees. Also, in a virtual enterprise, many of these critical processes are done by employees or partners outside the four walls of the company. Still, companies have to manage the overlaps, redundancies, inconsistencies, and white spaces among and between those many applications, people, and organizations.

In synthesis, the problems that businesses need to solve are:

- to tightly connect business execution with business strategy and objectives;
- to ensure the constant reliability of execution by orchestrating the behavior of people, systems, and business partners;
- to do this without disrupting the business's culture or preferences in terms of organization and infrastructure; and
- to avoid impairing the business's ability to change at the rhythm of market requirements, competitor capabilities, and internal or external innovation.

Without any doubt, it's a tall order.

The industry's initial approach to knitting these processes together (orchestrating their business services from applications) was to create a program that took data from one application and automatically put it into another. This approach got old very soon, primarily because of the enormous number of interface programs needed to make it work.

As an example, let's say that a company has the following applications: General Ledger, Accounts Receivable, Accounts Payable, Human Resources and Payroll, Manufacturing, Procurement, Inventory Management, and Billing. The initial reasoning was, "Let's make an interface program between each of the modules in each direction." So point-to-point interfaces were developed between General Ledger and the remaining seven modules, and then between the Accounts Payable and the remaining modules, and so on. When we were one-tenth of the way through this approach, we realized that we would have to build $8 \times 7 = 56$ interface modules. However, the problem didn't end there! These applications started having different versions, and so, each new version of each module implied fourteen new interfaces (seven incoming and seven outgoing).

It got ugly in a hurry. When industry analysts started calling it the "spaghetti interfaces" approach, we knew we needed a better way.

That new approach emerged in the late nineties when the pioneers of today's enterprise application integration (EAI) suites found a way to avoid creating an almost geometric number of interface programs. There are two common EAI approaches, Hub-and-Spoke and Messaging Bus, but they are based on the same basic concept that applications are connected to a single broker instead of among themselves. In this way, instead of having fifty-six interface programs to maintain as described in the example above, we would only need to create eight adapters or connectors to the broker; one for each application. Under this approach when a new version appeared, only a single new connector would be necessary.

The rationale was impeccable, but something went wrong. In early 2000, we started hearing the same analysts questioning this new approach that they had contributed to popularizing. "We went from spaghetti interfaces to spaghetti EAI," many observed.

Shortly thereafter, the big Internet economy bubble, already wobbling, burst completely. The "dot com" revolution had, in many cases, been unable to either create a viable revenue model or implement the adequate orchestration of their internal services to fulfill the model.

These problems were already obvious when we started to complicate things further by trying to create transparent marketplaces through business-to-business (B2B) exchanges that stressed the hub-and-spoke paradigm to the utmost. In B2C the spokes were implemented as Web sites and the only orchestration necessary was between the Web application and the back-end applications and people. In B2B, each spoke needed its own orchestration.

Besides, we soon discovered that companies wanted to continue to do business their own way and were less than eager to relinquish their existing models for a more perfect marketplace. The reason for failure becomes obvious when we consider the cost of integrating companies into exchanges, an average of about half a million dollars and requiring four months of effort. Although the business reasons for the failure of B2B exchanges are clear, we can't help thinking that the technological approach and its limitations played an important role in accelerating their demise.

We believe that the e-business revolution has just started. BSO will be a major advancement in making this revolution viable. It will provide an approach and tools that, although building on previous ideas and technologies, will greatly diminish the risk of e-business by improving the time-to-market of solutions and providing the flexibility needed for their continuous improvement. The causes of our present predicament are many and varied but, on the technical side, the rigidity of integration solutions is probably one of the most important. For some reason, early on, work flow and integration were divorced. BSO sustains that they are one and the same thing, and that services from people and services from applications need to be regarded under the same light as process activities.

One of the main causes of inflexibility is that the messaging approach did not completely replace the point-to-point integration programs as we thought it would. Although the point-to-point integration programs were many, they were programs, not connectors or adapters. What's the difference? The fundamental objectives of a connector or adapter are:

1. Take standard data from the broker, transform it so that the target application can understand it, and then call a procedure in the target application using the transformed data.
2. Take the output parameters from an invoked procedure, transform them into broker standard constructs, and then hand the result to the broker.

In contrast, the objective of a point-to-point interface program is much broader: To do anything and everything necessary to make application A work seamlessly with application B for a given transaction or set of transactions. The interface program might apply rules, manage exceptions, and drive the process of knitting together the two applications. Adapters or connectors simply cannot do this. The problem with an interface program is that it is tightly coupled and point to point. This makes the program difficult to change and requires a quadratic number of interfaces to be built as the number of applications grows, doesn't it?

Not necessarily. The quadratic multiplication of interface programs depends on the layer of abstraction in which the program is built. Initially, they were built as peer programs to the two applications that were being integrated. The issue was in the point-to-point nature of the interface programs, not in the fact that they lacked a central means of connectivity. The inflexibility of those programs had more to do with the fact that they were developed in programming languages rather than generated from process models that could be graphically constructed and changed on-the-fly as needed, and that they were designed as interfaces, not as overarching processes.

We should recall that the EAI approach was initially limited to passing data from one application to another, assuming that the content of those data and the queue in which they were published would suffice for the adapter to invoke all adequate procedures in the target application. For this to be true, two conditions would have to be met:

1. An adapter or connector to an application would have to connect to all methods of an application programmer interface (API), and that API would need to be exhaustively complete for whatever the external world might want from the application.
2. There could be no mismatch between what one application provided and what all others required from it.

When the difficulty of meeting these conditions became apparent, EAI vendors started adding a logic layer inside the brokers. They called it process logic. It should be called event-handling logic, and for a very simple reason: Most EAI vendors built this supplementary logic tier as a set of rules that reacted to the appearance of certain events on the bus. Therefore, it was logic driven by events, which is the opposite of activities driven by logic (which we consider to be the definition of process).

Although it is also true that a decade before the EAI vendors came up with the idea of integration brokers, work-flow vendors had pioneered the approach of integrating applications inside process definitions, the ability to interact with underlying applications was very poor at that time. The first work-flow products concentrated mainly on routing documents among people, applying process rules to manage the behavior of the document flow, and people activities. BSO sees applications as if they were service providers analogous to people. In today's world, there are already technologies and technology bridges that allow the process to manage the behavior of underlying applications as well as the behavior of people.

As customers realized that the passive-state engine logic as provided by EAI vendors was not enough, systems integrators ended up building auxiliary interface programs that connected to the bus and supplemented the lack of active logic, or they started putting this logic within the connectors or adapters. These addendums seriously compromised the maintainability and flexibility of the resulting constructs.

If the main reason for integrating those applications is to improve the performance of a company's processes, we should ask ourselves: Does it make sense to focus on connecting applications? Or does it make more sense to focus on automating a company's processes as the work-flow vendors did originally? What did we really achieve by trying to make these applications send electronic messages to one another? Haven't the results of this approach been highly redundant, overlapping, inconsistent, and clunky processes that are usually worse than the one driven by swivel-chair users or interface applications, and haven't we ended up building auxiliary interface programs anyway? Haven't we ended up distributing the logic and centralizing the technology, creating a maintenance nightmare, a single point of failure, and a scalability problem?

This critique implies that a partial approach (just throwing messages over application walls into a bus) is insufficient to drive and improve company performance. Even if it were possible to eventually make the EAI approach work by supplementing the magical event-driven scenario with the interface process logic that we were trying to eliminate, the effort necessary for event-enabling applications to be able to integrate them takes too long, costs too much, and is exponentially more difficult to maintain as the number of integrated applications grow. We have traded exponential point-to-point interfaces for an exponential maintenance nightmare.

What the industry needs today is a holistic and self-propelled approach.

The holistic approach starts by focusing on all of a company's generic customer-facing and interdepartmental processes instead of only the company's specialized user-facing applications. These customer-facing and interdepartmental processes are, by nature, cross-function, cross-division and cross-ecosystem. We call the approach holistic precisely because it starts by analyzing the complete end-to-end services to be delivered, rather than looking at the individual functions from specific applications. The holistic approach recognizes applications, people, and organizations as containers of a wealth of services that can be orchestrated into new, internal or external customer-facing services. This is done through the execution of a process model that automates the iterative and routine tasks that people have to perform to make sense out of disparate processes and data representations in their fragmented application base. It is an approach in which the orchestration engine acts as a hub that runs flexible process models. These process models invoke fragmented services from people and systems, through any technology, and apply business rules to them, transforming them into new and improved business services. This approach does not aggregate applications through one proprietary means of connectivity. Rather, it orchestrates services through process logic applied to existing services and exposed through any means of connectivity.

BSO is this holistic approach. BSO is not only a product or a product category. It is also an approach toward business integration that requires certain types of tools and technologies that respond to a specific architecture. We discuss this architecture in Chapter 3, and describe the approach by using a methodology framework in Chapter 4.

At its highest level, the BSO approach consists of seven steps for continuous improvement. Those are:

1. Identify and prioritize the critical services needed for company success.
2. Discover how the company fulfills these services (model the "as-is" processes).
3. Define the improvement objectives in terms of process metrics (cycle time, quality, volume, cost, etc.).
4. Modify the as-is process to try to meet those objectives by modeling the should-be process and determining the services it needs to invoke from the business ecosystem.
5. Identify any existing and useful services that can be provided by people, applications, or third parties.
6. Harmonize these services so they can be consumed by the should-be process.
7. Implement the process and put it into production. Monitor metrics. Return to step 3 and repeat as necessary.

For those who appreciate business process reengineering (BPR), this approach no doubt sounds very familiar. BSO derives a good part of its high-level methodology and approach from BPR, but the objectives and end results are different.

The primary objective of BPR is to help a company discover and streamline (reengineer) its internal processes. The results of a good BPR project are a number

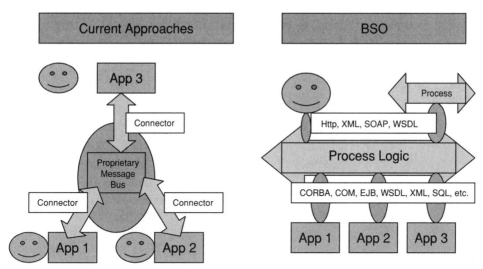

FIGURE **1.1. Current Messaging-Centric Approaches Versus the BSO Approach.**

of documents that specify a complete set of internal processes and policies. It's the company's responsibility to train its employees in those procedures, and the implementation of the process logic in the company's systems is done, if at all, through the trained employees. There is no way to enforce BPR processes on third-party organizations.

The objective of BSO is to use existing internal or external services (automated or not) to create a new automated service for any internal or external customer. The result of an orchestration project is a computer-driven process that uses services from people, computer applications, and other organizations to deliver a product or service. BSOs are process models and rules that, rather than being subject to human interpretation and execution, are executed by a computer. This execution is consistent, metrics driven, and easily adaptable to changing business conditions.

Orchestration is a departure from BPR because its goal is to create a computer-driven service. BSO needs the abilities found in traditional work-flow systems intermingled with the capabilities of traditional EAI and business-to-business integration (B2Bi) systems, but the BSO approach differs significantly from the traditional EAI approach because it focuses on creating processes that drive the execution of services, instead of creating adapters that listen to and create events on a centralized messaging bus.

Figure 1.1 compares current messaging-centric approaches with the BSO approach. We notice the following from this comparison:

- BSO focuses on improving company performance by orchestrating the corresponding services, more like work-flow solutions would approach the problem.

Data sources, employees, applications, and external systems alike are seen as containers of business services to be used as needed by the orchestration intelligence.

There is no distinction among EAI, B2Bi, and B2C. Under the BSO approach, companies build and use services – internal or external, human or automated, standard or nonstandard and from any technology – to improve enterprise performance.

For orchestration to be possible, BSO technologies must provide a capability that we will call *harmonization,* which we address at length later in this book. In essence, harmonization provides the ability of an orchestration to work with services from any type or origin.

Like work-flows, orchestrations are self-propelled; it is the orchestration engine that invokes business services from people, applications, and organizations and not the other way around; this allows processes to run independently of the implementation of the underlying services.

• BSO uses the process logic as the hub that drives the integration of people, applications, and organizations, therefore allowing this process logic and these services to be shared. This is in contrast to the EAI approach, which only shares data among application systems. Also, in contrast to the point-to-point interfaces that are peers with two applications instead of a layer of logic on top of many, it is in perfect agreement with the work-flow approach.

BSO is, in many ways, the opposite of current approaches, and herein lies the difficulty that people have in understanding it. It's a logical view, not a physical one. In this chapter, we want to make sure that we leave you an image that you can refer to as we get into more detail and the trees start hiding the forest.

Imagine a hub and its spokes. In the current approaches, the hub is in charge of connectivity through one technology and the spokes are in charge of process (applications), which in turn interact with people. People do not interact directly with the hub. In BSO the hub is in charge of executing process models and the spokes are in charge of connectivity *through any technology* to services from people, systems, or other process hubs. The orchestration engine in Figure 1.1 is clearly a generic connector *across many technologies.*

The fundamental difference between BSO and the traditional EAI approaches is that the traditional EAI approaches are technology centric. This is sort of a loaded claim because in IT, everything could be perceived as a technology. EAI, however, relies on proprietary technologies to build adapters and connectors to applications. This requires an IT department to make key strategic decisions on an integration platform. This is so because the adapters and connectors to the applications being integrated are proprietary. The BSO approach that we have talked about so far, and will continue to dive into, is IT-strategy independent because it relies on the process of harmonization across one or multiple strategies. As long as the services that are being integrated have been harmonized by creating metadata about them and populating standards' registries, they can be easily orchestrated. One might argue that you need technology to express metadata and discover services. That is true, but with standards-based technologies, such as Web Services Definition Language (WSDL) and UDDI, that can be used to describe metadata and discover it; and with synthesis tools that can discover metadata in already-existing component repositories such as CORBA, COM, Java, EJB containers, and others, orchestration becomes a logical configuration rather than a physical one.

Figure 1.1 should reinforce the concept of BSO as a holistic, logical approach toward orchestrating services from any origin through any enabling technology, which is, among other important things, the clear remedy to "spaghetti EAI."

1.2 BUSINESS SERVICES

Let's define what we mean by business services. Activities such as catering, transportation, and legal and financial work are classic examples of business services. However, for the purposes of discussing orchestrations, our definition of business services is broader.

At a high level, a business service is anything a company does to fulfill a request from an internal or external customer. This may include actions a company employee takes on behalf of an internal or external customer, a task a company system performs for an internal or external customer, or virtually any combination of the above. One characteristic of any business service is that the customer has the power to request it or not. Unsolicited activities are not considered to be business services. Those unasked-for actions are more properly called business waste or business noise.

To be usable by an orchestration engine, a business service must expose an interface that makes it accessible for invocation by a computer program. So, a more complete definition would be:

A business service is what a company does to fulfill to a programmatic request from an internal or external customer.

You might ask, "Are Web services business services?" The answer is yes because Web services provide a simple programmatic interface implemented on standard Web protocols and are addressable by a URL. Web services are the ultimate way to externalize business services on the internet. However, not all business services are Web services. There are business services that need not be exposed as Web services, such as database queries, the invocation of an API from an ERP system, or human services driven by the invocation of a graphical user interface. In this scenario it is illogical to try to make any technology, including Web services, the centerpiece of an orchestration. The centerpiece of any orchestration should be the orchestration itself. The services are the instruments that are being orchestrated into a whole. Therefore, as we said earlier, in BSO the hubs of multiple EAI approaches become the spokes, and the spokes with their integration logic become the hub.

For a more complete understanding of the new paradigm, and to provide vocabulary that we will be using throughout the book, let us classify business services according to the following categories: complexity, source, and enabling technology.

1.2.1 Classification by Complexity

What a customer sees of a business service, as we explained previously, is the service's programmatic interface. So, from the customer perspective, the complexity of a service is nothing more than the complexity of its interface. There are three basic levels of complexity in interfaces: discrete, composite, and orchestrated.

1.2.1.1 Discrete Services

These are services that present a discrete interface. This means that a single interaction with the interface completes the service, and this interaction is, to all intents and purposes, executed as a whole without parts. This is the case for services that consist of posting a message, listening for an event, or for some API services that return arguments. Examples include services that allow posting of an e-mail, returning of the temperature in a turbine, posting a message to a Pub/Sub bus, presenting a graphical interface to a user, geting a purchase order from a back-end system, etc. Discrete services can be synchronous or asynchronous.

1.2.1.2 Composite Services

These are services that require more than one interaction to be completed, and therefore consist of multiple parts. For example, some APIs that allow the customer program to query data in a back-end system return a reference to a record set. To get useful data, the program that invoked the initial service must also invoke a new service such as "get next record" from the record set. When programmatically querying a relational database, there are services such as open cursor and get next cursor that allow the calling program to read a set of selected records. In the same way, there may be human services that require a series of interactions to be completed, for example, a negotiation, where the customer solicits an offer and man makes counteroffers until an agreement is reached. From a technical perspective, composite services can usually be decomposed into their parts and their parts considered as discrete services. However, from a BSO perspective, it is important to try to abstract them into a discrete service that offers a single interaction.

From a business perspective, services must have a granularity that makes business sense, not technical sense. This is why any orchestration must accept, natively, composite services from people or applications as well as other appropriate discrete services, and compose them into a new discrete business-level service or, as we will see later, an orchestrated service. If this activity is done simply from an aggregation perspective without any orchestration, we can call it composition. These compositions also present either a synchronous or asynchronous interface.

Composition is done by creating intelligent business objects (IBOs) that abstract the complexities of one or more composite or discrete business services into an object that offers discrete services. We call them intelligent, not because they are inference engines, but because they "know" how to integrate with the native services from applications or people, making the implementation transparent to the process that uses them. Therefore, the process relies on IBOs to do the right things from the implementation perspective. From the academic perspective, it might be more appropriate to refer to them as "abstract business objects." We will talk more about composition in Chapter 3 and throughout the rest of the book.

1.2.1.3 Orchestrated Services

Certain services present the customer with a complex interface that requires a series of predefined, timed interactions controlled by a business-level protocol. We call these higher-level services *orchestrated services*. As an example, consider an order fulfillment service requiring the following interactions: Send the PO, wait for proposed delivery dates, accept or reject delivery dates, wait for bill of materials, notify when delivery is complete, wait for invoice. This is what we call multisynchronous interaction, meaning that it is composed of a sequence of synchronous or asynchronous interactions spread out in time, and always following a predefined protocol. The service that implements the above interface is by necessity an orchestrated service. Orchestrated services are essential when attempting to synchronize two business processes. There is no easier and more secure way of implementing orchestrated services than BSO.

1.2.2 Classification by Source

A fundamental step toward understanding the BSO paradigm is the ability to see people, systems, and organizations as sources of services or as "service providers." Therefore, it may be helpful to classify services according to these three primary sources.

1.2.2.1 Services from People

This category consists of actions taken by individual people for internal or external customers. These services can be invoked by computer programs, and can range from tightening a screw on an assembly line to handcrafting a piece of art or approving a multimillion-dollar contract. There are certain attributes that distinguish business services from other activities that people do.

First and foremost, a business service is performed for an internal or external customer, not necessarily for the edification or gratification of the performer. A certain level of quality and accountability is required for business services. Quality refers to the consistency, repeatability, and predictability of the service itself, regardless of who or what performs it. Accountability refers to the fact that the person who executes the service is held responsible for maintaining its quality and its timeliness. Business services can be monitored by the customer or by the organization. To ensure the quality and accountability of the services, the orchestrator must be aware of employee capabilities and must group those skills into appropriate roles. Business services should be invoked from people who are capable of fulfilling the required roles. Roles should be assigned on the basis of proven capabilities and not on the position or title of a person in an organization.

The second attribute of a human business service in the orchestration paradigm is that it is passive from the process perspective, which means that the human does not need to decide which service is required from him or her because the process rules will prompt the human dynamically for services as needed. The customer uses a computer program or an orchestration system to invoke and synchronize human services, not the other way around. This is very important, because at the root of the orchestration paradigm lies the ability to replace human services with automated services without the need to alter the process model. The orchestration engine is in fact indifferent as to whether a certain service is being provided by a human actor or by an application. So, in services from people, a computer program or the orchestration engine asks the employee to read a certain report, approve a certain invoice, tighten a certain screw, or write a contract and "check-in" the service as it is finished.

The primary means through which an orchestration engine solicits a service from a human is the work portal, which is nothing but a portal-based version of the well-known worklist handlers of traditional work-flow engines. Work portals dynamically notify employees of the services they should perform according to their roles in the company, and the state of the processes in which they are involved. A work portal can be implemented on any computer or on a wireless device with messaging capabilities. In essence, the orchestration engine invokes and monitors the execution of human services through the work portal. To facilitate the execution of those services, the orchestration engine also gives the human participants access to any auxiliary services from systems that they may need in order to fulfill their task. When this happens, the human participants act as internal customers of the auxiliary services. BSO must have the ability to create a directory containing the organizational structure of a company, the people in it, their roles, their working hours, vacations, calendar rules, and other variables, and to make all of this available to the orchestration engine. This is the part of the "harmonization" capability that BSO has when orchestrating services from people.

1.2.2.2 Services from Systems

This category consists of all services that are delivered by a system, with systems including but not limited to:

- applications that provide data services (RDBMS, directory services, file systems, etc.),
- applications that provide monitoring or management capabilities over applications or computer systems (application management systems, infrastructure management systems, etc.),
- applications that provide connectivity and communications (e-mail, messaging systems, streaming media systems, etc.),
- applications that provide horizontal business logic (ERP, CRM, SCM, billing, provisioning, etc.),
- applications that provide industry-specific business logic (medical systems, insurance systems, banking systems, telecom systems, etc.),
- personal productivity tools (word processors, presentation builders, spreadsheets, etc.),
- mechanical systems (bulldozers, lifts, airplanes, ships, etc.)
- intelligent human replacement systems (robots),
- plant automation systems,
- arms and guidance systems,
- communication systems,
- demolition systems.

To be readily available to the orchestration engine, system services must be exposed in the form of an API. Most modern applications supply a rich set of services through their APIs. Legacy applications can usually be invoked at a transaction level through gateways. Some situations might require the creation of APIs or the use of screen scrapers. In other cases, direct database access might be required to obtain a service from a legacy system.

There are three ways to invoke a service from any system:

1. through an existing API of any type (including proprietary protocols usually found in mechanical systems interfaces),
2. through the data flow between the user interface and the back end,
3. through its persistent data.

These are the only three access points that any computerized technology has for leveraging business services from an application. There are easy ways, and not-so-easy ways, to leverage these access points: Messaging middleware uses adapters or connectors to transform these services into messages in a proprietary messaging system. That's the hard way. BSO technologies must provide the ability to discover and introspect API and component interfaces, automatically generating proxies in a component catalog that contain all of the necessary bindings to connect to those services, local or remote, and exposed in virtually any technology. This ability to discover services in systems, introspect their metadata, and automatically generate component adapters to them through different enabling technologies under a single, homogeneous catalog is a basic necessity to fulfill BSO harmonization. As we said before, another important piece is the capability needed at an IBO level, which includes the ability to extend transactional contexts, perform transparent data mapping and translation, and manage persistency.

1.2.2.3 Services from Organizations

Some services are composed of a series of organized and intermingled human- and system-driven activities. These are services from organizations or services delivered through real business processes. Services from organizations can be defined as real business processes exposed through a programmatic interface. Orchestrating people and system services is probably the easiest and most flexible way to create services from organizations. Services from organizations can be implemented in many ways. Their implementation is hidden from the customer that invokes them. This is essential precisely because the customer does not want to know how the service is implemented. The customer just wants to know what the expected result from the service is in terms of product, time frame, quality, or some other variable. Let's consider an example:

Assume that an internal customer, for example, the director of product marketing, wants to invoke an internal hiring service to recruit a qualified product manager. A number of potential resources could be used to accomplish this task. Some companies might use a headhunter, whereas others might do their own recruiting. Some companies require temperament profiling; others require a number of references. In the end, however, what's important to the director of product marketing is to know that he/she will hire a qualified manager in a given amount of time, and that the hired person will have, at a certain date, everything he/she needs to start being productive. This type of deliverable – measured in terms of product, volume, time, and quality – is known in many environments as a "service-level agreement" or SLA. We will talk more about SLA as a key benchmark for any business service.

This ability to discover and catalog services from organizations and expose the processes that use them as Web services or accessible subprocesses is another key component of BSO harmonization.

1.2.3 Classification by Enabling Technology

Business services also can be classified by the technologies that enable them. The examples cited here are by no means *exhaustive*, but they do provide an indication as to those orchestration-enabling technologies available when this book was written. We start with the more traditional enabling technologies and progress into the more modern ones.

1.2.3.1 Messaging Technology

Messaging technology was devised to replace punch cards as a source of input for the first mainframes. Messaging became more and more sophisticated as time went by. It was originally a way to create electronic punch cards through an intelligent terminal; it evolved into what was called messaging systems (IMS) and eventually into transactional systems (CICS). These enabling technologies were basically designed to work on a specific platform, and so, as more and more platforms were introduced, the industry saw the need for a cross-platform messaging technology.

That is why MQ series and the modern clones, such as MSMQ, were developed. An evolution of queue-based messaging systems brings us to the more modern publish-and-subscribe and hub-and-spoke messaging brokers. In today's market, messaging has proliferated tremendously and has been the basis for most modern EAI approaches. We consider messaging technology to be a valid business-services-enabling technology, but a message- centric approach toward business integration usually falls short of all that is needed to achieve the business objectives. Its place is more as an integration-enabling technology than as an integration solution.

1.2.3.2 Gateways or Bridges to Transactions

These enabling technologies were created precisely to transform legacy messages for use in another messaging system or another enabling technology. They have been instrumental in allowing systems from different generations to talk to each other. There are many and of every type imaginable, and we will not attempt to address them at length in this book.

1.2.3.3 Persistent Data Stores

This category of enabling technologies includes everything from file systems and databases to document management systems and directory and name services. Each of these enables data storage and retrieval services within a particular realm of competency.

1.2.3.4 Gateways or Bridges to Persistent Data Stores

In this classification, we group the likes of ODBC and JDBC. These enabling technologies function to abstract a database and to provide a supposedly homogeneous subset of services that will allow an application to be agnostic of the database implementation.

1.2.3.5 Remote Procedure Calling (RPC) and Object Brokers

In this category we group the first technologies that enabled APIs. These include Unix RPC, CORBA, and COM.

1.2.3.6 Application Servers

This category encompasses the second generation of component technologies, including transactional services and object and RPC brokering. In today's world, application servers also include Web server and Web service capabilities.

1.2.3.7 Internet Servers

These are Web servers, news servers, mail servers, internet messaging servers, file transfer servers, peer-to-peer servers, and others.

1.2.3.8 Fat Clients and Web Browsers

These are mainly the technologies that enable human services through a user interface.

1.2.3.9 Screen Scrapers and Web Scrapers

These are technologies that enable automated systems to use the data that flow between the application and its presentation to interact with the system.

1.2.3.10 Orchestration Engines

These services are typically large-grain organizational services that can be exposed through the proprietary APIs of the orchestration engines. In the more modern implementations, these services may also be exposed through Web services.

1.2.4 Combining Business Services

With all the above classifications in mind, we can now describe a business service in terms of the combination of the three taxonomies; for example:

- a discrete service from a person through a Web-browser-based work portal,
- a composite service from an application through an application server,
- an orchestrated service from an organization through an orchestration engine,
- a discrete service from an application through a screen scraper,
- a discrete service from a third-party organization through a Web scraper,
- a discrete service from an application through an internet server (Web service),
- a composite service from a control system through an object broker,
- a discrete service from an mechanical system through a messaging bridge,
- a discrete service from a robotic system through a proprietary messaging server,
- a composite service from a health care system through a database server,
- a composite service from people through an orchestration engine.

The combinations can go on and on, but this foundation of what business services are and how they can be combined is important to understanding the process of harmonization for orchestration.

Before we discuss the process of orchestration in Chapter 2, we explore the reasons why BSO is important and its future.

1.3 MOTIVATING DRIVERS

A number of market realities are driving the need for BSO. In this introductory chapter, we address the key drivers.

1.3.1 Customer Centric Economy

In his book, *The Agenda*, renowned Massachusetts Institute of Technology professor and pioneer of BPR, Dr. Michael Hammer, notes several factors that have produced the new customer-centric economy.

First and foremost is that customers now typically have a great many product and service alternatives. Productivity has been growing to a point where supply exceeds demand in such a way that suppliers are forced to fight for customers. Today, customers not only evaluate the quality of the product, but also their overall experience with the supplier. That experience cannot be left to improvisation or subject to the mood of one or more persons.

Web sites and search engines now also give customers information on just about anything and everything. There are sites that compare automobiles, offer any type of used goods, sell every imaginable airplane or appliance, and provide information about any religion. Companies that expose their products or services on the Internet compete for both mindshare and search-engine share. They must also be aware of Web-based polls and benchmarks that may mention their products.

Dr. Hammer says that, for any company to survive in the long run, it must have an ETDBW (easy-to-do-business-with) attitude. He also says that, to survive, companies need to add more value to their customers on a constant basis. How do companies achieve this in a constantly changing and ever more complicated world where search engines and benchmarks may de-position their products overnight?

There is a simple solution with a tremendously difficult implementation: Continuously reduce unnecessary overhead, reduce time to delivery, eliminate redundant tasks (especially those required of the customer), improve quality, and add value by continuously innovating your product line to better meet your customers' needs.

In a customer-centric economy, every nook and cranny of the company – every functional silo, every individual contributor, every application, every data source, every external communication, every piece of equipment – needs to be tense and ready to perform for the customer. To survive, a company needs to be like a highly trained runner that has every muscle, every nerve ending, and every abstract thought focused on the finish line.

For the enterprise to be responsive to customer, it needs to have a unified and integrated view of all aspects of customer-related information. This typically results in swivel-chair operation where the customer-facing employees have to pull customer-related data from multiple systems and then piece the data together to get a complete view. Responding to customer requests that require updates is even more difficult because that often triggers a business process managed through swivel chairs. BSO is the latest approach to accomplish this responsiveness to the customer for those services that are critical to the company's success by enabling computer-driven control and automation of these manual business processes and providing an environment where human intervention can be aided, audited, and perfected.

1.3.2 Trend Toward Virtual Enterprises

Globalization, partnering, and outsourcing are facts of life these days. In this highly competitive economy, companies must go wherever necessary to produce high quality products or services at a competitive price. Companies also have global customers, and to make it easy for these buyers to do business with the company, the organization must satisfy their languages and cultural preferences. This may require overseas operations, but more often it can be accomplished by partnering with strategically selected business allies. Growing competition also requires companies to focus more closely on their core competencies. This means outsourcing those services that are not critical to the central mission.

These forces support the trend toward the virtual enterprise. Organizations are "virtual" when they become an orchestrated set of internal and external services. Company boundaries are already getting fuzzier and fuzzier. Which functional departments operate in-company, and which are outsourced, is now very much an open question. It wouldn't be surprising if, sometime in the near future, companies moved to outsource CEO services (as they understand that jobs in today's silo-oriented world).

The one thing companies cannot outsource is the creation and management of their core processes. Those are the processes that implement the critical services that compel their customers to buy from them, to remain loyal, and to keep them in business. However, these core processes do not have to be implemented in whole, or even in part, through internal company resources. In fact, in the most successful companies, these processes consistently orchestrate services from the best possible source available, and today, more often than not, those services are outsourced. Yet, for a company to establish and pursue its core mission, these processes must be created, managed, and evolved by the company's senior leadership. These crucial processes represent a significant part of the identity and the competitive assets of the virtual enterprise.

In the past, companies were typically managed in either a centralized or decentralized way through the use of hierarchical organizations. A key to the success of the U.S. economy has been the ability of employees and management to work and hire "at will." This flexibility has given hierarchical organizations the ability to adapt and change to meet new challenges.

In today's world of complex supply-and-demand relationships, companies cannot hope to control the hierarchies of external members of their value chain. You either buy from a given supplier or you don't. You sell to a given customer or you don't. You ally with a given partner or you don't. If changing a supplier, customer, or partner implies a major upheaval in your organization – and your organization cannot adapt quickly and easily – your future is at risk.

By creating an environment conducive to managed change, orchestrations allow the virtual enterprise to be as flexible and dependable as the self-contained hierarchical organizations of the past.

1.3.3 Pain of Mergers and Acquisitions

No matter how hard we try, it takes a long time to build a culture and even longer to change an existing one. It also takes a long time to build the infrastructure and systems needed to support a successful company.

In the ideal merger scenario, two different cultures and two different infrastructures combine seamlessly to form a single, better enterprise. However, in reality this is often a lengthy and difficult process, so much so that the lack of integration is, in many cases, the primary cause of a failed merger. The objective is usually to make $2 + 2 = 5$. Synergy (symbiotic energy) is what they call it. The harsh reality is that, more often than not, $2 + 2 < 4$. We call it "antergy" (antagonistic energy).

A Harvard Business School case study, "InterSoft of Argentina," illustrates the cultural differences between the Argentinian software development labs and their recently acquired Russian counterparts. "The productivity of the relationship was outstanding as long as we communicated only by e-mail," an InterSoft official noted. "As soon as we tried sending engineers there or bringing engineers to Buenos Aires, the culturally driven antagonisms kicked in. They or we didn't like the food, didn't like the management style, and didn't like the temperature or the way we related to our peers ... it was difficult: productivity went down. As we went back to e-mail and short stays ... productivity went up."

This all-too-common dynamic exemplifies the benefits of the virtualization of relationships to facilitate integration. E-mail facilitates a purely intellectual interchange and minimizes the potential personal or cultural difficulties that can complicate a business communication. The same principle applies to other organizations and their cultures. The goal is to maximize synergies while avoiding antergies altogether. One way to do it is by "virtualizing" the relationship. Obviously, this is not possible at every level of a company, since every organization must forge and personalize its identity. Corporate management must establish a set of common values and principles and communicate those ideals to the rest of the organization.

However, principles and values alone do not guarantee a smoothly running operation. Differences in culture and infrastructure can be most apparent, and most damaging, on the front lines of a company's operations. The front lines are also where orchestration can mean the difference between success and failure. BSO plays an important role in maximizing operational synergies while providing shielding from the factors that usually provoke interpersonal or interorganizational antergies.

1.3.4 Avoiding Commoditization

According to classical economic interpretations, products of a certain type become commodities when price is their main differentiator. Therefore, the value of a given commodity is its price, and price depends on the vagaries of the marketplace. Companies in today's world can best defend themselves from commoditization through innovation and customization.

Loosely defined, innovation is the act of creating a new product or service, or adding value to an existing product or service. Also loosely defined, customization is the act of configuring a certain product or service according to the requirements of a specific customer, thus adding specific value exclusively for that customer. Implementing an innovation requires innovation. Implementing mass customization also requires innovation. Innovation implies change. People and systems in general are resistant to change. This resistance phenomenon is called inertia, and it's a natural law. Inertia leads to faster commoditization.

So, how do companies avoid falling into the unceremonious ranks of commodity companies? They do so through innovation, customization, and by becoming agents of change. Becoming an agent of change implies beating the natural law of inertia. In transportation, it had to be done first with boats, then carriages, then trains, then cars, then airplanes. In communications, it had to be done first with runners, then with organized mail systems, then with the telegraph, then with telephones, then wireless devices, and so on.

In businesses it had to be done with all the above, then with the computer, then with applications, then with integrated applications, then with application integration (internal or external). Finally, the more modern way to drive change and beat inertia is BSO. Orchestration is the only approach that allows businesses, as change agents, to reconfigure their services on-the-fly to offer customized services and innovation to customers without having to drastically change their organization and embark in expensive substitutions or reimplementations of their precooked integrations. You might ask: "Aren't work-flow or BPM systems on the same track? Not really. Today, work-flow and BPM systems *rely* on integration systems to provide connectivity with third-party applications. The main idea behind BSO is to provide the necessary semantics in a single language and the necessary runtime capabilities to manage people transactions and system transactions under the SAME ENGINE, seamlessly. The moment you are faced with using a work-flow engine to manage human services and a different integration broker to manage automated services from systems, you have created the possibility of two flows where there should be one. In real processes, there are clear dependencies between what people do and what systems do. What can be abstracted is the IMPLEMENTATION OF SERVICES, not the flow of services. Having many different flow engines produces the same mess that we are dealing with today when we try to integrate different ERP, CRM, and SCM systems in spite of their disparate embedded work-flow and process logic. This does not preclude the possibility of abstracting flows in the form of black-box subprocesses. This is always good practice, but these subflows always cause human services to be intermingled with automated services, as a minimum, to deal with exceptions. Therefore, subprocesses are included in the same abstraction layer as the calling processes: the BSO layer.

1.3.5 Security Concerns

Computer security schemes were originally created to keep unauthorized users from information that was either confidential or that the user did not need. Security protected the computer and its files. With the advent of local area networks, wide area networks, and, ultimately, the Internet, intranets, and extranets, business needs a new and broader type of security. Hackers have created all sorts of malicious viruses, worms, scavengers, and other specialties. Online theft, fraud, and wrongful access are concerns for both consumers and businesses.

As a remedy, companies have created strict security policies and given great power to the security experts that enforce those rules. Surprisingly enough, these security experts have almost unanimously opted for the same security scheme: An external firewall, a demilitarized zone (DMZ), and an internal firewall. The idea is very simple: Nothing except HTTP, HTTPS, and SMTP or MMTP requests are allowed through the external firewall. Therefore, the Web servers, mail servers, and news servers need to be in the DMZ. From there, the security people can open other ports in the internal firewall, strictly under their control.

However, these policies are questionable. Is it easier to allow only text messages to come in via port 80, regardless of what those text messages are, or is it better to open a specific port for specific types of messages? Isn't it more difficult to monitor the type of message that is coming in when it comes wrapped as http among thousands of other character streams, or is it better to open different ports for different types of messages?

The truth is that security experts do not and cannot monitor every message that comes into the company. Therefore, the rationale for the trade-off is simple: Make sure that whatever comes in is only text. Binary can do a lot of damage. Of course, text-based messaging is not entirely safe, since the majority of recent viruses have been written in Visual Basic Script. The problem isn't in the type of message. The problem lies in the facilities that receive the message and what those facilities do with that message.

Now, if all messages came in to an orchestration engine, and the rules of engagement for differing message types were specified within the BSO engine, we would have much more effective security protection. This is what we call a *soft firewall*. A soft firewall is in charge of brokering requests to back-end systems in an intelligent way, through process logic that implements company policy on the treatment of any and all messages and requests. Although there may be other solutions to deal with these security issues, we believe that these rules are essentially high-level business process rules and belong in the BSO layer.

This orchestration-engine-based approach also solves the problem of trying to establish a relationship between two companies by adjudicating passwords to all the employees. Larger granularity is needed to achieve an effective, efficient security regimen. Engine-to-engine security goes a long way in diminishing the complexity of any security approach.

BSO provides the foundation needed to implement simpler and more rigorous security policies.

1.3.6 Current Approaches

As we said earlier, current integration approaches are data-centric. This means that the intelligence resides in the preexisting applications, and the integration effort consists of setting up an infrastructure that allows these applications to communicate via an integration broker. The benefits are clear: The elimination of swivel chairs and the provision of a mechanism that avoids exponential growth of interfaces as the number of applications grow.

The model for EAI is ERP. ERP systems started out being disparate modules, which over time were linked through data integration and work flow. However, these integrated systems have been very difficult to implement. Even when successfully implemented and stable, because of their functional complexity those systems are difficult to learn and use and pose an enormous training challenge. Virtually every user company complains that it is easier to change the culture in their organization than to change their ERP implementation.

With the emerging orchestration approach, companies can now more quickly and easily orchestrate existing ERP services into new services that evolve with the business, and are tailored to the usability needs of a particular group of people.

Current EAI and B2Bi practices have also been largely successful at data-level integration of disparate application modules. However, the typical problems with

EAI and B2Bi are the high cost of ownership and the inflexibility of the solutions. In hindsight the reasons for these problems are clear:

1. To begin with, EAI and B2Bi require an all-or-nothing approach. To integrate a set of applications, they must provide adapters or connectors to every participating application. Application connectors must leverage all methods in the exposed APIs, and those methods must be sufficient to execute any received messages. Precisely because it is an event-based metaphor, and you never know what event will be next, the chances of success are directly proportional to the number of methods that are made available to handle those events. Therefore, adapters are big, even if in reality only a small percentage of the methods is ever used. Although event mechanisms per se don't necessarily imply methods explosion, the application-to-application integration approach does. The issue is that, in this approach, the processes that are being automated are not explicit; therefore, if a new application is added and it creates an event that is not understood by the adapters of the remaining applications, the event goes unprocessed. This leads to an adapter design with a nearly infinite scope. Adapters need to foresee ALL the possible interactions with the application, and therefore implement event handlers for all possible situations. This in turn usually implies the utilization of the full API, not just those methods necessary for the implementation of services needed in an explicit process.

2. The objective of these approaches is merely to integrate applications, whereas the larger business goal is to improve performance by automating business processes. They are not the same, and reaching the business objective through technologies that were meant for a technical objective is almost always more costly than initially projected. Even cobbling a work-flow engine on top of the EAI suite does not do the job because, as we explained above, a real business process intermingles human services with system services in the same flow. During the ERP phase, this cost was partially absorbed by the customer at implementation, but mainly absorbed by the ERP providers at development. In EAI, the cost is paid primarily by the customer at both development and deployment.

3. Adapters or connectors are marketed as off-the-shelf solutions, but in fact are little more than templates. Most require substantial work by system integrators (SIs) to adapt them to the needs of the customer. This is not a surprise because, as we pointed out earlier, adapters or connectors are heavily dependent on their surrounding environment.

4. SI billings for EAI projects typically range from four to ten times the license cost of the EAI or B2Bi suites themselves. SIs were happy while the party lasted but, now that the party is over, they are having a hard time finding large professional services engagements that offer real value to the customer.

5. To integrate a single participant into a B2B supply chain costs about half a million dollars and requires more than 140 days of effort. So, for a supply chain of 10,000

participants, this would be $2 \times 140 \times 10,000 = 2,800,000$ person-days, or more than 7,671 person-years, at a total cost of more than $5 billion. A high price to pay for an industry that isn't all that interested in changing the way it operates in the first place. BSO is a totally different approach. With BSO, you orchestrate services into new services that *you* expose to the world just like you expose your Web site. As BSO matures, integrating a supply chain of 10,000 participants may take as little as one hour, and supply-and-demand chains will self-configure on-the-fly. You may ask: "Do you mean each of these participants with his or her own processes"? Yes, because the processes of these participants will be exposed as an orchestrated service in the form of a Web service, which will easily be discovered, introspected, and integrated by other orchestration engines. Obviously, this requires widespread adoption of the BSO and Web services approaches.

6. Probably the most difficult barrier posed by current approaches is that they have not been designed for continuous improvement. To all intents and purposes, once applications or partners have been integrated, they are cast in concrete. Any change in back-end applications or process logic causes tremendous delivery delays. This problem is compounded by the size and depth of the integrated value chain. With orchestration, any services within the BSO environment and many services in the supply chain itself can change, with no effect on the rest of the chain, provided that these changes do not impact the signatures of the business services interfaces. Orchestration will, in the future, be able to discover and catalog services on-the-fly as needed by the process in progress. For example, if a company needs to buy a widget, the orchestration engine will be able to search for services from companies that provide that type of widget, select the most appropriate companies according to their Level of Service agreements and catalog those services on-the-fly, send them an RFI, and continue the process.

Orchestration provides the means to integrate internal and external operations quickly, cleanly, and at a competitive cost. In fact, it may well be the only alternative on the horizon that addresses this crucial need. In its early implementations, the ratio of professional services needed to implement an orchestration versus the cost of the orchestration system licenses is no more than one-to-one. This means orchestration is from two to five times faster and cheaper than previous-generation approaches to EAI, and a multiple of that in B2Bi projects. This affirmation is based on serious comparative studies of the differences in implementation efforts between one of the pioneering BSO solutions and competitive EAI and EAI plus work-flow–based approaches.

1.3.7 New Technology

This driver is more than just a driver. It's also a necessary condition. Until recently, orchestrating business services was limited to what human managers could do on-the-fly using prepackaged software. Companies looked more like a series of karaoke singers than an orchestrated opera. Yes, karaoke is fun, and a great way to discover talent, and sometimes it does cause an impression (one way or the other), but it's in a different league than an orchestrated opera.

The best "karaoke companies" have some practice (formal training) and some may even read music and lyrics (process definitions), but their execution has always been improvised by the silo (solo) singer. Most karaoke companies just execute by ear. This said, many companies undoubtedly succeed using this impromptu approach. However, their success is more a tribute to their human capabilities than to the value of prepackaged solutions.

In today's world, companies must go beyond mere feedback systems, and beyond even the single orchestra described earlier. Today's world requires a hyperorchestra: an orchestra that is distributed across complete value chains. However, to execute an orchestration across a complete value chain, we first need global data connectivity. Thankfully, the phenomenal growth of the Internet provides this global data connectivity, and thus establishes the foundation needed to support BSO. Other key technologies, including digital multimedia and wireless messaging, also support the emergence of orchestration.

Directory services, registries, and similar technologies allow us to discover and bind these services in a programmatic way. The advent of data and metadata standards such as XML, XML/SOAP, and WSDL now deliver key orchestration connectivity. Java provides a simple write-once/run-anywhere object-oriented language that is essential in the multiplatform environment of a hyperorchestration. Legacy bridges allow an orchestration to cleanly and efficiently tap into existing functionality.

All of these technologies have only recently become widely available. They are the basis for creating and orchestrating business services. Their availability is one of its most important drivers for orchestration, not only because they make it possible, but also because they drive a paradigm change in the way systems will be developed and integrated and in the way businesses will organize.

1.4 FUTURE OF BSO AND DIGITAL TECHNOLOGY

We believe that, with the advent of Web services and the proliferation of Web-enabling standards, such as HTTP, HTTPS, XML, XML/SOAP, WSDL, and WSFL, the orchestration of existing business services will become the preferred method of both using and creating these Web services.

Web services generally will be implemented as orchestrations of business services as described above, and those services might include other Web services or orchestrated services. Those services will be enabled by Web servers, XML/SOAP, and WSDL. In this manner, slowly but surely, we will see the advent of a World Wide Web of services that invoke each other to form new orchestrated services in an infinite continuum.

We foresee this trend creating a fourth tier, or hypertier, of enterprise computing. The hypertier will enable unprecedented levels of flexible business interoperation: the World Wide Web of interoperating businesses.

For example, in a multilevel supply chain, you would find a hypertier of nested order fulfillment services from one company to another. Each order fulfillment service is likely to be orchestrated from people services, application services, and, of course, services from other organizations. You can easily see that the intricate nature of such complex supply chains would require eons of work with any of the current approaches, yet it is relatively simple and natural within the BSO paradigm.

We believe that the BSO paradigm will be to business execution, application integration, and B2B integration what the relational databases have been to enterprise applications. Orchestration will revolutionize the way companies do business, offer services, and, in the future, integrate and create internal and external applications. However, it will do it in a quiet, unassuming way.

Without any doubt there is a strong messaging-middleware culture out there that will need time to adjust to the changes brought to bear by the coming wave of orchestration. Even though most of the important EAI vendors have now added a work-flow engine to their offerings, these engines are loosely coupled with their integration brokers and their usage is more opportunistic than holistic. Even if they decided to wrap their offering with a top-down methodology (which would, no doubt, improve the overall productivity of current tools), the impedance mismatch between microprocess-enabled brokers and macroprocess-enabled work flows will still pose an enormous implementation challenge. It is our contention that the BSO approach and related technologies will succeed where these previous attempts have failed. Through the success of BSO, we will witness an unprecedented improvement in productivity. It will silently and unassumingly go beyond the improvement that business and financial analysts expected – and never got – from the initial fiasco of the "Internet economy."

The same Web crawlers that today create massive indices of Web sites organized by keywords will soon evolve into business services, and those services will allow orchestration engines to dynamically discover services and to conform value chains to meet various and dynamic product, service, and performance requirements. Life cycles will become even shorter than they are today. Companies will become more and more process driven. Silo organizations will not survive because they will be too slow.

BSO is the more modern paradigm for industrialization of software creation. Although it leverages all of the previous technologies that were built with this objective in mind, orchestration goes well beyond just building functional, user-oriented systems. BSO creates systems that *interact* on- line with services from people, systems, and organizations to greatly enhance productivity.

This vision is supported in the fact that BSO actually reduces the complexity of integration. Because orchestration abstracts implementations of services instead of exposing them in the fashion of previous approaches, BSO goes well beyond integration into the realm of interoperation.

Application systems will never be the same in the age of BSO. They will be orchestrations of services from myriad different sources, not monolithic constructs from a single provider. This fact will drive today's software leaders to transform themselves as quickly as possible. We are seeing this trend today as we write this book. Everyone is starting to catch on to the vision, but not everyone is adopting the right approach. Those who do will survive; the others will not.

During the creation of this book, Siebel Systems announced its entry into the BPM space with their application network. Web Methods has been actively reengineering its integration suite to comply more closely with the BSO vision. SAP also wants a piece of the pie, and the list goes on and on. However, the same way that database independence has been important for ERP, CRM, and SCM systems, independence from *any* specialized application or technology is crucial to the success of BSO. Beware of application or platform dependencies in BSO suites. They are just a manifestation of old ideas trying to hang onto a lifeline: good for them, bad for you.

Another notable consequence of BSO is that it will help reduce the current information overload. Today's collaboration is informal, mainly through e-mail and instant messaging. This is great when most of the messages received are business relevant and provide all the information needed to accomplish the collaborative task. However, it gets ugly when more than 80 percent of the messages received are either spam or redundant massive replies. With a more formal approach toward collaboration, a great amount of spam and information overload will be eliminated and work will be less of a continuous interruption and therefore more amenable to workers in general, developments that will further enhance productivity.

Because of the encompassing nature of the BSO vision and the diversity of sources of business services, it will be very difficult for any company or government to monopolize the design of processes. Precisely because BSO does not suppose the previous existence of any one dominating standard, it will allow for regional, organizational, and personal preferences. We don't believe it will be humanly possible to create a Tower of Babel based on any given standard. So, the ghost of Orwell's Big Brother is not haunting BSO as it did BPR, work flow, and ERP when the selling companies were out preaching the benefits of the one-size-fits-all best practices, work-flow standards, and the single-source integrated application. This is another reason we believe that BSO will be a huge and rapid success, much like the explosive success of the World Wide Web. The Internet itself had been around for decades and e-mail had been used for many years, yet standards bodies have tried to get rid of them. Those two advances did not enjoy mass market success until the arrival of the browser/Web server. Today, the World Wide Web of services is at a stage similar to where Mosaic was four years before the end of the millennium: Still dormant, but about to explode. The idea behind the work-flow paradigm has been around for many decades, but it was dismissed as the market that never was toward the end of the millennium, pretty much the same as TCP/IP was dismissed in the late 1980s, and we were all going to be communicating via ISO protocols.

Few people outside of early adopters and academic circles have used independent work flow successfully. Just like TCP/IP had not been used by a vast majority in the early nineties. Conventional wisdom swayed from the work-flow paradigm to the new standards: Messaging middleware-based integration (the ISO of the end of the millennium). This is a paradigm that is better understood by technical people, just like the three-tier client/server architecture was better understood by technical people than the World Wide Web during the early nineties.

Yet Web technologies and work flow have something in common: they are readily understood by business people and nontechnical users. They have something else in common: These paradigms, coupled with a services harmonization capability, give birth to BSO. BSO inherits from them and this idea of making life easier in a world of diversity by providing the harmonization capability, the ability of appealing to the nontechnical user – in other words, usability. This feature will be a major reason for the trend in future adoption of BSO. The lack of usability, flexibility, and time to market of current business integration technologies is the pain that BSO will silently but surely relieve.

However, first it's necessary to make the Kirks, McCoys, Spocks, and Scottys of this world comfortable with the concept. In general CEOs and businesspeople (Kirks, McCoys) are naturally comfortable with the concept and clearly articulate that there's really nothing like BSO out there right now and that they would love to apply the approach if what they hear about it is true. The reason for this is that they are intimately familiar with the management discipline and perfectly understand the idea of nonspecialized cross-functional processes.

The CIOs understand it but need to be convinced with proof; they've been burned too many times, and so, they delegate the investigation of the problem to their architects and engineers. Business analysts understand it and are completely skeptical about the possibility of any product ever supporting the vision. They will respond with phrases such as "This is what the old such-and-such CASE tool tried to do and failed," "This is just a revamped version of work flow," "Yeah, I read from the analysts that this is lightweight integration," but most of them doubt that it will ever work. When asked for an alternative, they usually respond: "good programmers."

The hard-core infrastructure software gurus will want BSO to be implemented in their specific choice of application server. This is a metaphysical impossibility if we want to maintain BSO as a cross-container, cross-platform, database- and application-independent approach, which it must be to fulfill its purpose.

As we write this book, there are already a good number of BSO success stories that claim outstanding reductions in development time and order-of-magnitude improvements in change, and a number of implementations that were geared toward solving usability issues in existing systems with outstanding results in TCO and ROI. As these real stories continue, the skepticism on the approach will tend to disappear and we think that there's a possibility of stampede adoption in the near future.

If through this book we are able to give the Kirks, McCoys, Spocks, and Scottys enough of an overview and a roadmap on BSO to give them an edge on the potential stampede, we will have accomplished our objective.

CHAPTER 2

Process of Orchestration

2.1 INTRODUCTION

At this point we expect the reader to be comfortable and familiar with what we call business services, the different classifications, and what we envision to be the future of technology.

In this chapter, we explain what orchestration is by explaining the process of orchestration and then contrasting the resulting paradigm against the integration, automation, collaboration, BPR, and Web services paradigms. Then, we talk about the impact of orchestration on information technology (IT) disciplines and the way we do business.

Without any doubt, orchestration is something that, as of today, only humans can do. It is a creative activity. Furthermore, in today's enterprise, services are being orchestrated on-the-fly. Who is doing this? People are. People request services from other people and/or systems to be able to perform a service for someone else. Among the natural orchestrations that people perform, there are those that are systemic and repetitious, and there are those that are "one-offs." These systemic, routine orchestrations can be performed by an orchestration engine, relieving people of routine, repetitious tasks. From this perspective, orchestrations consist of capturing the rules and sequences of how and when a person invokes services to render a new one. In other words, *orchestration consists of creating an executable process model that implements a new business service by harmonizing preexisting business services and managing their tempo.*

It's very important to dissect this definition.

2.1.1 Orchestration Is Creating an Executable Process Model That Implements a New Business Service

The purpose of orchestration is to create a new business service for an internal or external customer. This service is created by developing a process model. This means that, although we acknowledge that there are other ways to create business services, if this is not done through the creation of a process model that will be executed by an orchestration engine, we don't call it orchestration.

2.1.2 Harmonization of Preexisting Business Services Is an Integral Part of Orchestration

Harmony is an interesting concept: it means that two or more different notes sound well together. Extending the concept to business services, we can say that *harmonization is enabling a business service from any source, exposed through any technology, to work well within an orchestration.*

The first step in harmonizing a service is to make it understandable to the orchestration engine. Not being human, the orchestration engine doesn't really have taste or understanding of its own, but it can be prepared to understand a certain set of data formats. This means that the first step is creating an interface definition for a service that is understandable by a previously prepared orchestration engine. In good orchestration suites, this preparation is done automatically by a synthesizer facility that can automatically discover all the services that have been exposed through a certain technology on a certain computer and then automatically create an adapter or connector to that service through a standard interface definition that is stored in a catalog. We will call this "synthesizing a service interface."

The second step is to make the interface understandable by the orchestrator (a human, generally a businessperson who is creating a process model). This means that the IT people or domain experts who have catalogued existing services either document them and create usage templates or compose them into new, business-level services for which they create usage templates and documentation. This is done by creating the intelligent business objects (IBOs) that we introduced in Chapter 1.

Harmonization is not an attempt to create new applications. Harmonization consists of creating a set of business-level services by composing discrete or composite services from systems or people into an IBO. For example, we would like to create services around a purchase order component that are something like get-order, put-order, approve-order, prioritize-order, approve-credit, etc. We don't care where we get-order from (SAP, Seibel, I2, or others). We don't want to know if we put-order into one of the above or all three at the same time and under the same transaction or which of the native services we use to do it. We don't want to know in which of those three systems there's an approval flag or a different status file. We don't want to know how an order is priortized or how many people are involved in approving the credit. If we follow these basic "implementation-hiding" rules, we will have services that are reusable across different orchestrations and we will be able to reimplement the services (e.g., when we add another application to the soup) without disrupting the orchestration. All of this at runtime! All of this with zero latency!

In synthesis (no pun intended) harmonization consists of

- **Synthesizing services from persons.** Discovering available capabilities in employees and contractors and assigning the roles corresponding to types of services that they can provide as well as the needed user interfaces.
- **Synthesizing services from systems.** Discovering available business services that are exposed through a certain technology on a certain server, automatically generating a connector.
- **Exposing services.** Creating a usage template and documentation for those services that will be used in their native form.
- **Composing services.** Composing native services into business-level services grouped under an IBO, and creating the usage template and documentation for them.

What clearly distinguishes true orchestration from simple work flow or business process management (BPM) is the harmonization facility that automatically synthesizes application services that are immediately usable by the orchestration engine or by a more abstract business-level service. This approach, given that it avoids the need for an added – often extraneously – messaging bus/adapter layer, drastically reduces development and maintenance fees and therefore the total cost of ownership of an orchestrated solution.

An important difference with messaging itself is that exposed or composed services are not orchestration-engine-specific (unlike connectors or adapters that are specific to a messaging bus), nor are they application- and release-specific (as connectors or adapters are to a specific application release). They are open and reusable by any application and only tied to a technology so they can be automatically extracted from any application or system. They are essentially a business-level application programmer interface (API). We talk about the possible implementations of these APIs later. The obvious ultimate implementation is Web services.

2.1.3 Managing the Tempo of Business Services Through a Process Model Is Germane to Orchestration

Tempo is the rhythm, order, and dependencies that regulate the execution of business services so that they delight the customer who invokes them. We all know that, in the modern world, time is money. In that context, "easy to do business with" generally translates into "timely to do business with." Mind you, we did not say fast; we said timely. Timeliness has to do with predictability and dependability and meeting expectations or exceeding them in a positive way.

One way to create the rules of tempo is through a graphical, roles-based process model that exposes the time and business rules-based dependencies between the different services or activities that are orchestrated into a new one. These process models can be infinitely nested, going from the baseline down into each participant's "libretto" or music sheet. These process models can always have counterpoints with other processes. When this happens, we are in the presence of orchestrated business services that present a multisynchronous interface.

A pretty common experience of parents in the United States is enrolling their children in school bands. It never ceases to amaze them that after the first semester they are actually playing things that make musical sense! This is especially true if they are the type of parents who listen to the early notes from their child's instrument with a smile while internally regretting having rented the instrument. Music teachers and orchestrators need to be very virtuous people. The screeching of a violin, the teeth-wracking sound of brass and reed, the nerve-wracking sound of percussion, and the unhealthy disharmony of keyboards and strings in the hands of novices require high tolerance to pain. The ability to persevere and orchestrate that mess into something worth hearing requires great vision and trust in humanity.

The juniors, after a couple of months, are capable of following a melody line, without any harmony or counterpoints. The drums, brass, reeds, and strings play the exact same melody with the exact same rhythm (or at least that's the intention).

This is analogous to a high-level business process. In essence, it is designed without counterpoints or harmonization. It's flat. It has no elaboration. It can get better, it will get better, but it requires practice, feedback, and evolution. You start with the melody and then work on the variations, harmony, and volume and rhythm alterations, always looking to further impress your audience.

A good orchestrator can do this through continuously improving the process models that he or she discovers over the way things are done today ("as-is" process). A great orchestrator, such as Beethoven, Bach, Mozart, Tchaikovsky, Lennon, or Bacharach, can see and hear the music in four dimensions (space plus time). They hear not only the baseline, but also the variations and harmonic accents. They can imagine the sound coming out of each instrument and write the orchestration on-the-fly; they see the "should-be" process. These people are very few. There are not enough of them to fulfill the need for orchestrating business services. Therefore, a methodology is required so that normal talents can successfully orchestrate business services. Chapter 4 describes tools for a proposed methodology template, and so, we do not go into further detail here.

Yet, there is a polemic that is better addressed right here and now: top-down versus bottom-up. Orchestration can be done from the melody down to counterpoints and harmonization or from counterpoints and harmonization up to the melody. Genius-level orchestrators tend to see it all simultaneously, but normal orchestrators need to use a step-based approach. Which approach is easier and more cost-effective for normal orchestrators? It is undoubtedly the top-down approach, from the higher process level down to the native lower-level services from applications, people, and organizations. When going top-down, the design path is natural and rational at the same time. You go from commonsense business logic that is understandable by all to the sophisticated detail and nuances of dealing with natively disharmonic applications and people. Furthermore, the top-down approach allows the business people to solicit the services that are necessary for the business process, and thus IT people will avoid the work of generating unnecessary services.

So, in essence, managing the tempo of business services consists of a top-down effort to design the process models that govern it from the lower level of detail toward the higher level of detail, from longer to shorter activities, from abstract to concrete. An easy way to organize this effort is:

- Start at a high level, the level of the relationship of the company as a whole with its environment. At this level the process orchestrates services from customers, partners, and suppliers as communities.
- Drill down to the intercompany services, where there are some rules that differentiate the services from individual companies within the communities.
- Drill down to the interdivisional services, where the rules differentiate the services from divisions within the companies.
- Go down further to interdepartmental services, where the rules differentiate the services from departments within the companies.
- Finally, go to the interparticipant services, where the rules differentiate services from people and systems. In this step the orchestrator can determine what services he/she needs IT to synthesize and compose from people and systems.

There is still one caveat. Not everyone can do the above. You need a person with high-level business knowledge with the capabilities of both abstraction and analysis. Typically, in IT environments and often in silo-oriented management environments, these people are seen as "poor performers," because of the time it takes for them to get from the ecosystem level to determining what services need to be orchestrated. In the meantime, everyone will get impatient and try to solve "their own" problems at a much more comfortable "sea level" altitude (buying or building an application that they see adequate for their problem). These applications will tend to be siloed in their scope and oriented toward pleasing internal users with functionality instead of pleasing internal and external customers. In short, orchestration requires commitment and unwavering support from company leadership. It cannot be done otherwise.

That said, it is always wise to start bottom-up in terms of the scope of the service that is to be orchestrated: Start small, think big.

2.2 ORCHESTRATION AS A PARADIGM

Business services orchestration (BSO) is more than a technology product category. It is also a holistic approach toward improving business performance by extracting the full value of its existing assets. One doesn't work without the other. This approach is what we will consider the "paradigm." We all talk about paradigms and paradigm shifts. We all intuitively know what it means. We're all tired of hearing it, but we have trouble in agreeing what a "paradigm" really is. In the context of this book, paradigm means *exemplary model*. This definition is not far from any dictionary definition.

So, BSO as a paradigm refers to the exemplary model of how to create new business services that will delight your internal and external customers without changing or modifying your existing assets. We have given the first broad strokes of this model in the preceding paragraphs. Now, we would like to differentiate this exemplary model from other exemplary models that are in vogue as we write this book.

2.2.1 Differences from Application and Business-to-Business Integration Paradigms

2.2.1.1 Differences in Goals and Objectives
The goals and objectives of enterprise application integration (EAI)) and business-to-business integration (B2Bi) are to facilitate the automated interaction between disparate enterprise applications or interenterprise transactions. These paradigms see the existing applications as the primary interfaces to existing users and tries to eliminate swivel-chair operations where some users spend time moving data from one application (internal or external) into another to maintain the synchronicity and consistency of the data. This paradigm was created under the supposition that existing applications had all the necessary functionality to allow for the complete automation of business processes.

In contrast, the goals and objectives of BSO are to create delightful business services for internal and external customers from existing available services from people, systems, and internal or external organizations. It's clear that the scope of BSO is broader than the scope of EAI and B2Bi put together. It's also clear that BSO makes no assumption on whether existing applications are enough to completely automate a company's business processes. Quite the contrary, it assumes that as the business evolves they will be insufficient and new services will need to be built or bought. BSO sees people, applications, and internal or external organizations as sources of services. BSO, like its precursor, work flow, does not see existing applications as the source of intelligence to orchestrate automated processes. They may have pockets of intelligence that are usable and may simplify the orchestration, but this is not required for its success.

2.2.1.2 Differences in the Implementation Approach

EAI and B2Bi approach implementation from the perspective of replacing people as messengers and translators between applications with messaging brokers and adapters or connectors. As the approach matured, the more visionary companies started to realize that those swivel-chair operators did more than just translate and input transactions. They actually collaborated with others to deal with exceptional cases, looked up data in the systems to which they had access so they could make intelligent decisions about what to do with the transaction, and escalated the problem to a supervisor when pertinent. In short, those people – knowingly or not – were driving a business process. Therefore, those companies started looking for business process management engines that they could put on top of their EAI or B2Bi technology to try to replace the user in managing processes. The problem with this approach is that although the data transformation and routing paradigm is adequate for replacing a translator/router, it is not pertinent as a basis for driving business processes. Therefore, most of these suites ended up implementing event-driven processes rather than process-driven events.

BSO approaches the implementation from the perspective of replacing people as "repetitive and routine orchestration drivers" with an orchestration engine. People are not seen as messengers; they are seen as process drivers who are not passively awaiting a message to translate and pass on, but are actively and intelligently soliciting the services they need in order to fulfill a request from an internal or external customer. Therefore, the orchestration engine is not just a messenger and translator; it is an agent that actively invokes business services to produce a result for an internal or external customer. The orchestration engine needs to "know" what it is doing from a holistic business perspective. We're not trying to say that the orchestration engine needs to be self-learning, but it does need to be able to apply the appropriate business rules it has been given by an orchestrator through the orchestration model and those rules have visibility of all the services available from within and without the organization. It's very important here to talk about intentionality. The orchestration engine fulfills an intention, the business intention of the orchestrator. A messaging broker fulfills no other intention than getting a message from one application or organization to another. The problem with the traditional EAI/B2Bi approach is that it takes for granted that the receiving end will know what to do with the message. This is not always true. In fact, it usually is not true (as can be seen by the results obtained so far). This is why most EAI vendors are struggling to incorporate work-flow engines into their offerings.

The key difference between the implementation approaches is that BSO attempts to create a business service that will delight the customer by orchestrating other business services (which, theoretically, should also be delightful). With this approach, services nest into great levels of complexity without requiring the customer to know what is going on behind the supplied interface. However, the customer of the service knows what to expect when the service is invoked and therefore can invoke it intelligently, and knows that the result will be delivered consistently. There's synergy in the concept of creating services to satisfy customers. It's the ultimate competitive frontier posed by the digital age!

In B2Bi and EAI, the customer has the capability of putting a message into a messaging broker, but has no clue as to what will happen to it. This is why, to be able to have some knowledge about what will happen, we invent "standard message types": EDI types, RossettaNet PIPS, etc. Then we ask the service providers if they support the standard or we try to force them to do so. It's not the service provider that is competing for our business by offering a service that makes our life easier; it is we, the customers, who are limiting their capability to delight us by demanding standard "junk food."

We are not trying to say that standards are not necessary. They are, but they are necessary at a technology level, not at a business level. Don't tell your supplier how to build a readable invoice! Choose the suppliers who satisfy you with a service, one with which you'll be more successful, and they'll be more compelled to oblige. Put the onus on the suppliers. Expect them to come up with meaningful orchestrations, so that you can then turn around and delight your customers with a more elaborate one.

2.2.1.3 Implications

Both the objectives and implementation of EAI and B2Bi paradigms limit them to being exclusively integration paradigms. The improvement in business performance will come – if at all – from the improvement in applications, adapters or connectors, people, and organizations that are external to the integration broker, not from the integration broker itself. To function properly, EAI and B2Bi require the creation of business-level standards and the ability to translate from many to many thereof. This in itself poses a major impediment to the improvements that the external sources can provide because standards tend to settle at a minimum common denominator.

Besides this major drawback, at the implementation level there are serious problems that make the approach questionable. The EAI and B2Bi paradigm require handcrafted adapters or connectors to back-end applications. There is no way of making these connectors reusable in different environments because they are sensitive to the different implementations of the back-end systems. Therefore, connectors need to be "reconfigured," which actually means reprogrammed, for each implementation of a given application. This poses a major obstacle to rapid deployment of any solution based on the paradigm. However, it gets worse.

As we said earlier, the underlying need to work with standards and to be able to translate many-to-many standards makes the whole construct heavy, complicated, and difficult to maintain. Avoiding the pain of creating rules that drive services has only made things worse: we now have constructs that need to interpret what service a message is meant to invoke, hope that the underlying service will comply, invoke it, take the result and artificially create another message for another adapter to interpret, and hope it will invoke an adequate service. We have added a layer that does not reduce complexity, but compounds it!

Without any doubt, this layer was meant to reduce the number of interfaces to be built. It has been successful in doing that. It's questionable that it has been successful in building maintainable constructs at a reasonable price. The approach is optimistic because it is based on the belief that the applications, people, and organizations will know what to do with a message that they receive in a format they understand. Therefore, the resulting constructs were not designed to be flexible. They are, for all intents and purposes, cast in concrete. Future improvements will either have to be built on top of the existing structure or the structure will have to be dynamited. As we all know, there is a limit to the compression that concrete can withstand.

BSO, on the other hand, is a paradigm in which the orchestration model itself drives services for continuous improvement. It is also inherent in the paradigm that it be able to discover and synthesize (automatically create) harmonic interfaces to new and better services without programming. These services, in turn, are used as the elements that are orchestrated into a new and better service that can be published on-the-fly for usage by customers! Business performance improvement (BPI) is at the core of the paradigm not at the periphery. Business interoperation is absolutely natural to BSO.

BSO supposes that the world is imperfect, that not all necessary services are available in the existing infrastructure, and that those that are available need to be synthesized and may need to be composed into business-level services to hide the underlying complexity. BSO supposes that work needs to be done; rules need to be put in place to successfully integrate services from applications, people, and organizations. BSO does not expect messages or services in standard format; it harmonizes disparate services and provides the rules to deal with diversity.

BSO does not believe that installing a pipe that puts messages from one application into another will do the trick because BSO is a pessimistic approach. Having this type of infrastructure installed only hardwires solutions that may not be adequate in the near future because applications, people, and organizations change. Therefore, improvement needs to be continuous and orchestrations need to be flexible. Orchestrations can be dismantled as easily as they were constructed. The parts are reusable, composable, and orchestratable. They can be rearranged on-the-fly without the customer ever noticing anything but the improvement, without any downtime! This is because modern BSO tools provide the capability to run different versions of the same orchestration simultaneously. Old versions run the instances that were created during their life cycle and, as a new version is published, all new instances are created in it.

At this point, it is safe to say that BSO is a substantially different paradigm than EAI and B2Bi, and the first results validate this affirmation. BSO has produced EAI results two to five times faster than EAI, and B2Bi results in massive value chains an order of magnitude faster than the above! For the experimented reader this should come as no surprise.

2.2.2 Differences from the Service- or Component-Brokering (SCB) Paradigm

2.2.2.1 Differences in Goals and Objectives

Under the SCB paradigm, we group all technologies that in one way or another expose application services in the form of reusable functions or components. In this paradigm we find old remote procedure calling (RPC) mechanisms, more modern object request brokers, and the ultimate application servers. The objective of these technologies is to provide a platform where application services can run, can invoke each other, and can be invoked as components. The more modern the construct, the more prebuilt services are offered to make it easier to build business-level components while hiding the more technical-level services. For example, in modern application servers you will find prebuilt services to manage connections, user sign-on, server clusters, and load balancing, transactional integrity, and other capabilities.

Their main goals and objectives are to make it easy to develop new green-field applications implementing solutions under a three-tiered architecture (SCB) paradigm where the business logic is separate from the presentation logic and reusable. As with any platform, to obtain all of these benefits, it is necessary to build all of the new applications on the SCB platform of choice. SCB platforms are not really good at interacting with other SCB platforms. For this, they typically use messaging systems that they don't usually provide. SCB platforms respond to the three-tier client/server paradigm. This is an approach for developing new applications. SCB platforms do not provide an approach beyond this architecture; they let the buyers decide which methodology to use and do not care whether it is top-down, bottom-up, middle-in, or inside-out.

In contrast, the goals and objectives of BSO are to create business services for internal and external customers from existing available services from people, applications, and internal or external organizations. BSO does imply an approach toward orchestration. However, BSO can benefit from an underlying SCB paradigm in as much as it provides easy access to services or components with their associated services. BSO needs to be able to talk to services that are implemented on any platform, not just on one. Furthermore, BSO's objective is precisely to build new services based on existing services from *people* and all sorts of *systems* and *organizations*. Services from people can be received through the presentation tier. Therefore, BSO sees a presentation application as a service, a robotic arm tightening a bolt as a service, a drone dropping bombs on a target as a service, in the same light under which it sees services that may be hosted by application servers or object-request brokering servers or as a callable command in a remote computer. SCB is usually restricted to creating and using application services on the server side.

2.2.2.2 Differences in the Implementation Approach

Most RPC platforms have been implemented to work tightly coupled to one or, at most, two or three given hardware platforms and operating systems. They try to take advantage of the native services of their chosen environments to make business services developed on them more efficient. They were initially designed to deliver services across a local area network (LAN) to client-side presentation applications. As the World Wide Web has become more popular, most application servers have in themselves become servlet engines or dynamic Web servers. The reason for this last move is to become the one-size-fits-all platform because, now, business logic and presentation logic are served from the same platform, and the Web provides the thin client interface. In essence, they would like everyone to deploy their applications on their platform. BSO has no problem with this. To the contrary, wide deployment of SCB platforms makes BSO as easy as it can possibly get. Yet, until the moment when only one SCB platform is left ruling the world, BSO will be necessary to abstract them in the same way that ODBC and JDBC are necessary to abstract relational databases.

BSO implements its own engine, which is not a platform but uses services from any other platforms. Although a BSO platform could be implemented on a standard application server, it is seldom convenient. Each standard application server tries to provide some competitive advantage that makes it incompatible with its peers. BSO migration to new platforms needs to be easy and not limited by the idiosyncrasies of a given application server or object request broker. BSO is essentially platform- and application-independent. BSO leverages Internet protocols such as TCP/IP, HTTP, HTTPS, and XML/SOAP for engine-to-engine, and engine-to-user–facing presentation services. However, BSO must also be able to leverage internally facing service and message brokering technologies such as Java, EJB, CORBA, COM, SQL, LDAP, JTS, JMS, MQ-SERIES, MSMQ, TIBCO, and others. Finally, whereas SCB technologies are fundamentally oriented to develop new applications, BSO is fundamentally a paradigm to orchestrate existing systems, people, and organizational services. BSO can be used to create new applications from scratch, but its strength lies in building new services from a majority of existing ones.

2.2.2.3 Implications

There is great synergy between the BSO paradigm and the SCB paradigm. BSO leverages these platforms as component or service brokers from which the synthesis and use of services is easy, safe, and scalable. However, BSO must provide its own framework for cross-platform transaction management services, user sign-on services, registry and directory services, connection pooling services, clustering and failover services, and others. The reason for this is to avoid *forcing* customers to use a service from a given platform. Often, customers will want BSO to leverage the existing services in the preceding list from an application server of their choice. BSO should be able to implement the framework using any preexisting service without any problem, but it should be treated as yet another synthesized and harmonized service, not be hardwired.

Something that sounds like BSO is being implemented as services on SCB platforms. The drawbacks of such implementations will be the limitations that the platforms will impose to a paradigm that is essentially platform independent. For example, Microsoft is implementing BizTalk and .Net on the Microsoft platform. Although the intent is to create open services from their proprietary platform, most large companies also have legacy systems in a variety of operating systems and various flavors of Unix.

BSO should be able to create new services from services that preexist in all of those platforms, not just Microsoft's; therefore, we don't consider BizTalk in its current implementation to be true BSO. We do consider it to be an exceptional SCB platform that makes it easy and secure to expose services through a variety of technologies and create them through a variety of languages, but always *implementing* them on a Microsoft platform.

Another example is BEA. BEA provides a process management facility within its application server. For the combination of WebLogic and the process facility to become something similar to BSO, they would have to provide a platform-independent component representation that can be created on-the-fly without programming. They should be able to run COM components, CORBA components, and legacy components as well as EJBs or, automatically generate EJBs that expose the former component interfaces. They may evolve to something like BSO in time, but their focus would need to be changed. The focus of an application server is to provide a development and runtime environment for components that are to be *programmed for* and *run in* the platform (WebLogic) to be able to utilize a *fixed set of services* provided by it, whereas the focus of BSO is to provide a way to discover and catalog, *without programming, any available services* that *are provided by any platform or system as well as in people and organizations* and orchestrate them into a new service.

To comply with the BSO paradigm, WebLogic should become a process engine in the sense that its focus should be on using services from other platforms rather than hosting components built for itself. Furthermore, both should be able to seamlessly integrate services from other organizations that possibly have another platform strategy. This can be done eventually through XML/SOAP, but will the other companies be able to use MS components of WebLogic or BizTalk on their Unix System? It doesn't look like this will happen anytime soon.

In conclusion, we believe that BSO is to SCB platforms as suspension bridges are to their pillars, with only one difference. Given that BSO is in the digital world, platforms can be exchanged on-the-fly without the bridge falling to pieces. BSO is the solution paradigm; SCB is one of the necessary technologies. Furthermore, for the BSO solution, you typically use more than one platform. If you try to build the whole suspension bridge on a single pillar you've created either a see-saw or a dam – imagine something like that instead of the Golden Gate Bridge! It's impossible to conceive a true suspension bridge that doesn't rest on more than one pillar. At a minimum, it needs to rest on two endpoints (each shore) and one suspension point. If you're trying to build an obelisk, and only an obelisk, then an SCB platform is all you need.

2.2.3 Differences from the Collaboration Paradigm

2.2.3.1 Differences in Goals and Objectives

We include in the collaboration paradigm those approaches that are focused on managing human activities. This is the case of work flow in any of its flavors: collaboration, transaction, enterprise, or BPM.

The goals and objectives of this paradigm are to facilitate, manage, and, in some cases, analyze human and/or organizational interactions. There are applications that specialize in managing data, others that calculate algorithms, yet others that provide productivity tools to users, and so on. Collaborative applications then specialize in managing the flow of work among people and organizations.

BSO makes a higher-level abstraction; BSO is indifferent to whether the work is done by people, applications, or organizations. Work from any source is seen as a business service. Therefore, BSO makes no distinction among the types of systems that exist or will exist in the future, and certainly does not consider itself as a collaborative application. BSO is an approach toward orchestrating services from any type of systems, people, or organizations into a new service that can be used by any type of systems, people, or organizations. BSO can then facilitate, manage, and analyze the interactions between people intermingled with interactions with systems, intermingled with interactions with organizations, in a single seamless process orchestration.

BSO is concerned with continuous improvement of business performance using all the elements that a business uses to fulfill its objectives. BSO does not focus just on people or systems or organizations. It focuses on all of them at the same time and manages processes from a holistic perspective. The cost of not doing so is not only the multiplication of specialized technologies but, much more importantly, the complexity of making work flows and integrations created with different technologies work together.

2.2.3.2 Differences in Implementation Approach

Most collaboration engines have been implemented as centralized servers that provide work lists to human participants. Their focus is to coordinate human activities. In general, since human activities are facilitated through documents that help humans communicate among one another and track and trace the flow, collaboration engines' strength lies in providing or connecting with document management systems or forms systems. Also, performance usually is not an issue, given the huge latency of human activities when compared with automated activities. Therefore, collaboration engines are implemented for low volume of transactions and large volumes of simultaneous users. Typically, they are prepared for multisecond response time. Transaction work flows and BPM, because of their more systemic orientation, are an exception to this last statement. They follow the same paradigm as their human-activity-focused cousins or ancestors: They concentrate on routing documents (or messages), not on orchestrating services.

It is no wonder then that even the latest BPM standards, such as BPML (Business Process Management Language), – the most modern effort from a multivendor association called BPMI to standardize the description of BPM models using an XML-based standard – is based on message routing and incorporates program controls within itself rather than on invoking services that hide these controls.

The BPM vision continues to be that of a facilitator, but the real intelligence on how to execute services resides elsewhere.

BSO's vision is that the orchestration is the intelligence that manages large grain services, in other words, manages the interoperation between people, systems, and organizations. This requires a much more sophisticated engine than those used in collaboration. For starters, the implementation of BSO by force needs to be natively distributed, because the ultimate goal is for organizations to be interoperational; therefore, it needs to implement — *and hide* — all the transaction management, security, scalability, and high availability features of the most sophisticated enterprise and interenterprise systems.

Therefore, BSO must be implemented natively as a federation of BSO engines, not as a centralized implementation. BSO also must be aware of messaging as a possible implementation of a services interface, but it still sees it as precisely that: A possible implementation. Clearly, BSO must be implementation independent. BSO does not rely on a document management system or messaging system or a transaction monitor to organize the services it uses. It relies on its services catalog, its clustering, high availability, and transaction management capabilities, which may well use services that are implemented using a document management or messaging system.

Document management systems as well as messaging systems are data centric. Collaboration engines that rely on these systems as the main basis to implement collaborations end up being data centric themselves. BSO is service centric; therefore, it has to be able to hide data implementations without relying on any given technology to do so but using all of them.

2.2.3.3 Implications

Although BSO and collaboration are related from the perspective of their meta-model (business process viewpoint), they have completely different objectives and implementations. Collaboration has not been a very successful market segment. The reason is simple: Companies put more effort in increasing performance through automation than through collaboration. Therefore, the focus of BSO on intra- and intercompany interoperation rather than just collaboration will make it successful where collaboration has failed. From the implementation perspective, BSO requires a much more sophisticated set of capabilities than collaboration tools do. This is why, even in the case of orchestrations of purely human services, BSO engines are far more reliable than the typical collaboration engines. This is also why just slapping a collaboration engine on top of an EAI suite or an application server does not transform it into an orchestration engine, the same way that slapping a body over two motorcycles doesn't transform them into a car.

Enterprise applications that utilize work-flow engines such as some of the more popular enterprise resource planning (ERP), customer relationship management (CRM), and supply chain management (SCM) systems are not automatically fit for orchestrating business services; they are fit for orchestrating their own components and that's what they were built for. They are simply not sophisticated enough and they turn every attempted orchestration under their supervision into a highly complex and seldom successful EAI implementation. In essence, there is no specific application that can be a services orchestrator unless it has been built using one. The reason is simple: Service orchestration is in itself a way of building applications from existing services. Applications that are not built from the outset using this approach and adequate orchestration engines, do not have what it takes to orchestrate services from other systems people and organizations. Even worse is the case of applications that want to be, in themselves, the centerpiece of a BSO effort. They shortchange the market and themselves. It's as if the CFO of a company wanted to be the CEO and then proceeded to run it exclusively from a financial perspective, or the VP of Customer Relationships wanted to run the company exclusively from his/her perspective, or the VP of Procurement wanted to do the same thing. How long do you think the company would last?

2.2.4 Differences from the Process Reengineering Paradigm

2.2.4.1 Differences in Goals and Objectives
No doubt, there are a lot of good ideas that flow from BPR to BSO, but their objectives are very different.

- BPR applies sound engineering principles to a business problem, helping companies reorganize to increase performance and competitiveness.
- The ultimate goal of BPR is to create a cultural change in the way companies organize and operate that makes them more effective.

BSO applies similar sound engineering principles to an engineering problem: Creating information technology (IT) solutions that allow companies to interoperate with services from other companies, internal organizations, people, and systems. The ultimate goal of BSO is to enable the World Wide Web of interoperating virtual enterprises. Unlike BPR, BSO does not intend to produce a cultural change. If this should happen, it would be because BSO has enabled virtual enterprises that consist of many companies that interoperate and therefore change the realm of possibilities. BSO's main objective is to reutilize *existing services* from systems, people, and organizations, orchestrating them into a new, more sophisticated service. The objective is not to change the way things are done but, as in judo, to leverage them to produce something new. This said, the methodologies and tools of BSO are slight modifications of those you will find in many popular BPR methodologies. We add more detail and references in Chapter 4.

2.2.4.2 Differences in Implementation Approach
In the early stages of an implementation, BSO borrows techniques and ideas from BPR. Although BSO concentrates on discovering and prioritizing services in the

planning and project planning phases (instead of super system, process relation-ship, and functional relationship mapping), there is no doubt that it leverages the central ideas of BPR (such as aligning services with strategy through the analysis of critical success factors and critical business issues).

They both share the "as-is" process discovery, the gap analysis between "as-is" and "should-be" processes, and some of the "should-be" process design ideas during the analyze and design phase. However, here is where the similarity ends.

BPR relies on documentation and training to implement the designs as a change of organizational behavior. BSO relies on a BSO engine to implement the designs as an IT solution. Some work-flow vendors are trying to do the same thing, and without a doubt this may be useful for purely collaborative solutions also.

Furthermore, it is recommended that the planning and project-planning phases for the first few implementations of BSO be skipped, cutting directly to the analysis and design phase to solve "pains" that stick out as sore thumbs, generally in the application integration, or the ERP, CRM, and SCM improvement arenas. BSO, like collaboration, would have a tougher time trying to get consensus in companies to go through a collaboration or work-flow implementation, because the pain for these types of projects is less acute than for the aforementioned ones.

The right time to help companies with a methodology for planning and project planning is after they have experienced the benefits of the first BSO implementa-tion. We include a framework for such a methodology in Chapter 4.

2.2.4.3 Implications

It is clear that, in the latter days of BPR, it was used more as a methodology to implement ERP, CRM, and SCM or to facilitate ISO9000 certification or total quality management or Six Sigma implementations than as an end in and of itself. The reason for this is that our fast-paced modern society tends to understand instant gratification better than the pot of gold at the end of the rainbow; in a world that doesn't wait, it seems difficult to find the time for cultural change.

As we said before, it is not in the charter of BSO to produce cultural changes of any sort. Furthermore, BSO thrives in an environment of no cultural change and no change in the legacy infrastructure of a company.

BSO is not after cultural change; it is after flexible, modern IT solutions that leverage the existing assets of every company by improving the way they are orchestrated. Therefore, it is clear that it can successfully "borrow" some of the very insightful and useful techniques brought to bear by BPR, just like enterprise application implementations did.

Precisely because it is not attempting to change the way people think, it will. However, it will do so in time and, quite frankly, BSO couldn't care less. The extraordinary goal of BSO is to enable the World Wide Web of interoperating virtual enterprises or the World Wide Web of dynamic services. Just like the World Wide Web of data changed the world without intending to, BSO will change the world without intending to.

2.2.5 Differences from the Web Services Paradigm

2.2.5.1 Differences in Goals and Objectives

Business-relevant Web services will greatly impact the way systems are built, business is conducted, and the world economy evolves.

There are two main reasons why Web services will have such a huge impact:

1. The IT industry leaders are behind them.
2. Web services are much more acceptable to companies than EDI or other B2Bi techniques and tremendously more acceptable than EAI approaches because:

- Web services are noninvasive to companies or divisions, whereas the older techniques are invasive.
- Web services don't preclude company or divisional freedom, whereas older techniques do.
- Web services need to be implemented only once by the company or division, whereas older techniques must be implemented as many times as required by the companies with which you must do business. (If two must-haves use EDI, two Web Methods, and two Rosetta Nets, you need to implement all three).
- Web services work on well-established Web technologies and do not require per-transaction fees to a VAN.

There are many other good reasons why Web services will grow explosively and be standardized spontaneously, not only in exposure but also in their content, just like enterprise Web pages have done.

The objective of Web services is to leverage Web technologies to provide a single standard for intracompany and extracompany interoperation.

Discrete and composite Web services development and runtime environments will be offered by the leading platform vendors as well as BSO providers. It is not the objective of BSO to be a development and runtime environment for discrete Web services. BSO's objective is to be the easiest way to leverage existing discrete and composite Web services to build and run larger-grain orchestrated Web services. BSO is in the business of orchestrating any type of business service, regardless of its implementation. Therefore, BSOs support every well-established technology that exposes services from people, systems, or organizations, including Web services.

BSOs allow you the freedom of not having to wait for the Web services to become mainstream while leveraging them now and when they do.

Since the easiest way to create Web services is by orchestrating diverse services from people, systems, and organizations, BSO will continue to pursue the objective of ease of use like it has for enterprise application usability.

2.2.5.2 *Differences in Implementation Approach*

Web services can be implemented using myriad different toolsets and run using myriad different platforms. The content of Web services is a different matter. If Web services are to expose services from applications implemented on a single platform, then application servers may be the implementation of choice. If Web services are to expose sophisticated services that leverage several systems on several platforms and services from people and other organizations, then BSO will be the implementation of choice.

Therefore, we can say that BSO is both a possible implementation of Web services and the easiest way to blend existing Web services with other services into a seamless process that orchestrates a new, business-relevant service, be it exposed as a Web service or not.

2.2.5.3 *Implications*

Web services will contribute to the success of BSO and BSO will be a driving force in the proliferation of Web services! They are joined at the hip.

However, BSO includes a technique that goes beyond Web services in terms of its capillarity into small businesses. We will talk about interpretable XML objects (IXOs) in the later chapters of the book. At this point, it is sufficient to say that IXOs allow businesses that don't have a Web server and a firewall but work by dial-up or broadband through an ISP to participate in any process on- or off-line without needing to install an instance of any EAI or B2Bi spoke, and for free. It is good to understand that BSO is concerned with covering the *full spectrum* of business services, not only those that are on-line and implementable by medium or large enterprises, but also not limited to on-line, synchronous, asynchronous, or multisynchronous, mono or multimessage (on-line or batch), or any other form that a service can adopt. Web services, on the other hand, will find their sweet spot in mid- to large-size companies and on-line services.

2.3 IMPACT OF ORCHESTRATION ON IT DISCIPLINES

The impact of BSO on IT disciplines may be greater than we can initially imagine. Enterprise-level IT disciplines have traditionally been dominated by one or more of the following traits:

- data-centric architectures,
- functionality-driven design,
- centralized implementations,
- specification-centric project management.

These traits, having been useful for creating domain-specific applications, are in many ways opposite to BSO thinking:

- service-centric architectures,
- process-driven design,
- decentralized implementations,
- ROI-centric project management.

Let's examine the impact of BSO on these disciplines.

2.3.1 Impact on IT Solutions Architecture

The two fundamental impacts that BSO has on IT solutions architectures is that it introduces a new layer or tier and creates a realm of absolutely new possibilities in terms of IT applications. Client/server architectures evolved from two tiers to three tiers as they encountered scalability and reusability issues. The Internet poses a set of new challenges: Ubiquity, multiplicity of platforms, multiplicity of organizations, unforeseeable network topology, security, and a whole new adventure in scalability issues.

BSO becomes the fourth tier in the client/server architecture but becomes the hypertier in the internet context. We will talk more about the hypertier in the next chapter. Let it suffice to be said in this chapter once again that BSO is not just a technology. It implies a paradigm shift and within this paradigm shift a totally new way of designing solutions.

This new way will have huge impact not only on the formal aspects of the architecture, but also on the material aspects of it. In other words, it will affect not only the architecture, but also to what IT as a whole will be applied. Applications will change dramatically with the popularization of the emerging BSO technologies and methodologies. They will no longer "simulate" reality as, for example, enterprise applications do today; they will act on reality and be a catalyst for real-world execution. For example, a purchasing system in the future will not talk to itself to create a purchase order and then allow a human to print it and allow another human to send it. It will talk directly to the systems of the adequate suppliers for what it's buying. It will not need to have its own catalog of suppliers; it will use a UDDI service to dynamically select the most appropriate suppliers of a given product or service, given a certain level of service requirement.

This means that BSO opens the possibility of applications being not only componentized, but also enabled to dynamically build themselves by automatically selecting and binding adequate components available on the internet on-the-fly!

2.3.2 Impact on IT Solutions Design

The pendulum of procuring IT solutions has swung from custom building to buying prepackaged applications for several reasons. Some of these reasons have been addressed in Chapter 1, but there are others. One of these other reasons is the fact that the functional approach toward designing greenfield solutions has been excessively expensive, difficult to make them evolve in a systemic way, and very lengthy.

In the functional-approach, systems analysts who had failed to please the users with their own ideas would tend to abdicate the responsibility of determining the functionality of the "system to be" to the target users. Users, confronted with such a scary task, would cover themselves by coming to the table with a comprehensive wish list that typically had much unneeded and redundant functionality. To avoid scope creep, the analyst would thoroughly document the requirements of each user and make sure that they individually signed off on them. Then, the analyst would proceed to compile the requirements and try to determine which of them were redundant or unnecessary. This was a difficult and error-prone task.

The next step was to model an application that would be able to deliver the resulting compiled list of functionality. The problem with this approach is already stated in its name, "functional design." The analysts had the power to ask the users what functions they wanted, but not what they needed the functionality for nor how it related to the needs of the business, the customers, and other co-workers. This was considered to be the user's business, not incumbent to the analyst.

Therefore, in the cases in which they arrived at a reasonable design, it was due to an elaborate mix of domain expertise, personal capability, and sheer luck. The personal capability entailed having the insight to try to understand what the customer's business did and why it did it, and not just what a user's needs were.

An example will clarify why: Let's suppose the "analyst" is to design a vehicle that can carry a person, a dog, any other sort of animal, provisions, surfboards, a Kodak camera and film, a computer, a set of games, and Grandma. If the analyst knows the family well (domain expert), then he may be able to guess that they're going on vacation. However, if the analyst doesn't ask where they're going, where they're leaving from, what route they will follow to get there, where they're going to stay, how long they're going to be there, etc., he may end up designing the wrong vehicle. Let's suppose that the family lives in San Diego and they have three months to go to Hawaii by sea. Then, designing a boat would be reasonable. If the family lives in Des Moines, Iowa, and is going to Hawaii from there, a boat would be inadequate; if the family lives in San Francisco and is going to Yosemite, then an SUV would be adequate. Therefore, the functionality depends more on the process to be enacted than on the wishes of any or all users.

BSO, as we will see in Chapter 4, in the analysis and design stage, requires that the analyst ask all of the above questions; in fact, from a purely rational perspective, you cannot even begin to determine what functions a service needs until you have fully understood where you are going (the full deliverable of the service) and how you are going to get there (process model). BSO constitutes a middle ground between the rigidity of prepackaged applications and the potential lack of alignment with true business need of a purely functional approach toward design. In fact, one of the most popular uses of BSO today is to make existing applications more usable or more adequate for the business strategy without having to reimplement or change it.

We often have heard IT people saying that it's easier to buy prepackaged processes than to try to discover the ones in place in a company. True, but the consequences are visible to anyone who wants to see them: Unconnected, overlapping, incompatible, and difficult-to-use disparate processes that need to be integrated through a process that requires the design that was avoided. However, this time the design is more difficult because it is constrained by the processes in the purchased applications.

EAI is yet another attempt to avoid the inevitable. Why is it popular? Because at the beginning it promised that, through prepackaged connectors, there would not be a need to discover and improve the company's processes; the goals would be achieved just by connecting those that were already in the applications. This fallacy has been unmasked by the fact that not only are the original EAI tools incorporating process modeling and execution facilities, but the implementation of prepackaged ERP, CRM, and SCM systems themselves implement internal workflow facilities and have many times required the services of process-savvy systems integrators to be able to get them to work properly.

The effort of designing and implementing business processes is inevitable; it's like the Borg (in *Star Trek*): Resistance is futile. We might as well get it over with and take it on.

It is also true that, until recently, it was very difficult to go from the design phase to the implementation phase because the development environments and case tools available had artificially divorced the world of work flow from the world of data integration and data flow. This created various levels of processes to be designed. This is why often when people talk about their processes, they can mean any of the following: A screen flow, a work flow, a data flow, a procedure, something that a CPU does, etc. The reason is that existing tools address one or more of the above definitions separately.

Very seldom do we hear that a process is an organized set of activities that an organization performs through its people and systems or through other organizations to fulfill the requirement of an internal or external customer. This is the definition of a process that fulfills a business service according to BSO. A process model implements an orchestration of services that automatically drives the execution of all the activities necessary to complete the real process as defined earlier. A business service is the result of that process as seen by the customer who requests it.

This viewpoint for design implies that the process model should start from a high level of abstraction, as explained earlier, and progressively move downward to implement subservices in the form of either subprocesses or methods in IBOs.

Therefore, the impact of BSO on design is that it fully enables a top-down, process-centric approach toward orchestrating business services from any kind of people and systems. Design is made easier, faster, and more secure through the BSO approach. Not only does the procedure change, the content also changes. Orchestrated services can easily be monitored and measured to see if they fulfill the business need as well as the needs of the participants in the process.

2.3.3 Impact on IT Solutions Implementation

In today's world, IT solutions are platform centric. Developers think of developing a full blown application on a certain platform and, when needed, recur to messaging-oriented middleware to talk to applications that work on other platforms. This leads to the process segmentation to which we alluded earlier, due to disparity of platforms as well as to disparity of applications. Process segmentation should be driven by business needs, not by technology constraints.

For example, in an order fulfillment process, you have services from finance, such as credit approval and invoice creation. You have services from production, such as inventory reservations and inventory replenishment, and others. You have services from logistics, such as carrier selection and shipping. Typically, these services are fragmented by the applications that implement them. They may be further fragmented by the platforms that are in use. This common scenario is no problem for the Orchestration paradigm because each fragment is seen as a services container from which the Orchestration engine will invoke discrete services and coordinate them with other services. For message-oriented integration, each fragment is seen as a stand-alone know-it-all application that can be relied upon to know what messages to send and what to do with those it receives. This is not always true.

It all comes down to a matter of reasonability in terms of the granularity of the "black-box" services (those that will not be modified). The larger the fragments of hardwired processes or services, the lower the flexibility and reliability of the end solution; the smaller they are, the more complex the solution. BSO advocates seeing applications as a set of services that are *"business object" size*, allowing for implementations that are easily evolvable and understood by business people. Other approaches see applications as a whole and provide adapters or connectors to the monolith; these approaches are more akin to technical thinking in which the world is restricted to applications and infrastructure. This means that non-BSO implementations abdicate from the possibility of reconfiguring services within applications, and applications do what they do and changing that is a matter of changing the application. On the contrary, BSO implementations focus on what the business needs and try to find those services in existing applications, whether they are in a different module or running on a different platform, or, worst-case scenario, need to be supplemented.

In short, the most important impact of BSO on implementation is that it allows for a top-down approach. This approach starts by modeling the service that the business requires and then drills down through as many levels of subprocesses as necessary to reach existing, discrete services from systems or applications through the creation of IBOs. We will see more on this in Chapter 4.

The other great impact on implementation is that good BSO suites do not require application-specific adapters or connectors to those services once they've been identified. BSO suites are capable of discovering the required services within applications and automatically generate the connectors to those services without any human coding. This is much more reliable and faster than the traditional approach.

When dealing with services from people, BSO already provides through its work portal, the critical functionality required to deal with them. Views of work lists per role, search capabilities, security, and permissions are among the most important services that a good BSO system provides to be able to prompt for and handle services from people.

Some of the more sophisticated BSO suites also provide a Wysiwyg forms design capability that complements the work portal. The most advanced BSO suites also implement the ability to serialize these objects and their presentations into executable XML objects that can be sent via e-mail, FTP, instant messaging, or XML SOAP to any remote client allowing the client to work off-line and take it's part of the workload as well as eliminating the need for huge Web server farms on the server side and the need for the client to log into many Web sites to do any job. We discuss this capability in detail in Chapter 10.

The impact on implementation of the above features is huge because they enable BSO not only as a tier that lies between presentation and business logic, but also as a tier that is in charge of distributed presentation and frictionless B2B. This is very important because often what is needed is a uniform interface, regardless of whether it is for an internal user or for a B2B transaction.

The above, plus the fact that orchestrations can be published to and run on a federation of orchestration engines that are unknown by the programmer, makes BSO implementations transparent on the client side as well as the server side. This means in essence that there is no difference in the way BSO deals with EAI or B2Bi. Where processes and presentations will execute is a matter of configuration, not of programming.

2.3.4 Impact on IT Solutions Project Management

Project management has always dealt with issues such as sandbagging the project plan, avoiding scope creep, documenting delays due to user or customer procrastination, documenting delays due to external factors (such as infrastructure readiness), hiding inefficiencies of the development and/or implementation teams, and hiding the problems of or blaming the technology (depending on the situation). In any case, the idea behind project management was to set low expectations in terms of the functionality to be delivered and to set high expectations on the work that needs to be done to get there. In many cases, there was no attempt to determine whether the functionality required was what the company needed; this was implied in the fact that they were paying for the project. BSO does not suppose that the company knows what functionality it needs and tries to discover it by partnering with the incumbents, as set forth in Chapter 4. BSO pays more attention to the end result (customer satisfaction and ROI) than to the means toward that end result (functionality).

As we will see in Chapter 4, the BSO tremendously simplifies the calculation of the ROI of any given project. Still, there should be some sandbagging; it is usually a good trick to promise only a small percentage of the perceived potential upside.

It's easy to see which approach is more aligned with the interests of the target enterprise.

Much has been said about calculating ROI. Many have used this approach, but the truth is that, although the theory was all in place, until the advent of BSO the actual results were very difficult to measure.

BSO provides the user company as well as the project manager with tools to forecast the ROI and measure the actual results as the orchestrations go into production. Therefore, BSO techniques and technology enable the project manager to *prove* the accomplishment of company objectives in terms of ROI.

In this context, it really doesn't matter what the expected functionality was. What really matters is that this new orchestrated service is valuable to the company and justifies its existence by either top-line or bottom-line improvement. This proactive co-design of the "should-be" processes that implement an orchestrated service transforms the passive role of IT into a highly active role, and the role of a project manager into the role of a change agent that is focused on the benefit to the company rather than exclusively on the functionality wish list supplied by users.

2.4 IMPACT OF ORCHESTRATION ON BUSINESS

Much can be said on the impact of orchestration on business.

Perhaps the most important impact is that orchestration aligns what people and systems do to fulfill the strategic needs of the business and the requirements of the market. Before BSO, businesses needed to align their strategy to the requirements of their existing infrastructure in terms of systems and people. Reconfiguring that infrastructure to satisfy the market and changing company strategies was such a lengthy and onerous process that it usually didn't make sense to even attempt it. Instead, businesses embarked on BPR projects in the hope that trained humans could compensate for the shortcomings of IT solutions. However, businesses have never really had the time to train their constituents to the extent needed. BSO practically eliminates the need for training on changes in the company's business processes and practices. The orchestration engine actually invokes services that people and systems already know how to perform and provides the sequence and tempo needed to be effective. BSO does not rely on human memory and volition to set the rhythm of operations. It relies on an orchestration engine that can work 24-7 and has failover capabilities.

BSO also impacts business in the sense that it opens the door to virtual enterprise organizations. As we said earlier, for BSO the raw materials are services from people, systems, or organizations. It makes no difference to BSO whether those people, systems, or organizations are internal or external. As we said earlier, it's purely a matter of configuration. Therefore, services that today are done in-house can be outsourced by the company and driven by BSO with a very small effort.

BSO provides the ability to monitor, track, and trace who did what (or what did what), how long it took to perform the task, and other metrics. This means that BSO can be continuously monitored to propitiate continuous improvement.

All of the above impacts also have their repercussions in the relationship between operations, strategy, and IT. They become inseparable. IT enables operations to fulfill the strategy. IT works with operations to define the orchestrations that are needed. IT is no longer reactive to demands from operations but proactive in search of better processes to implement the orchestrations. Operations no longer hands off requirements; it participates in designing the processes that are going to orchestrate their activities.

Also, the enterprise as a whole interacts more fluidly with its environment. Business becomes more dynamic and, at the same time, more reliable!

People become more productive because they participate in the planning of the orchestrations and can then concentrate on the execution of services that are usually less repetitive and more creative. Managers who were only good at enforcing a recipe created by others (and many times tainted by their own convenience) will no longer have a job.

Counter to conventional wisdom, BSO unleashes business innovation. It creates the time and the peace of mind necessary for it and provides a framework to implement it.

BSO may well be the modern substance that produces *the freedom to innovate.*

CHAPTER 3

The Hypertier of Information Technology

3.1 INTRODUCTION

Much has been accomplished by designing information systems architecture as independent tiers that interoperate only with those that are directly adjacent. In this way, logic is boxed into a logical hierarchy that makes solutions more scalable and easier to understand, maintain, and change.

This thinking started with the client/server model. This model was used successfully at first in two different environments and for two different purposes:

- as a way to separate the database services from an application that uses them (in this case, the client is the application and the server is the database server),
- as a way to separate the presentation services on a workstation from an application that uses them (in this case the client is the application and the server is the presentation server).

As more modern enterprise applications evolved, the need for separating both the presentation layer and the data layer from the "business-logic" layer became self-evident, giving way to the so-called three-tier client/server model. The three-tier architecture has had many different implementations and has gotten more and more sophisticated.

Initially, the layers were simply the data layer, which consisted fundamentally of the database server; the presentation layer, which was basically a presentation server; and the application layer in the middle, which consisted of everything else.

The application layer still implemented many generic reusable services that could be distilled from it. As these services started being abstracted from the application logic, the concept of application servers as "business logic containers" became more popular.

The idea was that these containers would encapsulate and hide the implementation of low-level services such as database access, transaction management, connection management, high availability, clustering, application programmer interface (API) management, messaging, and, of course, presentation. In this way the applications built on these platforms could be totally independent of the different implementations of the services they used and the developers could concentrate on coding the business logic. Furthermore, this business logic could be exposed as services to be used by other applications that could run within the application server or not.

The application server providers, seeing the impressive adoption rate of Web servers as the preferred way to create ubiquitous "thin clients" that started to implement not only the presentation logic, but also some business logic (content management, screen flow rules, etc.), started scrambling to add this functionality to the application servers so as to create a single platform for everything.

Without any doubt, using the Web as the presentation tier, with somewhat of a fuzzy boundary between the business logic in the application servers and the presentation logic in the Web servers is presently the state of the art for constructing and/or front-ending enterprise applications. However, is it sufficient for orchestrating business services from disparate sources?

In the .NET model, it would seem that it is. The idea behind .NET is that as long as there is a standard way to interoperate between different application servers (i.e., XML/SOAP), you can orchestrate services from disparate sources by creating the business logic in any one of them that simply uses services from others that are exposed through a standard protocol. This metaphor counts on the fact that all application providers and all application servers will eventually offer a Web Services stack to interoperate with them. Is this going to happen? Maybe. There is one thing for sure: as we write this book, independent software vendors (ISVs) and application server vendors are not sure that they want to play this game. They have already spent plenty of resources in exposing their application programmer interface (APIs) through CORBA, COM, Java, EJBs, XML, messaging buses, and others. There are also other constraints: the architecture to support thousands of users is not naturally the same that you would use to support several hundred peer application servers. There are scalability and security issues to be addressed and, of course, there are some basic transaction processing issues to be addressed. How can the ISVs be sure that XML/SOAP is the last implementation they will need to support? ISVs cannot possibly support every new connectivity technology that is introduced; therefore, expecting ISVs to support not only fully functional APIs but also to expose them through every possible technology is not very realistic. Many will bet on XML/SOAP because of the hype and the backing from Microsoft, IBM, and Sun Microsystems. However, they will already have to support the two substandards that are being created for description and discovery: Universal Description, Discovery and Integration (UDDI), and .NET.

The idea of peer application servers connecting through a universally accepted standard protocol is not new. It was present in Smalltalk, CORBA, somewhat in DCOM, J2EE, and many other initiatives as old as Transaction Processing (TP) monitors.

What these approaches have in common is that they try to avoid the need for harmonization by establishing a new superprotocol, which, because of its beauty, or simplicity, or adoption on behalf of the market leaders, will tend to be adopted by everyone.

History proves that massive adoption of standards in this area has been an elusive goal. There is a sort of self-preservation instinct in all of us that makes us wary of losing our identity and differentiation; things have gotten better in this respect, but the tendency is far from eradicated. One notable exception is the stack of internet protocols. It is also an exceptional situation: Netscape offered a free browser and so did Microsoft, and therefore so did everyone else. This provided the context for companies to be able to reach every desktop effortlessly. Nobody under these circumstances was going to challenge the standards that enabled this free access.

Now a superprotocol for application interoperation is a different animal: no matter how super it is, it is as limited as its specification and as complicated as the evolution of its specification. Standards tend to start out being limited, but straightforward and simple, and often end up being extremely convoluted and complicated. A prime example of this is CORBA. XML/SOAP is a sophistication of HTTP and XML and it will probably get more and more sophisticated. When it becomes as complicated as CORBA, chances are that another standard protocol will be proposed.

There is no end in sight to the variety of "standard" interoperation protocols, and so, supporting only one of them (although we celebrate and welcome the initiative of Web Services) will not suffice; a new tier of logic that can interoperate with all "standard" protocols is necessary. This new tier is the *orchestration tier*, and what it does is *proactively harmonize services from disparate sources implemented on disparate technology stacks*, and allows you to easily compose these harmonized services into orchestrations that can be exposed (or not) as a new, larger granularity service. For these orchestrated services, we do suggest using the Web Services

Description Language (WSDL) as a way to expose their discrete services and any of the process description standards (BPML, XLANG, WSFL) to expose the public flow of the orchestrated services. The reason for this suggestion is the fact that previous process interoperability standards such as WfMC have not been widely adopted and that WSDL and the process description standards will enable *any* application to interoperate with an orchestrated service.

So, in the BSO model, we create the new orchestration tier or, in short, *the hypertier of information technology (IT)*. Although initially, BSO will be utilized inside the four walls, it will reach its maximum value as the neural network of interoperating enterprises becomes a reality. It is really here that it goes from being a tier of nested processes to a hypertier.

It seems self-evident that the current approaches that decouple the hypertier into internal and external data-flow tiers and a work-flow tier, or an enterprise application integration (EAI) tier, a business-to-business integration (B2Bi) tier, and a business process management (BPM) tier, are, once again, missing the right level of abstraction for a business integration solution.

Mark Theilken, CEO of Fuego Inc., put it succinctly by saying: "It's like trying to build a car by putting a couple of motorcycles (i.e., a Harley and a BMW) side by side and linking them with pipes." They may both perform beautifully on their own, but the joint performance will be underwhelming and totally lacking in usability. All you need to do is imagine the adapters that need to be built: differentials between the engines, a common transmission, a common gear-shifting contraption, common steering contraptions, a body without chassis, and on and on and on!!!

The hypertier needs to view all possible services under the same light. Although segmenting the aggregation of these services by technology or by origin may seem to reduce the complexity of the problem, the opposite is true!

This is precisely why BSO is counterintuitive for many great IT professionals. We have all been trained to segment domains vertically and then try to bring them together. This discipline of "divide and conquer" is the opposite of what is needed for orchestration: "harmonize, compose, orchestrate, and conquer."

Nobody in their right mind can think that orchestrating business services is a trivial problem no matter how it is approached. It is complex, and what we usually fail to see is that the nature of the problem requires a holistic approach. Most of what we have done previously has required a highly specialized approach. Therefore, if we rely on conventional wisdom for business integration we are condemned to end up (as we have) with "spaghetti EAI," dysfunctional B2Bi, and BPM on life support.

David McCoy from the Gartner Group has been trying to articulate this concept by saying that BPM will succeed as a feature set of EAI, but not on its own. We would like to embrace and extend this concept to say:

The architecture for BPM engines and integration brokers should be redesigned into a single BSO suite that, using a single engine for driving human activities and automated activities, orchestrates services from any origin exposed through any technology. The World Wide Web of processes hosted by such engines will become the hypertier of IT.

3.2 REQUIREMENTS

The hypertier of IT as defined earlier is where virtual enterprise interoperation comes together. Therefore, it needs to be a robust, dependable, and secure environment in itself and provide more dependability and security to the environments with which it interacts than if the actors of the environment interacted directly among themselves. We will examine how BSO implements this hypertier and why it needs to fulfill state-of-the-art availability, security, scalability, and flexibility.

3.2.1 Availability

An old adage says that a chain breaks at its weakest link. Therefore, in a long supply chain that interacts automatically, if any orchestration engine should halt its execution, the whole chain would be affected. A World Wide Web of interoperable enterprises is very demanding in terms of availability. Any breakdown may cost much more than the total cost of the infrastructure that sustains it in lost business. From this perspective, orchestration is mission critical and orchestration engines must comply with the expected availability of mission-critical systems. Precisely because orchestrations are close to real time, both the benefits to the businesses involved when the entire chain works flawlessly and the losses to the businesses when it ceases to do so are magnified far more than with old batch-interaction models. This makes high availability a must for BSO. BSO without high availability is like a monkey wielding a gun at the World's Fair: very dangerous.

Availability can be compromised by malfunctions or by implementation changes. To deal with malfunctions the hypertier must be composed of BSO engines that support failover capabilities that are absolutely transparent to users (be they human or other orchestrations). This means that a BSO engine must be able – given a fatal malfunction – to failover to another engine without any visible effect on the operation of internal or external, human, or automated users.

To deal with implementation changes in the orchestration, BSO engines must be able to run different versions of the same orchestration simultaneously and seamlessly. The more advanced BSO engines allow the publication and deployment of a new version of an orchestration on-the-fly (without bringing down the engine) and transparently (without the human or automated services being affected in any way or losing their consistency). This is done by setting a time at which all new instances of the process will start flowing through the newest version (usually the instant it is deployed). The old instances will continue to flow through the version or versions in which they were created. Because processes can be as granular as necessary, this is always done at the lowest possible level.

At least one of the BSO engines investigated in order to write this book completely fulfills the above requirements.

3.2.2 Scalability

In the same way that malfunctions can affect a whole chain, scalability issues in one BSO site will affect the whole chain. Therefore, BSO must be infinitely scalable. Scalability has many facets. Possibly the most obvious of those facets is the ability to attain linear scalability by clustering BSO engines and automatically balancing their load. However, like quality, scalability must also be achieved within each engine. This implies ensuring the scalability of simultaneous users to an engine, of interorchestration communications within an engine, of interengine communications, and of the systems and/or people that provide services to the orchestration.

The scalability of people and services may have constraints that are beyond the capability of BSO. Therefore, this needs to be dealt with at the design and implementation stage by ensuring that the scalability of the overall company infrastructure can deliver the level of service required by design. We dwell more on this issue in Chapter 4 when we deal with the methodology framework.

Leading BSO engines at the time this book was written and within the real-world implementations that we investigated are already more scalable than the back-end applications and databases and have been limited by their capacity rather than by the capacity of the BSO suite itself. Obviously, we are talking here of situations in which the BSO engine runs on either the same platform or one similar in power to the one on which the back-end systems are running.

3.2.3 Security

One of the reasons why the messaging metaphor has been more widely used until today than a services metaphor is because messages are perceived as innocuous and services are not. This means that the recipient of the message is in control of what is done with the message. The message itself does nothing. Services, on the other hand, do things. Although, in essence, implementing a service is nothing but creating the logic that knows what to do with a message (request), there is a false sense of security in the fact that, in a pure messaging paradigm, what the recipient does with a message is "the recipient's business" (private) whereas, in a services paradigm, what the recipient does with a message is public. It's a false sense of security because it is generally easier to construe what the recipient is going to do with an order message, an invoice message, etc.

Nevertheless, creating services that interface directly to back-end systems can be very risky. For instance, if we expose a SubmitOrder Web service that interacts directly with SAP we may forget to add process rules that detect abnormal behavior in the usage of the service. For example, if a certain company buys 100 widgets per month and we suddenly receive an order for 1,000,000 widgets, it is very possible that a malicious competitor has breached the identity security of the customer to compromise our inventory and take us off the market.

This type of heuristic is better created at an orchestration level than at a discrete services level because it may need historical data and human intervention.

BSO suites need to provide capabilities for enforcing this business-level security because, without a doubt, the business process paradigm is more adequate and closer to the problem than a discrete services paradigm.

We call his capability that needs to be present in BSO suites "soft firewall capability."

This capability does not preclude the need for BSO suites to adopt state-of-the-art encryption, signature, and non repudiation security strategies. One of the advantages of the hypertier model is that it is very easy to establish a trusted network of BSO engines, thus avoiding the need for certificates and return-receipts for every transaction, as would be the case for non-orchestrated Web Services.

At least two of the implementations of BSO that we have investigated have good encryption, signature, and non repudiation strategies. Only one has the ability to create a soft firewall at the BSO level.

We will take a closer look at these other mundane security requirements that must be addressed by a BSO platform. We discuss the security features of various platforms in detail in Chapter 5 and discuss security within the specific context of Web Services in Chapter 6. However, here are a few key requirements that must be considered:

3.2.3.1 Authentication

Authentication is a process of verifying the identity of an individual or a software entity – known as *principal*. The evidence required to establish the principal's identity is known as *credentials*. We describe two modes of authentication that should be supported by the BSO environment:

1. **Basic authentication.** The basic authentication of requires the client to identify itself to the server by providing a username and a password. In this case the username provides the identity of the principal and the password provides the credentials.

2. **Certificate-based authentication.** In this mode of authentication, the client or the server can be authenticated through digital certificates. These certificates

provide a set of authentication information and are obtained from trusted third party sites and establish the credentials of the principal. The information in the certificate itself is authenticated because the certificate itself is digitally signed by the trusted third party hence making it tamper proof.

3.2.3.2 Authorization

Once the identity of the service requestor has been established and verified, authorization can be performed. *Authorization* is the process of determining what rights the principal has in terms of being able to access the service functions. This is commonly referred to and implemented through *Access Control Lists*. BSO enhances this security by applying role-based and time-based rules. Furthermore, BSO determines not only the functions to which a certain identity has access but when, and under what circumstances this access is granted.

3.2.3.3 Message Confidentiality

This feature provides protection of the contents of the message itself. Message confidentiality is typically provided through encryption. The secure socket layer (SSL) infrastructure provides a complete solution for encryption, including the exchange of digital certificates. HTTP(S) leverages the SSL layer to provide a secure HHTP implementation. However, SSL imposes a significant performance penalty because it encrypts the complete message. However, in many situations, all the data in a message are not confidential data.

In particular, in an XML-based message exchange protocol, one may be able to identify only certain elements of the XML document (the message format) that actually need to be protected. A security mechanism for Web Services will allow protection of selective elements of an XML message.

3.2.3.4 Message Integrity

The platform should support the integrity of a message. A receiver should be able to verify that a message was sent by an authenticated user and also be able to determine whether a message was altered in transit. This is usually accomplished by being able to digitally sign either the whole message or parts of it.

3.2.4 Flexibility

The BSO model must be platform independent and, generally, technology independent. Only in this way can it adapt to the strategies of the companies that adopt it. As we will see in the following point of this chapter, the BSO suite makes use of:

- platforms as service servers;
- databases as process instance data persistency servers, and servers of historical operational data;
- directory services or databases as metadata and business logic repositories;

- web servers and/or servlet engines as presentation servers and of on-line analytic processing (OLAP) tools as process execution analysis tools.

All of these components must be configurable according to the existing infrastructure of the company that uses BSO in order to avoid the need to retrain IT personnel and infrastructure administrators. The objective of BSO is to facilitate enterprise integration, not to further complicate it by requiring new infrastructure.

By the same token, the BSO architecture should be designed so that the processes that implement the orchestration as well as the services that it utilizes can be changed on-the-fly without affecting overall execution. For example, if the implementation of a process that is invoked by other processes changes, the processes that call it should not be affected, and if the implementation of a component (service) that is used by one or more processes changes, these processes should not be affected. This architecture will provide BSO with the required flexibility to fulfill its objective as the hypertier of IT.

BSO should go one step further and allow for parametric roles as well as parametric subprocesses and parametric services. This would allow all of these implementations to be context sensitive at runtime and provide the utmost flexibility.

At the time this book was written, there was at least one BSO product that fulfilled this requirement.

3.3 BSO REFERENCE MODEL

To facilitate the discussion on the desired architecture, we propose a reference model for BSO Figure 3.1 and then use it to discuss various elements of that model.

We use the time-tested block representation of different tiers of the reference model. However, this is not a waterfall model, but there is a recursive relationship, as discussed in detail later, between some of the tiers. Figure 3.2 shows a more flow-oriented means of describing interdependencies between elements of different tiers. We leverage both figures to describe the reference model.

Now, let's consider each horizontal and vertical tier.

3.3.1 Operating Systems

This tier represents the most basic tier in our stack. This new architecture does not really impose any special or new requirements on the operating system tier.

3.3.2 Web Application Servers

The web application server tier forms the most core software element for component-based development. Web application servers are extremely important member of this reference model because they provide the development platform to

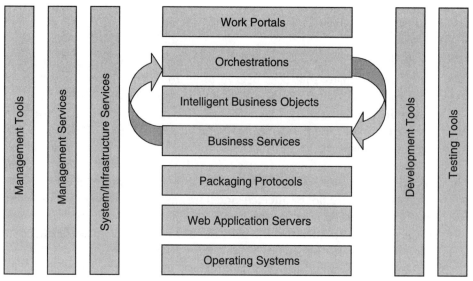

FIGURE 3.1. Reference Model for BSO.

build discrete business services. A typical application server integrates many core services that are usually required to build distributed component-based systems. The Web application server simply adds the web server to the application server and permits development of applications that can be accessed over the Web using packaging protocols based on HTTP.

We devote a considerable amount of time on application servers in Chapter 5. We briefly describe the core capabilities that we expect from the web application servers. Some of these capabilities may appear to be redundant because they are also part of either the system/infrastructure services tier or the management services tier. Although those generally are for the entire architecture, they are more specifically for the orchestrated services. In some cases, the products may actually integrate services similar to those provided by the development platforms under their tool sets.

- **Robustness and scalability**. These qualities are important at various levels. They are also given a first-class status in our reference and are considered an important capability of the management services tier for the architecture in general. However, the responsibility for robustness and scalability of the discrete business services that are being orchestrated primarily falls on the development platforms upon which it builds.

- **Metadata management**. This is so important that we devote an entire chapter (see Chapter 7) to it. In general, metadata for the development platforms is

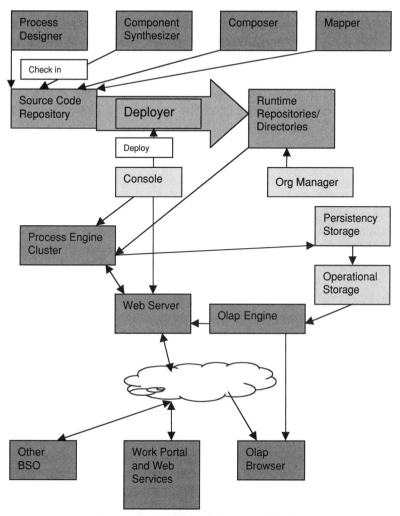

Figure 3.2. Elements of Reference Model.

for correct execution of the applications. These metadata may be things such as object-relational database mappings for persistence or various flags for correct delivery semantics. Quite often, to achieve better performance, these tools generate the metadata in code, which is then compiled rather than accessing repositories at runtime.

- **Security.** There is no single correct solution to the security problem. Security approaches almost always differ between business partners. Often, it will be different between various organizational units within the same enterprise. At other times, it depends upon the particular tools being used. In any case, the security services supported by the development platform are an important consideration.

3.3.3 Packaging Protocols

This tier provides packaging protocols. There are too many packaging protocols to consider. They are often confused with transport protocols, because many transport protocols also include packaging formats. However, we classify IIOP, RMI, and HTTP as carrier protocols. These protocols provide the basic means for transferring data from one end to another and perform connection management. IIOP also includes a packaging format that allows rich-context data to be passed along with the application requests.

Business services packaging protocols build upon the carrier protocols. Different protocols are important for different scenarios. We earlier warned against considering any single protocol as the superprotocol. Some protocols, such as IIOP, are very suitable for tightly coupled components within the trusted environment and high-performance on-line transactional systems. Other packaging protocols that are based on XML are very well suited for loosely coupled systems. XML-based protocols that are layered on top of HTTP, such as SOAP and ebXML, are particularly well suited for interactions between business partners when the requests have to go through firewalls. SOAP is discussed in detail in Chapter 5.

3.3.4 Business Services

This tier forms the business logic or the application tier. We spent a large part of Chapter 1 describing and classifying various kinds of business services. Business services are the centerpiece of our reference model. These are the business applications that are orchestrated to form solutions. These applications are the crown jewels of the enterprise and form the backbone of the IT. They may be custom-built applications, common off-the-shelf third-part applications, such as CRM and ERP systems, or legacy host-based applications such as IMS, TPF, or CICS applications that somehow have been resurfaced using new technologies.

3.3.5 Intelligent Business Objects

Intelligent business objects (IBOs) combine data representation and business logic to form intelligent objects. A user interface can be added to IBO to form visual business objects (VBOs). Every business object should have a companywide representation using IBOs or VBOs, whichever makes sense. For example, purchase orders, company invoices, company checks, bills of material, shipping manifests, functional specification sheets, and many others could be encapsulated in the form of VBOs. These objects provide an intelligent proxy to the business services and expose only the desired operations of the business services to the client. These objects can be serialized into interpretable XML objects (IXOs) that can be sent to a client environment and are capable of executing there, providing some simple services, such as data validation in the client's address space, without having to hop over the network for such tasks. Once the object has done what it was intended to do, the client can submit it for further processing. This process can be executed at the sender's orchestration engine or in any sequence of clients that the process has previously configured into the interpretable XML object. Both, IBOs and VBOs are capable of being converted into an IXO. IBOs and IXOs are discussed in detail in Chapter 6. VBOs are discussed in Chapter 9.

This layer also has a very pragmatic side. Although we discuss these objects in detail in Chapters 6 and 9, we briefly explain their rationale here also. As suppliers and consumers rush to integrate with each other to realize the promised benefits of integration and e-business, they are encountering a simple issue that has never been very well understood by IT architects – affordability. Electronic Data Interchange (EDI) was an attempt at making electronic business affordable for all companies, big or small. However, EDI grew so complex that only large companies were able to afford the costs associated with it. As a result, the small mom-and-pop shops were unable to integrate with the big boys. Again, today's integration brokers have become so expensive that the smaller organizations cannot afford to integrate with their suppliers.

The IBO tier, through its capacity to serialize objects into IXOs that are transportable through any internet protocol, is meant to address that hurdle, among others. The technologies in this layer allow a simple XML file that describes all the data required to fill out some forms and perform data validation. Simple and inexpensive plug-ins can then be provided to process these data at zero cost. Consider a small auto body shop that has only a computer with a dial-up internet connection and e-mail software. An insurance company, while processing a claim for an auto accident, sends an IXO to the auto shop via e-mail. The mechanic detaches the IXO from the e-mail and double clicks on the IXO. This causes the plug-in to be downloaded, if it is not already there, and the IXO is interpreted. The IXO processing results in a form being displayed to the client that captures the required input from the mechanic, and the "Submit" button uses any protocol (e.g., e-mail again) to send the resulting data back to the business service. This scenario demonstrates a real need to have low-cost solutions to integration for the B2Bi.

3.3.6 Orchestrations

Now we come to the centerpiece of the whole architecture. This tier sits between the business services tier and the presentation tier. This is what we call the *Hypertier*, primarily because orchestrations must be able to invoke services from people, systems, and other orchestrations, which in turn invoke services from people and other internal or external orchestrations, and so on. The two arrows in Figure 3.1, between the orchestrations and the business services tiers, show the recursive nature of orchestrations and the business services.

Orchestrations implement cross-functional and cross-company business process logic rather than the functional business logic that either already exists in installed systems or can be created on application servers. The orchestrations can themselves become discrete business services and can be further orchestrated by other orchestrations.

Orchestrations don't care where the services come from (people, systems, or other orchestrations), how they're implemented, or how they communicate. These last two issues are abstracted through the harmonization process. Therefore, well-designed orchestrations are reusable across environments. They allow for proactive harmonization, without waiting for all of your suppliers to adhere to a new standard. The services are typically harmonized through rules written in a scripting language that must have the capability of seeing all catalogued services as subroutines of the language and manage the data in the catalogued components as instance variables. In this way, the most complex business rules can be expressed with a few lines of scripting code. Ideally, the IBOs that we talked about earlier should be written in this language and used as a form of isolating the process logic from integration logic, and creating reusable rules.

This hypertier is basically composed of orchestration engines. These orchestration engines are to the World Wide Web of Business Services as *Web browsers with their human operators* are to the World Wide Web, with one huge difference: orchestration engines are usually mission critical and work on the server side; the Web Browser isn't and works on the client side. Orchestrations control the sequence in which services are performed. Therefore, they control a "custom protocol" for each process model they implement. This custom protocol drives what people, systems, and other orchestrations do and when they do it. It is no longer the duty of humans to drive these processes, and even less the duty of standard protocols. Once humans design the process, they can rest assured that the resulting orchestration of services will execute routinely and the ex-"human process managers" will be polled exclusively for services pertaining to their best abilities or to handle exceptional cases that exceed the capacity of the process rules.

3.3.7 Work Portals

The work portal represents the presentation layer of this architecture. It is to the World Wide Web of business services what the Web portal is to the World Wide Web of information. The work portal is the primary means through which the orchestration engines solicit services from humans, giving them a visual window into the orchestrations. Work portals notify human participants of the services they need to perform according to their roles in the company; they can be implemented on any computer or wireless device with messaging capabilities. In essence, the orchestration engine invokes and monitors the execution of human services through the work portal.

To facilitate the execution of these orchestrated services, the orchestration engine also provides the human participant access to the auxiliary services that are needed to perform the service on which they are working through the same work portal interface. Views of work lists per role, search capabilities, security, and permissions are among the most important services that a good BSO system provides to be able to prompt for and handle services from people.

3.3.8 System/Infrastructure Services

Architectures typically have been defined in terms of services that map more or less to purchased products. IT professionals have generally segmented these services by technology and/or by their origin. For example, those architectures almost always map the data services tier to database servers. As we stated earlier, that kind of architecture compounds the complexity instead of reducing it.

The architecture presented here views all services under the same light. This architecture places a huge amount of emphasis on *the service-oriented environment* where, as much as possible, services are exposed interface descriptions that can be shared by others, truly relieving them of their complexities.

Let us consider some of the important services that ought to be provided by the environment in which BSOs live and breathe in. We call these services system- or infrastructure-related services and place them in the vertical tier because they are leveraged by most of the horizontal tiers.

3.3.8.1 Data Management Services

Data management services are NOT database servers. There are many different kinds of data models that need to be managed. Some of them have to do with the business services that are deployed and others have to do with the environment. Some data elements are stored in database servers. Others may be stored in file systems as documents or proprietary repositories. How it is stored is not relevant for the logical model we are describing here because that model relates to physical implementation of those services.

3.3.8.1.1 Metadata and rules. Metadata are important and Chapter 7 goes into a considerable amount of detail. The literary definition of metadata is data that describe data. However, most often, metadata are used for information that systems may use to describe the systems they manage or services they provide. So, by that definition, the WSDL document for a web service may be its metadata.

Service contracts are an important form of metadata. Services running in an environment – system-level or business services – offer certain functionality to others who may want to use them. The functionality that they provide is described by their *service contracts*. WSDL is one form of a service contract, although we believe that a contract may include a lot of other information. In any case, some services have to be provided to store and retrieve these service contracts. In a service-oriented environment, systems are not bound to each other. In fact, they discover compatible services at runtime by using the discovery services provided by the environment. This search often will be driven by some criteria that are defined either by the application domain or the industry group and will most likely result in a compatible service contract being retrieved. UDDI is the de-facto standard for service contract management and discovery facility. As will be discussed in Chapter 7, although UDDI is a good start, it falls very short of the mark for the reasons discussed.

Orchestration definitions represent another form of metadata. There are many different initiatives in this area that are trying to standardize the orchestration definitions. These are discussed in Chapter 7 in quite a bit of detail.

Another important form of metadata that needs to be managed is the transformation rules. We discuss transformations in Chapter 4 in a lot more detail than we want to go in here. For right now, let us just say that as data are exchanged between business services, conceptually similar data are seldom structured the same way. A customer record in one system may not look entirely like a customer record in another system. For this reason, messages often have to be transformed from one form into another during the exchange. Most BSOs provide very powerful transformation capabilities. The data that describe details of required transformations have to be managed by the environment.

Another important kind of metadata is data validation rules. This greatly simplifies the application itself because the programmers or the designers can describe these rules and then the environment can manage them.

In more sophisticated BSO suites, the data validation and transformation rules are abstracted out of the executing business services themselves and can be changed on the fly, even after the business services have been deployed.

3.3.8.1.2 People and organizational data.

We have discussed in other chapters the importance of roles that people and systems play in orchestrations. A prime objective of BSO is to improve productivity by automating the manual participation of humans and eliminating swivel-chair operations. However, human services are still required but now they are coordinated by the orchestration engines. The part they play in the orchestration engine still depends on the role they have in the organizational structure.

This demographic data about the organization are managed by this service. A traditional architecture would have shown something equivalent to Lightweight Directory Access Protocol (LDAP) here. We insist on a higher-level service that has a well-defined service contract and is able to manage and mediate access to these demographic data through those well-defined interfaces. This service may very well be implemented over LDAP, but that is part of its implementation detail. In any case, LDAP is an access protocol; BSO-related data structures and functions still need to be defined as well.

3.3.8.1.3 Component synthesis data (component catalog). The component synthesis–based approach to generate interfaces requires storage of synthesis data. When an application is synthesized, two things may happen. First, the application is converted into a web service if it is not already in that form. This process of normalizing all application interfaces to Web Services is not necessary, but will help greatly and simplify the entire process. As part of this, WSDL is generated for the newly created web service. This Web Service and its WSDL and other contract-related information can be registered in the metadata and rules management repository. The next step in the process is to generate components that provide fine-grained object-oriented proxies (called components) to web services Later in Chapter 6, we discuss how these generated components are then used to build IBOs.

The generated components can be stored in the component catalog. The exact form of these generated components is specific to the particular BSO platform and its synthesis tools. Some may actually generate metadata; others may, in addition, generate a serialized object that can be used to create a runtime language-specific artifact whereas others may generate a programming language object with all the needed data generated in its code.

3.3.8.1.4 Operational data. As system and business services are deployed and execute, a lot of operational data are generated and need to be managed. Examples of some operational data for the orchestrations are the process instance-level data that are used by the orchestration instances to record their current state. Similarly, business services themselves may have some operational data of their own that they may need to store.

There may be a multitude of data management services to manage operational data of different kinds. For example, the orchestration engines might not want to share their operational data store with the applications for their operational data.

3.3.8.1.5 Application data. These data represent the data tier in the traditional three-tiered architecture. As you can see, our architecture removes that as a separate tier because we anticipate standard software services that will use, for instance, a relational database, but provide a higher-level interface to the applications. They may capture, as part of the metadata, the entity relationships between application components and may automatically keep the component model and the data model synchronized with in the context of transactions.

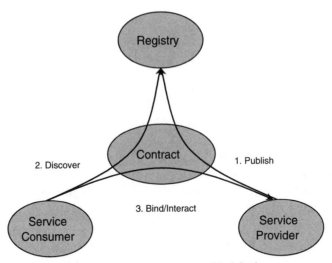

Figure 3.3. Publish–Discover–Bind Cycle.

3.3.8.1.6 System/environment data. There are other services that are provided by the environment/platform, such as load balancing and fault tolerance, that require management of some specific data. For example, an environment may allow clustering for load balancing and failover. However, that would require data associated with the configured orchestration engines and their current processing loads.

3.3.8.2 Discovery Services

Discovery service is the hallmark of the *service-oriented environment* in which the orchestrations dynamically discover each other and each orchestration discovers services that it can use and bind and with which they can interact. The endpoints of the applications are not hardwired into the client orchestrations. While making the orchestrations much more flexible, this feature also allows the environment to manage the scalability and failover by having the freedom to move the deployed services around according to the preconfigured policies.

Figure 3.3 describes the typical *publish–discover–bind cycle*. In this cycle, when a service is ready to be deployed, the service provider publishes it to a registry service. Often, this can be done as part of the deployment process. Publishing in a registry may mean several things, such as registering the basic information about the service that is generally fit for human consumption (e.g., contact information and textual description of the service). A key piece of information is the contract that the service implements. Another key piece of information is the endpoint where the service that is created during the publishing process is available. Once the service has been published, service consumers can discover that service through the registry.

Discovery normally involves using one of many ways to navigate through the registry and retrieve information. For example, one pattern might be for the developers to browse through the registry and download a contract. This contract then can be used by either manually coding client applications or using the built-in support in orchestration suites or other development environments to generate proxy code to interact with that service. Once the service consumer application has been built, it can again query the registry at runtime to retrieve the endpoints where the service provider is deployed. The proxy code can then bind to the service provider and interact with it. BSO and other tools are also now beginning to support dynamic stub generation instead of static stubs. This method lends quite a lot of flexibility to the consumer and is particularly well suited for orchestration engines. Using this method, the consumer code will actually download the contract at runtime and dynamically generate the proxy. This means that, as the contract evolves, the service consumer does not always have to be rewritten and can evolve on its own time line.

3.3.8.3 Security Services

The security issues have been discussed briefly in this chapter. It is discussed in more detail from the perspective of development environments in Chapter 5 and the capabilities expected from an integrated security solution for Web Services in Chapter 6. So, we are not going to say much about security here. The point of having security here is to highlight the fact that this architecture treats all capabilities under the same light and as deployed services from people, systems, or organizations. So, to that extent, we expect security capabilities provided by the environment to manifest themselves as deployed security services that can perform services such as authentication, authorization, and certificate management, among other things, for all categories of services.

3.3.8.4 Communication Services

In this category of services, the environment may provide implementations of sophisticated protocols for synchronous and asynchronous communications. For example, the BSO platform may provide implementations of SOAP, ebXML Messaging, or RosettaNet's RNIF, or may implement standards such as Java Messaging Service. These services may also include EDI facilities.

These are important capabilities that may either be beyond the scope for the business service to implement or too difficult for them to build. In any case, if the environment supports these communication services, then the choices for building business services increases hugely without increasingly their complexity.

In BSO, however, it's very easy to plug in components that provide these services as long as they have an exposed interface. They are simply synthesized and catalogued.

3.3.8.5 Orchestration Engine Services

This is the heart of the architecture and these services make it possible to build orchestrations. These services actually provide implementation of an *orchestrations container* that can retrieve definitions of orchestrations from the metadata repositories and execute them.

3.3.8.6 Transformation Services

These services act upon the transformation rules that have been specified and perform transformations at runtime. In BSO, because the orchestration engine operates with objects, transformation is done at a higher level of abstraction than it is with flat files. Each object may have contained subobjects, but they are abstracted when the transformation is being designed. Therefore, transforming one or more object to an object of a different class is a recursive process that is also top-down, like the rest of the approach. Furthermore, transformation in BSO does not distinguish between pure semantic transformation (associating field names) and translation of content (converting a Siebel customer number to an SAP customer number, or converting Euros to dollars). Transformations are dynamically loaded as needed to assign an object to an object of another class, and this continues recursively until the last conversion or translation has been accomplished. In this way, maps are created top-down and in a drill-down fashion, where each of the transformation rules that compose the map are reusable.

Most BSO suites accept transformation maps from popular transformation tools as if they were native. In effect, transformation can be seen as yet another service from a system.

3.3.9 Management Services

Management services build upon the core services that are provided by the platform environment. These services only differ from the core services in their intent because, whereas the core services are intended to ease the development of business services and to keep the deployed environment running smoothly, management services are intended to provide an additional level of control over how the environment functions and helps in reducing IT cost in managing those applications during their life cycle. Among these management services that we can mention are deployment, engine configuration, versioning, BSO cockpit services, and others.

3.3.9.1 OLAP Services

OLAP is used in many different contexts. First and foremost, it is used to describe the systems that take archived data, most likely from data warehouses, and provide ways to create multidimensional data cubes to analyze different aspects of business.

We apply OLAP to orchestration management. Orchestrations embody the cross-functional and cross-company business processes. The efficiency of those business processes can be the difference between survival or demise of the enterprise. OLAP in the context of orchestrations means the ability to monitor the efficiency of the business processes. There are legal and contractual ramifications to this also because the data collected as part of OLAP can also be proof of a company meeting or violation of contracted service-level agreements (SLAs). For example, a company may have signed legal SLAs to fulfill orders for its widgets within a certain time period. The OLAP tools can provide legal proof that the orders are being fulfilled within the contracted time. They can also be used to drill down to the problem step in the whole business process, if the process is not efficient.

Just like system performance tools can be used to identify deficiencies in the IT infrastructure, OLAP tools for orchestration can be used to identify inefficiencies in the business. These inefficiencies cannot always be discovered through analysis, and even if they are, the decision makers may need to see some hard proof. The OLAP services can be powerful tools in bringing about the change.

The OLAP tools for orchestration periodically concentrate historical data from different orchestration engines into an operational data store. These data are then exploited by an OLAP engine for process analysis.

3.3.9.2 Scalability Services

Some may question whether scalability is a service. However, since we insist on treating all capabilities or facilities provided by the platform environment as services, we choose to reflect the clustering capabilities and load-balancing capabilities provided by the platform environment as scalability services.

A BSO platform should provide a way to cluster a multitude of orchestrations of engines into one or more clusters so that load can be balanced between them. However, to make any kind of load-balancing decisions, the orchestration engines have to be instrumented to record their instance data. It turns out that orchestration engines need to record that kind of data anyway for their own state management as well as OLAP purposes.

3.3.9.3 Fault Tolerance

The ability to deploy clusters of orchestration engines not only provides the basis for load balancing, but also for fault tolerance. As we mentioned, the orchestrations embody critical business processes of the enterprise. It is extremely important that continuity of business be maintained in the face of hardware and system failures.

Fault tolerance services should actually be termed *business continuity services;* they not only allow the platform to provide business continuity if one server fails in the cluster by automatically rerouting the execution of the process instance to another server, but they also allow planned rerouting of requests to backup servers if the primary servers have to be taken down for hardware/software maintenance or upgrades.

3.3.9.4 Deployment Services

Deployment services allow configuration of clusters, copying of software code to servers, and setting up configurations on those servers. The real challenge in the deployment area is to enable deployment of new versions of the same services on-the-fly without affecting the overall execution. For example, if the implementation of a process that is invoked by other processes changes, the processes that call it should not be affected, and if the implementation of a component (service) that is used by one or more processes changes, these processes should not be affected.

3.3.10 Management Tools

Management tools make the management services easy to use and integrate multiple management services into task-oriented user-interface-driven tools. As with other tiers, the list that we identify is not exhaustive by any means but covers the most important tools.

3.3.10.1 Orchestration Deployment Tools

These tools allow deployment of orchestration engines in a single or clustered environment and allow the deployer to set the necessary parameters of the orchestration engine that are required for it to execute the necessary orchestrations, activate a new version of a process, roll back to an old version, monitor what versions are active, etc.

3.3.10.2 Service Management Tools

Service management tools provide the means to perform various tasks to manage business services. Those could range from deploying business services to starting and stopping them, rerouting messages to alternate services, and so on.

While the orchestration deployment tools deal with issues specific to orchestrations, service management tools provide general service management capabilities which are just as relevant for the business services tiers.

Additional tools in this area might allow setting up the organization's demographic data, such as users and their roles, and also setting up the security parameters for these users as well.

3.3.10.3 OLAP Tools

OLAP tools provide the ability to view the data related to the performance of business processes in multiple dimensions.

3.3.11 Development Tools

The intended users for the development tools are, of course, developers, and so, the tools are fine-tuned to improve programmer productivity. Again, this is a representative list rather than an exhaustive one.

3.3.11.1 Process Modeling Tools

This is probably the single most important tool in the whole architecture. It is really a modeling environment that lets developers use visual metaphors to model the processes that implement orchestrations.

There are many design notations – standard and proprietary – that completely, or at least partially, model orchestrations. Unified Modeling Language (UML) is the most important standard notation that allows modeling of the business processes using activity diagrams and the state diagrams. However, UML is a visual modeling language and lacks the ability to capture implementation details that are so necessary for a BSO implementation. We think that the only real standard for BSO modeling will be in the XML-based format for capturing the BSO definition. Once the definition has been captured in a standard way, it can easily be exchanged between modeling tools, which can render the definition visually using either UML or a proprietary modeling notation. Chapter 8 is devoted to defining a standard language for capturing business service orchestrations.

UML has many faults: It is too technical and not particularly business friendly and it doesn't provide a way for organizational or skills data to be captured, making it highly unlikely to be deployable, among others.

3.3.11.2 Component Synthesis Tools

We have consistently preached an approach to generate interfaces based on component synthesis rather than the standard connector/adapter model adopted by the run-of-the mill integration broker. However, this approach requires special tools to discover and catalog services from existing systems that can be used to fulfill required services.

Generally, these tools are based on introspection wherever possible. For example, such a tool can examine SAP's business object repository and generate required interfaces from it. We anticipate that these component synthesis tools will be able to generate business services (as Web Services) that are able to receive the requests and delegate those requests to the target applications. The contract of these Web Services includes only the desired functions and can be described in a description language such as WSDL. The upper layers of the architecture can then utilize these web services, completely oblivious to the actual implementation of the target systems. These generated web services can incorporate the integration of some of the core system/infrastructure services. For example, a web service generated for certain functions of the Human Resources module in SAP can also include some automatic use of some other core services such as billing and charge back.

Fuego, for example, provides a tool with which the programmer can enter the server, technology, ports, user, and password and browse all of the services that are exposed for that user under the given technology in the given servers. The programmer proceeds to select components to which he or she wishes to connect and the tool automatically generates a proxy in the component catalog with the selected services and data. For each service, the programmer can then proceed to create a template command in the Services Integration Scripting Language (SISL) such that it will be expanded automatically when the process designer double clicks on that method in the catalog. These services can be, for example, SQL services; COM services; JAVA services; EJB services; CORBA services; Web Services; XML objects exposed through any technology providing a DTD or an XSL description; Web page interception services (Web scraping); IBOs (called Xobjects in Fuego); CICS, IMS, VISAM, and ISAM services (exposed through ODBC); JMS messaging services; TIBCO services; MQ services; and others. All of these services are then accessed through a proxy that is generated automatically and is one of the components in Fuego's component catalog which is seen as a native library from the SISL.

3.3.11.3 User Interface Composition Tools

The composition tools allow composition of rich user interfaces attached to common IBOs. In our architecture, we describe IBOs as occupying a tier of their own. These objects are very mobile definitions of how the synthesized components can be used in a consistent visual manner and how they can be created from and instantiated as native objects in other systems, among other things. For example, an IBO for the Web Services described in the preceding subsection may incorporate a standard visual form to capture the human resources data required. These IBOs can then be serialized into IXOs and shipped to anyone, whether connected or disconnected, as an e-mail attachment, for example. With the help of a plugin, they come alive in the user's environment and can perform local data validation and then eventually be shipped back to the service that sent them. They can also offer an API so that the recipient can programmatically fill them or update back-end applications automatically.

Composition tools help with the user interface and data validation logic of the IBOs. They also might be used to customize the work portal to fit an organization's standards.

3.3.11.4 Mapping Tools

With mapping tools, powerful transformations are possible. These tools can provide everything from simple spreadsheet-style side-by-side mapping to XSLT-based mapping to very powerful heuristics-driven mapping. What's important in BSO is that we are faithful to the object-oriented abstraction practices. This will ensure that no unnecessary complexity is brought into the development tools.

3.3.11.5 Source Control/Version Management Tools

No tool set will be complete without paying attention to the team development environment for managing source code and version control. Most of these tools simply provide plug-ins for the third-party source code configuration management (SCCM) tools.

3.3.12 Testing Environment

Orchestrations are built into distributed environments. There are two important capabilities that a BSO platform should provide to help with testing orchestrations: interactive debugging and simulation.

3.3.12.1 Interactive Debugging

Most of the code that actually executes the orchestration code may be generated by the BSO platform. The transformations taking place may also have been specified through user interface–based tools using graphical metaphors. The BSO platforms do that to make it easy to orchestrate services. However, a side effect of that is that debugging becomes inherently more difficult. If there are some logic errors, they may become very difficult to trace because, first, it may be hard to control the manual execution of the orchestration engines and, second, it is hard to debug generated code.

It is important for BSO platforms to provide higher-level interactive debugging capabilities that will allow the user to debug business logic by providing the ability to break in the activities and examine the state of the process variables and message parameters rather than having to deal with programming languages.

3.3.12.2 Simulation

Business processes may integrate a large number of applications and may have several nested processes or subprocesses. Verifying the correctness of the flow of the business process and checking the effects of all possible execution paths in the business process require powerful simulation capabilities. The BSO platform should provide simulation capabilities that would animate the flow through a business process, allowing the analyst to provide varying parameters to test alternative paths through the business process.

Simulation can be a very powerful tool to validate the logic of business processes without costly and time-consuming field testing with different parameters. Although simulation is not an alternative to field testing, it shortens that period. The idea is to provide a way to easily simulate simultaneous users, automated components, and their possible behaviors. This can be very tasking because each state-full component will need to have possible datasets, and the methods will need to be simulated realistically. It doesn't get any easier on the client side, where latencies, incomplete data entries, and other situations must be put into the mix. We may see tools that deal with all of this at a higher level of abstraction, such as today's process modelers. However, the further from plausible, real cases the simulation is, the less its value.

3.4 Recursive Composibility

BSO is the hypertier of IT and not just the fourth tier, because process models can be infinitely nested and can be recursively invoked. This property of process models makes them tremendously flexible and reusable and provides unprecedented abstraction and inference capabilities for complex business-level rules. Furthermore, the nesting of process models can go on across companies, constituting a World Wide Web of orchestrated services. This Web can have clusters of trading-partner networks (TPNs) that interact more frequently and build in a highly organic and natural way.

3.5 Trading-Partner Networks

Orchestrations, the hypertier of IT, will, of course, first be implemented within the four walls of the enterprise. However, the nature of the business has already changed and the need to integrate and to do business electronically with business partners cannot be ignored. In any case, this business does not happen on an ad-hoc basis. We make several observations about the nature of electronic bonding between business partners:

- A lot of new technologies are being developed. Some of the key ones are SOAP, WSDL, and UDDI. However, these technologies are merely means to an end.
- Businesses do not become trading partners by simply discovering each other. They have to first establish trust by physical negotiations and over handshakes. However, once that has happened, business can be conducted electronically.
- Trading relationships do not remain static. Sometimes new partners are added to an existing set of partners for the same set of services and sometimes existing partners choose to no longer do business with each other. The computing systems of the trading partners have to understand and be able to deal with the dynamic nature of partnerships.

For a while, there was a mad rush toward B2B exchanges. However, that did not pan out for several business reasons:

- unwillingness of companies to relinquish historical partnerships in lieu of a perfect marketplace,
- unwillingness of companies to accept connectivity standards imposed by the big players,
- the epic proportions of the financial effort needed to set up these exchanges using current B2B technologies

The technological reasons are mainly the following:

- Current technologies require the constituents of an exchange or the exchange itself to create logic that knows what to do with messages that come with different flavors within the same standard and/or through different standards.
- All development that goes on to comply with those standards and their flavors do not signify any competitive advantage to the constituent or to the exchange, just the ability to continue doing business.
- Once that logic is in place it is difficult, if not impossible, to change.

In short, exchanges were based on the wrong paradigm for most business relationships. They were based on the "transparent marketplace paradigm" as set forth by stock exchanges. However, trading relationships are not always that simple. In fact they are seldom, if ever, that simple.

This is why TPNs without intermediaries that automate the trading policies already in place through the infrastructure already in place are much more viable than "transparent markets," at least in the short term.

The only way to create viable TPNs of this type is through the hypertier of IT. Orchestrations form the glue that binds the business partners.

Business partners, who agree to do business with each other, first need to establish trust between each other. This trust cannot be programmed. It is developed after lengthy meetings in boardrooms and is established over handshakes (and, of course, legal documents). Once that trust has been established, the business partners form TPNs. TPNs enable new business relationships to be forged and changed in response to a constantly changing business climate. They provide processes to discover new trading partners, discover the capabilities of the existing partners, and integrate new trading partners and electronically bond to them.

The role of TPN is not to define a hub to manage the flow of all business transactions. Perhaps a good example is the neighborhood association. It manages the general upkeep of a neighborhood, helps newcomers to integrate into the neighborhood, and maintains the neighborhood in general but does not regulate the traffic on the roads in the neighborhood.

The architecture that we described in the preceding section can be easily applied within the four walls of the corporation. However, this architecture is powerful

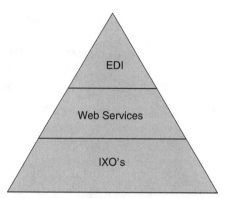

FIGURE 3.4. Technology Adoption Pyramid.

enough to be applied just as well to the TPN and it spans the full spectrum of B2B.

As can be seen in Figure 3.4, BSO deals with

- high-end companies that already have the infrastructure in place through EDI processing,
- mid-sized companies that have Web infrastructure using and providing Web Services,
- small or technically unsophisticated organizations by serializing IBOs into IXOs and sending them via any available carrier protocol, for example, e-mail, FTP, instant messaging, or XML/SOAP.

Given that 80 percent of the volume of B2B transactions is executed with small or technically unsophisticated organizations in today's market, dealing with these low-end partners in a paperless fashion can bring huge benefits to any company. IXOs provide this benefit. As we described earlier they are interpretable XML objects that can easily be interpreted by inexpensive software. These objects are encrypted and travel with their electronic signature. The implications are enormous: orders, invoices, shipping manifests, request for informations (RFIs), request for quotations (RFQs), bill of materials (BOMs), and virtually any document that today is sent by fax and subject to electronic or human interpretation errors can be replaced effortlessly and securely using IXOs. These objects know how to route themselves back to the sender or to other participants in the process, know how to print themselves where needed, and need absolutely no processing on behalf of the sender when they return with the desired information: they are a serialization of an IBO that is already a part of the orchestration. Note here that these objects *need* to be IBOs because, not only are the data serialized, but also the class logic, because the object needs to execute off-line on the receiving computer. Therefore, this class logic needs to be available to the BSO engine, and this would be very difficult to achieve from external APIs that run on other application servers or platforms. We talk at length about IXOs in Chapters 6 and 9.

One of the great advantages of the BSO model is that the provisioning cycle of integrating a partner into a partner network is simply an orchestration of services such as partner identification, validation, approval, and registration. This provisioning service can be as automated as the business acumen allows.

CHAPTER 4

BSO Methodology: Orchestrating and Interpreting for Success

4.1 INTRODUCTION

No groundbreaking work on business services orchestration (BSO) would be complete without establishing a robust underlying methodology. We have developed a specific methodology for orchestrating and improving business services, which, when used with a specific orchestration suite, results in the greatest return on investment (ROI) for clients.

This comprehensive approach is the culmination of many implementations of orchestrations accomplished by developing and using a BSO toolset. It focuses on the fundamentals of services analysis and design and process modeling as a form of orchestration implementation. It includes specific techniques and tools that we have developed by modifying the best approaches to services discovery and design.

Among the initial results of applying this methodology, we can mention the renewed role of the chief information officer (CIO). CIOs who master this approach and make it an integral part of their mode of operation cease to be seen as the nay-sayers in the company. They no longer adopt the role of gatekeepers and fire extinguishers. Instead, they become agents of change. They become the hinge between the company's strategy and the implementation and continuous improvement of the services that execute it. They no longer act as a service center for the company's users; they become the catalysts for improved services to the company's customers. There are companies where the CIO does not have the business wherewithal or interest to take on this catalyst role. In those companies, the LOB managers, the COO, or even the CEO should take ownership of the initiative.

This chapter provides a high-level overview of the BSO methodology and explains a unique approach for:

- discovering/documenting the enterprise's *as-is* processes that implement a service,
- defining the enterprise's *should-be* processes to implement a better version of a service.

Although this approach evolved from business process reengineering (BPR) methodologies, it caters to the creation of process models that will execute on a BSO engine. BPR essentially applies engineering principles to the organization of a business. BSO applies an engineering approach to an engineering problem: the creation of information technology (IT) solutions that automate and manage processes. It is not our intent to influence the culture or the organization of an enterprise through paper and training. The objective of BSO methodology is to facilitate the adequate design of integrated and collaborative solutions for the virtual enterprise by orchestrating its business services.

This is why BSO finds a better home in enterprises that fully acknowledge that in today's world:

- they need to manage for change;
- they don't have the luxury of time to reengineer the entire enterprise; and
- they need to build new, innovative services based on their existing legacy of people, organizational structure, and systems.

BSO encompasses and extends the business integration capabilities of enterprise application integration (EAI), business-to-business integration (B2Bi), Web services, and business process management (BPM) and inherits methodology ideas from BPR. Therefore, this methodology is oriented toward facilitating automated business integration more than cultural or organizational change. Obviously, automation always brings change to an organization. So, there will be an influence, but it will be indirect, as a result of orchestrating business services, not as a prerequisite.

The core of the BSO methodology focuses on developing service models and the process models that implement them – these are charts that will fill in the blanks that we just described. Only when necessary, we start at the highest level, looking at the enterprise in the context of its environment of suppliers, customers, and competitors, and analyzing social, cultural, economic, and political influences. We use a tool called a super-services model to do this. Using other special service model templates, we work down through the layers of the enterprise until we zero in on a particular BSO that we want to redesign and improve.

Many times the pain is clear (the service that needs improvement stands out like a sore thumb) and all of these preliminary steps are totally unnecessary. In these cases (which we deem to be not less than 80 percent of the cases), it is very important to ignore Phases 0 and 1. These phases defeat the purpose of rapid solution development and continuous evolution because they tend to get stuck in political feuds. Typically, if the organization needs to complete Phases 0 and 1 to detect an orchestration problem, it probably is not yet sufficiently aware of the problem to go and solve it. So, why do we include them? It is our experience that, because of the spectacular initial results that all BSO customers achieve, they usually adopt the approach as the mandatory IT improvement strategy. These customers then need a more comprehensive, strategic approach so they can include BSO in every IT project. This is the only intent of Phases 0 and 1. We recommend that BSO rookies skip these phases and go directly to Phase 2.

The process modeling work in Phase 2 is the bedrock on which this methodology rests. We spend a lot of time making sure we really understand the current state of the business process, which implements the service we want to improve, and how it works. Then, we proceed to design the business process that will achieve the goals set forth for the project and produce a positive net ROI within 12 months.

4.1.1 Silo Phenomenon

Traditionally, managers only see their organizations vertically and functionally and they tend to manage them that way. More often than not, a manager who heads up several units directs those units on a one-to-one basis. He or she sets independent goals for each function. Meetings between functions are limited to activity reports. In this function-oriented environment, managers tend to perceive other functions as obstacles rather than as assets in the battle to deliver better services.

In addition, most of the information systems that these managers rely upon reinforce and support this purely functional approach. This is because most of the information systems in use today were designed to reflect this theoretical, function-based business model. Therefore, they tend to perpetuate the silo phenomenon.

The metaphor of silos describes the organizational structures built around departments. Silos are tall, thick, windowless structures. These organizational silos tend to prevent peers at levels below the manager from resolving interdepartmental issues. Management must then devote an inordinate amount of time to resolving these conflicts, thus diverting their attention from higher-priority customer and competitor concerns. As a result, most cross-functional issues do not get resolved.

As managers strive to meet the goals of their individual functions, they get better and better at attaining their objectives. However, this functional optimization often contributes to the suboptimization of the organization as a whole.

Here are some typical examples of this tendency:

- building products that customers don't want;
- sales promising products or features that the company can't provide;
- managing cash with administrative efficiency but with total insensitivity to employee needs;
- creating programs for business development that overlap with the company's core business;
- throwing the same support recipes to small and large, critical and noncritical customers;
- approving the same transaction from the same point of view in multiple departments without the knowledge of the other departments.

It is very interesting to see how the notion of function affects performance. It is a very deeply rooted notion because managers and employees alike are known to state one of the following:

- "Sorry, that's not my job. I can't help you"
- "This is *my* job. Please do not interfere!"

For some reason the notion of function implies separation and segregation.

The notion of service is precisely the opposite. The notion of service implies alignment and unity of purpose: "How can I be of service?" "Thank you for asking." "Thank you for your business." "I appreciate the opportunity (to serve you)."

So, as we said in preceding chapters, having the ability to describe what the enterprise does (what process it follows) to fulfill requests from internal or external customers, and providing the ability to drill down into the processes that orchestrate the lower-level services that comprise them, is an alternative way of charting the organization of an enterprise. The advantages are many:

- Unlike functions, services are focused on a specific set of customers.
- Unlike functions, services exist only if they are requested by internal or external customers.
- Unlike functions, services are inherently prepared to be composed into higher level, more complex services. Therefore, services that are not orchestrated or in themselves oriented to an external customer, stand out like a sore thumb. Functions are like collection items (often unutilized assets).

FIGURE 4.1. Managing Processes Through Functional Silos.

- Unlike functions, services convey a distinct idea of responsibility and accountability for enterprise performance beyond the performance of any individual or organization per se.

4.1.2 Managing Processes Through Functional Silos

An organization can be world class within a silo, but if disconnects (deficiencies in the integrity of the process) in the white space between silos exist, the organization will perform services that are below its potential. In this template, we seek to counter this problem by providing tools to:

- identify those core services that an enterprise provides today;
- determine which key players (people, systems, or organizations) are responsible for these services;
- discover the processes that implement the core services by orchestrating subservices;
- recommend improvements to the processes and subservices, so that the enterprise can begin evolving its information systems on the basis of service effectiveness rather than on functionality.

Figure 4.1 depicts a process-driven enterprise where core business processes are managed through functional silos instead of just within them.

Our approach involves designing processes that orchestrate existing services into new ones in a perpetual motion toward excellence. It is our experience that when enterprises begin to align their services across functional silos through process instead of just within them, they improve customer satisfaction and business

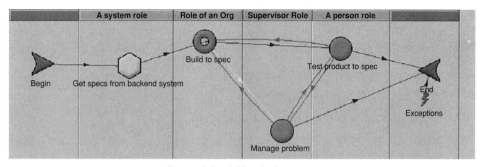

FIGURE **4.2. A Simple Process.**

performance. Still more surprisingly, they greatly improve employee morale and motivation. What is utterly incredible, however, is that IT starts getting a good rap!

CIOs who use BSO experience changes in their role in the company. They progress from being seen as the stick in the wheel, who was always responsible for being late to market with the required IS functionality, to being seen as the most proactive agent of change in the company. They no longer accept functional requirements at face value from any user. They successfully encourage the users to identify the company services in which they participate and what is needed for their participation to be optimal. To their surprise, users are delighted with this new approach! To better accomplish this they create a cross-functional team of users who are involved in the service and discover the "*as-is*" process with them and get to a consensus on the "*should-be*" process that will implement an improved service with an expected ROI.

What exactly is a process? A process is a sequence of activities that can be performed by combining services from people, systems, and partner organizations to fulfill a service request from customers or partners. A process model is a graphical representation of those activities; their sequence, types, and dependencies; and the time constraints involved.

Many notation standards for process model design exist today. Figure 4.2 was created with the BSO toolset's process design tool produced by authors' company, Fuego Inc. The yellow hexagrams represent services from systems; the orange circles represent services from people, and the blue donuts represent services from organizations. The columns (swim lanes) represent who should perform those services, and the arrows represent transitions between them. Transitions in this model are color coded: blue are unconditional, red are conditional and have a Boolean expression embedded, and yellow are time triggers and have an interval constraint. These process models are used to illustrate the methodology throughout the chapter.

4.1.3 Traits of Process-Driven Enterprises

Enterprises that have successfully gone through a transformation employing BPR methodologies or total quality management (TQM) exhibit the following traits:

- Departments cooperate and share information.
- Decision making is pushed lower in the organization.
- More people are authorized to conduct transactions between departments.
- Most work is done by teams.
- Employees are encouraged to communicate directly with their peers in other departments.
- Managers focus on facilitating the performance of their team for their internal and external customers.
- Cross-functional collaboration is rewarded.
- Problem solving focuses on root causes; i.e., disconnects in a process.
- Major issues are routinely addressed by cross-functional teams.
- Human performance systems support optimum process performance.
- Customer needs and concerns dominate business decision making.
- Corporate services improvement is fundamental to fulfill a strategy.

The objective of BSO is not to transform the traits of an enterprise; therefore, look for enterprises and organizations that already have these traits to be early adopters of BSO. In time, BSO will, as a lateral effect, foster these traits in the enterprises that use it, but it will be a natural, bottom-up transformation that will be comparatively painless.

As we said before, one of the unique aspects of the approach is that organizations can use it to optimize services at *any* level. We actually encourage you, our readers, not to immediately embark on an enterprisewide transformation, integration, or orchestration project. Instead, we encourage you to focus on the *low-hanging fruit* – one or two key services that you can easily redesign with the least impact on the enterprise and highest impact on customer satisfaction. Once you have picked these low-hanging fruit, you can select other services in order of their degree of impact to the enterprise's critical business issues.

The methodology that follows is an approach that organizations can use to find and prioritize these critical services, but we *strongly recommend* that an organization not undertake the planning and project planning phases for its first BSO project or projects. These phases are appropriate for a BSO rollout as an enterprisewide strategy after having obtained consensus because of several smaller successes. Things that are born big are usually isolated and left to die. History demonstrates that resistance to change is only overcome by extreme necessity. The need to radically change an enterprise's complete strategy only occurs when it

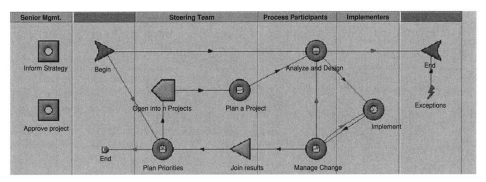

FIGURE 4.3. BSO Methodology Model.

is too late; therefore, resist the rational temptation of enterprisewide integration, reengineering, or transformation. Enterprises that rely on any of these to survive have their days counted anyway.

4.1.4 BSO Methodology Outline

Just like many compilers are written in the language that they are supposed to compile, we illustrate the methodology for BSO as a process itself. The process model shown in Figure 4.3 illustrates the flow of the approach. Each round *doughnut* shape represents one of the BSO methodology's five phases as a service from an organization whose role is in its swim-lane title. They are represented as subprocesses or subservices from organizations.

Two activities from senior management (depicted as square donuts) have the ability to start the process: Approve Project or Inform Strategy. The first is typically the case of approving a proof of concept through a project that's a high priority. The latter is when the organization has already embraced the approach and wants to apply it to all IT projects.

The default transition from the Begin node of the process is to the Analyze and Design activity that is performed by the participants in the process that was selected by senior management. This starts a short cycle where, after the Analyze and Design activities are finished, the implementers implement and the participants manage change until more budget is needed or a new strategy is in place.

A long cycle is initiated by senior management when they inform the company strategy to a steering committee that will be in charge of prioritizing the adequate services and planning the projects for each one of them before handing them off to the participants in the processes that implement those services.

We explore each of these phases in detail in the next sections. At the beginning of each section, we show Figure 4.3 with the phase on which we are currently focused circled in red.

Note: This methodology is based on our experience with many clients over the years. In addition, we have amplified and derived a framework for our approach through research in the field of business process redesign.

Here are very brief descriptions of the steps or activities and the required services in each of the five phases of the BSO methodology model.

Phase 0: Plan Priorities

INPUT: Business strategy, overall IT budget, time line
ACTIVITIES:
1. Validate and clarify strategy.
2. Identify and document the business's critical success factors (CSFs) and critical business issues (CBIs).
3. Identify the critical business services (CBSs) that address them.
4. Prioritize the CBSs.
5. Develop a Services Improvement Plan.

OUTPUT: Services Improvement Plan. A document that includes strategy, budget, CSFs, CBIs . CBSs, priorities, and plan.

Phase 1: Plan a Project

INPUT: Services Improvement Plan
ACTIVITIES:
1. Model services context.
2. Identify critical service issues (CSIs).
3. Identify service boundaries.
4. Document constraints and assumptions.
5. Establish service goals.
6. Determine time lines/commitments.
7. Define project roles (agree on participants in the process).
8. Develop project plan.
9. Orient participants.

OUTPUT: Project goals, project roles, description of each service to be worked on, and a Service Improvement Project Plan.

Phase 2: Analyze and Design

INPUT: Project plan for a given service (often, this project plan already exists if the pain is big enough; therefore, rookies start here with the best possible project plan definition)
ACTIVITIES:
Phase 2.1: Business Services Orchestration Impact Analysis (BSOIA)
1. Define the deliverables of the business service.
2. Discover and document the *as-is* process that implements it.

   3. Define success metrics and estimate ROI.

   4. Present BSOIA to customer for go/no-go decision.

Phase 2.2: Prototype

   1. Design *should-be* process.

   2. Validate running prototype with customer (devoid of production interfaces to people and systems).

   3. Create list of necessary discrete services from people and systems with documented deliverables and use cases.

   4. Estimate orchestration effort, reassess ROI.

   5. Make go/no-go decision on whether to implement.

OUTPUT: Implementation roadmap for a given service, including project plan, *should-be* process design and list of necessary discrete services as well as expected ROI.

Phase 3: Implement

INPUT: Implementation roadmap

ACTIVITIES:

   1. Discover and/or implement necessary services and compose intelligent business objects (IBOs).

   2. Obtain approval from participants on implementation-level design.

   3. Assess and recommend infrastructure setup.

   4. Test iteratively, going from lowest level to highest level of services.

   5. Obtain participants' committee approval of production worthiness.

   6. Prepare production environment.

   7. Train participants.

   8. Rollout. Assess and recommend infrastructure setup.

OUTPUT: Service in production

Phase 4: Manage Change

INPUT: Services in production and monitoring tools

ACTIVITIES:

   1. Monitor production services, customer requirements, and environment for improvement opportunities.

   2. Assess business impact of the improvement.

   3. OUTPUT: Business improvement recommendation. Based on this recommendation,

   4. If impact is to a specific service at a service design level, go to Phase 2.

   5. If impact is only to implementation, go to Phase 3.

   6. If impact may change services priorities, go to Phase 0.

   7. If impact may change company strategy, end. Start new BSO.

4.1.5 Advantages of the BSO Methodology

Before we examine the BSO methodology model in detail, let's review some of its advantages over other more traditional approaches:

- **Fits into the enterprise's or system integrator's existing objectives and methodology.** Our approach is oriented toward facilitating orchestration of existing services from people, systems, and organizations. Therefore, we provide tools that have not always been available in methodologies oriented towards single-origin application development.

- **Acknowledges and encourages cross-functional and cross-enterprise collaboration.** It captures those white-space transactions between functions; those areas where many valuable business transactions occur.

- **Delivers orchestrated services that map directly to the enterprise's CSFs and CBIs.** The redesigned services immediately impact the organization's pain points and are reflected in improved metrics, such as delivery time, yields, volume, and quality, which translate into measurable ROI.

- **Focuses on people's/system's capabilities.** The approach focuses on people's and systems' capabilities to perform a service, rather than just their functions. The approach sees people, systems and organizations (a set of cooperating people and systems) as service containers or service providers.

- **Orchestrates bottom-up harmonization.** Our approach is to orchestrate services rather than to ship and transform data. This means that the focus is enterprise interoperation and cross-enterprise interoperation rather than just data synchronization. This approach clarifies what services are needed from people, systems, and/or organizations.

- **Enables business agility and performance.** This approach gives managers a way to define, change, and implement a business service with agility and consistency. It allows teams to design dynamic service implementations that can change as conditions change. Therefore, this approach is designed for rapid and continuous improvement rather than for static perfection.

In summary, the BSO methodology attempts to provide members of an organization with the knowledge and tools to effectively and efficiently orchestrate the enterprise's business services so that they respond to CBIs and align with the overall enterprise strategy and customer needs. The methodology represents an attempt to respond to the changing conditions of today's customer-driven marketplace, and the new ways that enterprises must conduct business in this age of globalization and virtualization. It is an attempt to modify more traditional approaches to process modeling, delivering a framework more suited to produce valid IT solutions for these highly connected and changing times. Its purpose is to improve an enterprise's performance through the automation and optimization of its services. The BSO methodology can be used to orchestrate services either from the top, at an enterprise level, or from the bottom to help improve a single process. Key differences from more traditional *BPR* approaches include:

- The use of an engineering approach to an engineering problem: IT solutions.
- Cultural change, if any, is obtained as a result of the solutions and isn't a prerequisite to them.

Finally, the impact on the role of the CIO is huge. CIOs who use BSO start speaking a language that COOs and CEOs can understand and appreciate. They also get much more insight into the company's real problems, not only those imagined by the users of IT. Senior management begins to look on IT as proactive help for business execution rather than as an infrastructure that is slow to respond to business needs. In a nutshell, the BSO methodology and solutions attainable from it align IT to the business strategy and customer needs more than ever before.

Many feel that there is not enough evidence of this through the argumentation set forth so far in the book, but the claim comes from transcribing statements from CIOs that have implemented the BSO approach and the business people with whom they work. Possibly the reason for this, even in companies that have previously engaged in ISO9000 certifications or TQM or BPR projects is that the process models are the EXACT code on which a BSO engine runs. This is possible because the process model does not need to be modified to be able to manage services due to the harmonization capabilities of BSO. A BSO process model is the contract between business strategy and IT aided execution.

4.2 PHASE 0: PLAN PRIORITIES

This phase itself involves several different steps that are further explained below.

4.2.1 Introduction to Phase 0

The BSO methodology planning phase ensures that strategic and operational priorities generally (although not always) drive target market requirements and the environment in general. During Phase 1, the steering team discovers the service requirements based upon the enterprise's strategy and exposes the necessary elements. In contrast, Phase 0 emphasizes validation and clarification of the enterprise's or unit's strategy and goals in terms of the services offered and applicable

CSFs and CBIs. We do this so we can focus on a set of services that, when improved, will have the greatest impact on customer satisfaction and overall enterprise success. The goal is to produce a services plan that contains a prioritized list of services, along with an overall budget, time line, list of potential projects (groups of the services that will be addressed together), and list of project owners. This basic planning helps the orchestration team stay on track and stay aligned with the enterprise's priorities. (Note that the orchestration team comprises the people who currently feel the pain in the existing process or process participants and are eager to improve it; this team is actually applying the methodology to the project.)

Finally, this phase also helps to get senior management on the same page with respect to needed activities and priorities.

The caveat to be dealt with in this phase is the *credibility* issue. It is of no use to know what needs to be done in terms of BSO if BSO itself has not previously proven to be effective. For this phase to be effective, management as a whole needs to *believe* that it can act on the enterprise's reality through BSO techniques and technology. This is why we suggest that service orchestration teams initially apply BSO to a clear outstanding "pain" *before* they start the planning effort. Although there is clear value in prioritizing the critical services to be improved to attain the enterprise's goals, there is an order of magnitude more incentive for doing so if the team realizes that it can truly improve them.

Once clear incentives are established, the work necessary for Phase 0 becomes effective. The team interviews senior executives, the steering team, and functional managers who *believe* that BSO can help them. The results of these interviews are documented in several kinds of service models, which as a whole, illustrate the virtual enterprise's organization in terms of its services from organizations:

- super-services model;
- series of services composition models; and
- series of services orchestration models.

Although the need for in-depth planning may seem self-evident at the beginning of the project, it is useful midway into a project to be able to refer back to this information to make sure that the team is still on course and the project is still oriented toward its primary objective. If no initial documentation exists as to the project objective, it is easy after several weeks or months to lose sight of the original goal. At this point, it is useful to be able to refer back to the Services Improvement Plan and the list of CBIs/CSFs to see if the team is still on course and working to meet those original objectives.

In many cases, enterprises already have a Services Improvement Plan, although they may call it different names, such as Process Improvement Plan, Business Reorganization Plan, or Total Quality Plan. In these cases, Phase 0 is unnecessary.

4.2.2 Inputs to Phase 0

The inputs to Phase 0 include:

- business strategy;
- IT budget; and
- time line.

4.2.3 Activities for Phase 0

The stepsor activities for Phase 0 are as follows:

1. Validate and clarify strategy.
2. Identify and document the business's CSFs and CBIs.
3. Identify the CBSs that address them.
4. Prioritize the CBSs.
5. Develop a Services Improvement Plan.

These are detailed in the following subsections.

4.2.3.1 *Validate and Clarify Strategy*

The first step in the planning process is to validate and clarify the organization's overall strategy. When a senior executive or an executive leadership team distributes the enterprise's strategy, or if a functional manager distributes a particular goal to the services orchestration team, the members need to clearly understand:

- the steps and associated metrics for reaching this strategy/goal,
- any dependencies that may impact the reaching of this strategy/goal,
- any constraints or assumptions associated with the strategy/goal.

In essence, the orchestration team is trying to fulfill the organization's strategy through a high-level set of services. Once it has all the information it needs, it can create a set of master services that fulfill the organization's strategy. This set represents what the enterprise delivers for its customers, employees, shareholders, partners, suppliers, and other stakeholders. It also includes, at a high level, the services from others that it needs in order to fulfill its deliverables.

Enterprises behave as *adaptive systems*. They are processing systems that convert various resource products and services into product and service outputs. They provide these outputs to receiving systems or markets in the form of a new, orchestrated service. The enterprise also provides financial value in the form of equity and dividends to its shareholders. The enterprise is guided by its own internal criteria and feedback, but is ultimately driven by the feedback from its market.

Service models are tools to help the enterprise or organization plan and guide its BSO. They are like road models: They help make work visible. They improve communication and understanding and provide a common frame of reference. They show how services are currently organized. They are analysis tools to help an enterprise understand:

- what needs it fulfills;
- what it needs from the surrounding ecosystem to fulfill them;
- what risks and opportunities are created by investors, suppliers, competitors, and partners;
- what restrictions are imposed by the public sector;
- what the composition of its core services is;
- what the dependencies between the services that comprise core services are.

Finally, and most importantly, they can show how work is, and should be, performed.

We recommend specific types of models to guide orchestration teams. These models form the cornerstone for the planning phase of the BSO methodology:

- super-services model (model of critical high-level services to and from the enterprise),
- service composition models (models of services to and from internal or external organizations that are necessary to fulfill a given super-service),
- services orchestration models (process models representing the orchestration of super-services in the composition models).

4.2.3.1.1 Super-Services Model. This type of model provides a context for the enterprise within the larger environment. It is useful for framing a discussion with senior executives to determine the enterprise's CSFs and CBIs, and whether the enterprise is meeting the key success factors for its industry. It helps focus on the *why* of the services improvement project. Orchestration teams will later use it as a discovery and discussion tool during meetings with key stakeholders.

Figure 4.4 provides an example of a super-services model. This model is a variation of super-system models, such as those proposed by Rummler and Brache, among others. The reason is that, in a services model, the return for the service is implied and not explicit. A super-services model depicts the enterprise as an adaptive system in relation to its external environment. It basically consists of depicting what services it delivers to and receives from the environment. It also depicts what services competitors and partners provide to the enterprise's target market. It is important to understand that the money flows in the direction opposite to that of the services. For example, if an external service from investors is providing capital, the produce of that service (dividends) will go back to the provider. In the case of the super-services model, if a certain service (i.e., obtaining capital) is critical to the enterprise, the analyst must focus on the services that the enterprise

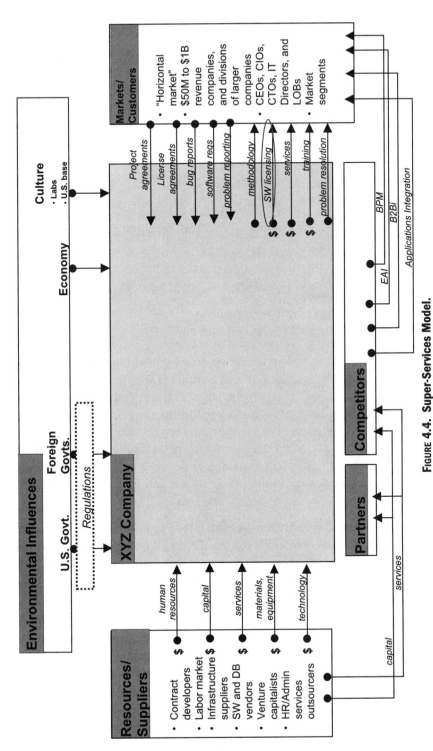

Figure 4.4. Super-Services Model.

needs to provide (i.e., to investors) in order to obtain this service from them. The model is used to:

- provide focus for executive strategic planning;
- show how an organization interacts with the outside;
- understand, analyze, improve, and manage relationships with such external influences as
  - markets,
  - customers,
  - resources,
  - competitors,
  - environment (e.g., governmental, political, regulatory);
- answer the questions,
  - What's the pain?
  - What's the threat?
  - What's the opportunity?
- identify CSFs for the industry as a whole;
- identify CBIs that are for the enterprise in particular.

To build this model, we recommend starting by drawing the services that the company offers to its target markets and customers. Having done this, continue with the services that are offered by the target markets and customers. The next step is to determine what services are offered to the same market by competitors and partners. Then we proceed to identify the services from investors, suppliers, and partners that are necessary for the company to be able to deliver its services to the target markets and customers. Finally, it's important to determine the services that the company must offer to the public sector and which services the public sector offers in turn.

4.2.3.1.2 Services Composition Models. This type of model helps focus on the core business of the enterprise in terms of a specific service that it delivers and how it is comprised of services from and to internal and external organizations. It shows what the enterprise's services hierarchies currently are and how they actually work across functions, departments, and enterprise boundaries, without getting into the detail of their dependencies. Figure 4.5 shows an example of a services composition model.

Among other things, the service composition model explores:

- How do areas of the company and external partners and suppliers work together?
- What subservices are available and who are the supplier and the customer of those services?
- What is the priority in terms of impact on customer satisfaction?

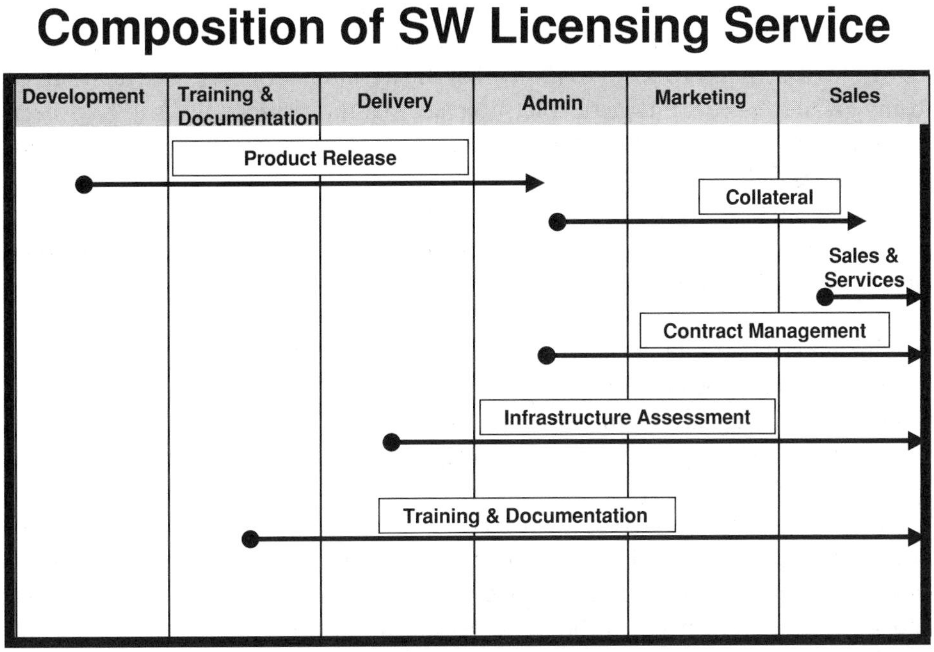

Composition of SW Licensing Service

Development	Training & Documentation	Delivery	Admin	Marketing	Sales
		Product Release			
				Collateral	
					Sales & Services
				Contract Management	
			Infrastructure Assessment		
		Training & Documentation			

FIGURE 4.5. Services Composition Model.

Services composition models show the business from the viewpoint of the services it needs from internal and external organizations to fulfill the services that are critical to its mission/vision/values/strategy. Senior executives can also use them to envision *what services* they should analyze because they compose their core business services. Such models can serve as master blueprints for the orchestration team. These models do not imply any sequence to the services necessary to fulfill the higher-level service; it just shows which services are necessary and who the internal or external customers of those services will be. They answer the question of *who should deliver what to whom* from an organizational standpoint to fulfill a service.

4.2.3.1.3 Services Orchestration Models. These models take the services from the services composition models and organize them according to the time line for their ideal execution. They answer the question of who *needs to do what and when*, to perfectly fulfill a critical service. As with the previous models, the team is still working at an organizational level, still without any attempt to analyze which specific people and/or systems should deliver the service. It's important to avoid the temptation to lower the scope of these models because the intent of these models is to facilitate blueprints for the *should-be*. When the level of abstraction descends below the organization line, we tend to design for the *as-is*. The other temptation that needs to be avoided is to see these models as implementable.

Their scope should be limited to depicting the dependencies between abstract services and should not be seen as orchestrations of real services. For example, in Figure 4.6 the intention is not to imply that the development cycle is synchronized to any given sales effort. It just depicts the fact that the product needs to have been developed before it is sold, by hinting to management to check the development cycle if sales difficulties appear.

Services orchestration models further refine the assessment of which services will have a greater impact on the enterprise's overall performance because they clearly depict the following:

- which services from internal or external organizations are reused in implementing more than one critical service,
- how critical they are on the time line of the service,
- which services they need from other organizations and how critical they are.

Figure 4.6 illustrates a completed services orchestration model. The model defines how services from different organizations interact and what their dependencies are. As can be seen in the figure, Development is done before Documentation, and Documentation needs to be done before the Beta Program is launched and this Beta Program needs to be successful to build the corresponding collateral and release the whole product. When calling on a customer, Sales will interact with Marketing to supply the whole product, with Services to assess whether the infrastructure is adequate for the product to be installed, and with Administration to negotiate contractual clauses. Once all of this is done to the customer's satisfaction, Sales delivers the product license and closes the deal.

The importance of this chart is that it helps to assess, from a dependency perspective, what services have impacts on the content, cycle time, quality, volume, or predictability of the overall orchestration.

4.2.3.2 Identify CSFs and CBIs
The second step in Phase 0, Plan of the BSO methodology, is to identify industry-standard critical CSFs and CBIs that can differentiate a particular enterprise from the competition.

CSFs are those variables essential to world-class performance in the environment in which the enterprise does business. They serve as a guide as for the orchestration team to identify the core services in the next step. Benchmark data from industry associations, reports on competitors, and interviews with industry experts and analysts also help determine these CSFs. Examples are:

- effective delivery,
- effective sales,

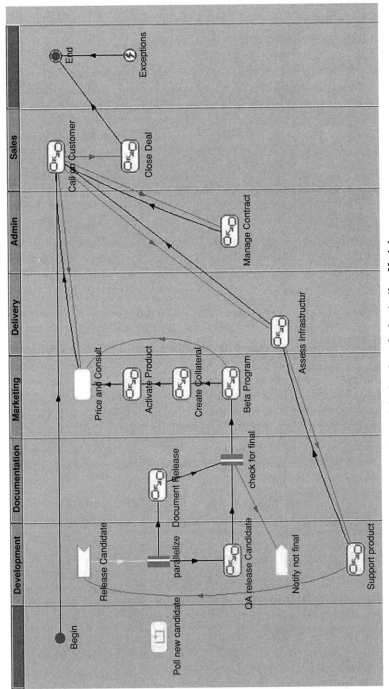

FIGURE 4.6. Services Orchestration Model.

- market recognition,
- effective recruitment,
- leadership in product development.

CBIs are the threats or opportunities that are most pivotal to the success of a strategy. Often, CBIs are not service-specific because they usually have enterprisewide implications. CBIs usually relate to revenue, profits, or market share. Examples include:

- positioning/messaging,
- leveraging of partners,
- recruiting/hiring/evaluation,
- market intelligence,
- competitor analysis,
- understanding market requirements.

Once the team understands the CSFs for enterprise's industry, it can focus on the enterprise's CBIs. When the enterprise is not performing well in terms of a particular industry wide measure, this is a red flag for probing deeper and identifying service performance issues. Identifying the CBIs can help pinpoint barriers that are keeping the enterprise from performing at the expected level.

4.2.3.3 Identify and Prioritize Services

The third and fourth activities in Phase 0 are to determine which services most affect the enterprise's CSFs and/or CBIs and then prioritize which processes should be selected first for improvement. One way to do this is by applying the Services Value Alignment (SVA) form to the six most important services of each model.

The purpose of this planning phase is to determine which of these services are critical. Critical services are those that are central to the success or failure of the business and have a major impact on the business's CSFs and CBIs.

The orchestration team needs to find any services that either must be or cannot be considered critical services due to preexisting conditions in areas of legal compliance, security, customer relationships, where the service fits into the enterprise value chain, etc.

There are literally hundreds of potential business problems and, in a typical business, there are usually dozens of large-grain services that could be improved.

Once the CSFs, CBIs, and opportunities are known, the orchestration team uses the SVA form (see Figure 4.7) to create a list of critical services.

The approach is to use the SVA form to prioritize the super services and then drill down to the services composition models of the prioritized services. This is repeated with the services included. The result is a clear idea of which services are best aligned with the CSFs and CBIs of the enterprise.

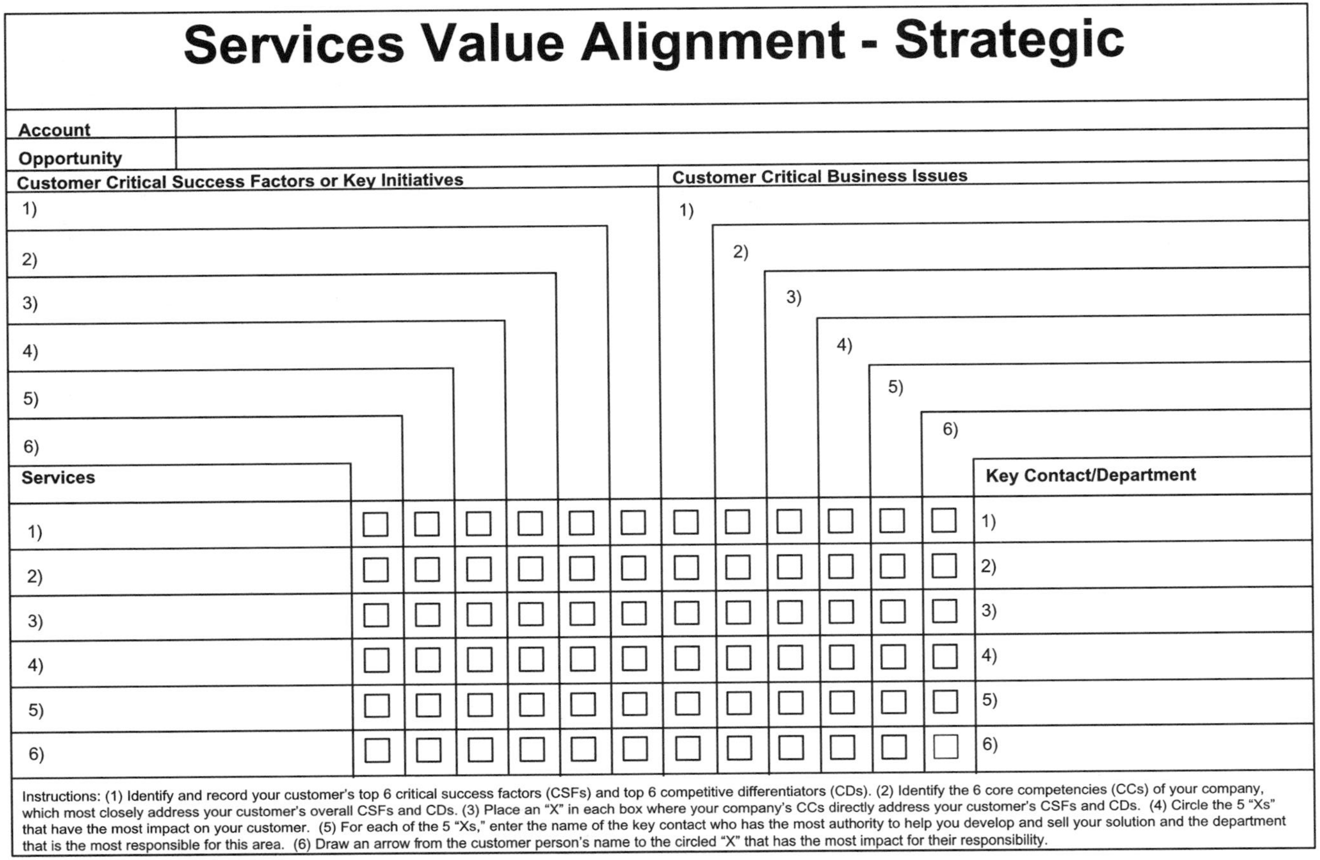

Services Value Alignment - Strategic

Account

Opportunity

Customer Critical Success Factors or Key Initiatives

1)
2)
3)
4)
5)
6)

Customer Critical Business Issues

1)
2)
3)
4)
5)
6)

Services

1)
2)
3)
4)
5)
6)

Key Contact/Department

1)
2)
3)
4)
5)
6)

Instructions: (1) Identify and record your customer's top 6 critical success factors (CSFs) and top 6 competitive differentiators (CDs). (2) Identify the 6 core competencies (CCs) of your company, which most closely address your customer's overall CSFs and CDs. (3) Place an "X" in each box where your company's CCs directly address your customer's CSFs and CDs. (4) Circle the 5 "Xs" that have the most impact on your customer. (5) For each of the 5 "Xs," enter the name of the key contact who has the most authority to help you develop and sell your solution and the department that is the most responsible for this area. (6) Draw an arrow from the customer person's name to the circled "X" that has the most impact for their responsibility.

FIGURE 4.7. Services Criticality Matrix.

111

Upon realizing which services have the highest alignment, the orchestration team can determine which have the most impact on the CBIs identified in step 2. By using the services orchestration models of the selected services, the orchestration team can determine which subservices are critical to their fulfillment and take the enterprise's current metrics for each of these critical services to determine those with the most negative impact on the CBIs. The orchestration team can use a matrix similar to the one shown in Figure 4.7 to rank and prioritize which services to analyze. This information will be the input to the next and final step of Phase 0.

The way to use this matrix is to put the CSFs on the upper left and then the CBIs on the upper right. After this, critical services should be listed on the lower right and boxes checked where they align with CSFs or CBIs. The services for which the box lines have more checks or more important checks would have the higher priority.

In addition to evaluating the critical services in terms of their impacts on the enterprise's CBIs and success factors, another important factor to weigh is how difficult work on the services will be. The difficulty can be measured in terms of the operational complexity involved, impact to key stakeholders, or other considerations.

For doing this, we recommend a four-quadrant matrix that groups the services in one of the following quadrants:

1. critical and easy,
2. critical and difficult,
3. noncritical and easy,
4. noncritical and difficult.

This matrix can become part of the documentation and it should help the team prioritize the services on which it will be working.

The next and final activity/step in Phase 0 is to develop the Services Improvement Plan.

4.2.3.4 Develop Services Improvement Plan

The Services Improvement Plan is the culmination of the work completed in the first three steps. It is the recommendation regarding which services should be analyzed at a people and systems level, and the order in which they should be analyzed. Also included is the rationale for making this recommendation, including a summary of all work completed in the previous four steps of Phase 0. The Services Improvement Plan is simply the steering team's recommendation regarding which services should be analyzed first. It is not to be confused with the project plan. Detailed project planning occurs during Phase 1 of the BSO methodology.

The Services Improvement Plan should consist of two parts:

1. actions that will be taken to address the CSFs and CBIs through service improvements,
2. actions that will be taken to manage those critical services that do not require any improvements.

4.2.4 Outputs of Phase 0

Two major deliverables should be produced in this phase:

1. strategy document that contains the validated strategy; CSFs; CBIs; super-service, service composition, and service orchestration models; and a Process Improvement Plan;
2. Services Improvement Plan that contains
   - SVA forms,
   - Services Criticality/Difficulty Matrix,
   - prioritized list of critical services to be improved,
   - budget,
   - time line,
   - list of recommended projects,
   - list of proposed project owners.

4.3 PHASE 1: PLAN A PROJECT

4.3.1 Introduction to Phase 1

In Phase 1, we start with the enterprise's validated and clarified strategy or goals, CSFs, CBIs, and approved Services Improvement Plan containing the prioritized list of critical services slated for improvement. Selecting one of the high-priority critical services, we create a detailed project plan for its improvement.

The project plan describes the selected critical service and the relevant CBIs, which are restated in terms of Critical Service Issues (CSIs). Assessing the way that all the critical services that comprise the selected service affect a CBI, rendering a list of CSIs, does this. The project plan also contains a precise description of the service boundaries, a list of project constraints or assumptions, project goals, budget, time line, and project team roster.

The caveat to this step is that it is liable to fail unless senior management has already experienced the huge benefits that BSO can obtain for the enterprise. Therefore, we recommend that this step also be skipped if the enterprise has not previously orchestrated at least one service that did not require a project planning effort (typically, lower-level services that have to do with application integration and/or enterprise application improvement and for which the benefits are self-evident).

The intent of Phase 1 is to fully define the project parameters and achieve consensus and buy-in on these parameters. This phase helps prevent costly rework and scope creep. Services that are clearly defined and described with clear request and delivery points are a definite preventative against scope creep. Likewise, it is critical that the key stakeholders give their buy-in and reach consensus on specific, measurable goals before each project is kicked off. This ensures the viability and justification for the project. It also lets everyone know when the project is complete. Otherwise, the project team could continue tweaking the service orchestration indefinitely. Remember that orchestration is an ongoing process, and so, a balance between time to delivery of the project and its goals is warranted. Wrapping all of this into a project plan is also valuable as a reference tool for future projects. Teams can refer to this plan to synchronize their work.

4.3.2 Inputs to Phase 1

The input to Phase 1, the Services Improvement Plan, comprises critical processes identified as having significant impacts on a particular CBI. During Phase 1, the CBI is converted to a CSI, which is process specific. For example, the CBI to *increase market* share *from 32 to 38 percent* may spawn a CSI such as *reduce new-product time-to-market to nine months*. This CSI drives the creation of a project plan, which is the output of this phase.

4.3.3 Activities for Phase 1

The activities for Phase 1 are the following:

1. Model services context.
2. Identify CSIs.
3. Identify service boundaries.
4. Document constraints and assumptions.
5. Establish service goals.
6. Determine time lines/commitments.
7. Define project roles (agree on participants).
8. Develop project plan.
9. Orient participants.

4.3.3.1 Select Specific Critical Service to Work on

This is a hidden activity; it happens in the split node in the process. The steering team will work on one project at a time.

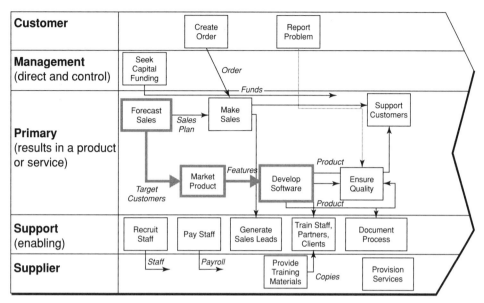

FIGURE **4.8. Service Context Model.**

4.3.3.2 Model Services Context

The Phase 0 models aid in the discovery of how a service influences and is influenced by other services. This is important because it helps with key stakeholder identification. Key stakeholders are individuals or organizations that provide or receive services that compose the critical service under scrutiny. Identifying them in the project plan is important to allow proper scoping of the service and the level of effort.

Figure 4.8 shows how two services, Market Product and Forecast Sales, impact the Develop Software service This knowledge is important in order to scope the service, gauge the proper level of effort, and identify all key stakeholders. In this step, the steering team discovers how processes influence, and are influenced by, other processes.

4.3.3.3 Identify CSIs

The inputs to this phase are a CBI and a service identified as having a significant impact on that CBI. During this phase the CBI is converted into a CSI, which is service specific for the critical service and for those services from organizations that compose it.

For example, a CBI to *increase market share from 32 percent to 38 percent* may spawn these three CSIs:

- Reduce new-product release time to nine months.
- Shorten the product management cycle.
- Increase testing to improve quality of alpha releases.

Phase 0 - Planning				Phase 1- Project Definition
Mission/ Vision Value	**Strategy**	**Critical Business Issue**	**Process**	**Critical Service Issue**
To be market leader	Identify and grow key markets	Losing market share	Develop New Products Fulfill Customer Orders	Reduce cycle time for developing new products

Why?

FIGURE 4.9. Establish CSIs.

The SVA chart developed in Phase 0 helps the orchestration team determine which services impact the CBI.

Note: More than one service may affect a CBI, but this stage should focus only on the critical service that most affects the CBI. If more than one service has a more or less equal effect on the CBI, the orchestration team should still select only one service at a time. This approach is predicated on having one orchestration team work on one service at a time. Once a service has been reorchestrated, the same team can work on other services.

Figure 4.9 shows a table that can be used as a tool for establishing CSIs.

Tip: Extracting CSIs from CBIs may take some probing. Some orchestration teams treat the CBI as an initial problem statement – it is useful to drill down into the initial problem statement to make sure the root problem is targeted. One useful technique involves a series of questions – The Five Whys.

```
Critical Business Issue: The Five Whys
"We're losing market share" = Initial problem statement

1. Q: "Why?" A: "Our market share is down."

2. Q: "Why?" A: "We're losing customers to our competi-
   tors."

3. Q: "Why?" A: "Our products are outmoded."
```

---

4. Q: "Why?" A: "Product development time is too long."
5. Q: "Why?" A: "Our R&D cycle time is too high." =
   Root Problem = CSI

Obviously with this CSI in mind, the orchestration team can ask "Why" for every service that comprises it. For example: "Our R&D cycle time is too high" (referring to the QA service).

1. Q: "Why?" A: "Our QA service is not as good as it should be."
2. Q: "Why?" A: "Because the Alphas have too many bugs."
3. Q: "Why?" A: "Because they don't test the user-side tools in depth."
4. Q: "Why?" A: "Because there are no automated procedures to do so."
5. Q: "Why?" A: "Because QA doesn't have it as a high priority" = root problem.

This is the critical service issue for the QA service.

4.3.3.4 Identify Service Boundaries

The boundaries are the start and stop points of the service loop. It is particularly important that the scope of a service, which can start and stop at a number of places (such as product development and order fulfillment), is manageable and only addresses the CSIs established in the previous step.

At this point, an efficient way to identify service boundaries is to use the services orchestration models developed during Phase 0 to confirm the service boundaries with all the pivotal organizations that need or nurture the service.

A clear understanding of the service boundaries also helps the orchestration team key in those stakeholders within the intervening organizations who are experts for at least some aspect of that particular business service, and especially those who are customers of it. If these people can be convinced to join the project team, they can add tremendous value to the orchestration team. Since they have a deep understanding of the current business service and its requirements, they are more attuned than anyone to any deficiencies in that service. As a result, they will be highly motivated to improve the service and can help design an improved orchestration of that service that truly meets the needs of the business. In the example in Box 4.?, talking to the right person in QA will certainly help assess what needs to be done to increase the priority of the user tools within the QA process.

4.3.3.5 Document Constraints and Assumptions

The steering team needs to document any underlying assumptions (e.g., "80 percent of customers will continue to be aerospace enterprises" or "the user components will commoditize") and to know whether any solutions (e.g., reorganization or changing computer platforms) are off-limits due to project constraints.

4.3.3.6 Establish Service Goals

After the CSIs have been established and constraints and assumptions documented for the project, service goals must be established. These offer a clear, unambiguous measure of the service improvement. As the orchestration team works through the service orchestration, it tests the improvements against the service goals to determine whether the improvements are on target. If it finds that it cannot make substantial progress toward attaining those goals, it should consider leaving the service as is or redefining the goals. The service goals go beyond the CSI to numerically specify the *current* and *required* service performance. The service goals require service performance in terms of improvement over current service metrics. These goals should be quantifiable. They could consist of metrics pertaining to such indicators as financial metrics, product volume, cycle time, or number of customer complaints received. All goals should be SMART (specific, measurable, attainable, realistic, and time-constrained).

Frequently, the service goals for processes that are changing from an old style to a new one (especially e-services) are unrealistic in terms of cost and execution time. Services that took a day, people now want in a matter of seconds and often not for the benefit of the customer. It's always a good idea to benchmark the goals against market reality and to set goals that will enable the company to perform better than the market, but if those goals seem TOO high, it's important to look at the potential quality of the proposed service – there may be something wrong.

4.3.3.7 Determine Time Lines and Commitments

Before work can begin on developing the project plan, both the steering team and the orchestration team must agree and buy into a project time line with deliverable commitments. These will be documented in the project plan, so that any changes to them must take the form of a formal change order.

This means also that each individual involved with the project must make a clear commitment to the amount of time she or he can work on the project, so that the project plan can be correctly loaded with resources. In addition, it is critical that each individual's supervisor has a clear understanding of that individual's time commitment to the project and authorizes that commitment to the steering team *in writing*. Unfortunately, it is all too common for managers to authorize their

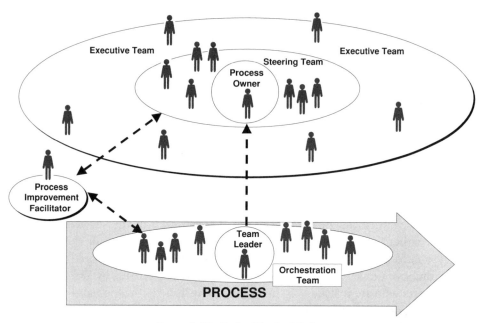

FIGURE 4.10. Typical Project Roles.

personnel to work on a project team with an implicit assumption that this work is above and beyond their regular duties. All parties need to clearly spell out and agree upon the exact planned commitment in terms of hours per week.

4.3.3.8 Define Project Roles

4.3.3.8.1 Team model. Figure 4.10 shows recommended project roles for, and organization of, a service orchestration project.

4.3.3.8.2 Organization. The large oval at the top of the diagram indicates that the process owner and steering team should be comprised of members of the executive team who are directly affected by the process changes. The steering team provides direction, oversight, and approvals for the project. The smaller oval in the large arrow at the bottom depicts the orchestration team. The orchestration team actually performs the analysis and design of the process. It should be a mix of business experts who are directly involved on a daily basis with the processes being redesigned, the consultants, and the programmers and other IT specialists.

Following is a list of typical project roles (each is defined below):

- **Executive team**. Membership on this team depends on the level of the service. If the service is high level, enterprisewide, then the executive team will probably comprise the highest-level decision makers in the company, with the CIO as their visible representative. If the service is at a lower level, delivered by a single business unit, then the executive team will probably comprise senior functional managers led by the CIO. Their role is to support the service owner and the steering team, including making decisions about changes that impact the entire enterprise/business unit.

- **Service owner.** The service owner should be the person that represents the users of the orchestrated service (the persons or organizations that can request it, in essence, the internal or external customers). They are motivated to advocate for the success of the service orchestration effort because they are the ones to whom the shortcomings of the current service are causing the most pain. She or he serves as the chairperson of the steering team. It is critical to correctly determine who the service owner is. The service owner must be the person who is rewarded on the success of the orchestration of the service he or she owns rather than on the success of his or her functions in it or outside of it. As such, during the project, the service owner will be motivated to protect the orchestration team from obstacles and barriers put up by the functional managers who are resistant to the change. This is a vital responsibility because many, if not most, of the orchestration team members will be outranked by the functional managers and thus will be vulnerable if not protected by the service owner. Because of this, the service owner should have at least equal or greater rank in the company than the functional managers involved in it.

- **Steering team.** Depending on the level of the service being orchestrated, the steering team is made up of either senior company executives or functional managers who own the services that are being orchestrated into this new service. The company's executive team usually chooses these. The service owner leads them. The steering team provides direction, oversight, and approvals.

- **Service improvement facilitator.** The service improvement facilitator is an expert in the BSO methodology. This person should be as neutral as possible. That is, he or she should have nothing to gain or lose as a result of changes to the service orchestration. The ideal candidate is an outside consultant, or an individual who has no direct input into the service itself and knows *little* about the service being analyzed. His or her role is to provide the methodology, guide and challenge both the steering and orchestration teams, and document their input.

- **Orchestration team leader.** This person must be credible. He or she serves as the communication point between all the teams. He or she must have project management experience, must be from the business, and must not be an IT person or a programmer because he or she will be advocating for the reorchestration of the service from a business, rather than a technological or programming, point of view. It is also very important that this person be proficient in the methodology and concepts of orchestration. Our experience has been that these people tend to design functionality for users rather than focusing on services for internal and external customers and their orchestration.

- **Orchestration team**. The orchestration team is composed of two groups:
  - *Process participants*. Functional managers should nominate persons from their departments who are considered experts in services that compose the process that is being reorchestrated. All on this design team are equal in rank. This group should be comprised of knowledgeable, team-oriented individuals who work across the spectrum of the process that orchestrates the new service and are motivated to make the necessary changes. They will do the analysis and design and will participate heavily in the implementation during the testing phases. They are also in charge of monitoring the services in production and managing change for continuous improvement under the direction of the service owner About eight to twelve is the best number of members for the group.
  - *Implementers*. The CIO should nominate adequate domain experts on the systems side, and a small group of developers. This group is mainly involved in the implementation phase, but must supply input to the design phase, especially when dealing with the capacities and constraints of the existing infrastructure.

4.3.3.9 Develop Project Plan
The project plan serves to encapsulate and summarize all of the information captured during this phase into one document. It contains a meaningful plan of action in terms of scope, objectives, roles, resources, budget, schedule, and targeted outcomes.

4.3.3.10 Orient Project Participants
A series of kick-off or orientation meetings is held for all participant groups just prior to the project's start. These meetings ensure that all project team members are fully informed of the project's scope and their roles in the project. The outcomes of the meeting(s) should be that participants buy into the benefits of the project and receive a brief overview of the BSO methodology. In these meetings, the service owner:

- briefs the participants about the CBIs impacted by the project;
- stresses the value of the work they are about to perform in terms of addressing these CBIs;
- briefs the participants on the expected outcome of the project in terms of project goals (the gap between the before and the after of the service metrics);
- informs the participants of the target ROI by assigning a value to the improvement of the project's service metrics;

- Encourages a sense of teamwork and value among the participants through distribution of giveaways, such as shirts.

4.3.4 Outputs of Phase 1

Three major outputs or deliverables are produced in this phase. These are a list of project goals, a roster of project roles, and a precise description of each service to be analyzed and if necessary reorchestrated. This information is compiled into a Service Improvement Project Plan, followed by a kick-off or orientation meeting for the project team after the steering team approves the plan.

4.3.4.1 Project Goals

Project goals are based on the improvement expected on current service metrics, and are quantified in terms of ROI. They require service performance improvement. They are quantifiable and consist of metrics pertaining to commonly used indicators such as financial measures, product volume, cycle time, or number of customer complaints received. Every effort should be made to make all goals SMART (specific, measurable, attainable, realistic, time-constrained).

4.3.4.2 Project Roles

Project roles should be agreed on, and should include a roster of specific individuals for consideration as team members. These individuals and their managers should be formally notified and the terms of their participation documented and agreed to.

4.3.4.3 Service Descriptions

The orchestration includes a precise description of each service to be worked on. This description should contain a list of all subordinated service requests and fulfillments, and which functional organizations in the enterprise are affected.

4.3.4.4 Service Improvement Project Plan

Unlike the Services Improvement Plan, an output of Phase 0, the Service Improvement Project Plan deals with only one of the critical services identified in Phase 0. This makes the project manageable and minimizes disruption to the business. Trying to tackle more than one service at a time results in a project that is too complex and prone to failure or abandonment. This is the nontechnological reason why organizations fail to complete most EAI projects.

This document should be fairly straightforward. However, we recommend that the project plan include the following elements:

- description of project service hierarchy and an organizational-level orchestration of the services,

- list of CSIs to be addressed by the plan for each of the critical services within the hierarchy,
- description of service boundaries for each of the services,
- list of constraints and assumptions,
- list of quantifiable project goals,
- detailed budget,
- projected ROI,
- time line showing resource loading and major milestones,
- project team roster.

4.4 PHASE 2: ANALYZE AND DESIGN

4.4.1 Introduction to Phase 2

In Phase 2, Analyze and Design, the orchestration team first discovers and documents the current, *as-is* service in the form of a hierarchy of process models and notes any flaws, redundancies, unwanted loops, or disconnects in the processes. The team next analyzes the root causes of problems and then determines the feasibility of achieving the project goals through process improvement. If it satisfied with the analysis, it proceeds to design a *should-be* process model that orchestrates the improved service. This done, the team reestimates the cost of reorchestrating the services involved and the ROI. Finally, the team makes a series of recommendations in a preliminary implementation plan, which is presented to the steering team.

Through analysis of the *as-is* business process hierarchy we can pinpoint disconnects, incomplete services, redundancies, unwanted loops, unforeseen exceptions, automation opportunities, and other issues that, if fixed, will improve the service it implements. As we redesign the business process, we can do so in such a manner that sustainable process change is possible. This means that the processes will be designed so that that they can be continuously improved in real time as they continue to operate, so that there is minimal downtime or disruption to business operations upon successive improvements to the service. The work to design the *should-be* process forces the providers of services to get involved (the persons, systems, and organizations that provide services to the process). Phase 2 is a collaborative process with room for all to negotiate and leave the table feeling that all of their WIIFM (what's in it for me) issues have been addressed and at least partially satisfied. As the *should-be* process emerges, improved metrics will be validated as feasible and will be manifested as benefits to the business that will be irresistible to management.

This phase should be the entry point for any first-time BSO initiative. The reason for this is that it usually takes only fifteen to twenty days from the beginning of this phase to the moment at which a sustainable estimate of the ROI can be established. Chances are that, if the pain that led to the project is big, the ROI will be attractive to management. In this way, the customer will see the potential for returns – if it exists – in a relatively short time, and this will sustain the motivation for success for enough time to finish the project.

Before we proceed further, let's introduce a few key terms and how we define them in the context of BSO:

- **Business process**: A sequence of business services orchestrated to fulfill the delivery of a higher-level business service. The business services that are orchestrated by the process can be performed by people, systems, or organizations (in the form of orchestrations or subprocesses). They are the participants or actors in the process. In short, the process is the way an orchestrated service is implemented.
- **As-is process**: The fully discovered process currently in use by the enterprise (also referred to in the literature as "current," "is," and "in-place" processes).
- **Should-be process**: A defined, but not yet implemented, process that is recommended for implementation and continuous improvement (also referred to as "to-be" "could-be," and "should" processes) .

4.4.2 Inputs to Phase 2

The input to Phase 2, Analyze and Design, is the project plan to improve a CBS. A project plan and should contain the following elements:

- description of service hierarchy to be analyzed,
- list of CSIs to be addressed by the plan,
- description of service boundaries,
- list of constraints and assumptions,
- list of quantifiable project goals,
- project budget,
- time line showing resource loading and major milestones,
- project team roster.

In some cases (especially when Phases 0 and 1 are skipped), the orchestration team may have to compile this information from various sources. Incomplete or inaccurate information may indicate that the work that should have been accomplished in Phase 1 has not been satisfactorily completed. If this is the case, it is sufficient to have the service hierarchy to be analyzed and a sense of the goals; the budget and time line are more important for the Design and Approve Prototype subphase of Phase 2 and they can be supplemented as a part of the go/no-go decision in the BSOIA phase. The orchestration team may need to obtain the rest of the data during its *as-is* process discovery. It is also recommended that there be a project kick-off meeting with the orchestration team, not only to explain the project plan, but also to go through the details of the steps in this phase.

Once the orchestration team has a project plan with at least the minimum stated above, the team focuses on the two subphases of Phase 2: BSOIA and, if the estimated ROI justifies it, prototype creation.

4.4.3 Activities for Phase 2

There are two subphases for Analyze and Design, as described below:

> *Phase 2.1: BSOIA*
> 1. Define service deliverables.
> 2. Discover and document the *as-is* process that implements it.
> 3. Define success metrics and calculate ROI.
> 4. Present BSOIA to customer for go/no-go decision.
>
> *Phase 2.2: Design and Approve Prototype*
> 1. Design *should-be* process.
> 2. Validate running prototype with customer (with simple prototype interfaces to people and systems).
> 3. Create the final list of necessary discrete services from people and systems with documented deliverables and use cases.
> 4. Estimate orchestration effort and reassess ROI.
> 5. Make go/no-go decision on whether to implement.

4.4.3.1 Business BSOIA

First, the project plan (which defines the scope or hierarchy of services to be analyzed) should be formally approved and the approving authority should sign off it. In most cases, this approving authority should be the process owner on the steering team, but it could be anyone on the steering team, any of the directly affected functional managers, or a senior executive in the enterprise. What is most important is that the plan and scope be formally approved and documented.

In addition to this formal approval, there should be a checkpoint meeting with the approving authority to ensure that he or she has a complete understanding of the project.

4.4.3.1.1 Define Scope and Deliverables

- **Clearly define service deliverables as a first step.** Before starting the *as-is* process discovery, it is important to determine the expected deliverables of the service that is being analyzed. This initial round of discussions is germane to determining the service's real content. An example would be if the orchestration team asked what the deliverable is for a human resources (HR) recruiting service. The obvious answer is a "new employee." However, if the team knows that a service objective is reducing turnover that results from hiring under- or overqualified individuals for certain positions, then it knows that the real deliverable here is not simply a new employee, but an employee with the talent, personality, and experience to fulfill the job requirements, that is, one who is a good fit for the job. However, depending on the endpoint of the service, HR may be required to provide the working quarters and tools also. So, the deliverables must be documented in detail.

- **Interview project management.** The orchestration team meets with the project steering team and/or the internal or external customers to determine and gain consensus on what they think are the key deliverables of the service to be orchestrated. The team must take the time to discuss these required deliverables with the owners of the subservices. This step is critical. If this is not done, the steering team or stakeholders may resist or attempt to sabotage any proposed process redesign because they may believe that it does not represent their best interests. If the orchestration team skips this stage or does not get buy-in on the deliverables, it runs the risk of defining a *shouldn't-be* process.

- **Deliverables.** *Expectations versus reality.* The orchestration team uses the service deliverables definition as a basis of comparison at the end of *as-is* process discovery. By establishing in advance what the deliverables are, the team sets a desired end result, and begins with the end in mind. This allows the team, during discovery of the *as-is* process, to find disconnects between the deliverable and the process that supposedly produces it. Therefore, the real delivery may not be the same as what the service owner or senior management thought it was. They may also find that, although it is the same deliverable, it is not as complete or as relevant as they thought. They could find that the deliverable does not meet customers' expectations because the process to produce it has many disconnects or is inefficient and cumbersome. They may find that the deliverable that the process produces is fine but that it is produced too slowly, without enough quality, or too expensively. Of course, they could find that the existing process is efficient, works perfectly a it is, and cannot be improved. This last outcome is possible, although highly implausible, because if this were the case, management probably would not have singled out this service for review in the first place.

- **Revisiting the steering team.** Once the service's scope and deliverables have been determined, the orchestration team should revisit the steering team and make any last-minute additions or deletions based on the implied services hierarchy needed to produce the deliverables.

> **Scope:** We consider the order fulfillment process that goes from the creation of the order to the delivery of the product.
>
> **Deliverable:** The service exposed by the computer manufacturer delivers a computer manufactured to the desired specifications and shipped to the customer's shipping address along with the invoice posted to the manufacturer's ERP system and charged to the buyer's credit card.

4.4.3.1.2 Discover and Document as-is Process. Before we start discussing the mechanics of documenting the *as-is* process, it is useful to spend a moment discussing why we bother documenting this process at all. Indeed, many process designers insist that this is just a waste of time. They think that the most effective course is to plunge ahead and immediately design the new *should-be* process. We call this approach "jumping to solution." Our belief is that, to design an effective solution, the orchestration team must first fully understand the problem. To do this, it must play the role of "gumshoe" detective and use the *as-is* process discovery methodology presented below. This accomplishes a number of things. It provides the basis for a gap analysis that will ultimately provide a sustainable estimate of ROI. Through a thorough discovery process, the team can effectively document the actual *as-is* process and easily identify the "pain points," or the parts of the process that are inefficient or broken.

Once the team has identified these, it can estimate the impact of improving the service by simply fixing disconnects, redundancies, missing services, and unnecessary services or iterations. This is important because the team can actually improve the process enough to obtain sufficient ROI while causing minimal disruption in service to the business's operation. Even more important, the team will be regarded with the respect that people with true knowledge of the business deserve, instead of being regarded as clueless innovators who disrupt business and require employees and customers to undergo extensive retraining in something that may not work.

- **Efficiencies across processes.** In addition, the sort of careful *as-is* process discovery described below yields other rewards. It helps the orchestration team find commonality of services used by this process and other processes in the enterprise. This reduces the level of effort required for the project team when it moves on to other processes. Accurately assessing the current process helps reduce pushback later on because, as part of the discovery process, the orchestration team interviews many key stakeholders, both from management and end users. By doing this, the team includes them in the process and, to a certain extent, addresses or at least acknowledges their needs and ascertains the services the team expects them to provide for the process.

- **Inclusion of stakeholders.** Moreover, "working backward" using the *spider* technique, which we discuss shortly, the orchestration team not only verifies the point of inefficiency in the process, but it gets at inefficiencies or disconnects upstream in the process. This enables the team to assess the benefits of reorchestrating the service. By identifying each point of pain, the team should incrementally create a foundation of support and buy-in for the *should-be* process because the *should-be* process will have validity for those key stakeholders who have expressed their perceived problems with the process. Note also that the design of the *should-be* process will always be undertaken with the customers' convenience and service in mind, but the process will also address many of the "pain points" identified through the interviews, which should in turn address many of these WIFFM issues of the stakeholders and participants.

- **More fresh ideas.** The spider, an *as-is* process discovery technique, consists of a computer-assisted set of interviews with people who either provide a human service or are domain experts on the services from systems that are needed. Good ideas for improving the process will naturally emerge as a result of interviewing people who have an in-depth knowledge of their services to the business process under study. These are people who understand the nature of their businesses, including the subtleties and nuances associated with many of the tasks they perform. A *should-be* process that incorporates the subtleties and complexities of the particular business for which it was defined is a more complete solution, and one that will most effectively address the enterprise's critical process issues. As we discussed in the introduction of this section, without any *as-is* process discovery, there is a tendency to just "repave the cow paths" of the existing processes with new technology without making any substantive process improvements.

- **Identification of baseline metrics.** Finally, taking the time to discover the *as-is* process allows an opportunity to revalidate and make more discrete the project goals identified in Phase 1. The orchestration team identifies suitable points of measure at different points in the process. It then documents the metrics for each point and uses them as a baseline or point of departure for the "*should-be*" process design. For example, perhaps one project goal is to reduce the order-to-ship cycle time to three business days. If the team discovers a bottleneck in shipping, it can set the current baseline for this point in the process and then begin by improving the process to reduce this bottleneck and increase the rate of throughput.

FIGURE 4.11. A Simple Process Showing Roles.

Step 1: Identify participants and their roles

The challenge in this step is to discover the key roles in the process. The orchestration team, with the documented deliverables of the service in hand, interviews individuals to determine what roles they assume in the process. The reason that this is done first is that discovering roles helps simplify *as-is* process modeling. This approach also meshes well with the mechanics of the BSO toolset's process design tool when we use it to graphically model the process. Figure 4.11 shows simple process roles. A swim-lane metaphor is used to identify the roles and activities related to each role. The roles shown in this figure are Interviewer, "Hiring Manager, CFO, and Candidate.

A suggested order of actions follows:

1. Create a list of everyone involved in obtaining the final deliverable.
2. Conduct interviews with each person.
3. Find out what service the person fulfills for the process.
4. Focus on roles, not individuals.

Once the team identifies the primary roles for the process, it starts documenting the *as-is* process by completing the spider form.

> These are the roles discovered through the above interviews:
>
> - **Sales** — Tasked with interfacing with the customer during the entire order fulfillment process. Sales creates a new order when the customer first calls, thus triggering the order fulfillment process.
> - **Order Fulfillment** — The nerve center of the order fulfillment process. Order fulfillment is responsible for coordinating activities between finance, warehouse, manufacturing and QA.

- **Finance** — Finance is responsible for verifying a user's credit and eventually billing the user's credit card for the order and updating the ERP system.
- **Manufacturing** — Manufacturing is responsible for actual assembly of the product.
- **QA** — Once the product has been manufactured, QA inspects the product to make sure that it meets various government and company standards and the product works as claimed by the company.
- **Warehouse** — Warehouse maintains an adequate supply of the parts necessary for a continuous stream of orders. Daily reports are generated for the inventory-at-hand. These reports are then examined and orders are placed with the parts suppliers to stock up inventory.
- **Shipping** — Once the product has been inspected, the shipping department uses one of the package carriers to ship the product to the customer.

Step 2: Complete the spider form

In this step, the orchestration team documents the results of participant interviews by filling out a spider form, shown in Figure 4.12, and then graphically creating an activity flow. The form helps the orchestration team discover the *as-is* process by allowing it to record the services performed by, or the involvement of, a participant in each activity from the inputs to the activity, or what a participant needs in order to begin the activity, the activity itself, and the outputs – the results of his or her activity. To document the spiders, the team always starts with outgoing services, then inquires about the activity, and finally asks about necessary incoming services. These incoming and outgoing services are the "legs of the spider."

In process discovery and design for BSO, we need to think upside down – we always think that people are pushing things but, actually, in the BSO world, the process is requesting (pulling) services to create a new service that is being requested from it.

The incoming and outgoing services define the activity. What we are defining is what the participants produce, how they produce it, and what they need in order to produce it. We do not worry about chronology just yet.

> The spider form in Figure 4-12 is the result of an in-
> terview by Waqar Sadiq with the Sales Executive, Felix
> Racca.

In the form in Figure 4.12, the box in the center represents the activity (the abdomen of the spider). In this box, you will find the following fields that need to be filled in:

- **Interviewee**: The person who is being interviewed.
- **Role**: The role of the person who is being interviewed.
- **Activity**: The name of the activity (it needs to be expressed in the form of an action). This field may be associated to a subform where more detail of the activity is provided.
- **Duration**: The mean duration of the activity according to the interviewee.
- **Interviewer**: The person who does the interview.

In the columns to the left, labeled "Input needed," you need to fill in a row for each input in the following way:

- **Source role**: The role that originates the input. These roles, if they are performed by human participants, need to be one of the roles discovered above. If not, they must be entered anyway because they constitute a typical disconnect. It's important that the interviewer have the list of roles at hand and makes sure that the interviewee is positively indicating a role

Inputs needed				Outputs produced		
Source Role	Deliverable			Condition	Receiving Role	Deliverable
Customer	Order			Bad Historical Date	Supervisor	Escalated Order
System	Order Screen			History OK	Orderfulfillment	Order
System	Customer Historical Data	Interviewee: Felix Racca Role: Sales Executive		History OK	Orderfulfillment	Credit card information
		Activity: Create order in system				
		Duration: 15 minutes				
		Interviewer : Waqar Sadiq				

FIGURE 4.12. Spider Form.

that is different from any on the list. If the source is a system, then this column should have the name of the system, module, submodule, etc. The source can also be a business partner, in which case the role should express the category of business service that it provides.

Deliverable: The product (in the form of data or materials) that the source role delivers to the interviewee. This column typically has an associated sub-form that adds detail about the deliverable and catalogs it to avoid nomenclature disconnects. In the example, "Process Design" should always be called by that name because it is a key to the unraveling process. In the columns to the right, labeled "Outputs produced," you need to fill a row for each output in the following way:

- **Condition**: The role to which the output produced will go. It's usually a logical condition. Use the key word "Always" to denote that the outputs will be sent concurrently to two or more roles or activities within a role. If you do not put anything in the condition, then it is understood that the output will go only to this route if none of the other conditions are met. In some cases, you may need to send the output to "parametric roles" meaning that, where you send the output will depend upon a parameter. The way to denote this case is, as you will see below, to indicate the parameter name in the role column.
- **Receiving role**: The role of the person or system that receives the output. This role can be parametric. In that case, it would be indicated as a role with a parameter between parentheses, such as System (name). This would indicate that the output would be sent to as many systems as there are names that we pass as parameters.
- **Deliverable**: The item to be delivered (data or material) to the receiving role.

If different persons that you have decided to interview have the same roles in an organization, the team may discover inconsistencies in the spiders. This is a desired outcome and the team should not correct this while it is creating the spider forms. The team should focus on obtaining all the inputs and outputs for one role at a time (fill in as many spider forms as roles the person has). This will keep the documentation of the spiders better organized. It is important for the team to remember that it is still documenting the _as-is_ process. It needs to make sure that the interviewee is describing what he or she does today, not what they would like to do.

When the interviewing is complete, you will have created a database that holds all of the spiders.

Next, we create an activity flow that graphically shows the current _as-is_ process. One way to do this is by taking the spider forms and working

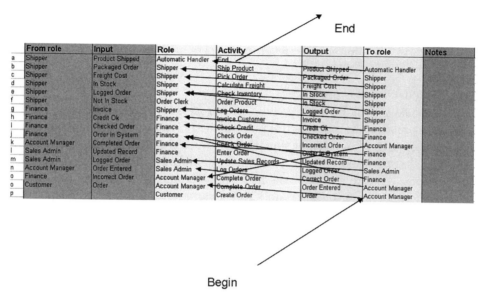

FIGURE 4.13. Unraveling the As-Is Process.

backward from the end of the process, trying to match the input legs of each spider with the output legs of others. We start with the final desired output or outputs of the process, and then we look at the activities that produced those outputs. We look at the inputs to these activities, and match these to the same outputs. We continue this recursive process until we have included all of the inputs, activities, and outputs listed in our database and have created an activity data flow similar to the one shown in Figure 4.13. This step is known as unraveling the *as-is* process. There are tools that completely automate the creation of the activity flow based on the input of all the spiders.

The spider and the activity flows described in this methodology are very rudimentary, and are meant to be aids toward designing the *as-is* process.

There are tools that are more sophisticated and need more information for the spider, such as the conditions for the output legs that we depict here. These tools are meant to practically automate the creation of the *as-is* model as well as some obvious disconnects.

Figure 4.13 is an example of a portion of an activity flow taken from a set of spiders that were built for an order fulfillment service. The objective of the figure is to illustrate the matching of inputs to previous outputs. We don't recommend doing the unraveling this way. Many times it's better to do it in a room with sticky spiders and actual participants, to quickly stick the spiders on a whiteboard and draw lines to the matching inputs and outputs.

This can be done pretty quickly in a short session with comments from the participants. If the BSO suite provides an unraveling tool, the best way to go about this is to project the resulting process model on a screen and discuss it with the participants.

Step 3: Model the *as-is* process

The next step in documenting the *as-is* process is to perfect the model of the *as-is* process. The input for this phase is the activity flow from step 3. In some cases, activity flows can be imported by process modelers so as to be able to visualize the *as-is* process. The best way to do this is to use modelers that support cross-role process models. We recommend developing this model in the BSO process design tool. The advantage of doing it this way is that the team can use this as a starting point when it starts designing the *should-be cross-role* model. However, the model can also be drawn manually on wall chart paper or by using a PC graphics tool such as Visio or Microsoft PowerPoint.

> Figure 4.14 shows the *as-is* process diagram of the order fulfillment process example after all of the spider forms have been unraveled.

In Figure 4.14, the disks represent activities performed by each of the roles. The square shape with the hole in the center represents the creation of a new instance of the process. The large arrow shapes at each end represent the beginning and end of the process. The lines with the arrows in the middle represent the transitions between activities.

Modeling the *as-is* process is iterative. Even when the model is automatically generated, teams seldom model the process correctly the first time. The best practice is to get something on paper or in a process modeling design tool, and then refine it. Another good technique is to create a "parking lot," or list of all activities or inputs/outputs that do not have a clear place in the process. Unraveling software does this automatically.

This cross-role model shows the *what* and the *who* of the process as it currently is. It helps the orchestration team completely understand the current *as-is* process. The graphic format also highlights potential problems. In the same way, it is a useful tool when the orchestration team meets with decision makers. The team can get a good overall concept of the *as-is* process, and can easily point out and explain problems in the current process to these decision makers.

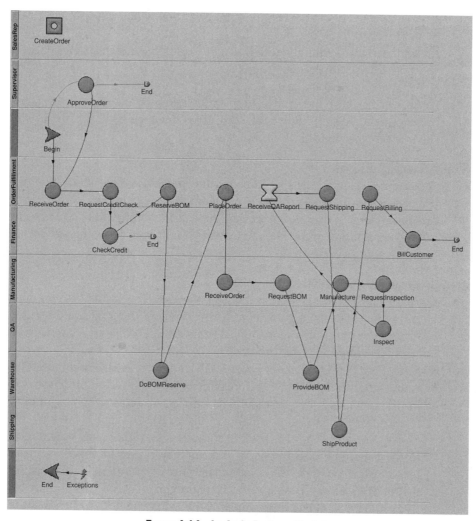

FIGURE 4.14. An As-Is Process Model.

After completing the *as-is* process model, the team asks the following questions:

- Does the process fulfill the deliverable? If not, what other services does it need in order to do so?
- What concludes the process?
- What triggers the process to begin?
- Who are the "players" in the process?
- How long do the activities in the process take?
- What cost, quality, service, or speed issues exist?

- Are there any disconnects or redundancies that would imply unnecessary services?
- Are there any seemingly unnecessary delegations or escalations?
- Are there any unnecessary loops?
- Are there any manual tasks that could be automated?

By answering these questions, the team assesses the viability of the target improvement. To simplify, we call all of these deficiencies in the integrity in the process "disconnects" from now on.

Step 4: Identify disconnects

A disconnect is anything that impedes the effectiveness or efficiency of the process. It may be an input, a step, or an output that is missing, unnecessary, or substandard. It may be something done at the wrong time, done by the wrong organization or people, not executed well, or done manually when it could be automated.

Step 5: Identify optimization opportunities

Once the orchestration team has modeled the *as-is* process and has identified all of the disconnects, it is ready to further explore the model and identify structural optimization opportunities. Some typical problems readily apparent just from looking at the process:

- *Series flow*. This is a series of activities that are processed sequentially. This is time-consuming because, before performing a task, each role has to wait for the previous role to complete its activity. An improvement would be to allow for the parallel processing of these tasks.
- *Churn*. The term churn is used to indicate a loop that goes back almost to the beginning of the process, and thereby causes each activity to be performed again. This is not an efficient use of resources. An alternative would be to allow a back-and-forth transaction between two primary activities. We will show an example of this when we design the *should-be* process.
- *Unnecessary approvals at executive level*. This is also known as white-space handoff, because it means that the manager must approve the order before it can be transitioned between departments – in this case from the finance department to the shipping department.
- *Manual tasks*. An excessive number of manual tasks or activities probably means that some of these could be automated to increase the efficiency of the process.

The team must look at the *as-is* process critically and challenge anything that seems unnecessary or questionable. Too often one will look at an *as-is* process model and assume that everything depicted was purposefully designed that way. To the contrary, in many cases *as-is* processes have evolved and mutated over time, and bear little resemblance to, or are unaligned with, the process relationship model developed in Phase 0. The team must take the role of iconoclast and be willing to challenge and question everything on the *as-is* process model that seems problematic.

A final point – at this stage, we are still just documenting the *as-is* process. We are still only identifying problems here. We must stop short of making recommendations until we our findings have been validated and our success metrics have been defined. Making recommendations at this stage would be premature. For example, if we take the example above and recommend that several manual tasks be automated, we may find out during the process of validating our findings that the issue of automating these activities has already been subject to a cost/benefit analysis, which found that the cost of machinery to replace the workers was prohibitive.

Here is a suggested order of actions as the team goes about identifying problems in the *as-is* process design. Note that the results of this discovery work should be relayed back to the steering team in a way that frames how they impact the enterprise's CBIs. We recommend the following steps:

1. *Provide background on as-is process documentation method.* Present the list of deliverables associated with the process. Distribute a list of who was interviewed to determine the *as-is* process. Explain the methods used to discover the *as-is* process, including interviewing techniques, the spider, and the *as-is* activity flow diagram.

2. Show *completed as-is cross-role process map.* Explain symbols and conventions used in the map and provide a brief overview of the current process. Check for validation at this point.

3. *Point out "pain" in current process.* Point out disconnects and other problems, explaining what they mean to the efficient and successful completion of the process and deliverables.

4. *Present as-is process metrics.* Frame the metrics in terms of how they impact the critical business issues facing the company. For example, in an HR recruiting process, a current metric could be how many days it takes from initial job posting to receipt from applicant of a signed offer letter. Another metric could be the number of people who accept offers per month or per year.

5. *Reach consensus about which metrics reflect CBIs.* The key decision makers should be familiar with and able to articulate the CBIs. As you review the metrics with the key decision makers, seek to reach consensus regarding which of the metrics indicate inadequacies or inefficiencies in their current process and reflect the CBIs. Make note of these metrics for future reference when you begin to define the project success metrics. For this, you can use the SVA form from Phase 1.

6. *Identify flaws in the current process that correlate to metrics.* Highlight for the key decision makers those flaws in the current process that, if corrected, would help bring process metrics into an acceptable range. In addition, explain that this analysis of the current process performance will provide a benchmark against which to gauge process improvements once the processes are redesigned.

7. *Present a value proposition of should-be process.* By identifying and framing problems with the *as-is* process in terms of how the current process metrics impact the company's critical business issues, you have built a value proposition for proposing a redesign of the current process. Identifying and then pointing out inadequacies in the current process in terms of the metrics already in place better position you to reach broad-based buy-in to your proposed redesign.

4.4.3.1.3 Define Success Metrics and Calculate ROI. In this activity we assess which disconnects enable us to make the process better and what the impact of this would be on the current process metrics.

Step 1: Define success metrics.

After the *as-is* process has been documented, the next major step in the Analyze and Design phase is to define success metrics (including the expected ROI) for the project's service. The project steering team typically performs this activity. The steering team can use the current process metrics discovered as part of the *as-is* process documentation in the previous step. It can use these as a baseline for process improvement. However, sometimes the metrics currently in place do not properly address the enterprise's CBIs and new metrics need to be developed. Success metrics are necessary because, over time, they help determine trends. Metrics also help to determine stability, measure improvement, bring important issues into focus, and identify problems. More importantly, though, they help to estimate the benefit to the enterprise in terms of the ROI of improving the service.

At the same time, however, the importance of developing metrics must be balanced against the effort required to monitor and report them.

In any case, measures of performance will need to be defined. Typical quantifiers include:

- cycle time,
- volume,
- quantity,
- revenue,
- cost of revenue,
- cost of lack of quality, and
- cost of people.

Project constraints such as hardware and software constraints, scalability limitations, system resource availability, and volume capacity must be factored into the proposed success metrics as well. We show gap analysis based on the above metrics, but there is also ROI based on cost avoidance due to constraints to company growth. We call this opportunity-cost-based ROI, but we do not enter into detail about this calculation in the book. In addition to project constraints, the steering team must also determine what is within the enterprise's sphere of influence to control. Issues that must be considered include:

- Is there sufficient time to implement the needed changes to make the success metrics viable?
- Is there sufficient budget to implement the changes necessary to make the success metrics attainable?
- Are sufficient measures in place to allow the success metrics to be effectively measured?
- Do the success metrics impinge on another functional area in the enterprise that is either unwilling or unable to provide the needed information?
- Do SEI/ISO regulations preclude the attainment of some of the success metrics?
- Are there government regulations that will impact the success metrics?
Here is a list of questions useful to ask when establishing process success metrics:

Revenue
- What revenue does the process generate?
- Could it generate more revenue per instance of the process? How?
- Could we reduce the revenue of each instance if we increased the volume?

Cost
- What does it cost to operate the process?
- Which services cost the most? Why?
- Which services add the most value and which add the least?
- What are the causes of cost in the process?

Cycle time
- How long does it take?
- Which services consume the most time? Why?
- Which services add value and which do not?
- Which services are redundant, are bottlenecks, or add complexity?
- Which services cause delays, storage, or unnecessary movement?

Quality
- How many errors occur in this activity?
- Is variation common?
- Why are people doing the same activity differently?
- What are the causes of defects?

- What variables need to be managed to have an effect on quality?
- How can we change the process to reduce or eliminate variation?
- What is the cost of customer complaints by type?
- How many payments have been posted incorrectly?
- How many incorrect new-account documents have been generated?

Metrics				
	As-is		Should-be	
Cycle	15d		2d	
Quality	90%	10% Error	97%	3% Error
Person-hours/order	800		20	

Step 2: Estimate ROI

Once the team has defined the project's success measures, it should reassess the ROI of the project based on the difference between the targeted success metrics and the known *as-is* metrics. There is an example of how to do this in Figures 4.15 and 4.16.

As can be seen in Figure 4.15, we calculate the gap between the *as-is* and what it *should be*, based on conservative estimates of what would happen if we fixed all the disconnects and made the improvements suggested above.

> Figure 4.15 provides a form that calculates monthly returns based on the process improvement suggested earlier. The following data need to be supplemented:
> - *Metrics column:* In the example, we supplied cycle time, quality and person-hours per month.
> - *As-is column:* This has two subcolumns — measure and impact per unit. You must input the current measure of cycle time (as an interval), quality (in percentage), and person-hours per month (as hours). In impact per unit, you put revenue per unit as a positive money field and cost per unit as a negative money field.

> • *Should-be column:* This has three subcolumns —
> measure, impact description, and impact per unit.
> In measure, you input the expected measures after
> fixing the process problems in the same units as
> above. In impact description, you have the de-
> scription of the impacts of cycle time, quality,
> and personnel variations caused by fixing the
> process problems. In impact per unit you need to
> input the expected revenue per unit or cost per
> unit as positive or negative currency.

After these inputs have been completed, you add the subprocesses that
the process uses in the impact description column and map their total gap
per cycle field in the Gap column. This is done recursively if subprocesses
call other subprocesses (if any).

Finally you input the *as-is* volume in terms of cycles per month in the lower
left-hand box and the expected *should-be* cycles in the lower right-hand box.
These values should be propagated to the subprocess spreadsheets, if any.
The calculation will render the total gap per cycle, or the monthly return in
this case.

In Figure 4.16, we try to assess what the ROI will be after twelve months of
having the process(es) in production. For doing this, we sandbag an estimate
of the development cost and the implementation and BSO license costs and
we offset it to the monthly returns of Figure 4.15.

BSO Per Month Gap Analisys For: Fulfillment process

Metrics	As-Is		Should-Be			Gap
	Measure	Impact/u	Measure	Impact Description	Impact/u	Impact/M
Cycle Time		$1,500.00		Revenue	$1,500.00	$300,000.00
	15d	-$750.00	2d	Cost of direct material	-$750.00	-$150,000.00
Quality		-$100.00		Cost of return processing	-$80.00	$280.00
	90%	-$325.00	97%	Cost of throwaway	-$325.00	$20,800.00
Person/h/ Month		-$20.00		Mean cost FTE/hour	-$25.00	$18,600.00
	800	-$10.00	20	Associated costs Cost/hour	-$12.00	$9,312.00
TOTAL Gap Per Cycle						$198,992.00
Expected Increment in number of cycles per month	1000		1200			

FIGURE 4.15. Initial Gap Analysis.

Cost of Development	-$500,000		
Cost of Licenses and Rollout	-$1,000,000		
Total Cost	-$1,500,000		
Monthly Gap (Recovery)	$198,992		
	Bal+Int	Amort	Balance
Month 1	-$1,500,000.00	$198,992	-$1,301,008.00
Month 2	-$1,311,849.73	$198,992	-$1,112,857.73
Month 3	-$1,122,131.55	$198,992	-$923,139.55
Month 4	-$930,832.38	$198,992	-$731,840.38
Month 5	-$737,939.05	$198,992	-$538,947.05
Month 6	-$543,438.27	$198,992	-$344,446.27
Month 7	-$347,316.66	$198,992	-$148,324.66
Month 8	-$149,560.70	$198,992	$49,431.30
Month 9	$49,843.23	$198,992	$248,835.23
Month 10	$250,908.86	$198,992	$449,900.86
Month 11	$453,650.03	$198,992	$652,642.03
Month 12	$658,080.71	$198,992	**$857,072.71**

FIGURE 4.16. BSO ROI Initial Calculation.

In the Figure 4.15, you input the cost of development and the expected costs of licenses and rollout, all as negative currencies. The spreadsheet automatically calculates the total cost. You also input an interest rate (see Figure 4.28), The monthly gap (recovery field) is mapped from the appropriate spreadsheet and the system automatically calculates the balance plus interest, amortization, and balance for each month.

> In the example the project practically breaks even in the eighth month of production, produces $857,072 at the end of the first year, and produces $2,387,904 every year after the first.

Step 3: Create BSO Impact Report
   The following items are compiled into a BSO Impact (BSOI) report:
   - service hierarchy name,
   - cover letter,
   - service scope,
   - service deliverable,
   - list of participants interviewed,
   - spider interview forms,
   - *as-is* process model,

- disconnects and problems to be addressed by *should-be* design,
- success metrics, gap analysis, and estimated ROI
- recommendation,
- go/no go document.

Once compiled, this report is presented to the customer for a go/no-go decision.

4.4.3.1.4 Seek go/no-go decision. Before the team proceeds any further with the methodology, it must firmly believe three things:

1. **The process needs changing, there is ROI, and there is consensus about both things**. If this is not the case or if there is no consensus that the process needs to be changed or that the service will benefit substantially from being orchestrated and exposed programmatically, the team should immediately terminate the project. This complacency indicates that the pain doesn't yet exceed the perceived effort. Until that balance changes, there is no point in proceeding because the project will probably fail due to lack of support.
2. **The orchestration team has the ability to work with others to make the process better**. The team must believe it can work with the various stakeholders to improve the process and the services that it orchestrates. If there is uncertainty about the team's ability to negotiate change and overcome resistance, it is better not to start the design just yet. By its very nature, this work requires butting up against the status quo and pushing at times (albeit diplomatically and gently) to overcome resistance. If the team believes that it does not have the tact and skill to work with others in this fashion, it is best to stop now. Process redesign efforts are difficult, and although the new technologies that allow BSO make it easier to implement and easier for the process to evolve, the ultimate driver for all these projects is the volition of senior management and the consensus of those who intervene.
3. **The orchestration team can garner support to make the change happen**. The team must have sufficient executive sponsorship to see the project through. This support must be more than just lip service. Senior management must repeatedly convey a strong message that the project is important to the enterprise and that everyone affected should cooperate with the process design team or else face the consequences. Positive reinforcement is preferred over the threat of negative consequences. This can take the form of recognition and financial incentives offered by the executive team to those who actively work to make the project a success. If senior management does not offer this positive advocacy, the team should stop, because without it, one resistor (typically, a mid-level manager, but sometimes even an end user with a lot of informal power) can stop the project. The active endorsement of senior management is required to override such

resistance. Services orchestration implies subverting how functional managers and IT users think of themselves: They think they have the power to require services from IT, BSO is an IT effort, and therefore they tell *the team* what to do. However, they don't have this power. They and the IT people are responsible for delivering the services that have been orchestrated into a new service and you (the service owner) represent the customer. This is unsettling for them. Often, we have had to pound on a table in front of the process participants and paraphrase John F. Kennedy's famous line: "Ask not what your processes can do for you; ask what you can do for your processes!!!."

Often, this has worked, but a few times it has not.

If the team has not answered, "Yes" to all these questions, it should shelve the project because there is a high probability that it will fail. However, if the team has answered "Yes" to all three questions, it proceeds to present the BSOI report to the customer, seeking a go/no-go decision.

4.4.3.2 Design and Approve Prototype

The Design *Should-Be* Process step is the final step before making the go/no-go decision about whether to move into the implementation phase of the BSO methodology. There are three major goals to be obtained by this step:

1. an approved *should-be* process prototype,
2. a document with the service interfaces that are to be used by the *should-be* process for its implementation into production,
3. a set of documents that result in a credible revised ROI estimate.

4.4.3.2.1 Design and Publish the Should-be Process Prototype. The following steps apply to *should-be* process design and prototype creation:

Step 1: Define *should-be* process value proposition.

The arrows in the Figure 4.17 represent inputs to the *should-be* process design. All of these inputs should be addressed to ensure buy-in from key decision makers.

Let's discuss these further:

- *Benchmark data.* A through review of benchmark data regarding how other enterprises approach this business process should have been reviewed as part of the *should-be* process design. practices from other enterprises that are deemed an advance over the current *as-is* process should be included, if appropriate.

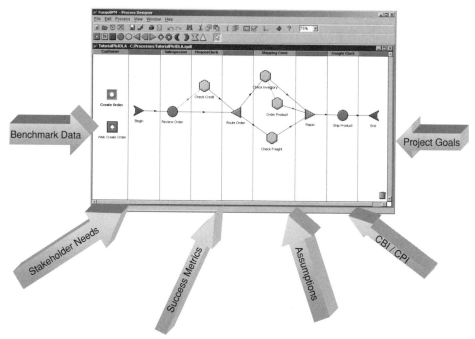

FIGURE 4.17. Inputs to the Should Be process design.

- *Success metrics.* The design of the *should-be* process should achieve the success metrics and the impacts of their gap with the current metrics, as calculated earlier in this phase.
- *Stakeholder needs.* Stakeholders needs as determined throughout the discovery phase and documented in the creation of the spider must be incorporated into the design. This is very important. The process design should always be to delight stakeholders as well as customers.
- *Assumptions.* All the project constraints and assumptions as documented in the project plan should be reviewed before design of the *should-be* process begins.
- *CBI/CPI.* The CBIs and the CPIs must be reviewed to make sure that the *should-be* process design addresses them.
- *Project goals.* The *should-be* process must have performance levels that attain the project goals, as documented in the process project plan. Align process objectives with the enterprise's overall objectives.

Step 2: Modify *as-is* process model to define should-be process.

The orchestration team uses the spider form, such as shown in Figure 4.12, to compare the listed roles with the *as-is* process model roles. As the team starts transforming the *as-is* process model into a *should-be* process model, it revises the roles listed, adding any not already there and deleting or changing those already shown, as appropriate. Only those roles necessary to operate the process should be displayed on the cross-role process model. The roles should only reflect the organizational structure, not reproduce it exactly.

As the team analyzes the *as-is* process, it focuses on activities that it can either eliminate, streamline, combine or complete with fewer handoffs, automate, or have completed by a supplier or customer.

It is also useful to consider what steps should be added to improve communication within the business process, and what steps, if added, would allow those who are part of the process to be more proactive. The team asks the questions:

- What would the process look like if one person had to do all the work?
- What activities upstream could be improved?
- What if the work was done right the first time?

One question should always be paramount: What work does the customer really care about? We can have the best internal processes possible, but if we do not significantly improve our level of service or value to our customers, all of our work is meaningless. This is why, when performing process analysis and design, we always work backward, starting with the end product or deliverable to our customers. Adding value to our customer relationship is the only reason most enterprises are in business, and this is the overarching guiding principle that guides all of our process redesign work.

Seek opportunities for improvement. As the team designs the *should-be* process, it continues to find opportunities to

- automate activities;
- make the enterprise easier to do business with (ETDBW), more efficient, and more competitive;
- increase efficiency and reduce the amount of information exchanges between information systems that employees must perform manually (swivel-chair operations);
- improve efficiency and profitability to meet shareholder and management concerns;
- reduce the cost of doing business;
- fulfill any government regulations in a more efficient and cost-effective manner.

Think perfect versus *–as-is*. The team considers the ideal state for the process or "crafts a vision."

Don't design in exceptions. Avoid the ever-present temptation to try and account for each exception.

Get the junk out. Remove the "noise" in the process – all of those activities or checkpoints that do not add value. All of these slow down the process and add up to expensive delays.

Go after the top 80 percent. The team should ask, "Is it worth going after the last 20 percent to design a perfect process?" In most cases, the team might try to follow the Pareto principal and wind up spending 80 percent of resources trying to fix that last 20 percent of the process. They should avoid this trap. A well-designed *should-be* process that captures 80 percent of business transactions should free enough resources to allow it to individually troubleshoot the remaining transactions. In most cases these transactions require individual attention anyway.

Make sure the *should-be* process model is complete. The team only gains agreement/approval of a proposed solution if it is displayed in the process model.

As can be seen in Figure 4.18, the order fulfillment process no longer has any manual intervention in the coordination of the work that other departments do. The manual activities have been replaced by subprocess calls. The process model itself is in charge of coordinating what the different departments do.

Another difference to be noted is that, in the *should-be* process, we have parallelized credit approval and reservation of inventory parts, and the whole process is at a higher level of abstraction. In fact, with the exception of the submit order activity and the QA activity, all of the rest of the activities are subprocess calls.

Because of this higher level of abstraction, the implementation of credit approval or reservation of parts or manufacturing or shipping can be modified without affecting the design of the order fulfillment process, or vice-versa

Finally, note that, in the *should-be* process, we include the handling of the possible exceptions as

> notification. Therefore, if the parts, for example,
> take too long to arrive and fulfill the level of
> service agreement, the instance in the subprocess will
> expire and throw an exception that will be handled by
> the notify-exception activity in the main process.

Figures 4.18–22 show a *should-be* cross-role process design of the order fulfillment previously shown in Figure 4.14. Note some significant differences from the *as-is* process design shown in the preceding section:

- *Two create options.* We have determined two create options for starting the process. One is the traditional one, where the customer initiates the process by faxing, mailing, or calling in an order. The other operation takes advantage of the enterprise's Internet capabilities. Instead of a sales-order clerk performing a swivel-chair operation and manually reviewing all incoming Internetorders, the new process automatically monitors these

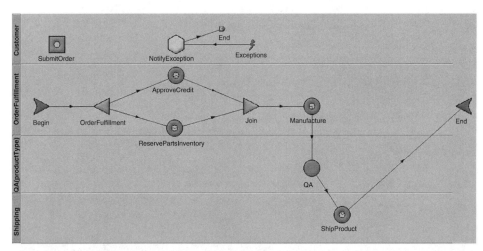

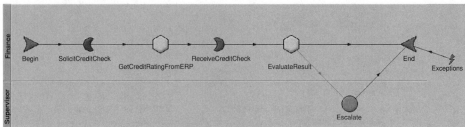

FIGURE **4.18–4.22. Cross-Role Process Model.**

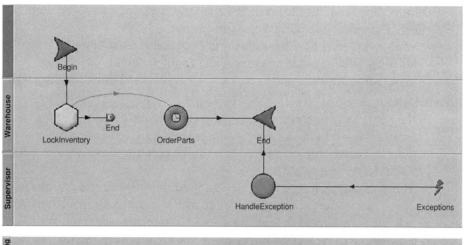

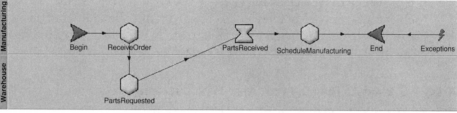

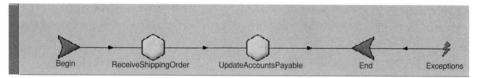

FIGURE 4.18–4.22. *(continued).*

incoming Internet orders and kicks off the order fulfillment process as soon as the order is received.

- *Automated activities.* Note the hexagon-shaped activities on Figures 4.18–4.22; they symbolize automated activities. Manual intervention is no longer required.
- *Join and split activities.* The triangular-shaped activities on Figure 4.18 indicate concurrent processing. In this example the check-inventory and check-freight activities can now be processed simultaneously and independently of each other. In the *as-is* process shown earlier, the check-freight activity could not be started until the check-inventory activity had been completed. This considerably slowed down the process.

During design of the *should-be* process, the orchestration team should continually ask: "Is this the most efficient and effective process for accomplishing the process goals?" In the preceding example, we have eliminated duplicate effort, unnecessary steps, and disconnects by

- eliminating sales administration and direct sales order entry,
- allowing parallel order processing and credit checking,
- eliminating multiple order entry administration and order logging steps.

Step 3: Publish process and create the running prototype.

In this step, the team creates the running prototype in a testing environment. This running prototype focuses on the process flow, indicating the services that are necessary for the process goal to be accomplished (service that it orchestrates to be fulfilled).

This running prototype has little or no interaction with real services from systems, but it must show one or more of the suggested interactions with people with an attractive user interface to which the customer can relate. If the customer is reluctant to believe in the ability of BSO to interact with back-end systems, one or more interactions with must be added, but solely to help the customer understand how much easier it is to integrate with systems using the BSO approach, not to implement a real service orchestration.

4.4.3.2.2 Validate Running Prototype With Customer. Before getting into the analysis and documentation of the required services for the process, we must ensure that we have customer buy-in for the *should-be* process design. To get it, we present the customer with the running prototype of the *should-be* process that we created in the preceding step. The objective here is to make sure that we're going to incur in the effort of designing services for the *right process design*. This step also helps refine the services required for each activity. In general the participants will demand more services and options from the process. The team will take note of these services and options and see if they are actionable.

```
In the process shown in Figure 4.23, which replaces the
credit approval process in Figure 4.19, the users de-
tected that we were repeating the credit check that had
already been done by accepting the credit card of our
retail customers. This was solved with the transition
to end of the subprocess and the escalation to the su-
pervisor by the "escalate" activity.

In the process shown in Figure 4.24, which replaces
Figure 4.22, we fix the lack of notification activities
at the warehouse that are necessary before shipping.
```

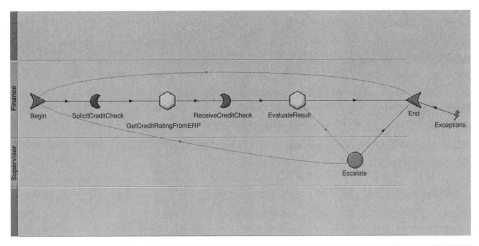

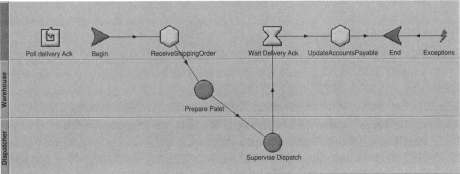

FIGURE 4.23–4.24. Validated Subprocesses.

4.4.3.2.3 Create list of Required Services. In this activity, the team creates a list of required services and their interactions with the orchestration as well as the documentation of the deliverables of each of the services in the list. The required services may be from people or from systems. This activity documents their use cases and deliverables.

To do this, we recommend the creation of a use-case scenario per task for every activity within the process. Use-case scenarios are a widely used technique to define the expected behavior of objects and people in a specific usage scenario. This technique was introduced by Ivar Jacobson in his first book on object engineering and has become an integral part of the unified object-oriented software engineering methodology. There are many tools that facilitate the graphical representation of use-case scenarios, the most widely used being Rational Rose.

We will not get into the detail of creating use-case scenarios, but, to help in their creation, we will give some guidelines for those who choose not to use a specific tool.

In BSO process models, activities represent a service that is rendered through the usage of existing services. If the activity is interactive, the service is delivered by one or more humans who complete a list of tasks. These tasks can be mandatory or optional, and repeatable or nonrepeatable. For each task, a use-case scenario can be created.

If the activity is automatic, the service is delivered without any human intervention, and typically consists of a single task. This task also requires the creation of a use-case scenario. In this case the process engine must be considered as an actor.

We also recommend the creation of use-case scenarios for all of the other activities in the process where, with the exception of a "grab"-type activity, in which a human participant takes control of the process instance regardless of its state in the process, the process engine must be considered as a participant.

The following sequence of seven steps is what we recommend for a successful description of the necessary services:

Step 1: Document the deliverables of each activity.

> In this step the team should create a deliverables description exactly like the deliverable description of any service for the specific activity. The customer for the service deliverable is the process.

Step 2: Determine the list of tasks and their classification for interactive activities.

> It may be evident from the deliverables that one or more of the interactive activities need to be created in discrete tasks or that discrete tasks are needed by the human participants as inputs to fulfill others. This leads to the need for analyzing the list of tasks necessary for an interactive activity to fulfill its deliverables.

Step 3: Determine the actors for each task.

> The actors in a use-case scenario are people or systems that participate in it, those who provide a service that contributes to the fulfillment of the task. Once we have the deliverables per activity, and the list of tasks that comprise it, we can determine the actors that are needed. The actors should be described in terms of their roles if we're expecting a service from a human and as the name of the system/module/submodule if we're expecting a service from a system.

Step 4: Create the services graph for the use case.

> For each task, describe the services that the actors perform to fulfill the task by drawing a line from the task to the actor and labeling the line with the service description.

Step 5: For each service description, identify the input and output objects that are needed.

For the first time in this chapter, we dive into data modeling. The first step is to identify the objects that need to be passed as parameters or received as parameters from every service. It's sufficient here just to identify them by name, without getting into the detail of their content.

Step 6: Create an object/service chart.

In this step we identify the objects that are going to be reused in more than one service in the current process.

Step 7: Create the use-case scenario description for each task.

In this step we describe the actors, the services, and the objects that intervene in the task. After that description, which includes the pertinent use-case graph and object/service charts, we describe how the orchestration engine will utilize the services to fulfill the deliverables for the task.

In most BSO design tools, this documentation is created by use of process design tools and is stored along with the *should-be* process design, making it easy to find and change as needed.

4.4.3.2.4 Estimate Orchestration Effort and Reassess ROI. In this activity, we take the list of actors (roles and systems) and the list of services that we need from them, and, applying standards, we reassess the orchestration effort by classifying the services as in Chapter 2, for example:

- discrete service from a supervisor through the work portal,
- discrete service from SAP through COM,
- discrete service from the Personnel schema in Oracle through SQL.

We put these services into a table, as in Figure 4.25, where, for each activity and each task within an activity, we assess the person-hours necessary to implement each one of the "necessary services," putting them in as many different columns as we have different specialist rates.

We add up the columns, and then proceed to estimate the effort of using the Component Integration Language (CIL) to orchestrate the services for each task, creating a table that has the task/effort in terms of person-hours. We multiply the different person-hours by their rates and add them up, and then we add up the resulting prices.

At this point we have an estimate of the cost of professional services needed for the effort.

After this, we calculate the cost of licenses and rollout implementation, as in Figure 4.26. In this figure, we have the following columns:

Order Fulfillment Cost Estimate

Activity	Hours Quality Assurance	Task	Hours Scripting and Testing	Required Services Complexity	Origin	Enabler	Domain Expert	Archi- tect	Coder	Tester
Submit Order	10.00	Enter Order	5.00	Discrete	ERP	Com	3.00	1.00	4.00	4.00
				Discrete	BSO	Work Portal	1.00	4.00	2.00	1.00
		Assess Historical Data	5.00	Discrete	BSO	Work Portal	3.00	4.00	5.00	2.00
				Discrete	AR	Com	5.00	2.00	1.00	4.00
Begin	2.00		1.00							
Order Fulfillment	1.00		1.00							
Approve Credit	2.00		1.00				21.00	28.00	35.00	14.00
Reserve Parts	2.00		1.00				35.00	14.00	14.00	28.00
Join	4.00		4.00							
Manufacture	2.00		1.00				40.00	21.00	14.00	35.00
QA	2.00	Approve Product	2.00	Discrete	QA System	Java	1.00	2.00	4.00	4.00
Ship Product	2.00		1.00				35.00	14.00	14.00	14.00
End	1.00		1.00							
Notify Exception	2.00		2.00	Discrete	Email	Java			1.00	1.00
Total of Hours	30.00		20.00				144.00	90.00	94.00	107.00
Cost/Hour	$130.00		$110.00				$1,200.00	$150.00	$110.00	$60.00
Column Cost	$3,900.00		$2,200.00				$172,800.00	$13,500.00	$10,340.00	-$6,420.00
Cost of Service										$209,160.00

FIGURE 4.25. Service Development Cost Chart.

- *Service*: This is the name of the process that implements the service.
- *Concurrent users*: This has two subcolumns – N^* (number of concurrent users expected in the process) and ERT (s) (expected response time in seconds)
- *Instances*: This also two subcolumns – N^*/s (expected maximum number of instances per second) and ESI (kb) (expected maximum size of an instance in kilobytes)
- *Engines*: This has three columns – F/Users (automatically calculates the number of engines or processors that would be necessary to support that number of concurrent users at the desired response time), F/Inst (automatically calculates the number of engines or processors that would be necessary for that number and size of instances) and For Tot (the number of engines that you estimate will be necessary, taking into account whether the users are the same for two processes [as in the example, you only need two processors for both processes], and whether the instance volume and size can be absorbed by those processes).
- *Integrity test*: This column attempts to calculate the effort in person-hours for each specialist who will be involved in doing the final testing before going

Service	Conc. Users		Instances		Engines			Integ.Test			
	N*	ERT (s)	N*/s	ESI (Kb)	F/Usrs	F/Inst	For Tot	User Hs	D.E. Hs	Arch Hs	Code Hs
Order Fulfillment Service	100	3	40	100	2.00	1	1	200	20	20	40
Approve Credit	1	3	40	100	0.02	1	1	200	20	10	20
Reserve Inventory	1	3	40	100	0.02	1	1	200	20	10	40
Manufacture	0	3	40	100	0.00	1	1	200	20	15	35
Shipping	100	3	40	100	2.00	1	1	200	20	5	35
Other	50	3	100	100	1.00	2.5	1	50	100	50	50
Totals							6	1050	200	110	220
Unit Cost							$128,000	$50	$120	$200	$100
Ccst per Col.							$768,000	$52,500	$24,000	$22,000	$22,000
Total Cost											$888,500

Table title: **Orchestrated Services Rollout Cost**

FIGURE 4.26. License and Rollout Implementation Cost of a Service.

into production. In the example, we have four subcolumns – User Hs (hours expected from the users of the process to do the testing, create test data sets, etc.), D. E. Hs (hours that domain experts dedicate to testing if the services invoked from applications are producing the right results), Arch Hs (hours expected from systems architects who test the infrastructure configuration), and Code Hs (estimated hours of corrections to the process model or code).

The final five subcolumns are multiplied by the cost of each unit and then consolidated into the total rollout cost.

We are also in a position to recalculate the monthly returns in a more accurate way than before, based on an assessment of the impact of the *should-be* process on the metrics gap analysis. We do this using the chart in Figure 4.27.

Some BSO suites provide simulation capabilities that allow you to run the *should-be* process based on the parameters set forth in Figure 4.26, such as number of concurrent users, instance size, and latency parameters for each user and system involved in the process. The process simulation and process metrics collection tools are very useful to assess a realistic return from the gap analysis.

As can be seen, the finer calculations of development, license, and Implementation costs have rendered a lower investment, and the finer calculation of the gap has rendered a higher return than in the BSOIA part of Phase 2.

This is the way it should be. Less experienced orchestrators will tend to be overly optimistic after discovering a lot of disconnects in the BSOIA phase. This enthusiasm is not good. It's important to set expectations low during BSOIA. It should be barely high enough to move forward into the prototype. After the prototype phase, expectations can be set a little higher (always sandbagged), as in the example.

> Now our monthly return is $283,376, almost $90,000 more
> than in our initial estimate, but we have more data
> and less risk of missing details in our estimate. Our
> costs have come down from $1.5 million to just over $1
> million, which is approximately another 50 percent re-
> duction. All of this renders a break-even in month 4, a
> twelve-month return of $2.35 million, and a return of
> $3.4 million each year thereafter.

Note: In this methodology, we don't show a complementary chart that can be added for long-life-cycle implementations. This chart is the recurring cost chart. It includes maintenance fees, support fees, reserve for system repairs, and other recurring costs that add to the TCO. It supposes that the current version of the process will survive beyond the twelve months already included in this calculation. The reason we don't include it is because we suppose that the application of this methodology and the facilities of advanced BSO suites (zero latency change) will encourage the user to revamp the processes at least once every twelve months. In this scenario, the TCO and ROI will be recalculated before any of the yearly recurring costs kick in.

4.4.3.2.5 *Make go/no-go decision.* At this point, a final go/no-go decision needs to be made on whether to implement the BSO or not. We create a document with the process design and all the charts of the previous steps as well as the process prototype and prepare a presentation and a proposal for the customer.

BSO Per Month Gap Analisys For: Order Fulfillment						
	As-Is		Should-Be			Gap
Metrics	Measure	Impact/u	Measure	Impact Description	Impact/u	Impact/M
		$1,500.00		Revenue	$1,500.00	$300,000.00
Cycle Time	15d	-$750.00	1d	Cost of direct material	-$750.00	-$150,000.00
		-$100.00		Cost of return processing	-$80.00	$320.00
Quality	90%	-$325.00	98%	Cost of throwaway	-$325.00	$24,700.00
Person/h/		-$20.00		Mean cost FTE/hour Associated costs	-$25.00	$18,900.00
Month	800	-$10.00	10	Cost/hour	-$12.00	$9,456.00
BSO Per Cycle Gap Analysis for subprocesses called by this process				Approve Credit		$20,000.00
				Reserve Parts		$10,000.00
				Manufacturing		$10,000.00
				Shipping		$40,000.00
TOTAL Gap Per Cycle						$283,376.00
Expected Increment in number of cycles per month	1000		1200			

FIGURE 4.27. Monthly Gap Analysis.

BSO ROI Calculation Sheet (after Prototype)

Interest Rate For Calculation:	10%		
Cost of Development	-$209,160		
Cost of Licenses and Rollout	-$888,500		
Total Cost	▸ -$1,097,660		
Monthly Gap (Recovery)	$283,376		
	Bal+Int	Amort	Balance
Month 1	-$1,106,807.17	$283,376	-$823,431.17
Month 2	-$830,293.09	$283,376	-$546,917.09
Month 3	-$551,474.74	$283,376	-$268,098.74
Month 4	-$270,332.89	$283,376	$13,043.11
Month 5	$13,151.80	$283,376	$296,527.80
Month 6	$298,998.87	$283,376	$582,374.87
Month 7	$587,227.99	$283,376	$870,603.99
Month 8	$877,859.02	$283,376	$1,161,235.02
Month 9	$1,170,911.98	$283,376	$1,454,287.98
Month 10	$1,466,407.05	$283,376	$1,749,783.05
Month 11	$1,764,364.57	$283,376	$2,047,740.57
Month 12	$2,064,805.08	$283,376	**$2,348,181.08**
		$3,400,512	

FIGURE **4.28. ROI Estimate.**

4.4.4 Outputs of Phase 2

Several major deliverables are produced as a result of the activities in this phase. These are as follows:

- **As-is process documentation**. This documentation includes a description of the scope of the process, a definition of the project deliverables with associated quantifiers, and a cross-role *as-is* process model showing
  - roles;
  - activities, including inputs, outputs, current metrics.

- *Success metrics*. The metrics defining the success of the project should be documented. Exact and agreed-upon measures for all quantifiers should be listed. Typical quantifiers include
  - cycle time,
  - volume,
  - cost,

- quantity,
- cost of lack of quality,
- activity response time.

- *Should-be* **process design**. This documentation should include a description of the scope of the process, a definition of the project deliverables with associated quantifiers, and a cross-role *should-be* process model showing
  - roles;
  - activities, including inputs, outputs, current metrics.

- **Use cases.** If appropriate, use cases should be delineated for the process.

- **Service interfaces.** A list of the appropriate service interfaces should be included as well.

- **ROI calculation forms.** The forms to reassess ROI and make the proposal to the customer should be included.

4.5 Phase 3: Implement

4.5.1 Introduction to Phase 3

In the Implement phase of the BSO methodology, we tackle the implementation of the business services that were specified in Phase 2, Analyze and Design. In this phase, we close the gap between the process design and the physical implementation. The key issue in this phase is translating the process design into reality. Just as when an architect finishes the design of a building and hands the blueprints over to the builders to transform his vision into a bricks-and-mortar building, so too does the implementation team receive the *should-be* process design and implementation plan from the project design team. The implementation team then sets to work developing, testing, configuring, and deploying the combination of hardware, software, and people to create the new BSO.

So far, the BSO methodology that we have presented has been independent of a particular BSO environment, although we have used our product for demonstration purposes. However, because this phase bridges the gap between design and implementation, this phase is more closely coupled to the BSO suite in use than any other phase. In Phases 0 thru 2, we have been able to get away with writing a methodology that is quite independent of any technology. In fact, all three phases can be executed practically without the use of any technology. In contrast, practically all of the implementation phase is done using the specific BSO suite at hand.

We continue to use our tool of choice, Fuego 4 from Fuego Inc, to discuss the implementation, but we focus on concepts and implementation tasks rather than the tool.

The implementation dependencies don't end here; we realize that many of the decisions around implementation tend to depend on the needs of the client and the particular situation. Because of this need to best fit a client's existing infrastructure, architecture, and environment, each implementation will necessarily vary a great deal from client to client. Accordingly, there is little use in trying to impose a strict set of rules or procedures for implementation. What follows are some guidelines and best practices on how to approach the implementation of a BSO design. These are the results of our experiences with a large variety of clients. We hope that you will take this information in the spirit intended and use it as you see fit while working to devise an implementation solution for your own project.

Following is the sequence of steps in our approach to implementation using Fuego 4 as an example. In the rest of this section, we examine each of these in greater detail in the order presented.

Development stage:
1. Refine services definitions until they are discreet and able to be implemented in the chosen environment.[1].
2. Implement interfaces – introspection (for services from existing systems), presentations (for services from people).
3. Package the services as IBOs.
4. Implement IBOs.

Testing stage:
5. Conduct unit testing of services.[2]
6. Conduct integration testing.[3]

Configuration stage:
7. Develop strategy for distributing process(es).[4]

Deployment stage:
8. Physically deploy.[5]

QA stage:
9. Conduct QA testing.[6]

Regarding the preceding sequence, please note the following:

1. Business services will be derived from the use cases received as inputs from the analysis and design phase.
2. Unit testing is done by the developer.
3. Integration testing occurs in a testing environment that has visibility to all systems from which services are used.

4. Configuration strategy depends on what has been specified in the analysis and design phase.
5. Deployment stage should implement what has been specified as the strategy for prioritizing the measurements defined in the previous stage.
6. QA work is done by the business analysts or, alternatively, some group other than developers. This is done in a controlled beta testing production environment and one process a time.

This can be done in Fuego 4 because processes are loosely coupled with one another to make it easy to snap them in and out.

4.5.2 Inputs to Phase 3

The inputs to Phase 3 are the "*should-be*" process design and an implementation plan. This information is typically contained in the following documentation:

- **As-is process documentation**. This documentation should include a description of the scope of the process, a definition of the project deliverables with associated quantifiers, and a cross-role *as-is* process model showing
  ○ roles;
  ○ activities including inputs, outputs, current metrics.

- *Success metrics*. The metrics defining the success of the project should be documented. Exact and agreed-upon measures for all quantifiers should be listed. Typical quantifiers include
  ○ cycle time,
  ○ volume,
  ○ cost,
  ○ quantity,
  ○ cost of lack of quality,
  ○ activity response time.

- *Should-be* **process design**. This documentation should include a description of the scope of the process, a definition of the project deliverables with associated quantifiers, and a cross-role *should-be* process model showing
  ○ roles;
  ○ activities including inputs, outputs, current metrics.

- **Use cases**. The use-case scenario documentation of Phase 2 should be included.

- **Service interfaces**. A list of the appropriate service interfaces with their input and output parameters should be included along with the object/service charts.

4.5.3 Activities for Phase 3

4.5.3.1 Development Stage
4.5.3.1.1 Refine services. The first step involves refining the services that are received from the process designers in the form of use cases and service interfaces until they are discreet and able to be implemented. emember that we are still in a discovery phase; we are not yet in an implementation phase.

The *deliverables* for this step are the set of refined, discreet services. These should be based on specified services, and should identify services discreet enough to be implemented. Identifying these is an iterative process that continues until all discreet services are discovered. The difference between processes and procedures is important. Procedures are a sequence of steps executed by the same role. Procedures should not be implemented as a sequence of activities, but rather as a unique activity with multiple tasks or one unique long task.

When we talk about a unique activity here, we mean that there is no context change within an activity. Basically, the process is interacting with a set of actors and does not change state until these interactions (tasks) are finished and the process successfully transitions to another activity. In other words, a unique activity is a procedure where a series of tasks are performed without changing the state of the process instance.

The following *guidelines* should be useful:

* Based refinements on one point in time.
* Represent discrete services as methods on an IBO. These IBOs need to be objects that are recognizable by a business person: order, invoice, shipping manifest, bill of materials, acceptance form, check, transfer notice, etc.
* Check whether needed services are already available as default methods of components in the BSO toolset.
* Look at refinement as a top-down strategy with a bottom-up attitude.
* While refining, keep in mind reusability and abstraction.

Note: Abstraction is a way to provide a user-friendly interface. It also encourages reusability. At the same time, however, we should not expose implementation details from the execution layer to the process layer that is invoking the services.

4.5.3.1.2 Implement interfaces. One of the main objectives of BSO is to automate processes by integrating business services. The required application programmer interfaces (APIs) of these business services to accomplish the task at hand are synthesized from the repositories of those business services creating a homogeneous component catalog. Most BSO tools provide rich synthesis capabilities for creating these interfaces. Fuego 4 provides a Component Manager that uses introspection to synthesize business services. The following discussion examines various approaches to interface creation.

Interface designs are the *deliverables* that follow services refinement. Some of the interfaces include

- HTML and JSP for presentation interfaces to human services;
- JAVA, CORBA, EJB, COM, XML, Web Services, and other forms of automation for system and data manipulation;
- SQL for data manipulation;
- Common objects for abstraction and reusability.

For *interfaces to human services*, Fuego 4 provides a rich set of input invocation capabilities natively from its CIL. These input capabilities generate an HTML form on the fly. The forms are not full featured and are not adequate for externally facing user interfaces, but they do the job for simple, internally facing ones. Note that CIL is specific to Fuego. Some other tools use other proprietary programming languages; for example, SeeBeyond uses MONK scripting language.

CIL is a very powerful language that borrows its syntax from Visual Basic and hence presents a pretty low learning curve. Fuego 4 also provides a composition facility to predesign presentations that are full featured, allowing the generation of background, fully featured widgets and the ability to perform validations using CIL. Where the native input statements fall short, these presentations may be the answer. Still, they may fall short of the requirement for the interface and the designer may opt for using JSP, ASP, or Flash to create these interfaces. If using Fuego 4, this approach should be the last resort because these interfaces will need to be maintained separately whereas the ones mentioned above are part of the BSO maintenance. Also, building these presentations in Fuego automatically makes them available to be sent by e-mail as executable forms that can work off-line. This greatly facilitates the interaction with customers, suppliers, and partners who don't have Web infrastructure.

Fuego accomplishes *automated services interface synthesis* through introspection. Interface introspection encompasses methods and attributes. For APIs that the BSO toolset can generate and automatically catalog from existing metadata, we use the BSO toolset's native synthesis capabilities (Java, EJB, SQL, CORBA, COM, XML, Web Services, etc.). The introspection approach used by Fuego greatly simplifies the process of generating interfaces. However, other BSO products have equivalent approaches, although they are more difficult and expensive to maintain. For example, SeeBeyond requires event-type definitions (ETD) to be designed first. ETDs represent the data that are exchanged with the business services. Actual interface is enabled by designing a collaboration that uses its proprietary Intelligent Queues (IQ), MONK code, adapters, and the ETDs to interface with the business services. Vitria adopts a similar approach, where the developers have to configure the relevant connectors with the transformation logic written in Java and a set of publish/subscribe channels. MQ Series uses a loosely coupled MQ workflow facility that has the ability to send or receive messages that are defined in the MQ messaging system. It layers NEON in the middle so that rules can be written to transform messages and manage data flow. All three are independent engines. The MQ stack is a premium example of loosely coupled engines that multiply the complexity of the problem.

Although none of the last three tools is the ideal for interface synthesis, there is no doubt that they can be used to implement the BSO approach.

The BSO synthesis toolset should also able to use already-developed Web applications using Web interception capabilities apart from components enabling connectivity with technologies such as JSP.

For APIs for which the toolset cannot perform introspection (i.e., C++, C, COBOL, or other languages that do not provide introspection capabilities), there needs to be a decision on the best way to interface with them: that is, by creating Java wrappers, by using proprietary third-party products that provide connectivity with the back-end application with which you want to interface (i.e., MQ Series, MSMQ, Mainframe Gateways, etc.), by interfacing directly with the database, and so on.

Be aware of the security managers within the BSO engines for Java components that run within them. For example, in Fuego 4, Security Manager exists to prevent undesired behavior of components from producing side effects on the engine execution.

An introspection-based approach is preferable to creating prepackaged application-specific adapters, or creating wrappers to native interfaces in an application server, because it avoids all the complexities of managing and synchronizing different versions of connectors or adapters for versions of business services. Introspection is fast and creates discrete entities to deal with back-end applications or systems. Figure 4.29 shows Fuego's Component Manager, which can perform introspection of business services and generate interfaces for them.

The creation of interfaces by introspection in Fuego 4 is fast and practically failsafe. The interfaces created in the component catalog by this method hide the complexity of the implementation of connectivity and the protocols, allowing implementers to be able to concentrate on the business logic rather than the plumbing.

Fuego 4's introspection capability automatically creates adapters that expose the selected methods (with input and output arguments and their types or classes) and attributes from the selected components of any exposed object repository such as COM, CORBA, JAVA, EJB, or WSDL. In the case of data-oriented introspection such as XML and SQL, Fuego 4 automatically creates adapters that expose the

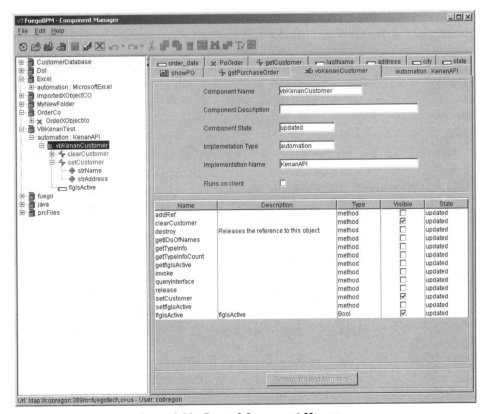

FIGURE 4.29. Fuego 4 Component Manager.

selected stored procedures (if pertinent) and attributes, as well as some standard methods such as insert, delete, update, store, and select (also where pertinent).

So, in Fuego 4, you create a catalog that contains components that may have native methods, inherited methods, attributes, enumerations, transformations, and presentations, and in the case of SQL, stored procedures, views, and tables.

Mapping tools provided by a BSO vendor are used to configure transformations. Fuego 4 provides advanced transformation capabilities that are triggered recursively as needed by the resolution facility, depending on the patent-pending business data types or classes that are being assigned. So, any object knows through its transformations what it can be converted into and what it can be created from; if those transformations assign other objects of certain business classes or business types, the pertinent transformations are invoked. In Fuego 4, transformations and data conversions or translations are one and the same thing. For example, we have a simple business-level Order Object of business class myOrder that contains the following data:

- Customer Number (an integer of business type myCustomerNumber)
- Date (a string of business type myDate)
- Order Number (an integer of type myOrderNumber)
- Items[] (an array of objects of the business class myOrderItems)
- Price (an integer of business-type dollars)
- Tax (an integer of business-type dollars)
- Total (an integer of business-type dollars)

And we have, for instance, an SAP Order on which we perform introspection and catalogue as a business class SAPOrder that has the following fields:

- CustNo (an integer of business type SAPOrderCustomerNumber)
- (a date of business type julianDate)
- OrderNo (an integer of type SAPOrderNumber)
- OrderItems[] (an array of objects of business class SAPOrderItem)
- Subtotal (an integer of business type germanMarks)
- VAT (an integer of business type germanMarks)
- TransTax (an Integer of business type germanMarks)

We catalog the following transformation: MyOrder <- SAPOrder is:

- Customer Number <- SAP.CustNo
- Date <- SAP.Date
- Order Number <- SAP.OrderNo
- Items []<- SAP.OrderItems
- Price <- SAP.Subtotal
- Tax <- SAP.VAT + SAP.TransTax
- Total <- SAP.VAT + SAP.TransTax + Subtotal

When the transformation is invoked, what happens under the covers is this:

- **Customer Number**. Fuego 4 resolves the conversion between an integer of type SAPOrderCustomerNumber and myCustomerNumber. Typically, this will be implemented as a procedure that looks up myCustomerNumber corresponding to the SAPOrderCustomerNumber in a cross-reference table. If the SAP number is not found, the system throws an exception and allow the user to find or create the equivalent "myCustomer" and add the appropriate entry in the cross-reference table.

- **Date**. Fuego 4 will resolve the conversion between the string, myDate, and the date, julianDate, by invoking a conversion procedure.

- **Order Number**. Fuego 4 will resolve this in pretty much the same way as it resolved customer number.

- **Items[]**.Fuego 4 will resolve this by iterating through SAP.OrderItems and invoking the myItems <- SAP.OrderItems transformation, which may in turn need other recursive transformations or conversions for the data elements, as seen in the above data elements. In any case, if any conversion or transformation should fail, the system throws an exception, allowing the user to complete dictionaries and even create procedures by exception!

- **Price**. Fuego 4 resolves this conversion by, for example, invoking a procedure that uses a currency exchange Web Service to convert from Marks to dollars.

- **Tax and Total**. Fuego 4 resolves the expressions to a compatible type (Marks) and then converts to dollars.

Fuego 4 also has the ability to use third-party graphical mapping and transformation tools that create Java classes as a way to implement these transformations.

Other BSO tools offer different ways of performing transformations. Vitria, for example, provides a host of prewritten Java transformers that can be selected to perform the transformation. Alternatively, the programmer can write his/her own Java transformation code and plug it into the connector. In either case, the transformation is performed inside the connector by the connector container, and all the functionality is hard-linked at design time.

In Fuego 4, when cataloguing a component, you can create a usage template for each method that will expand into the calling syntax of the CIL when you double click on the method. What Fuego 4 does not have, and is absolutely necessary for large projects, is a search engine that allows the developer to find adequate services by typing keywords into a search engine.

Synthesis capabilities offered by some tools may be a lot more powerful than the ones offered by others. Hence the selection of a BSO tool will greatly influence the implementation strategy and, in turn, the total cost of a solution.

IThe following are tips for performing introspection with Fuego:

- Use only the part of the API that you need. When Fuego or others don't provide the knowledge-base capability, use a domain expert!
- Click only on components prespecified by the business analyst and interpreted by the domain expert.
- Do not select unnecessary methods. Select only those prescribed by the domain expert.

The next step requires transforming the abstract business services into what we call business-level services by defining IBOs that package the business services and pertinent data. IBOs were introduced in Chapter 3 as intelligent proxies to the business services. In Fuego, IBOs are defined using CIL to code their methods, and a WYSIWYG form designer to create associated presentations. IBOs' methods, attributes, and transformation and presentation properties are created so that a higher abstraction layer can be used to isolate the implementation specifics of any discrete service, and to provide objects that are familiar to business people. IBO technology enables data (object structure), methods (object behavior), transformation (object creation and state modification), and presentation (externalization of object state through graphical interfaces) in one single solution. Furthermore, in Fuego 4, IBOs can be sent to customers, suppliers, or partners as IXOs (interpretable XML objects) that can execute presentations or transformations remotely and off-line on third-party systems and know how to return to the process that sent them or wherever it indicates without the need for a footprint of Fuego 4 on the receiving computer. Your business associates – be they people or companies – can download a plug-in from your Web site that is used by the e-mail front-end of choice of your associates to present them with the work they need to do. We talk more about IXOs later in the book, but what's important for this implementation discussion is that they allow remote off-line execution of user interfaces (forms) or system interfaces (transforms) associated with any IBO in a secure way that contemplates signature, encryption, and non-repudiation. This is very useful for companies that deal with small companies that do not have an Internet Infrastructure other than a PC and a dial-up connection. Furthermore, these IXOs are also capable of performing some client-related tasks, such as data validation, strictly on the receiving computer or computers.

4.5.3.1.3 Implement services. *Deliverables* associated with the implementation of services include:

- providing implementation for services using introspected interfaces;
- encapsulation of the behavior of systems to be connected, which is related to abstraction or information hiding and has a significant benefit at maintenance phases;
- ensuring that the business service layers have an object-oriented approach to using IBOs;
- coding of reusable business rules.

Fuego's implementation for IBOs is provided through the BSO toolset's Component Manager, which allows the developer to create them in the component catalog. In Fuego, IBO methods are implemented with CIL. This enables the usage of other catalogued components that are able to create an abstraction layer using components that may be implemented in different technologies. Use-case rules are implemented within the BSO toolset designer, invoking discrete interfaces or components previously catalogued.

IBOs allow for ease of language for method implementation. They also provide flexibility at time of change by creating a middle object-oriented business service layer. Coded methods are easier to change. They provide the ability to wrap components that have been implemented in different technologies. An IBO may be associated with multiple presentations for one data model. An IBO that has been enhanced with visual presentation knowledge is known as a visual business object (VBO). IBOs/VBOs allow for fast object definition cloning. Finally, they are stored in an XML format that allows easy interchange among developers. These serialized forms of IBO/VBO are called interpretable XML objects (IXOs). IBOs/VBOs in Fuego can be serialized automatically into Fuego's implementation of IXOs called UXO's (unidentified XML objects), which can be shipped encrypted and signed to any registered partner ,and in serialized format to any unregistered partner.

The following *guidelines* should be useful:

*   To enforce reusability, use an object-oriented approach toward implementation with IBOs.
*   Think always in an abstract way so that you do not expose the internal implementation details of services. Encapsulate object state within the implementation of the service.
*   Based on use cases, code the specified business rules using defensive programming.
*   If APIs are nonblocking or synchronous, use process capabilities to make a nonsynchronous component call into something that is synchronized. Another possibility is to wrap this asynchronous component call into something that is synchronous, for example, an IBO method.

Defensive programming means that when a component is called, the returned value is checked. If an error code is returned, the error should be handled in the best way possible. An "on" statement in CIL manages exceptions – a small bit of code for "on" or "if," as appropriate, can be added. Given the integration nature of the BSO toolset, there is an extreme need for "defensive programming." As such, exceptions and errors should be managed comprehensively. Component exceptions and process exceptions should be appropriately trapped and all component return results should be checked for error codes.

4.5.3.2 *Testing Stage*
Unit testing should be the developer's and, when pertinent, the domain expert's responsibility. The developer should do integration testing, but the business analysts

should perform a thorough quality assurance test of the work at this time as well. System testing should be done by the business analysts and then (after they receive training on how to use the new system) by a representative sample of end users. Use the following guidelines when conducting testing.

4.5.3.2.1 Conduct unit testing of services. The primary *deliverable* associated with the unit testing of services is the verification that services meet the desired behavior set forth in the use cases. Use cases should have a testing section to complete the unit testing. This is achievable by using the CIL debugger within the BSO toolset environment, and through direct component testing outside of the toolset environment. A secondary deliverable, but one that is also important is a thorough inspection of the implementation. Conducting a code walk-through should accomplish this.

Most BSO products provide powerful debugging facilities. Fuego 4 provides debugging capabilities in its CIL editor. The CIL editor can validate syntax of each business rule and provides an interactive debugger that allows conditional and unconditional breakpoints, real-time syntax checker, variable inspection feature, and step-by-step debugger.

Vitria provides a powerful debugger that allows a process model to be debugged during development, allowing breakpoints to be specified. It also provides a process animator that can change the color of various activities in its console, as those activities are executed.

Here is the recommended sequence of steps for conducting unit testing of services:

1. Validate syntax for each CIL module by executing Check CIL in the CIL Editor. This ensures that the code actually matches the systems being integrated with the interfaces under introspection and exposed by the BSO toolset's Component Manager.
2. Unit test each CIL module using the CIL debugger. This validates that the components being invoked from a CIL actually work as expected and also that the use case being implemented delivers what was specified for it.
3. Validate the business logic in each CIL module by "code inspection" or "code walkthrough." Whenever possible, this should be done by a developer other than the person who wrote the original code.

Note: At this phase of unit testing, we assume that the catalogued components being used to build business rules for the desired processes have been tested and are working correctly. If this is not the case, component testing in a more isolated environment is needed.

During unit testing of the services, testers must verify that the syntax validation matches the defined interfaces. During debugging, they must check:

- that components are answering as expected,
- response times,
- returned values,
- that tests follow the test scenarios set forth in the use cases.

4.5.3.2.2 Conduct integration/systems testing. The primary *deliverable* associated with the integration testing is that the end-to-end desired behavior is delivered. The results of this integration testing for each redesigned process should be documented and should be validated with the end users. All testing should use performance metrics (as defined in Phase 2 of the BSO methodology) to measure the effectiveness of the integration.

All integration and systems testing should be done in the testing environment. As the integration/systems testing allows end users their first contact with the system, the team needs to ensure that when it responds to end-user feedback, it remains aligned with the business objectives. Although end-user objectives should be noted and documented, you should remember that the main goal of the process redesign is to support the enterprise's business objectives.

By using the Audit Trail functionality of the BSO toolset work portal during integration/systems testing, we can ensure that service-level agreements (SLAs) are achieved. At the same time, we can use this to check how underlying systems are responding to the demands of the instances flowing through the processes. Information that can be derived by using Audit Trail during integration testing includes:

- number of persons involved in the completion of a process instance,
- response time of each of the participating users,
- time it takes to execute automated and nonautomated activities,
- number of participants obtaining a lock to execute an activity and thereby preventing other participants from executing it,
- time required for the execution of each one of the tasks (if multiple) within a process activity,
- state of instance within a process,
- status of instance within nested levels of processes.

The work portal is used to present tasks to persons involved in a process. The ability to test human interaction with processes is achievable by using the BSO toolset's work portal. End users can interface with the activities presented to them. Activities for the end user to execute are presented on the basis of role assignment to enforce security and task visibility. The integration/systems tester can use the work portal to verify if all the needed information is routed correctly to all the steps or activities of the process.

Process performance problems, such as bottlenecks, can be detected during systems/integration testing by using the on-line analytic processing (OLAP) tool. The tool can be used to assess the "hit" ratio (e.g., number hired vs. number interviewed). Any metrics not met may indicate a problem earlier in the process. The OLAP tool can be used to check that the process is performing as expected. and to make sure that an instance rejoins after bifurcations or conditional splits. The OLAP tool is also useful for flagging results that were not planned or expected based on analysis metrics or graphics. Metrics obtainable with the OLAP tool include:

- degree of productivity of users within a same role, for example, how many requests each user is answering;
- number of approved and rejected orders after a specific action within a process;
- average time to answer a request;
- average time to complete a client request;
- wait time , that is, how long a particular step within a process is waiting to be completed before moving to the second step within a process.

Given the metrics (similar to the ones explained above), we can check in advance whether we are achieving basic expectations and detect problems before moving to the next step (deployment of processes). These tools allow detection of process performance bottlenecks and provide the data required to meet SLAs. Fuego and Vitria, for example, both provide a process analyzer. However, to actually use it, the developers have to do a significant amount of programming.

Without any doubt, process simulation can help solidify the solution by greatly simplifying the testing procedures and ing BSO solutions much more dependable. An optimal configuration of the orchestrated services is desired to achieve the expected performance results. A simulation capability allows the network architects to simulate the loads on the system for stress testing and gather data that allow the architects to develop a process distribution strategy for the deployed environment.

4.5.3.3 Configuration Stage

The main focus of this activity is to develop a practical strategy for distributing processes over the available network resources. The primary intent of the configuration activity is to develop identify a network topology and resource locality. High-availability requirements for the whole architecture are identified.

Finally, the deployment environment is configured on the basis of specified parameters.

4.5.3.3.1 Analyze Results of Integration Testing. The most valuable input for developing an effective process distribution strategy is provided from the integration/system testing activities. Simulation tests result in a lot of valuable data for system performance and are critical in identifying potential bottlenecks. Performance metrics reported by OLAP are checked against the ones proposed and defined in Phase 2. This information is used to:

- establish a strategy based on performance metrics;
- determine whether transactions are performing as expected, e.g., determine whether transactions are being executed with acceptable response times;
- identify possible bottlenecks and determine if load balancing is needed If bottlenecks occur when subprocesses are invoked, then load balancing is probably necessary.

4.5.3.3.2 Identify Network Topology, Resource Locality, and Availability. In this step, the team develops a network topology that fully includes failover plans and system redundancy for load balancing and fault tolerance.

There are many issues the team needs to consider while developing this topology. These include the following:

- **Distribution of integrated systems and users.** This is important to provide the users optimal performance. If a user in Europe has to access servers in the United States to do some work, that naturally would degrade the performance for that user.
- **Network bandwidth** (network capacity). This is important because those tasks that require a large amount of data to be exchanged in order to complete a task or activity would naturally impose a larger burden on the network, reducing its overall performance.
- **Reliability of resources** (high availability of used resources to support 24 × 7 operation). If certain resources need to have high availability, then the architects have to develop a system of redundant and replicated services so that, in case of failure, the business continuity is maintained.
- **User and system concurrency** (support for volume of transactions at the same time). If there is a large number of concurrent users, than scalability of the system becomes important. Since each user consumes a certain amount of resources, the network architecture has to support the creation of multiple instances of engines to support load balancing among them to support the high number of concurrent users.

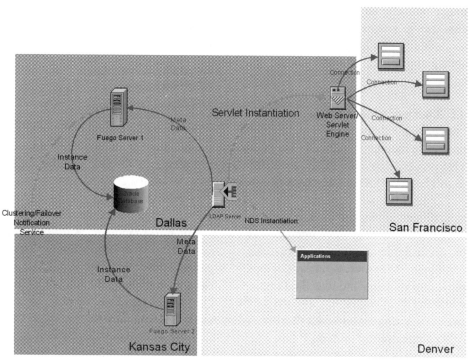

FIGURE **4.30. Network Topology, Resource Locality, and Availability.**

- Configuration of deployment based on performance metrics.
- Implementation process distribution using BSO toolset programmatic load balancing capabilities (if needed).
- Language and preferences in each locality or per user in each locality.

At this point it's important to have test cases for the different localizations. Although Fuego 4 allows very simple localization through Unicode and dictionaries for everything including process design and documentation, the completeness of those dictionaries is an implementation issue.

Figure 4.30 shows a typical network topology with Fuego 4. The topology really cannot be generalized and will vary drastically from BSO platform to BSO platform.

4.5.3.3.3 Resolve Execution Engine Considerations. By using the BSO toolset's process programmatic load-balancing functionality, you can distribute processes among different BSO toolset execution engines and thus provide greater reliability and better response time. Before you do this, you should study process usage carefully so that you can distribute the workload evenly among different engines. To ensure higher availability, you can plan to implement Failover BSO toolset's engines. For this to happen, you need to ensure that there is a high availability of resources in order for the BSO toolset's engines to run. There can be "n" failover engines.

4.5.3.4 Deployment Stage

The primary *deliverable* associated with the deployment stage is to make the project's process(es) available for production following the deployment strategy. This process deployment should be reliable and secure. It should have the ability to roll back performed deployment operations if necessary.

The BSO environment should provide tools to publish the orchestrated services in difference environments, such as testing, QA, and production. The process distribution strategy developed earlier is now put into practice by using the appropriate deployment tools. Figure 4.31 shows such a distribution strategy, which configures three orchestration engines. As a general rule, processes should be deployed in multiple engines. In Figure 4.31, two engines share the same database while the third engine has its own database. This strategy makes the trade-offs between performance and data sharing. A database is often the slowest moving device in an orchestration system. If two engines share the same database, there may be better load balancing across those two because the state of the business process is shared in between the two through the shared database and hence any incoming request for the same process instance can be processed by either one of them. However, this has the adverse affect of the database becoming the performance bottleneck as well as the point of failure. By assigning each process engine its own database, it is made independent of the others and can scale better. However, load balancing becomes more complicated and constrained.

4.5.3.4.1 Deployment Sequence in Different Environments. In general, the first environment that has to be deployed is the development environment. This is generally the most unstable environment because the programmers may be performing nightly builds and the code may be changing very rapidly and may be full of bugs. Once the orchestrated services have been developed, the testing environment is configured. QA environment is configured next and production environment last.

4.5.3.4.2 Deployment Sequence for Processes and Resources. Each developer will be testing the process that he or she has been assigned on his or her desktop or environment. Once developer testing is complete, you can move to an integrated testing environment. After development has been approved in the testing environment, you provide the new inserted modifi-

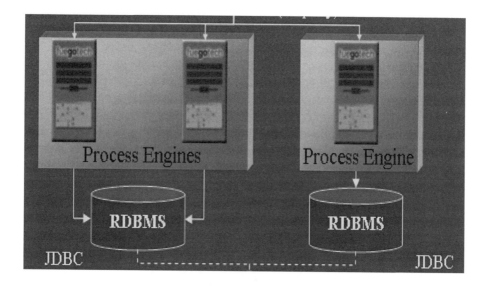

- Configuring deployment based on performance metrics
- Enabling deployment with High Availability

FIGURE **4.31. Process Distribution Strategy.**

cation to the QA group. The QA group then approves/disapproves production deployment.

4.5.3.5 Quality Assurance Stage

4.5.3.5.1 Conduct QA Testing. The primary *deliverable* associated with the QA stage is to debug the process in production in a small, controlled environment as much as possible before rolling it out to User Approval and Testing (UAT) environments.

The following *guidelines* should be useful:

- Although this is done in a production environment, conduct the QA testing in a small locale with as many localization issues and bottlenecks as possible.
- Regard this as a beta test of an application system.

4.5.3.6 Outputs of Phase 3

The major *deliverable* of BSO methodology Phase 3 is the production process or processes. Each interim deliverable leading up to the final deliverable needs to be produced, completed, and approved before work can commence on the next stage's deliverables. Here is a list of the interim deliverables for Phase 3:

Development Stage

- document with refined discrete services
- document of the component catalog

Testing Stage

- unit testing approval document
- integration/systems testing approval document

Configuration Stage

- document with the strategy for distribution of processes

Later Stages

- QA log of bugs and corrections, QA sign-off for massive deployment

4.6 PHASE 4: MANAGE CHANGE

4.6.1 Introduction to Phase 4

Phase 4 of the BSO methodology, is the post-implementation phase. It is the responsibility of the people who run the business. This is the phase where, once the process is implemented, you practice continuous improvement. You respond to feedback and requests for changes to the process from customers, end users, database administrators, and others. This feedback could range from requests for minor changes or improvements to processes to requests for the creation of an entirely new process or set of processes.

All of these requests will come from either of two directions. Some could come directly from the steering team, if it determines that a change can be made without having to go through the Phases 0 through 2 once again.

Requests for changes could also come to Phase 4 from the implementation team working on a process in Phase 3 of the methodology. These requests for changes or modifications could come as a result of an inability to implement some aspect in the process design. If the requested change is deemed just a matter of refining the design, then it would be sent back to Phase 2 for further design work. If the design issues associated with the change affect other processes and are deemed to have implications beyond a simple redesign, they could be sent back to Phase 1 for consideration as a new project.

Feedback on physical deployment is also received in Phase 4. Any additional training and documentation are developed in Phase 4 as well.

This phase allows for continuous improvement. Moreover, it is at this point in the methodology that ownership of a process is truly transferred from the project team to the process owner. He or she is responsible at this point for monitoring the change and ensuring continuous improvement. At the same time, however, a real advantage to this phase in the methodology is that it provides a clearinghouse for changes because not all changes will be accepted for implementation. Flexibility is built into the model to allow the process owner to discern whether the change is substantial enough that it must be sent to the steering team for consideration as a new project, or whether it can be returned to the implementation team or the process design team for further modification.

4.6.2 Inputs to Phase 4

The inputs to Phase 4 are the processes put into production. Associated with this process (or processes) are the current success metrics and gap analysis. The change management team will use these metrics as a baseline with which to monitor the process. Additional inputs will be requests for process changes coming from either the implementation team or the steering team.

4.6.3 Activities for Phase 4

The following is a summary of the activities that constitute Phase 4:

- **Check feedback from process owners.**

- **Manage organization as integrated system of processes.** At some point, all of the individual process management efforts have to be integrated with each other and with the goals at the organization level.

- **Manage individual processes for optimal performance.** Each process must be individually managed by its process owner according to a process improvement plan with set strategy/goals, work plans, and budgets, and with all necessary resources in place.

- **Clarify process owner and process management team roles.** The process owner is someone with clout in the organization who is responsible for looking at, and then taking action to improve, the performance on an entire cross-functional process. The process management team meets regularly to identify and then implement process improvements.

- **Plan, support, and manage performance.** Managers use their relationship and process models as tools for planning and implementing change to improve performance.

- **Ensure that measurement systems are in place.** Measurement system must be process based. Managers must routinely ask about the effectiveness and efficiency of processes to which their departments contribute.

- **Practice continuous improvement.** Individual core processes are continually analyzed and improved.

4.6.4 Outputs of Phase 4

The following are *deliverables* for Phase 4:

- documented feedback from process owners,
- description of changes in business requirements or strategy,
- documented feedback from administrative infrastructure on physical deployment;
- knowledge transfer from implementation team to end users and to new IT specialists through training and documentation, and
- a change requirement document that includes one or all of the above.

As can be seen in the process model in Figure 4.30, this output will go either back to implementation or back to analysis and design or directly to plan priorities where it may be reprioritized or sent to end users waiting for a new strategy definition.

Although the output goes either to Implementation or to Design, we consider the process to be in a continuous improvement phase. If it gets reprioritized, there may be a discontinuity, but, in any case, we still consider it to be in the continuous improvement phase. Now, if the steering team wants to require a new strategy and budget, there may be some serious discontinuity in the process improvement.

4.7 SUMMARY

Reasons for change should ALWAYS have their risk analysis. Some of these reasons may include:

- business change defined by the enterprise;
- need to upgrade underlying back-end applications;
- need to change underlying back-end applications;
- need to change BSO toolset version;
- need to install patches for underlying applications or BSO toolset;

- need to improve cycle time, quality, and/or cost.of a service;
- need to improve usability or response time.

In any case, true BSO suites should make these changes seem like a walk in the park. If your BSO suite fails to do so, it's probably an old version and you may want to investigate changing it for something more modern.

CHAPTER 5

Basic Applications and Data Services

5.1 INTRODUCTION

Applications in our context are defined as software that is developed by programmers to solve specific business problems. These applications generally implement business logic which is either not available in off-the-shelf applications, or some special constraints such as performance or security, which are otherwise not met by the COTS applications have to be considered.

Figure 3.1 describes the reference model for BSO. Our discussion in this chapter relates to developing software that resides in the Business Services tier and the tiers above it. Most orchestration products provide an orchestration engine, a sort of maestro, which reads the BSO definition and then manages the flow of activities. In some implementations, the orchestration engine as well as business logic code may execute inside a container environment. We discuss application and data services in this chapter as seen not only by the application containers but also by the orchestration container and the orchestration engine.

Products in this functional category, discussed in Section 5.2, relate to the *Web application servers* layer of the reference architecture presented in Chapter 3, Figure 3.1. Programming languages discussed in Section 5.3 are important for all layers of the reference architecture. Technologies discussed in Section 5.4 are again important for all layers in the reference architecture but relate more to the *packaging protocols* layer of the stack.

5.2 APPLICATION DEVELOPMENT PLATFORMS

An application development platform is a comprehensive set of services to develop, host, and manage applications. Any distributed application should be built using a robust application platform. In most application development efforts, more than 50 percent of the time and money is spent solving generic infrastructure-related issues such as managing transactions or managing persistence. An application development platform provides a set of application-infrastructure-related services, thus leaving the applications that are built on top of the platform to focus on business functionality.

In this chapter, we discuss the three front-runner modern application development platforms for distributed systems. These are namely Object Management Group's Common Object Request Broker Architecture (CORBA), JavaSoft's J2EE, and Microsoft's .NET environment. All three platforms offer capabilities fairly close to each other, but with various degrees of complexity and ease of use. Before we discuss the capabilities of these three environments, let us first review the important capabilities that are desirable in an application development platform.

5.2.1 Capabilities of Application Development Platforms

5.2.1.1 Robustness and Scalability
Any development platform acquires robustness and scalability over time. Although all architectures try to learn from other efforts and try to design for robustness and scalability, the true feedback is obtained only after field deployment of the systems.

Scalability of an application depends on two factors. First, an environment can provide scalability with features such as clustering, load balancing, and queued components. These features should be transparent to the applications while the application benefits from them just by virtue of using the platform. The second aspect of scalability deals with the application design itself. Distributed applications have application components distributed in a managed environment. Since these components interact with each other in an interprocess/intermachine environment, the application architecture should try to reduce the coupling and conversational communication between them. Scalable applications are generally composed of discrete components that provide large-grained, stateless services to each other, as opposed to fine-grained, statefull shared objects.

Features related to high availability include advanced redundancy capabilities. Redundancy allows multiple instances of a component to be instantiated so that, if one fails for some reason, control can immediately be shifted over to the other ones. This kind of fault tolerance is generally a critical requirement of mission critical systems that need to provide 24×7 services.

The ability to have planned downtime is another important aspect of robustness. All systems need maintenance. Most of the time the downtime is to upgrade the software release, but it could also be due to regular hardware-related maintenance or important patches to software for functional or technical reasons. In any case, planned downtime allows a replacement instance of the application to be created temporarily and the traffic to be diverted to it in an orderly manner. This is different from fault tolerance. In a failure situation, unfinished transactions will always be aborted. In a planned shutdown, unfinished transactions will be allowed to finish while new transactions are diverted toward the temporary instance.

The ability of the applications to be managed either through tools provided by the platform itself or through common system management software is also very important. A managed application should be able to log its critical events, raise critical events, and be restarted in case of failures. Advanced applications should support configuration and performance management through such management tools.

5.2.1.2 Metadata Management
Metadata management is an important service needed by large and complex capabilities. Metadata in general is discussed in Chapter 7. In a service-oriented architecture, the most important metadata are those that describe the service contracts and any other information needed to enable communication between two peers. Some examples of this kind of metadata are interface descriptions, Web service descriptions, BSO definitions, and trading-partner agreements.

An application development platform should allow capture of the important metadata and allow queries to be issued to retrieve metadata at design time and runtime.

5.2.1.3 Database Connectivity
There are hardly any large and complex systems that do not use a database. Whether the database is used by the application to store its data or by the platform to store its transient data, it is used extensively.

Over the past couple of decades, relational databases have matured a lot. Databases such as Oracle, DB2, and SQL Server are very scalable and robust. They can generally handle a very large number of users, can optimize queries fairly well, and can be mirrored and replicated.

A database, however, is a scarce and expensive resource and its use must be optimized. Often, the same instance of a database may have to be shared among multiple applications. This represents an interesting evolution of business systems, with present-day business applications sharing a database rather than owning it. This requires the use of sophisticated techniques for database connection pooling and concurrency management.

An application development platform should allow the state of application objects to be stored in the persistent storage, which is most likely to be a database but could also be other things such as memory mapped files, either of which should be transparent or quite easy to use. In particular, it should assume the responsibilities for database connection pooling and transaction coordination.

5.2.1.4 Distributed Transaction

Transaction coordination and resource management are critical capabilities of development platforms. Transactions are defined in many ways. For example, transactions are often used to mean business-level units of work. There are also database-level transactions that ensure database-level consistency. The meaning that we use describes *distributed* transactions that support two-phase commit between all participants. These transactions have the ACID properties:

- **Atomicity**. A transaction provides an *atomic* unit of work. When several activities are done as one logical unit of work, either they are all successfully completed or none of them are performed.

- **Consistency**. A completed transaction should never leave the databases or applications that participated in a transaction with any inconsistencies.

- **Isolation**. When a transaction is being executed, its final outcome is not known until all phases of the transaction coordination are concluded. Any data modifications made during this time are not available together until the transaction either commits or rolls back. It is as if the transaction was performed in complete isolation from the rest of the world.

- **Durability**. This means that the effects of the transaction are lasting and cannot be lost. It implies that the effects are made permanent by committing the changes to stable storage before the transaction finishes.

Transactions allow many disparate data sources to participate in a coordinated manner to accomplish a logical unit of work. From that point of view, the transactional capabilities can be split into two distinct parts: (1) transaction coordination and (2) resource management.

XA defined by X/Open defines the two-phase commit protocol that defines how multiple data sources and object systems participate in distributed transactions. We will not go into the details of this protocol here. However, it is worth mentioning that this protocol consists of two phases (as the name implies). The first phase is that of preparation, in which all the involved resources vote whether the transaction should be allowed to proceed or not. If any resource votes not to proceed, the transaction is stopped there. Once all the resources vote to finish the transaction, the next phase begins. In this phase, all the resources are asked to commit their work. As you can imagine, there is a role for a coordinator. This coordinator drives the two-phase commit process. Various objects, representing applications and data sources, are registered with this coordinator. It supports the operations to begin, commit, or rollback the transactions.

The second aspect of the transactions is resource management. Most of the time, the resources represent data sources such as databases. These non-object-based transactional systems provided resource managers that can be registered with the transaction coordinator and can in turn manage their native resources.

Transaction coordination is extremely important for BSO. For example, an activity in the BSO may require three different systems to be updated with certain information. This may be one unit of work, which needs to be completed as a unit. If a failure occurs while in the middle of these updates, the work already completed may have to be rolled back. A transaction coordinator will be able to drive this process and allow the application to either roll back the whole transaction or complete it in its entirety. However, a development platform cannot always manage these transactions, and the applications may have devised various ways to remedy the situation. As long as all resources involved in the transaction support a two-phase transaction process or, at most, one of the resources supports a single-phase transaction, a transaction coordinator can manage failure. However, if more than one of the applications involved in the transaction do not support the two-phase commit protocol, which is usually the case in real life, then a transaction coordinator does not help much. In that case the business applications themselves have to employ a technique, called *compensating transactions*, to compensate for the rogue applications. In compensating transactions, when a failure occurs, the driving business application usually invokes a method on the applications, which have already finished, negating the effect of the earlier work.

5.2.1.5 Messaging

Most enterprise systems require a variety of communication patterns. The communication patterns can be largely categorized as request/response and messaging. Either pattern can be synchronous or asynchronous. Messaging is the decoupled form of communication, where both entities are termed as clients. In that sense, messaging is truly peer-to-peer as opposed to request/response, which is more client/server-like. Furthermore, although a communication style can be either synchronous or asynchronous, messaging is mostly done in an asynchronous manner and request/response is mostly used in a synchronous manner.

Asynchronous messaging is extremely important for business services orchestration (BSO). Most processes being managed by orchestration engines are long-running processes that may in some cases take days to complete. For example, an order fulfillment process may take several days to finish. During this time, various systems may interact with each other. The orchestration engine may send the order to the material resource planning (MRP) system to start manufacturing. In response, the MRP system may execute some of its local processes and may come back in several days with the notification of the completion. The engine process cannot be expected to block for so many days. Messaging is perfectly suited for situations in which work has to be performed and notifications have to be sent later when the work is done.

5.2.1.6 Security

Security is, undoubtedly, the most important requirement on enterprise systems. Most enterprise systems make valuable information about the business and its employees and clients available to the relevant people. Some of those people also need to change this valuable information.

Security in itself is a very large area of technology with many different features. Lets us briefly describe some of these features. When a user starts to interact with an enterprise system, he or she needs to identify himself to the system. When the client itself is another system, such as a process engine that is trying to invoke some methods on an enterprise system during the execution of some tasks, it is acting on behalf of a user and takes on the identity of that user. *Authentication* is usually the most basic security feature and it is almost always required. It ensures that a user is who he or she claims to be.

Another quite basic feature of security services is called *authorization*. A user interacts with a system so that he or she can invoke some methods on the system. All users are not created equal. Once authenticated, some users may be allowed only to view or change some information that pertains to them whereas others may be allowed to view or change more information. As a typical example, in a human resources system, an employee may be allowed to view his salary information but not that of others. However, his manager may be allowed to view salary information of everyone on the team and also may be allowed to change it. A security system that supports authorization allows the system to determine an authenticated user's access privileges. Once the user has been authenticated, the application can then determine the access privileges of the user and decide to what functions the user will be allowed access.

Distributed applications communicate with each other over networks. These can be local area networks (LANs) or wide area networks (WAN) over leased lines or that use the public Internet. Although LANs are usually safe, most WANs and public Internet are inherently unsafe. Malicious individuals can actually snoop the communication lines and intercept the communications. Then, they can use this information to crack the password and assume that individual's identity.

For this reason, critical information being exchanged between a client and a service provider should be *encrypted*. There are various encryption algorithms that are quite safe and are based on a system of keys and digital certificates. Perhaps the most-used protocol for exchanging information between distributed entities in a secure way is the Secure Socket Layer (SSL). SSL applies authentication, authorization, and encryption under the covers and provides a safe medium for information exchange. A security service must support SSL but should also allow individual application of these security features. For example, SSL encrypts entire messages. Encryption, although very safe, is quite expensive in terms of performance. Often, the whole message, especially when it is large, does not need to be encrypted. For example, when sending user information to a shopping Web site, only the credit-card-related information may need to be encrypted. A security service should also allow encryption of individual elements of the message.

A security system should also support other security features such as audit trails, which hold users accountable for their actions. Another important and related feature of the security services is called *nonrepudiation*. Nonrepudiation services deal with evidence of actions, such as proof that some notification was sent to a recipient and that the recipient did receive that notification, and therefore no one can deny that the data were received.

5.2.1.7 Web Service Support

Most development platforms have historically focused on making things work very well together inside the network environment of the enterprise. However, to embrace the truly global nature of today's business environment, technologies have to allow applications to enable the extended enterprise, which encompasses its business partners as well.

Web services technologies outshine everything else in that area. The key Web services technologies are SOAP, Web Service Description Language (WSDL), and business registries. We discuss SOAP and WSDL later in this chapter. Business registries are discussed in detail in Chapter 7.

5.2.2 CORBA

CORBA was the groundbreaking technology of its time. Prior to CORBA, distributed computing environment (DCE) provided the computing environment of choice. Many component models were layered on top of DCE, of which DCOM is the most notable. CORBA provided a comprehensive architecture for distributed computing.

The Object Management Architecture (OMA) defines the context for all CORBA-related specifications. It provides the conceptual foundation upon which the rest of the specification is based on. Figure 5.1 shows the OMA reference model.

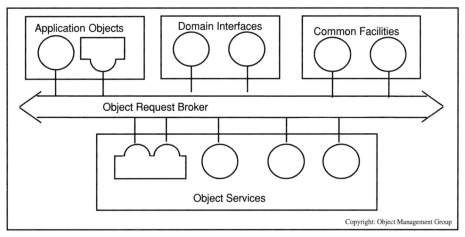

Copyright: Object Management Group

FIGURE 5.1. OMA Reference Model

The OMA reference model includes the following components:

- **Object request broker (ORB)**. ORB provides the basic mechanism by which messages may be exchanged by objects existing in different address spaces. Each address space is served by an ORB, which communicates with other ORBs to relay messages. A client invokes a service by sending a request through an ORB. The ORB on the server side receives the request and then dispatches it to service implementation.

  The interface definition language (IDL) captures the contract of the service implementations. The mapping of IDL expressions to different programming languages is defined by OMG language binding. IDL is perhaps one of the two most important technologies defined as part of the CORBA standard.

  The key to interoperability is the general inter-ORB protocol (GIOP). This is the communication protocol that describes how data are encoded and decoded and what messages are exchanged between two CORBA implementations. GIOP must be implemented on a communications transport layer. Although GIOP is an abstract protocol, the Internet inter-ORB protocol (IIOP) is a concrete protocol that defines how GIOP is to be implemented for a TCP/IP transport layer. Other transport layers, such as DCE-CIOP, may be used, but ORBs are required to support IIOP to comply with the CORBA specification.

- **Object services**. When objects are distributed across a heterogeneous network, operations that are otherwise quite simple in a single computing environment become inherently more complex. For example, in a single computing environment, objects can simply be created in language-specific syntax. However, this becomes a daunting task in a distributed environment. In fact, objects in a client's environment may be proxies to server objects. Their life-cycle management can itself become fairly complex.

Object services are supporting components and services necessary for the development of consistent applications in heterogeneous environments. These object services may be used to construct either applications or higher-level facilities and object frameworks. OMG has so far defined Collection Service, Concurrency Service, Time Service, Event & Notification Service, Naming Service, Licensing Service, Life Cycle Service, Persistent State Service (PSS), Property Service, Query Service, Security Service, and Trading Object Service & Transaction Service.

As with all specifications that are part of OMA, these are only specifications of service interfaces and not implementations. Vendors implement these service interfaces using different strategies that better suit their products. However, because all of these services use the core ORB infrastructure, the services are guaranteed to interoperate with each other through IIOP.

- **Common facilities.** Common facilities are application components that provide functionality that occurs frequently in application requirements, such as facilities for distributed document management. In a sense, the key difference between object services and object facilities is that the object services are fundamental building blocks of distributed applications whereas object facilities are shared by applications but are not their fundamental building blocks.

  To date, the Internationalization and Time facility and Mobile Agent facilities are available.

- **Domain interfaces.** The OMG has defined various industry-specific task forces. Currently, specifications are available for industries such as finance, health care, manufacturing, life sciences, telecommunications, transportation, and utilities. These interfaces are grouped as domain interfaces.

- **Application interfaces.** The application segment represents the actual business applications that operate in this environment. It is not an area that the OMG intends to standardize. However, it is shown as part of the OMA to provide the proper context.

5.2.2.1 Scalability and Robustness

None of the OMG specifications specifically addresses scalability and robustness. These features are generally attributes of an implementation. Since OMG defines only a specification in terms of the service interfaces captured in IDL, these features cannot be expressed.

CORBA products have been around for a while now and are quite mature. They have been used in high-volume business applications from banking to high-performance systems such as satellite base systems. As mentioned earlier, scalability depends not only on the underlying product but also on the application architecture and design. CORBA does not dictate, prevent, or suggest any style of application design. However, all CORBA services are designed as large-grain service objects. Large-grain service objects are inherently more scalable than fine-grained entity objects.

OMG has recently floated the RFP for load balancing. There are many systems that have implemented various kinds of load-balancing schemes for CORBA-based systems, ranging from simple round-robin schemes to more sophisticated cost-based load balancing. With the load-balancing service, OMG will be formalizing load-balancing specification as part of the core service.

5.2.2.2 Metadata Management

The key metadata in an ORB environment are the interface definitions. An ORB requires the interface definitions to correctly process a request. These metadata can be provided to it either by specifically hard coding in the stubs or dynamically through a metadata repository.

Often, hard-coded stubs are not an option, specifically for clients who have been written as generic clients without stubs or for dynamic servers, which can process any kind of request, such as gateway servers.

More specifically, an ORB may use these metadata:

- to provide type checking of request signatures,
- to create a request for a dynamic client,
- to assist in checking the correctness of an inheritance graph and to properly narrow objects,
- to provide interoperability between different ORBs.

In CORBA, these metadata are managed by the *interface repository (IR)*. IR provides persistent storage for these interface definitions and provides a set of IDL interfaces. The IR actually consists of a set of interface repository objects that represent information in it.

Most of the repository objects are container objects. The top level module for the repository is called `Repository`, as shown in Figure 5.2. The `Repository` object contains all global constants, typedefs, exceptions, interface or value type definitions, and modules. A `RepositoryId` is a string identifier that uniquely and globally identifies an interface repository object. A `ModuleDef` object maps to an IDL module and represents a collection of interfaces, value types, constants, typedefs, and exceptions defined in an IDL module. An `InterfaceDef` object maps to IDL interface and contains lists of constants, types, exceptions, operations, and attributes. The `AttributeDef` object describes an attribute of an interface

```
org.omg.CORBA.ORB orb = org.omg.CORBA.ORB.init(....);

org.omg.CORBA.Repository root = null;

org.omg.CORBA.Object obj =
orb.resolve_initial_references("InterfaceRepository");

root = org.omg.CORBA.RepositoryHelper.narrow(obj);
```

FIGURE 5.2. Getting Access to an Interface Repository

or a value type. The `OperationDef` object defines an operation on an interface or a value type. It contains a list of parameters to that operation and a list of exceptions raised by that operation. An `ExceptionDef` defines an exception. There are other objects representing value types, constants, and typedefs besides the ones mentioned here.

There are three ways of getting an `InterfaceDef` object:

1. If an interoperable object reference of an unknown type enters an ORB implementation, the application can get the `InterfaceDef` for that object by directly invoking the `get_interface` operation, which obtains the `InterfaceDef` directly from the ORB.
2. Another way is to obtain the root to the IR, as illustrated in Figure 5.2, and navigate through the contained modules and through the interfaces contained in them.
3. There are situations in which an ORB implementation may use multiple IRs. This may be because an application may use two different ORB implementations and each ORB may have a different requirement for the IR implementation. In some cases, an object implementation may choose to provide its own IR and in other cases it may be desirable to store some additional information in another IR. In either case, globally unique repository identifiers can be used to obtain the `InterfaceDef` corresponding to the same interface from the different repositories.

5.2.2.3 Persistence Management

For large applications, managing persistence of data can become quite complex. Object-oriented languages allow inheritance, which further complicates persistence management.

PSS manages the persistence of CORBA objects. PSS is slightly different from other services in that those services focus on defining interfaces. However, persistence is essentially an implementation problem. It allows the state of the object implementations to be stored. A client of a CORBA server does not deal with PSS.

```
abstract storagetype Person
{
  state string name;
  state string address;
  readonly state string social_security_number;
  key unique_key (social_security_name );
};

abstract storagehome PersonHome of Person{
  factory create(social_security_number);
};

catalog People{
  provides PersonHome personHome;
};
```

FIGURE 5.3. PSDL

However, the PSS deals with the interface between CORBA server components and the external databases.

To understand this, let us compare some of the concepts in PSS specification to relational database concepts, which everyone understands so well. A *storage object* in PSS is semantically equivalent to a row of data in a table. A CORBA object that is created from these data could be thought of as a *storage object instance*. A table in a relational database provides a home for all the rows of data of a particular format. A relational table equates to a *storage home*. Of course, a relational database would be a *datastore* in PSS. A database connection is represented by a session in PSS. PSS has *catalogs* that roughly equate to data dictionaries or database schemas in the sense that it groups related storage homes together. Each storage object has an ID unique within its storage home and a globally unique ID. The scope of globally unique ID is the entire catalog.

Persistence of these objects can be quite complex. It would be counterproductive to burden the application with that complexity. For that reason, PSS defines a new language called Persistent State Definition Language (PSDL), which is a superset of the IDL and defines some extra keywords such as *abstract storagetype, abstract storagehome,* and *catalog*. Only those objects that need to be persistent are defined in PSDL using those keywords. However, because PSDL is an extension of IDL, you can use IDL descriptions with PSDL. Once the objects are defined, a PSDL compiler automatically generates the objects required by the PSS implementation. A compliant PSS implementation must be able to generate a default implementation from the PSDL-provided definitions. Figure 5.3 shows an example of a persistent object.

In the Figure 5.3, `Person` defines a persistent type. It has three persistent attributes (`name`, `address`, and `social_security_number`). The access to `social_security_number` is restricted to read-only. Person also has a key that comprises its `social_security_number` attribute. `PersonHome` defines the home for the Person. It defines a factory to create `Person` objects. Since the `social_security_number` attribute is a read-only attribute, the create method takes it as an argument and initializes a new instance of `Person` with it. A `catalog` groups all homes to form a related set.

PSS is integrated with the object transaction service (OTS, discussed in the next section), and the storage objects can be accessed in the context of these transactions. A PSS implementation may register a resource on behalf of the CORBA server with the OTS transaction and write out its state when the transaction commits to or rolls the changes back when the transaction aborts.

5.2.2.4 OTS

OMG distributed transaction is a fairly complex transaction service that supports two-phase commits and nested transactions and provides complete interoperability with non-object-oriented XA-based transactional systems. One of OMG's goals has been to mandate that all CORBA services try to use other CORBA services and interoperate with them. A good example of that is strong coupling between the PSS and the transaction service.

There are two modes of using transactions. The first one is implicit. In that mode, the objects are not necessarily transaction aware. No transaction context explicitly appears in the method signature. An originator application starts a transaction, which then gets associated with the originator's thread. When the originator issues a remote request to a transactional object, the transaction context associated with the invoking thread is automatically propagated to the thread executing the target method. Each thread is associated with only one transactional context at a time. When the transaction is terminated, by either being committed to or rolled back, the transaction context is disassociated from the current thread.

Most of the interactions for OTS clients are with the `Current`. `Current` is used to manage the transactions. It has methods to begin, rollback, suspend, and resume a transaction. Furthermore, if more control of the underlying transaction systems is needed, `Current` can be used to get the `Control` object, which can then be used to do more sophisticated things. The `Current` always either represents the currently active transaction or is used to start a new transaction.

Figure 5.4 illustrates how to get access to `Current` and then begin a transaction. A client does not have to cache the `Current` object, because this is effectively a singleton object.

Most applications that use OTS will want to utilize the two-phase commit support of the underlying database to do the heavy lifting of all transactional matters. A client of an object implementation may control the scope of the OTS transactions but the data are written out to the database by the implementation. OTS does not really specify how an implementation might involve a resource

```
org.omg.CORBA.ORB orb = org.omg.CORBA.ORB.init(…);

org.omg.CosTransactions.Current current = null;

org.omg.CORBA.Object obj =
orb.resolve_initial_references("TransactionCurrent");

current =
org.omg.CosTransactions.CurrentHelper.narrow(obj);

current.begin();
```

FIGURE **5.4. Getting Access to Current**

manager, which is provided by an underlying database in the current transaction. In any case, the implementation will get an XA-compliant connection to the database. For example, an application using JDBC will get the object of type `javax.sql.XAConnection`. Once this connection has been obtained, the object implementation can save its data over this connection. After the point when the transaction is committed, the OTS implementation should send a series of messages to the XA resource manager as part of the two-phase commit protocol.

In many cases, the application may need to register its own resources. For example, an implementation may be saving its state using a third-party interface or a database that may not provide an XA manager. In other cases the object implementations may have their own transient data that may need to be preserved transactionally. For example, an object implementation may have attributes that hold values using very expensive calculations, such as graphics processing. If this implementation is in the process of calculating a new value of its attributes in a transaction and the transaction rollback, it may want to revert to its old value rather than lose everything. Such an implementation will provide its own resource object and will register that resource object using the `Current` in the transaction. A resource object implementation provides an implementation of key operations such as `prepare`, `commit`, and `rollback`.

5.2.2.5 Messaging

CORBA defines two services, event service and notification service, which provide a decoupled message exchange between suppliers and consumers of messages.

An event is a fundamental concept here, although it is not represented by any physical data structure. An event is basically an occurrence that may be of interest to other parties. Events are described by data that are exchanged between suppliers and consumers through event parameters.

Event Service describes two models for event communication, the `push` and `pull` models. As might be evident from the names, in a push model, the suppliers

```
Class TestPushConsumer extends
omg.org.CosEventComm.PushConsumerPOA{

  Private org.omg.CosEventComm.PushSupplier supplier;

  Public TestPushConsumer(org.omg.CosEventComm.PushSupplier supp)
  {
    supplier = supp;
  }

  public void disconnect_push_consumer()
  {
    supplier.disconnect_push_supplier();
  }

  public void push(org.omg.CORBA.Any data)
  {
    String string_data = data.extract_string();
    System.out.println("Received event data: " + s);
  }
}
```

FIGURE 5.5. A Generic PushConsumer

of events take the initiative and send data to potentially interested consumers by calling back on them. In a pull model, the consumers take the initiative and actually query the event supplier for new events. In either case the communication between the suppliers and the consumers may be either generic or typed. In generic push or pull, all event data are communicated through generic methods that take a single parameter that packages all event data. In the case of typed push or pull, the push and pull operations are defined in OMG IDL and the data are communicated through their parameters.

An *event channel* plays the role of an intermediary between the supplier and the consumer. If the suppliers and the consumers are directly connected to each other, then they become strongly dependent upon each other's availability. With an intermediary, that dependence is removed because it provides an intermediate routing point, and the consumers and the suppliers can interact with each other asynchronously. An event channel itself is both a supplier and a consumer of event data.

In Figure 5.5, a push consumer using a generic push model receives data through the push method, which takes a single argument of type Any. This method is invoked on the TestPushConsumer asynchronously when the data arrive.

Figure 5.6 illustrates the main programming steps, skipping error handling other initialization steps, which a PushClient needs to take in order to receive events. A push client needs to obtain a reference to an event channel. An instance of event channel is shared between the supplier and the consumer. There may be various ways to create an event channel and register it in the

```
// get the root POA and then get EventChannel Factory
org.omg.CosEventChannelAdmin.EventChannel channel; // assume
initialized

org.omg.CosEventChannelAdmin.ConsumerAdmin consumerAdmin =
                channel.for_consumers();
org.omg.CosEventChannelAdmin.ProxyPushSupplier supplier =
                consumerAdmin.obtain_push_supplier();

TestPushConsumer consumer = new TestPushConsumer(supplier);

Supplier.connect_push_consumer(consumer._this(orb));

Orb.run();
```

FIGURE 5.6. Main Program for a Push Client

naming service or use some other application-specific method for registering it and sharing the event channel. Once the event channel has been obtained, the client invokes `for_consumer`, which returns `ConsumerAdmin` interface, which provides administrative functions for the client. The client then invokes `obtain_push_supplier`, which returns the proxy to the supplier. The client then connects its specialization of `PushConsumer`, `TestPushConsumer` in this case, which then results in the push method being invoked on it whenever there are new event data.

A push supplier is also very similar to the push consumer. A push supplier extends `PushSupplier`. A push server program obtains the shared event channel using a commonly agreed method. It then invokes the method `for_suppliers` on it and gets an `SupplierAdmin`. The `SuuplierAdmin` is then used to obtain a `ProxyPushConsumer`. The event supplier can then invoke the `push` method on this proxy object.

The existence of this event channel allows mixing of different models. For example, the event channels support a push supplier and a pull consumer. The push supplier will push the event data on the event channel. However, the event channel will not push those data to the event consumer. Instead, the event consumer will go and pull the data from the event channel when it needs to.

OMG's notfication service extended the event service by providing several additional features:

• The event service allowed typed push and pull communication but it meant that the data could be pushed or pulled using typed methods defined in IDL rather than generic `push` and `pull` methods. However, the specification did not allow the structured event data. The notification service allowed the transfer of events in the form of well-defined data structures.

- The notification service allows the client to attach filters to select the events that are delivered to them rather than have all the events delivered. Most of the time, these event filters are co-located with the event channel itself, thus significantly reducing network traffic by filtering out the unwanted events for a particular consumer.
- Suppliers acquired the ability to discover the event desired by consumers attached to a channel. This way, the suppliers do not have to produce events in which a consumer is uninterested.
- Quality-of-service properties can be configured on a per-channel, per-proxy, or per-event basis.

The notification service extends the event service without changing any of its semantics.

5.2.2.6 Security
CORBA defines a fairly comprehensive security service. The service is split into two packages:

- **Level 1**. This package provides security for "security unaware" applications or for those with minimal requirements for implementing their own mechanisms for authentication and authorization. The entry-level security functionality in Level 1 includes security of invocations between client and target object, message protection, some delegation, access control, and audit.

- **Level 2**. This package allows applications to control the security provided at object invocation. It also includes administration of security policies.

An ORB must implement security at one of the preceding two levels to qualify as a secure ORB. Object invocations are mediated by appropriate security functions to enforce policies such as access control.

5.2.3 J2EE
Java 2 Platform, Enterprise Edition (J2EE) is a completely Java-based application server environment to build enterprise-grade Java applications. J2EE brings many key enterprise technologies under one standard umbrella and integrates them to provide an application development environment. The J2EE environment not only allows development of Java applications, but it also defines service for developing Web applications in Java, browser-based Java clients, and regular Java client applications.

Figure 5.7 illustrates J2EE architecture. J2EE architecture can be divided into four separate runtime environments, each represented by a container. In addition,

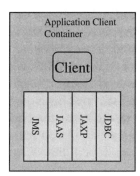
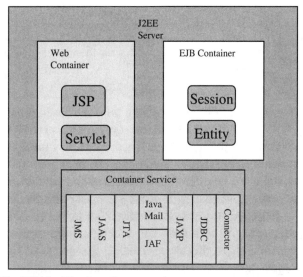

FIGURE 5.7. J2EE Architecture Components

there are several services that are provided by the J2EE architecture, and different container environments make those services available to the Java components that execute inside the respective container environments.

Programs require execution environments in which to run. J2EE containers provide that execution environment in such a way that the container also provides a number of services. Various J2EE application components do not directly interact with other J2EE components but rather always use protocols and methods of the container to interact with each other and the platform services. This allows the container to transparently implement services such as transactions and security.

The four major components are:

1. **EJB container**. The Enterprise Java Beans (EJB) container provides the managed execution environment for application components that contain the business logic. These components can be either session beans, which essentially model large-grain service-oriented concepts, or entity beans, which are finer-grained entity concepts that have a state tied to database tables.

2. **Web container**. Web containers support technologies more suitable for serving requests from Web clients. Most of the times, these Web clients are based in a browser, but the Web container does not really know that. The components known as *Web containers* are usually accessed over HTTP(s) by the Web clients.

Typically, these Web components are used to accept a request from a Web browser and generate a response that consists of a dynamically generated HTML Web page, which the browser then displays. Servlets are written as Java code which can accept prespecified HTTP commands, such as HTTP-GET and HTTP-POST, and then execute some application logic to generate a response. Java Server Pages (JSPs), on other hand, are server-side scripts, which can have Java code embedded in them. These scripts are transparently translated into servlet code by the Web container and executed.

3. **Applet container.** A simple browser-based client can use HTML to execute its client-side logic. HTML can only support HTTP request/response-style communication. If a more sophisticated display needs to be created or the interaction with the server needs to be more conversational, then Java applets can be used to implement client-side technology. Applets are Java classes that are automatically downloaded to a Web browser and executed there. Because this is Java code, executing in a client's Web browser, this Java code can open the data stream to the server, can receive asynchronous messages, and can configure a display in the browser using the powerful user interface capabilities of the Java language. This is called an *applet container*.

4. **Application client container.** This is a regular Java client that communicates with J2EE components in either a J2EE Web container or a J2EE EJB container.

As mentioned before, J2EE provides a number of services that are then made available to Java code running inside those environments. These services include Java connector architecture, database connectivity, transactions, naming, security, and messaging, among others. We discuss key services, as they relate to building BSOs later.

5.2.3.1 Robustness and Scalability

The J2EE platform has certainly been used to build enterprise-grade applications. J2EE provides a component model for development that is easy to scale up. By providing session EJB, J2EE provides an abstraction to build highly scalable stateless services. At the same time, the applications also have the option of building fine-grained transactional applications using entity EJB. This provides a fairly rich component model for applications to build upon.

Although load balancing and clustering are not part of J2EE specification, most J2EE products have features such as clustering and 24 × 7 availability. This is a further testament to the fact that J2EE is a solid platform for building enterprise-grade applications. The leading J2EE products are also fairly mature and have been around for several years. The product maturity comes from use in real environments.

5.2.3.2 Database Connectivity

Java Database API, which is based on X/Open SQL CLI, provides programmatic access to relational databases in a database-independent manner for Java applications. This API allows programmers to execute SQL statements, retrieve rows, and create or update rows in the underlying relational database. JDBC is a set of Java interfaces as well as a number of concrete classes that use those interfaces. Each database vendor implements those Java interfaces for their underlying data source.

JDBC service is available in the application client container as well as the J2EE server containers. When used in the application client container, the application is completely responsible for interacting with the JDBC driver. When used in the J2EE server, the J2EE server provides automatic persistence management of entity EJBs. For entity EJBs, the application server can pool connections and manage distributed transactions with very little help from the application. Furthermore, database is updated in a transparent manner. Most other uses of JDBC service in the J2EE server are similar to its use in the application client container.

5.2.3.3 Transaction Management

J2EE specification provides support for transactions in the J2EE server, for the components executing in the Web container and the EJB container. A servlet, a JSP, or an EJB may demarcate a transaction through the interface `javax.transaction.UserTransaction`. J2EE specification also defines JDBC, Java Messaging Service (JMS), and XATransaction to behave as transactional components that may be shared by multiple applications in the same transaction. However, this support for transactions is not available to the applet container or the application client container.

The user-visible API specified by the J2EE specification is called the Java transaction API (JTA). This API defines the `javax.transaction.UserTransaction`, which can be obtained from the Java Naming and Directory Interface (JNDI) by accessing the `java:comp/UserTransaction`. This object provides the application with the ability to control the boundaries of the transaction by being able to start and end a transaction. A transaction started like this is associated with the current thread. The `UserTransaction` is managed by the *transaction manager*. The transaction manager is the nerve center of the transactional activity and provides the functions required to start and stop transactions, associate the transactions with calling threads, propagate transaction contexts on the outgoing invocations, start new transactions on incoming invocations carrying a transaction context and managing the transactional resources. A transaction resource manager participates in the transaction by implementing the transactional resource interface that is used by the transactional manager to coordinate transaction and recover work. J2EE requires JDBC and JMS providers to implement that interface.

```
// A session context is passed to an EJB through the //
// method setSessionContext.

UserTransaction currentTxn = ctx.getUserTransaction();
```

FIGURE 5.8. User Transaction in J2EE

EJB servers expose UserTransaction to the application through EJBContext. Figure 5.8 illustrates how to get the user transaction in an EJB.

Figure 5.9 shows how the user transaction can be obtained from any other element of the J2EE server.

Regardless of how the UserTransaction is obtained, it can be used to perform various functions such as beginning a transaction, committing or rolling it back, getting the transaction status, and setting timeout.

An application server manages transactions automatically for entity beans through a set of transaction-related properties declared at the time of its deployment. For example, through those properties, it can be instructed to automatically start a transaction for a bean if one has not already been started or can mandate that a transaction always be started by the calling client.

5.2.3.4 Messaging

Java Messaging Service is a client-side API that is designed to provide reliable point-to-point messaging as well as publish-subscribe service. JMS is designed to be a client-side interface to various service providers who provide the actual point-to-point and publish-subscribe service and then implement JMS interfaces to provide a client-side API for their clients. Since messaging is essentially a peer-to-peer concept, all users of JMS are called JMS clients (whether they are producers or consumers of messages). They are distinguished from the JMS providers, who provide the actual messaging services and implement the JMS interfaces that the clients use. JMS does not attempt to define the common features of existing messaging systems but rather defines essential concepts and facilities required for enterprise messaging systems. Figure 5.10 illustrates the general JMS architecture in which two peers produce and consume messages that are supported through a service provider.

```
Context ctx = getInitialContext();
UserTransaction currentTxn =
ctx.lookup("java:comp/UserTransaction");
```

FIGURE 5.9. Obtaining a UserTransaction from a Client Container

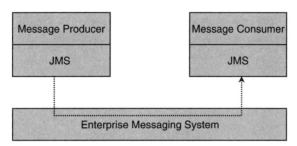

FIGURE 5.10. JMS Architecture

JMS defines two models of messaging:

1. **Queues**. JMS supports point-to-point messaging through queues. A queue establishes a communication channel between exactly one producer and one consumer of messages.

2. **Topics**. A publish-and-subscribe paradigm is supported by JMS through topics. Multiple publishers can publish messages to a topic and multiple subscribers can subscribe to a topic. When a publisher publishes a message to a topic, it is immediately distributed to all the registered subscribers.

As mentioned earlier, JMS is designed to be a Java library for clients of enterprise messaging systems. Since the underlying messaging systems are probably quite different from each other in terms of how they are administered and how connections are established, in order to keep the JMS clients portable, the specification defines two objects as administered objects, which are created by the administrators and registered in JNDI. These two administered objects are:

1. `ConnectionFactory`. This object is used by the client to establish a connection with the JMS provider.

2. `Destination`. This object specifies a destination that could be either a *topic* or a *queue*. The client uses this object to specify the address of the destination required to send or receive the messages.

Figure 5.11 illustrates the key steps that a JMS client takes to publish a message. A client first looks up the `ConnectionFactory` and the Destination in the JNDI namespace. Once the `ConnectionFactory` is retrieved, the client uses it to establish a connection with the provider. This connection can then be shared among multiple threads in the same application. Generally, you need only one connection to the provider in one application because the connection is designed

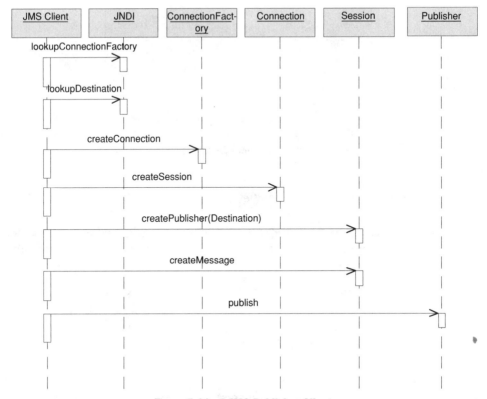

FIGURE 5.11. A JMS Publisher Client

to be used from multiple threads. The connection can then be used to create a session. JMS sessions are not to be used by multiple threads. Typically, a thread of control will create a JMS session, use that session to create JMS topic or queue publishers with the specified destination, and then be released. This works well because transactions are supported by JMS sessions. Since transactions are usually associated with a thread, JMS sessions are also associated with a thread of control. JMS defines several kinds of messages, including text messages, object messages, among many others. JMS does not define XML messages because they are just text messages. Once a message has been created, a publisher object is used to actually publish the message on the topic or the queue.

A JMS message is composed of a header, a set of properties, and a body. A JMS header contains a set of fields used by the JMS client and the provider for routing and delivery of the messages. The JMS header contains fields such as JMS Destination, the delivery mode, message ID, and timestamp. Typically, the JMS API fills in all the JMS header fields. However, a client may also use or modify some of the fields. For example, a client may save a message ID and later set the correlation ID of an outgoing message to indicate a reply to a previously received message. The use in that case is between the two peers – the producer and the consumer of the message.

JMS messages contain built-in facility to support message properties. JMS specification further specifies a mechanism to filter on the properties to provide a selection mechanism. This allows a JMS provider to filter the JMS messages on behalf of a client, using application-specific criteria. This in turn reduces network bandwidth by not burdening the network with all messages and makes the message consumers easy to develop and consume fewer resources also. They receive only the messages that fit their criteria rather than all the messages published on the topic. Properties are name-value pairs, where the values can be any one of the primitive types such as Boolean, byte, short, or long. There are some reserved properties that may be supported by a JMS provider. These properties' names begin with "JMSX." In addition, a JMS provider may also reserve property names beginning with JMS_<vendor name> prefix.

JMS provides a message selection mechanism for the clients to specify a selection criterion for the message that can be delivered to them. The message selector can reference the fields of the message header and the properties but it cannot reference the contents of the message body. The selection criterion is provided by using a query language that is a subset of SQL92.

JMS allows five kinds of message bodies: stream, map, text, object, and byte. The session object is also the factory object for creating messages. JMS does not define an IDL to define the structure of its messages.

5.2.3.5 Security

The security in J2EE is supported at the Java Development Kit level. That means that you do not necessarily need to have full installation of J2EE to take advantage of the security features. This section therefore describes the security features provided in the Java 2 SDK Standard Edition (J2SE). The discussion below assumes that users are familiar with security features such as principals of encryption, message digests, and digital certificates.

* **Java cryptography extensions** (JCEs). JCEs are based on the design principles of Java cryptography architecture (JCA) and provide a framework and implementations for encryption, key generation and key agreement, and message authentication code algorithms. The API provided in the JCA package covers various encryption algorithms such as DES, RC2, RC4, and RSA and provider-based encryption. Figures 5.13 and 5.14 illustrate a program that takes input data from the screen, encrypts the data, and then writes the data to a file. Let us consider a set of complementary programs. One program reads input data from the screen, uses a randomly generated private key to encrypt the data, serializes

```
1. KeyGenerator keygen = KeyGenerator.getInstance("DES");
2. SecretKey myKey = keygen.generateKey();
3. FileOutputStream kfw = new FileOutputStream(keyFile);
4. ObjectOutputStream ostream = new ObjectOutputStream(kfw);
5. ostream.writeObject(myKey);
6. ostream.close();
```

FIGURE 5.12. Generation of Private Key

the private key to a file, and then writes the encrypted data to a file. The other program, re-creates the private key from the file and uses it to decrypt the data previously written to the file, and writes it back to the screen. Figure 5.12 shows how to generate the private key.

- **Java certification path API**. This Java package provides classes and interfaces to handle certificate chains. The API defines interfaces and abstract classes to create and validate certificate chains, but does not provide an implementation of the API.

- **Java Secure Socket Extensions (JSSE)**. JSSE provides a framework and an implementation for the Java version of SSL (v2.0 & v3.0) and Transport Layer Security (TLS v1.0). JSSE provides functionality for data encryption, message integrity, and optional client authentication. JSSE is based on the same design principles as JCA. JCA provides support for message digest, signatures, keys, digital certificates, and encryption algorithms. JSSE encompasses the same concepts as JCE but automatically applies them underneath simple stream socket API.

- **Java Authentication and Authorization Service (JAAS)**. JAAS is used (1) to authenticate users so that the identity of the user currently executing the Java code can be determined regardless of whether the code is running as an application, an applet, a bean, or a servlet; and (2) to determine access control rights of the user to determine the functions or methods to which the user has access.

- **Java GSS-API**. The GSS API is a Java implementation of Generic Security Services API defined by RFC 2853. It allows applications access to a variety of underlying security services such as Kerberos.

```
1. Cipher cipher = Cipher.getInstance("DES");
2. cipher.init(Cipher.ENCRYPT_MODE,myKey);
3. FileOutputStream fostream = new FileOutputStream(file);
4. CipherOutputStream cos = new
      CipherOutputStream(fostream,cipher);
```

FIGURE 5.13. Creation of a Cryptographic Cipher

```
1. while (true){
2.      String data = getNewInput();
3.      if ( data.equals("quit") == true ){
4.         System.out.println("Quit signal received....");
5.         ostream.close();
6.         break;
7.      }
8.      System.out.println("YOU TYPED: " + data);
9.      ostream.write(data.getBytes());
10.     ostream.write(Character.LINE_SEPARATOR);
11.     ostream.flush();
12.}
```

FIGURE 5.14. Encrypting Data Using Cipher Streams

The next few figures describe various steps required to perform data encryption. Figure 5.12 demonstrates a how private key can be generated to use for encryption. Lines 1 and 2 create a random key for a DES encryption algorithm. Lines 3 and 4 create an output stream to serialize the key-object-in and Line 5 actually writes out the key to the file.

Once the key has been created, a cipher for the DES object is created. A cipher object is the core of the JCE functionality and provides the functionality of a cryptographic cipher for encryption and decryption. Figure 5.13 shows how to create a cipher. Line 1 creates the cipher, using the previously generated key. Line 2 initializes the cipher for either encryption or decryption. Line 3 creates an output file stream. Line 4 creates a cipher stream that can encrypt the data as it writes the data out to a file.

Once a `CipherOutputStream` has been created, any data written to that stream will be encrypted and then written to the attached `FileStream`. In Figure 5.14, Line 2 reads the data from the input console. If the user types "quit," the stream is closed and the program stops. Otherwise, data are written to the stream.

For decryption (see Figure 5.15), once the private key used to encrypt the data has been deserialized from the previously written key file, the cipher can be created for decryption.

The remaining steps involve creating `FileInputStream` and `CipherInputStream`, which automatically reads the data through `FileInputStream` and then decrypts it.

```
Cipher cipher = Cipher.getInstance("DES");
cipher.init(Cipher.DECRYPT_MODE,myKey);
```

FIGURE 5.15. Cipher for Decryption

5.2.3.6 Web Service Support

The Java community has been working on various standards, all aimed at providing support for the Web-services-related technologies in J2EE. The following sections provide a brief discussion of the key Web services and XML-related standards that are either in the process of being accepted or have already been accepted:

5.2.3.6.1 Java API for XML Processing. JAXP enables programmers to process XML documents using the XML processing model of their choice. JAXP enables processing of XML documents using standard APIs. There are two models for processing XML. The first is a W3C technology called the Document Object Model (DOM). This model loads the hierarchical structure of an XML document into the program's memory as a tree structure, which can then be traversed. The other model is Simple API for XML (SAX) which is a faster and an event-driven model. In this model, the parser does not read the entire document into the memory but, rather, calls back user code when it encounters various XML constructs. SAX-based processing turns out to be more complex to code but results in less usage of memory and faster speed. These models are, of course, very different from each other and require completely different programming models. However, JAXP hides the configuration and creation of these parsers, which usually turns out to be very parser-implementation specific. The specification provides two pluggability layers, one for SAX and another for DOM. Through these layers, various parser implementations can be plugged in, keeping the code itself portable to the parser implementation.

In addition to supporting DOM and SAX, JAXP also supports a number of other World Wide Web Consortium (W3C) technologies. The most important, of course, is the XML specification itself. In addition, JAXP also supports XML namespace specifications and XSLT. The API provides several classes to process transformation instructions and transform the source into the result.

5.2.3.6.2 Java API for XML Binding (JAXB). XML is the platform-independent mechanism for describing data. Java is a platform-independent way to build programs. A Java binding for XML then becomes natural for the two powerful technologies. XML is mostly used to describe data structures. To facilitate programs written in a programming language manipulating those data structures, it would be helpful if that program did not have to worry about parsing the XML documents all the time and just had to deal with the data as represented in the programming language being used. XML data are usually described in some form of XML schema. Figure 5.16 illustrates a simple definition of Address in W3C's XML Schema Language.

Figure 5.17 shows a simple Java mapping to that Address structure.

The idea behind defining the data binding is that the programs should never have to worry about XML documents. If a client program interacts with a service

```
<complexType name="Address">
   <sequence>
      <element minOccurs="1" maxOccurs="1" name="streetNum" type="string"/>
      <element minOccurs="1" maxOccurs="1" name="streetName" type="string"/>
      <element minOccurs="1" maxOccurs="1" name="city" type="string"/>
      <element minOccurs="1" maxOccurs="1" name="state" type="string"/>
      <element minOccurs="1" maxOccurs="1" name="zipCode" type="string"/>
      <element minOccurs="1" maxOccurs="1" name="phoneNumber" type="string"/>
   </sequence>
</complexType>
```

FIGURE 5.16. A Simple Address in XML Schema

such as Universal Description, Discovery and Integration (UDDI), which describes all its data structures in XML Schema Language (XSD), the client program always uses a Java equivalent of those data structures and some magic happens that serializes the language parameters of the outgoing calls into XML and deserializes the incoming XML parameters into Java structures.

There are several ways of accomplishing this. The JAX-RPC standard, described in the next subsection, handles that situation with SOAP-based services, which have been described in WSDL. WSDL is described in more detail later.

5.2.3.6.3 Java API for XML Messaging (JAXM). JAXM provides API for XML-based messaging that uses SOAP 1.1 with attachments. JAXM does not imply any particular high-level messaging standard but rather allows customization of exchanged SOAP messages based on configuration files called `Profile`.

There are generally two styles of communication. First is the remote procedure call style, in which the interaction takes place between the two peers. The service exposes some methods that can be invoked. Those methods carry signatures that include the method name and its parameters. The method may also return some data as a return type. This method requires the interacting peers to be more tightly coupled to each other. The second style is document-centric computing. In this style the peers exchange documents with each other rather than method parameters. The content of these documents provides the data that need to be exchanged

```
Public class Address{
   Public String streetNum;
   Public String streetName;
   Public String city;
   Public String state;
   Public String zipCode;
   Public String phoneNumber;
}
```

FIGURE 5.17. Java Mapping to Address

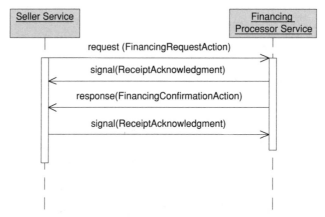

FIGURE 5.18. Request Financing Approval (Source: RosettaNet PIP 3C2)

between the peers. The messages themselves do not have any parameters, but the document containing the data is carried with the message as an attachment. This style of computing allows the interacting peers to be more loosely coupled. Usually, the response to a received message is provided by another message going in the reverse direction. Often, there is a protocol that describes how messages are acknowledged. Figure 5.18 illustrates RosettaNet's PIP 3C2 for requesting financing approval. This kind of interaction is more suitable for business-to-business computing with business partners in an extended enterprise.

JAXM defines API to send and receive document-centric messages. JAXM supports various kinds of message exchange patterns:

1. In the fire-and-forget scenario, the sender sends a message, possibly with some data. The requestor does not expect any acknowledgment or a response.
2. In the next type of the message pattern that is supported, the sender sends a request. The only expected response to that request is an acknowledgment from the receiver that the request has been received. The request can be sent either synchronously or asynchronously. When the request is sent synchronously, the sender waits for the acknowledgment. In asynchronous mode, the acknowledgment arrives later on in a separate message.
3. Another messaging pattern that is supported is a request in which the sender sends a send a request to do some work. The receiver performs the requested work and sends the results of the request in a response document. As in scenario 2, in synchronous mode the sender blocks until the response is received and in asynchronous mode, the sender receives the response later.

JAXM requires all providers to implement SOAP 1.1 with Attachments specification and use the same transport bindings such as HTTP or SMTP. In addition, the providers may be implementing a higher-level interaction protocol, such as ebXML Messaging Service. JAXM refers to this adherence to the higher-level standards as *Profiles*. For two peers to interoperate, they must implement the same Profiles. SOAP specification is described in more detail later in this chapter.

5.2.3.6.4 Java API for XML-RPC (JAX-RPC). Whereas JAXM provides XML-based messaging using SOAP 1.1 with Attachments specification, JAX-RPC provides an API to do RPC-style computing. JAXRP can be used to write a SOAP-RPC client as well as a service implementation. It provides full support for WSDL and service implementation.

5.2.3.6.5 Java API for XML Registries (JAXR). As industry attention has shifted toward developing technologies for Web services, attention has also been focused on business registries. Business registries are used mainly to store information about Web services that would be considered necessary for selecting them for use and for binding to them.

Various competing registry standards have emerged, providing various levels of functionality. They also require very different programming models. For example, ebXML Registry & Repository and UDDI are two competing registries with very different capabilities. A program using one would not be able port from one to the other, however. We discuss the evolution of registries and issues surrounding the modern-day registries in detail in Chapter 7. However, without going into detail here, the different models exposed by the registries are not desirable.

JAXR defines an API for accessing XML-based business registries using a canonical information model and a consistent service interface. This shields the client application from the underlying registry. A client does not really program to the underlying registry. The clients programs to the programming model of the JAXR and uses the capabilities provided by JAXR implementation.

5.2.3.6.6 Enterprise Web Services (JSR 109). This specification defines the model for implementing, deploying, and using Web services from within J2EE. For that reason, this specification heavily leverages JAXM and JAX-RPC and provides the model for supporting SOAP-based Web services natively in a J2EE container.

One of the important requirements of this specification is to build a Web services façade for existing J2EE-based applications in an easy, seamless, and nonintrusive manner. Additionally, the specification focuses on building new Web services and deploying them into the J2EE container.

5.2.4 .NET

.NET is Microsoft's new computing platform in which there is a unified platform for various programming languages, devices, services, and applications. This platform

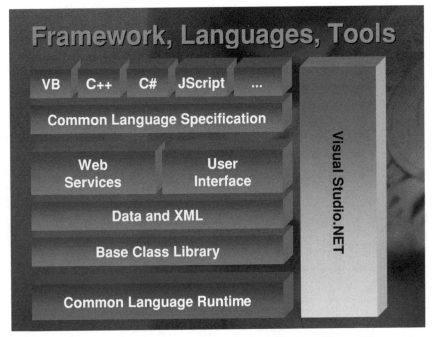

FIGURE 5.19. Components of .NET Platform (Source: Microsoft)

integrates Web-based computing with user interface applications and interactive applications into one unified platform. The key component of this strategy is the .NET infrastructure, which includes the .NET Framework, development tools such as Visual Studio.NET, .NET Enterprise Servers, and a variety of client devices. Our discussion here is limited to .NET Framework. Figure 5.19 shows the components of .NET platform.

The .NET Framework consists of a Common Language Runtime (CLR) and .NET Framework classes, which are also called base class library. The CLR is the key to .NET giving an equal status to all programming languages. CLR accomplishes this arduous task by Common Language Specification (CLS), which is a set of rules that all languages must adhere to. Because of CLS, a VB.NET and a C# program can interoperate with each other. Developers can write portions of an application in VB.NET and other portions in C# and then make a single executable out of those. When a program is built, CLR-compliant compilers compile into Microsoft Intermediate Language. Within the EXE or DLL of a .NET application, a special instruction is placed at the entry point of the executable to execute a CLR main function. This function, when executed the first time, compiles the remaining code into a real executable and then caches it.

Another built-in capability of .NET-supported languages is metadata. All CLR-compliant compilers embed the metadata about the program itself into the

The .NET Framework

System.Web	
Services	UI
Description	HtmlControls
Discovery	WebControls
Protocols	
Caching	Security
Configuration	SessionState

System.WinForms	
Design	ComponentModel

System.Drawing	
Drawing2D	Printing
Imaging	Text

System.Data	
ADO	SQL
Design	SQLTypes

System.Xml	
XSLT	Serialization
XPath	

System			
Collections	IO	Security	Runtime
Configuration	Net	ServiceProcess	InteropServices
Diagnostics	Reflection	Text	Remoting
Globalization	Resources	Threading	Serialization

FIGURE 5.20. Enterprise Services in .NET (Source: Microsoft)

compiled code. This way, the runtime has complete metadata available to it. Although this was never a problem for interpreted languages or byte-compiled languages such as Java, the compiled languages such as C and C++ always lost their type information upon compilation. These metadata can be used to provide aspect-oriented programming, supporting runtime features such as persistence management, Web service descriptions, and security. Custom metadata can also be used to provide new features and capabilities.

Another feature of the .NET environment is that the languages themselves do not provide any services. CLR-compliant compilers take all services provided by the traditional compilers away from the compilers and package them into framework class libraries. A CLR-compliant compiler does not perform even the simplest task. All capabilities are part of the framework class libraries, which are then implemented in each language separately.

5.2.4.1 Enterprise Services in .NET

Figure 5.20 shows the enterprise services available in .NET. Microsoft's .NET Enterprise Services provide support for many advanced application-server features

```
Using Microsoft.EnterpriseServices;

[ObjectPooling(Enabled=true,MinPoolSize=2,MaxPoolSize=10)
]

Public class MyScalableClass : ServicedComponent{
}
```

FIGURE 5.21. An Object Pooling Example

today. Enterprise Service leverages the mature, COM+ Services technology to provide object management, pooling, events, load balancing, queued components, transactions, and object constructors.

COM+ Services provide high-performance capabilities at a binary level via a technique called interception. Interception captures calls to components with low-level wrappers with the same binary-level interface as the component. Interceptions can do pre- and post processing on all component calls, allowing support for transaction management, queuing, auto-commit transactions, and role-based security. COM+ Services are used in the fastest implementations of many benchmarks, such as TPC-C.

COM+ services also provide enterprise-scale support for applications, although their ability to scale up is limited because the current Windows platform is limited to 32-processor systems. Horizontal scaling is typically used for the largest applications that utilize COM+ services. Although COM+ Services is a native feature of Windows 2000 and Windows .NET Server, Microsoft also provides Application Center Server 2000 to support component load balancing of COM+ components.

5.2.4.2 Robustness and Scalability

.NET leverages COM+ services to provide scalability features such as object pooling and transactions. Transactions are discussed in detail in a later section. Object pooling is a key scalability feature that allows stateless objects to be created in an object pool. The incoming requests can then use one of the objects from the pool and the object can be returned to the pool after the request is completed. These objects can share a common context such as open data base connections (ODBC). COM+ services are available to objects that derive from `EnterpriseServices.ServiceComponent`.

The code fragment from Figure 5.21 shows a class that derives from `ServicedComponent`. When an instance of this class is created from a managed client, the .NET CLR creates a COM+ application for this class and configures it with the specified attributes. In the above case, a pool of object instances will be created, initially with two objects. This pool is created as soon as the containing application starts. As demand is increased, more objects will be created in the pool, up to 10. This allows servicing of a larger number of concurrent clients, spreading the cost of creating objects over many clients and invocations. This is beneficial only if creating the objects is a time-consuming process, requiring acquisition of expensive resources such as database connections.

5.2.4.3 Metadata Management

For the most part, our discussion of metadata in this chapter has been about the application/Web services rather than metadata provided by language compilers. .NET provides full support for WSDL to describe Web services. .NET automatically generates a WSDL document for Web services built, regardless of the language in which they are built. Furthermore, .NET also provides extensive facilities for automatic generation for WSDL proxies. If the WSDL for a Web service, regardless of whether it was built using .NET, is available, either directly from the Web service itself through a URL or from a local file system, Microsoft .NET can generate a proxy for it in any CLR-compliant language.

There is support for searching Microsoft's UDDI repository, test or production, in .NET. You can perform a simple search, looking for different Web services available under a category or you can perform a more advanced search. In either case, it returns a list of Web services. After examining details of those Web services, you can simply add a reference to one or more Web services to the current project simply by clicking on the provided button. Once you create a reference to a Web service in your project, .NET generates a proxy for that Web service and adds it to the project. This proxy then can be used to interact with that Web service. However, Microsoft .NET does not provide a UDDI registry implementation out-of-the box with the standard .NET platform that can be deployed in a private environment; nor can a service be automatically registered in a public or private UDDI registry when it is deployed. However, .NET server contains a private UDDI registry along with other enterprise tools.

There is a separate download available for UDDI Standard Development Kit (SDK) for .NET. This SDK provides a client-side API for accessing UDDI from .NET-based services whether written in VB# or C#.

5.2.4.4 Database Connectivity

Database connectivity in .NET is provided through the database connectivity framework known as *ADO.NET*. As with most other .NET technologies, XML is natively supported in ADO.NET. ADO.NET provides two class hierarchies, separating data representation from data manipulation.

The first core element of ADO.NET is the `DataSet` that forms the basis for providing a disconnected model to access the database. The native serialization format for `DataSet` is XML, which makes it an ideal mechanism for transferring data between a database (SQL Server) and a Web service. A `DataSet` object can in fact be populated either through an XML document that contains the data or through a database. `DataSet` provides a consistent data representation of the relational programming model, regardless of the data source. There are a number of classes in this class family, which represent everything from a relational table to primary keys. The schema of a data set is defined in XSD. You can generate an XML schema from a data set or you can create data sets from existing XML schemas.

The second core element of ADO.NET is `.NET Data Provider` and it provides data manipulation and data access. This family contains classes such as `Connection`, which provides connectivity to the database and manages transactions on that connection. The `Command` object executes database commands against a data source. The `DataReader` class provides a forward-only, read-only, stream of data from a data source; and, finally, a `DataAdapter` populates a `DataSet`, providing `Select`/`Insert`/`Update`/`Delete` commands on the DataSet.

A `DataAdapter` is specific to a data source. The SQL Server .NET data adapter is highly optimized and uses its own protocol to communicate with the database. Microsoft also provides OLE DB .NET DataAdapter, which can be used to access any OLE DB data source through OLE DB. There is also ODBC .NET DataProvider for ODBC data sources.

5.2.4.5 Transaction Management

.NET provides support for distributed transactions through its transaction processor, which is called Microsoft *Distributed Transaction Coordinator (DTC)*. DTC sits in between a transaction-aware application and multiple resources and streamlines network communication, connecting multiple clients to multiple applications that could access multiple data resources. Each machine that has participating resources has a local component called *Transaction Manager (TM)*. The transaction manager is tasked with tracking incoming and outgoing transactions on that computer. Although the TM can coordinate the transactions, it does not manage the data directly.

The data are managed by the *resource managers*. Each different type of data source (such as a database or a messaging queue) has its own resource manager that, when requested, knows how to commit or roll back the work performed. For example, the respective resource managers would know how to store data and perform disaster recovery in a database, durable message queues, or transactional file systems.

Transactions are declarative. For example, a developer of a Web service will declare the transaction properties of a method by declaring `TransactionOption` property of a `WebMethod`. When the system receives a method invocation request, it examines the object context and looks for the current transaction. Then,

TABLE 5.1. Transaction Option Values of `TransactionOption` and Description of System Behavior	
TransactionOption Value	Description
Disabled	Any transaction is ignored and the presence or absence of a transaction has no effect on the execution of this method.
NotSupported	The system creates a new context with no governing transaction and invokes the method in that context.
Required	If a transaction already exists, then the system shares that transaction. If a transaction does not exist, the system starts a new one automatically. A newly started transaction is committed if the method executes successfully and is rolled back if the method throws an exception.
RequiresNew	With this value, the system always starts a new transaction, even if one exists. A newly started transaction is committed if the method executes successfully and is rolled back if the method throws an exception.
Supported	With this value, the system shares a transaction if one exists and does nothing different if one does not exist.

based on the value of the `TransactionOption`, the system takes some action. Table 5.1 describes various values of `TransactionOption` and the system behavior.

In automatic transaction control, the transaction boundaries are controlled automatically by specifying the values of different methods. Similar attributes can also be used to declare the voting policies of the methods. For example, `System.EnterpriseServices.AutoCompleteAttribute` causes an object participating in a transaction to vote in favor if the method returns normally. If the method throws an exception, then the transaction is aborted.

.NET also allows manual control of transaction boundaries. Manual transaction control, although a lot more work, allows complete application control over transaction boundaries and resource enlistment in transactions and determines the outcome of the transaction.

5.2.4.6 *Messaging*

.NET provides full support for messaging by leveraging Windows Message Queuing and provides a comprehensive set of classes to send or receive messages over asynchronous queues and to create, administer, and monitor those queues. All of these classes are provided through the namespace `System.Messaging`.

One of the core classes is called `MessageQueue`, which provides a wrapper over the physical queue. The class can actually be used to create a message queue or can be instantiated with a preexisting queue. In either case, the queue must have been created before the instance of `MessageQueue` can be used to send or receive messages. `MessageQueue` can be used to receive messages either synchronously or asynchronously. Synchronous reception causes the current thread to block until the message is received or the call times out. Asynchronous reception, on the other hand, allows the application to provide a callback method, which can be called when a message becomes available on the queue. Besides providing methods to send and receive messages, the `MessageQueue` class also provides methods to create, delete, and purge the message queues. These administrative methods are class-level methods and thus an instance does not need to be created before a queue can be created.

A `Message` object represents the actual message that is transported over the message queue. A message actually consists of a message body (which carries the payload) and a set of properties. The message body can contain any kind of data, be it text or binary, encrypted or not. There is an upper limit on the size of the message though, which is 4 megabytes, including the body and all the specified properties.

.NET Messaging requires the data to be serialized into any format allowed for transport and storage by the message queues. This is an intelligent design. It means that the data types that can be supported by the messaging system are really extensible because you can write your own serializers. In general, for sending messages, the formatters serialize data into the native queue format. On the receiving side, the formatter deserializes the data into the expected object.

The .NET messaging system initially provides three formatters, which cover almost all interesting cases. The first one and the default serializer, is `XmlMessageFormatter`. For sending messages, `XmlMessageFormatter` can serialize a System.Object into an XML string. The conversion of the data object into an Xml string follows the mapping that Microsoft has specified for various languages such as Visual Basic and C#. When `XmlMessageFormatter` is used to send a message, the content of the message body received is the XML. To properly deserialize this message, you provide the `TargetTypeNames` and `TargetTypes` so that the appropriate object data can be instantiated from the XML payload. Only one of these two needs to be specified. In either case, they tell the formatter which schema to use to create the target object with the XML data. If the data elements in the XML document do not match the schemas specified in the types, then the system throws an error. The use of `XmlMessageFormatter` achieves a loose coupling because it does not require the same type of object to be used on both sides as long as the data elements match each other.

The other available formatter is `BinaryMessageFormatter`, which can serialize or deserialize an entire graph of objects using binary format. Binary formatting is generally more efficient than XML formatting because it avoids the text-based processing for the XML document. The main disadvantage of this formatter is that it results in a tight coupling because the type of the object on the sender side has to be the same as on the receiver side. This in turn requires the sender to distribute the DLLs to the receiver containing the code for the objects being transported over the message queue.

5.2.4.7 Security

Although .NET supports various security features at the code level also, we are mostly interested in security at the application level. At the application level, .NET supports directly or indirectly all the required features and will be supporting more integrated security specifications for the Web services. ASP.NET supports all available security mechanisms, such as SSL, digests, and digital certificates.

- *Authentication.* .NET supports several options for securing Web service security of applications. The first form is windows based, where the supplied username and password are checked against the account of the windows authentication system. ASP.NET also supports certificate-based authentication, where digital certificates are obtained by a trusted third party and used for authentication. These digital certificates can also be optionally mapped to Windows accounts. XML Web services can also support custom authentication schemes by utilizing the *SOAP Header* to send the credentials to the XML Web service for authentication. Although not suitable for Web service applications, Web sites built with ASP.NET can also be secured by using the Microsoft authentication service called *Passport*.

- *Authorization.* The .NET Framework provides two mechanisms for authorization that are *File Authorization* and *URL Authorization*. File Authorization allows setting of permissions in IIS on a per-file basis and can be used in conjunction with Windows Authentication. URL authentication provides access support on a URL basis, including asmx files. In addition, custom authorization solutions can be provided in a manner completely independent of the transport protocol.

- *Code-access security.* The .NET Framework provides a security mechanism called code access security to help protect computer systems from malicious mobile code, to allow code from unknown origins to run safely, and to protect trusted code from intentionally or accidentally compromising security. Code access security allows code to be trusted to varying degrees, depending on where the code originates and on other aspects of the code's identity. Code access security also enforces the varying levels of trust on code, which improves security. Code access security can also help minimize the damage that can result from security vulnerabilities in your code.

- *Role-based security.* Applications can provide access to data or resources based on credentials supplied by the user. Typically, such applications check the role of a user and provide access to resources based on that role. The .NET CLR provides support for role-based authorization based on a Windows account or a custom identity. This is available in all .NET languages.

- *Cryptographic services.* Microsoft .NET supports advanced cryptographic capabilities such as private- and public-key encryption, digital signatures, hashed values, and secure random numbers. For example, this can be used to protect data by preventing the viewing or modification of messages.

- *Security_policy_management*: The .NET platform supports permissions for user objects and system objects. For example, explicit permissions are required to access files, perform a DNS lookup, or to access unsafe code. The .NET Framework allows all languages to request permissions either programmatically or declaratively (via metadata).

- *Directory support*: Microsoft .NET also provides directory services functions, such as directory lookups against LDAP-based systems, such as the Active Directory, and for other systems that support the Active Directory Services Interface.

5.2.4.8 Web Service Support

Microsoft .NET provides a very comprehensive support for Web services. First, there is built-in support in .NET-based languages for Web services. Figure 5.22 illustrates a C# source file that contains the source code for a Web service.

```
public class MyService : System.Web.Services.WebService
{

    [WebMethod]
    public void addAddress(string personName,Address address)
    {
    ...
    }

}
```

Figure 5.22. C# Source Code Class for a Web Service

Figure 5.22 shows a very simple and rather incomplete C# class that represents a Web service. Notice the [WebMethod] method attributes. .NET generates a WSDL document that describes a service interface containing all methods in the associated language files that have this attribute.

Within the Visual environment provided by Microsoft Visual Studio.NET, many features provide direct support for Web services. First, there are many templates for projects for building Web services. Within the environment, Web references can be created for other Web services so that they can be easily used. The environment also automatically generates test pages for testing Web services. Figure 5.23 shows the support provided for Web services in .NET.

The strongest support for Web services comes from the native support for XML in .NET. .NET provides built-in support for XML schema with complete data bindings defined for C# and VB#. Datasets in .NET can serialize their data in XML, and vice versa.

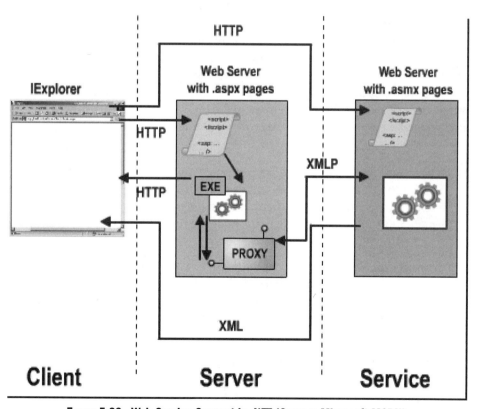

FIGURE 5.23. Web Service Support in .NET (Source: Microsoft MSDN)

5.3 PROGRAMMING LANGUAGES

There are many attributes of a language that are necessary to build orchestrated services. Although different kinds of applications impose different kinds of requirements on the language environment, we can examine those attributes of the languages that are important to building highly dynamic applications.

5.3.1 Important Attributes of Languages to Support BSO

As our discussion proceeds, it will become evident that many of these important language features are very easily handled by languages that are either interpretive or are compiled into intermediate byte code. On the other hand, most of these important features become very difficult for languages that are directly compiled into machine code, such C and C++.

5.3.1.1 Complete Object Model

Object-oriented programming took the software industry by storm in the early 1990s. As is usually the case with a new technology, initially there was a lot of hype and the proponents oversold to the skeptics. However, object-oriented programming has continued to impact design of language systems and systems architectures. All modern languages, or at least the popular ones, fully support object-oriented programming. We make the object-oriented features of programming languages a mandatory requirement for BSO. Let us define then what are the attributes of a programming language that make it object oriented:

- **Abstraction**. Abstraction is a fundamental way to deal with complexity. Abstraction focuses on the visible characteristics of a system. A well-abstracted system removes the need for the user of that system to look at its internal implementations. Programming languages deal with abstraction in many different ways. Section 5.3.1.2 deals with abstract interfaces in more detail.

- **Encapsulation**. Whereas abstraction focuses on an outside view of a system, encapsulation hides the internal details of the system from its users. Object-oriented programming languages provide encapsulation by providing the ability to make some methods, which are internal to the implementation, unavailable to the user of the code.

- **Inheritance**. Inheritance is a fundamental concept pioneered by object-oriented programming. It is the prime mechanism to enable reusability of object-oriented programs. It is also fundamental to the important late binding feature discussed in Section 5.3.1.3.

- **Polymorphism**. Polymorphism is again an invention of object-oriented programming and is related to inheritance. Polymorphism simply means that, in an object inheritance hierarchy, a derived type can be used anywhere that its base class is expected. This implies that polymorphism essentially requires all objects to derive from one superclass.

5.3.1.2 Abstract Interfaces

Programming is all about writing code to do certain tasks. If that task is a service provided by that code to whomever calls it, then the exposed API to that code becomes its public contract. Consider a class in any object-oriented language. This class has public methods that describe its exposed API. It also has many private methods that describe its private implementation. Abstract interfaces focus on capturing the public API (or public contract) of a class. This is an important capability because it completely separates a public contract from its implementation.

Once the contract has been captured in an abstract interface, a client can be written to this contract, completely independently of the implementation of that contract. Indeed, there can be many different implementations of a contract and we consider one example in the next section where abstract interfaces can be used to provide flexibility.

5.3.1.3 Late Binding and Dynamic Loading

Execution of a program generally is not linear. There are many paths a program may take, and each path may execute a different piece of code. Late binding and dynamic loading are two related concepts, which basically mean that the code to be executed is either loaded in or selected for execution based on runtime needs.

Dynamic loading has been available in language systems for a while. "C" on UNIX systems enabled dynamic loading through shared libraries and later Windows adopted it with dynamically linked libraries. It was a giant step forward because all of the code did not have to be linked in the executable program at compile time but could be loaded into the process memory as needed, resulting in much smaller size of executables.

Late binding was later used by C++ to enable polymorphism. Other early languages that supported late binding were Ada and Smalltalk. Our definition of late binding is slightly different from the typical definition used by the language designers. In their terms, late binding is where the names or variables are not known until runtime, where the actual type may be different from the apparent type. This is a very low-level definition for our purpose. So, we take it up a notch where late binding means that the code to be executed to accomplish certain tasks can be written independently of the caller code and may be changed at will.

In modern systems, late binding allows fairly complex and configurable systems. Consider a service that collects metrics about other services running in its managed environment, so that it can perform load balancing. This is a pretty common need of large programming systems, where large numbers of transactions have to be processed and a large number of users have to be supported. To make matters worse, the load patterns are uneven so that you cannot permanently allocate resources. This service may perform some simple cost-based load balancing, starting new services as needed. However, a customer may want to plug in some more sophisticated algorithms for load balancing. The dynamic-loading or late-binding feature of the language system, combined with abstract interfaces, will allow this kind of scenario. The load-balancing service may be written to dynamically load some other classes that implement some predefined abstract interfaces. The prepackaged load balancing service may be provided information about the code that will implement those abstract interfaces, to be loaded through some configuration mechanism, and it would happily load it when the time comes for it.

5.3.1.4 Introspection

Any programming system, be it a language or a framework, has metadata that describe the structure of entities within that system. The concept of metadata was quite weak in older compiled languages, such as C and C++. For the most part, once the compiler had finished compiling the source code, all the type information was lost. Since some form of metadata is essential to enable object-oriented features such as polymorphism, compilers such as C++ played great tricks to save some type of meta information to enable those features.

As language designers have realized the power of metadata and processor speeds have become fast enough to overcome inherent overheads of byte-compiled languages such as Java and C#, the notion of metadata has become very strong. Reflection is the ability of a language system to make its type system metadata to the programmer at runtime. Byte-compiled languages usually compile the metadata into the generated source code. At runtime, when the byte-code execution environment loads this compiled code, it first reads the metadata and then internally uses metadata to execute the code.

Reflection is not only important for programming languages. OMG's CORBA was one of the early distributed architectures to fully enable reflection. Since CORBA is not a language system but, rather, distributed architecture, it enabled reflection through its interface repository. Interfaces in CORBA are described in its IDL. As IDL compilers compile these interfaces, they also populate the interface repository with the metadata. CORBA-based services can later query this interface repository to get all the available metadata.

This technique of using a repository to save metadata is also used by many BSO systems. The metadata in which they are interested goes beyond the language systems and usually pertains to the business services that they integrate or invoke.

A description language, such as IDL or WSDL, contains all the metadata that are required to describe a service. Standards for business services tend to store the description document itself in the business registry. The runtime can then parse these description documents and make use of the metadata as appropriate.

5.3.1.5 Garbage Collection

Garbage collection is the ability of a language system to clean up after itself. In any complex systems, during the course of its execution, a large number of objects may be created. Not all of these objects are needed all the time. However, it can be programmatically quite difficult to keep track of the objects that are being used and remove the ones that are no longer needed.

Garbage collection is very hard for compiled systems to perform and the burden is entirely on the programmer. As a result, when a large number of objects are created and then are no longer needed, a lot of memory is wasted. However, byte-compiled and interpretive languages can handle this task very well. This is probably the single biggest improvement that Java language brought to the C++ developers.

Garbage collection is more important for orchestrated services because they do not run for a short period of time and then exit. A typical orchestrated service manages long-running transactions and hence may run for hours or days or weeks. In this course, it may create hundreds or thousands of objects. Not having to deal with reclaiming memory associated with objects no longer needed vastly simplifies the user code for these systems.

Garbage collection is implemented differently across different language environments. Recent optimizations in this area, such as the multibin garbage-collection strategy used by .NET, can make performance very good.

5.3.2 Java

Java language enjoys the status of one of the most used programming languages in the world. From the beginning, Java came with a lot of additional classes, such as networking packages. For this reason, early on, there was a lot of confusion about the language. Some considered it a very powerful programming language whereas other considered it a distributed architecture. In the early days, comparison of Java with CORBA was a favorite topic at various technical conferences. Over the time period, the language has matured a lot and its context has been cleared also. CORBA programmers are no longer defending CORBA against Java but are happily using Java to write CORBA services. Meanwhile, J2EE has emerged as the component architecture more native to the Java language.

The biggest reason for the slow initial reception for Java for IT applications was its speed. Java source code is compiled into byte code by a Java compiler. This compiled code is then executed into a process called Java virtual machine

(JVM). Although this execution of intermediate code slows the execution down, it is also the reason for many of the rich features that the language has. As the performance of JVMs have improved, processor speeds have increased, and memory has become cheaper, the execution speed of Java has become a nonissue for most applications.

5.3.2.1 Portability

The big promise of Java was *write once, use anywhere*. This had a lot of promise because its immediate predecessor, C++, was not very portable and, because it was a compiled language, it could not be run anywhere. Portability is important because, today, software vendors deliver applications for many different platforms. It is simply not cost effective for them to have to maintain different versions for different platforms.

Java is a byte-compiled language. That means that a Java compiler compiles the source code into an intermediate byte code. This byte code is independent of the platforms. At runtime, a JVM executes this byte code. All the platform-specific services are provided to the compiled code by the JVM. SUN Microsystems and a handful of other companies provide the JVM for each specific platform.

5.3.2.2 Interfaces

Java provides strong support for separating an object's contract from its implementation. C++ did not have this clear separation. Sure, you could have classes that were completely abstract, but Java gives first-class status to interfaces. A Java interface can be used only to declare methods. The interface cannot have attributes or any kind of implementation.

Interfaces in Java are the primary means of abstraction. Interfaces can inherit from other interfaces. Java learned quite a few lessons from C++. Although multiple inheritance in C++ was much praised, in reality it proved of little use. Multiple inheritance in C++ resulted in more problems and issues with ambiguities than it had benefits and, as a result, the programmers did not use it as extensively as first anticipated. Learning from C++, Java allows multiple inheritance of interfaces but not of implementation. So, although interfaces can inherit from multiple interfaces, a concrete class cannot. A concrete class actually can only singly inherit from other concrete classes. However, it can implement multiple interfaces. Figure 5.24 shows how Java interfaces can be used. `OutputHandler` is an interface that is implemented by the class `DatabaseHandler`.

5.3.2.3 Introspection

Introspection is supported in Java through its reflection API, which is a small but powerful API to construct new classes, access and modify fields in objects and classes, and invoke methods. Every type in Java is an object and has reflective information available for it.

```
Public interface OutputHandler
{
    void initialize(Hashtable props) throws RemoteException;
    void process_data(Object data) throws RemoteException;
    void shut_down() throws RemoteException;
}

public class DatabaseHandler implements OutputHandler
{
    private String jdbcDriverClass_ = null;
    private String jdbcProtocol_ = null;
    private String jdbcSubprotocol_ = null;
    private String jdbcDataSource_ = null;
    private String username_ = null;
    private String password_ = null;
    private Connection  connection_ = null;

    public void initialize(Hashtable props) throws
        RemoteException
    {
// open data base here
    }

    public void process_data(Object data) throws
        RemoteException
    {
// write the data out to the database
    }

    public void shut_down() throws RemoteException
    {
    }

//////////////// Other private methods ////////////////
    private void open_connection()
    {
    }

    private void close_connection()
    {
    }
}
```

FIGURE 5.24. Use of Interfaces in Java

There are three core classes in the reflection API: Field, Method, and Constructor. These are core classes that cannot be further specialized and, furthermore, only the JVM may create instances of these classes. These classes are used to get reflective information about the underlying objects, get and set their values, create new instances, and invoke methods. Additionally, there are methods in the class Class that can be used to create new instances of Field, Method, and Constructor. There is also the class Array, which provides methods to create and access Java arrays.

```
Class c = Ingeter.class;
Method [] methods = c.getMethods();
For ( int I = 0; I < methods.length; I++ ){
   Method method = methods[I];
   System.out.println("Method name: " + method.getName();
   System.out.println("Return type: " + method.getReturnType();
   Class [] parmTypes = method.getParameterTypes();
   For ( int pi = 0; pi < parmTypes.length; pi++ ){
   System.out.println("Parameter type: " +
        parmTypes[I].getName();
   }
}
```

FIGURE 5.25. Using Reflection to Get Method Metadata

Reflection in Java is most helpful in doing useful things with classes that are not necessarily known at compile time. Reflection allows you to determine the class of an object, whether an object is actually a class or an interface, its superclass (the class it extends), and the interfaces that a class implements. It allows a client to query a class for its methods and their signatures and allows the dynamic invocation of those methods.

Let us consider an example of a process engine that needs to execute a user-provided class to perform the actions when a transition fires. Let us assume that, through a graphical user interface (GUI), the user provides the class name and the method name and its signatures to the process engine. In fact, the GUI interacts with the user and as soon as the user provides the class path, it presents a list of methods available in that class. The user can then select a method and map its required parameters to the process instance variables. The execution engine may then save that information. At runtime, the execution engine may then retrieve this mapping, construct an instance of this class, and, using the process instance variables, invoke the required methods.

Figure 5.25 shows how to get metadata about a given class. Given any class name, its class object can be obtained by calling the static method on Class object `Class.forName(String className)`. An instance of the class object holds all the metadata about that class and acts as the factory for the core reflection classes.

Invoking a method requires obtaining an instance of the class `Method` and then invoking it with the required parameters. First, the class has to be queried for the desired method. Calling `Class.getMethod` and passing it the method name and its signatures do this. Once the method has been obtained, it can be invoked. If it is an instance method, then invoking it requires a target object to be passed to it. Otherwise, for a static object, null is passed for a target object. The parameters to the method have to be in the proper order, as declared in the class declaration; otherwise, the query and the invocation will fail.

```
Public Object invokeStaticMethod(String className,String methodName, object
[] parms)
{
   try{
      Class [] parmTypes = null;
    If ( parms != null ){
      ParmTypes = new Class[parms.length];
      For ( int I = 0; I < parmTypes.length; I++ ){
         ParmTypes[I] = parms[I].getClass();
      }
   }
   Class c = Class.forName(className);
   Method method = c.getMethod(methodName,parmTypes);
     Return method.invoke(null,parms);
   }
   catch(Exception e){
      System.err.println("Error: } + e.getMessage();
      Return null;
   }
}
```

FIGURE 5.26. Method Invocation Using Reflection

Figure 5.26 shows a Java method that can be used to invoke a method on an object and provide its return value.

5.3.2.4 *Dynamic Loading*

Dynamic loading is the capability of loading in code as needed. This capability is closely related to reflection and, in fact, the ability to load new code and create instances of code during the runtime are part of the reflection API.

Java allows instantiation of a class instance in pretty much the same manner as method invocation. A short way is provided to create an object with its default constructor. An object instance with nondefault constructor is created by querying the class for the constructor with the right signatures, just like a method, and then invoking a method on that.

In Figure 5.27, if the provided parameters are null, it is assumed that the default constructor needs to be invoked. In that case, we simply execute the `newInstance` method on Class itself. However, if some parameters are provided, then we first build up an array that contains the types of the expected arguments in the correct order and then retrieve the `Constructor` object and invoke the `newInstance` method on it, passing to it the provided parameter values.

In the preceding section, we described a scenario for a business process execution engine that needs to execute some user code at runtime. For all nonstatic methods, the methods are invoked on an object instance and hence the object has to be created. We are calling this ability of the execution engine dynamic loading because it loads the class at runtime when it needs it. Strictly speaking, Java uses dynamic loading all the time. For classes whose types are known at compile time,

```
Public Object createInstance(String className,Object [] parms)
{
   try{
   Class c = Class.forName(className);
   If ( parms == null ) // use default constructor
     Return c.newInstance();
   Else{
     Class [] parmTypes = new Class[parms.length];
     For ( int I = 0; I < parmTypes.length; I++ )
       ParmTypes[I] = parms[I].getClass();
     Constructor ctor = c.getConstructor(parmTypes);
     Return ctor.newInstance(parms);
   }
   }
   catch(Exception e){
   return null;
   }
}
```

FIGURE 5.27. Creating a New Object.

the JVM uses its internal class loader to load classes in its memory and to create object instances as needed.

5.3.2.5 Garbage Collection

As described earlier, garbage collection is the ability of a language system to reclaim unused objects. When an object is no longer referenced in a JVM, it is considered unused and is marked for garbage collection. Java supports garbage collection in single JVM. For example, if a variable references an object and that variable goes out of scope, then that object is no longer referenced. Internally, the JVM maintains a reference count of objects and the object is considered unused only after that reference count goes to zero. An object also can be explicitly marked for garbage collection by setting it to null.

When an object is no longer referenced, it is not immediately dropped. It is simply marked as eligible for garbage collection. The JVM usually has a spread thread that runs a garbage collector. This garbage collector runs automatically, at frequent intervals. Under some situations, the program can explicitly try to invoke the garbage collector by executing the static method System.gc().

Before the garbage collector reclaims the memory associated with an object, it gives the object a final chance to clean up after itself by calling its finalize method. If the object is holding any valuable resources such as open file handles, finalize is a good place to clean up those kinds of resources.

5.3.3 C#

Pronounced C-Sharp, C# holds a lot of promise for the .NET platform. On the surface, C# is very similar to Java: Both are based heavily on a simplified form of C++ with garbage collection, and the syntax between the two languages is very similar. However, there are some innovative new semantics, such as first-class component support, versioning, XML-based documentation, and attributes within C#.

Like Java, C# is also compiled into an intermediate language. Just like JVM, the C# byte code runs in Microsoft's CLR. Microsoft has actually made the CLR the common environment for over twenty-five languages, including Visual Basic.NET, Jscript.NET, and Managed C++. CLR also supports languages from other vendors, such as Fujitsu Cobol.NET, Fortran.NET, Eiffel, and Smalltalk. One important difference between CLR and the JVM is that CLR precompiles the intermediate code and executes native machine code, as opposed to interpreting byte code.

.NET defines a unified-type system called the *common type system (CTS)* which not only defines the types that all compliant languages need to implement but also defines the rules that are followed by CLR with regard to how the applications declare and use those types. One of the important benefits of CTS is that all the compliant languages easily share data with each other without any need for type conversion. Parts of a large .NET project can be implemented in C# and others in VB. Each one can then be packaged into separate assemblies and can freely cross-reference each other without any problems.

In CTS, everything is an object. There is really no difference between primitive data types, such as integer or float, and those types that are implemented by users using classes. Treating all types (intrinsic or user-defined) in a consistent manner avoids the problems that arise when separate classes are required to hold intrinsic values. Since all types derive from the common root class `System.Object`, it becomes easier to inherit from primitive types and enable polymorphism across specializations of primitive types.

CTS defines two categories of types: *value* and *reference*. A variable of a value type contains actual data. These variables are always passed by value and an assignment of a value to such a variable actually results in the value being moved into the memory allocated for the variable. C# defines several value types, including enumerators, structures, and primitive types. Reference types, on the other hand, are type-safe pointers to areas of memory. When you declare a variable of a reference type and allocate memory for it, you are just allocating memory big enough to hold the pointer. The value itself is stored in a different memory location and the value of the variable points to the address of the memory location. C# defines several reference types, such as classes, arrays, delegates, and interfaces.

References in C# are type-safe, and direct access to pointers is almost never allowed. There is an option to use C-style pointers in C#, but this requires that the developer explicitly embed the pointer code within an "unsafe" token. Unsafe code, since it might use pointers, cannot be executed without very specific, high-level security access. That is, code downloaded from the Internet normally would not be able to run unsafe code, unless this was explicitly enabled by administrators for some reason (not recommended).

Having the option of support, unsafe code provides the ability for C# to easily take advantage of existing software written in C or C++ if this option is required.

5.3.3.1 Interfaces

C# supports interfaces in a manner similar to Java. Interfaces can be used to define behavioral characteristics of design entities. Language classes can then implement those interfaces by providing the actual code for that behavior. Like Java, C# does not allow multiple implementation inheritances of classes. However, a C# class can implement multiple interfaces.

A class that implements an interface is required to implement all its methods in order to become a concrete class. The interfaces themselves can derive from other interfaces. This is a useful mechanism for combining several interfaces to produce interfaces with richer functionality.

Since C# does support multiple interface inheritance and metadata via attributes, some advanced runtime techniques can be employed to "inject" or "attach" implementation code prior to execution. This is an interesting option, although an advanced one.

5.3.3.2 Introspection

C# provides powerful support for metadata and reflection. When a C# compiler compiles the code, it also compiles metadata into the executable, which is then available to the runtime environment. The applications can then discover these metadata at runtime.

Reflection in C# is provided through the `System.Reflection` namespace. The key class in the namespace is called `Type`. Any class instance can be asked to provide its type or, alternatively, `Type` also has a static method to get a type by name. The `Type` has many methods to get information about a class, its methods, and its inheritance hierarchy. Figure 5.28 illustrates how an instance of a class can be dynamically created and methods on it be invoked.

The class `Activator` is used to create instances of types. If an object has a default constructor, then the `Activator.CreateInstance` can be created. Otherwise, a constructor can be invoked to create an instance. Once an instance has been created, methods can be invoked by first obtaining information about instance methods and then invoking them. It is not necessary to have a target object to invoke a static method.

5.3.3.3 Attributes

C# provides the very powerful feature of annotating a class with metadata that can be queried by the class implementation later at runtime. Typically, this is

```
public class TestClass
{
   public TestClass()
   {
   }

   public void display(String message)

   {
      Console.WriteLine("Message: " + message);
   }

   public static test()
   {
      // get the type information
      Type t = Type.GetType("CSharpCosoleApp.TestClass");

      // create an instance of the object
      Object obj = Activator.CreateInstance(t);

      // get the method information
      MethodInfo info = t.GetMethod("display");

         // construct its parameters and invoke method
      Object [] parms = new Object[1];
      parms[0] = "method invocation test";
      info.Invoke(obj,parms);
   }
}
```

FIGURE 5.28. Dynamic Creation and Invocation of a Class

design-time information that is essentially an integral part of the class itself. The mechanism is quite generic and the class designer can use it for other things as well, such as runtime information.

Figure 5.29 illustrates an attribute being declared at the class level. The name of the attribute is ObjectPooling and it has three fields associated with it. The first field is Enabled and has the value of true. The second field is Min-PoolSize with a value of 2 and the third is MaxPoolSize with a value of 10. The designer also implements a class that represents that attribute and derives from the System.Attribute class. This then becomes class-level meta

```
Using Microsoft.EnterpriseServices;

[ObjectPooling(Enabled=true,MinPoolSize=2,MaxPoolSize=10)
]

Public class MyScalableClass : ServicedComponent{
}
```

FIGURE 5.29. Example of an Attribute Declaration

information, and each instance of the class created has that meta information because an instance of the attribute object is also created. Each class then can use C#'s reflection API to query the presence of these attributes and obtain the corresponding instance.

These attributes are not just limited to class level. In fact, the attributes can also be attached to fields and methods in the class. This gives a fine level of granularity in terms of attaching metadata to the constructor to which they relate.

5.3.3.4 Explicit Interface Implementation

C# allows a class to inherit from a single base class, and it allows multiple interfaces. Sometimes there are namespace collisions between interfaces and/or classes. To avoid these collisions, C# supports implementing multiple versions of the colliding methods by using explicit interface implementations. For example, instead of simply defining `Save()` as a method, one could implement `IFlightInfo.Save()`. This might be useful if there are multiple `Save()` methods defined in the class hierarchy.

5.3.3.5 Value Types and Boxing

In languages such as Java, there are classes and primitive types. For performance reasons, classes are always created on the heap and primitive types are created on the stack Primitive types in Java do not derive from any base class – they are defined in the language as primitives.

In C#, all types derive from `System.Object`, and are considered objects. However, for performance reasons, there are a number of low-level data types that are *implemented* as stack-based primitive types, but that *appear* to be objects. This happens through the magic of a compiler technique called boxing and unboxing. For example, the literal constant "5" can be considered a number, but it is also an object. One could write "5.ToString()," calling a method against it. This works, system treats everything as an object, but it does not slow down performance since certain types are implemented as value types on the stack.

In C#, there is a keyword called `Struct` that allows one to create new data types that are stored on the stack, but that also derive from `System.Object`. This might be useful if there are certain common data objects that one does not want to store on the heap. Storing objects on the heap requires garbage collection, and might incur unwanted performance costs. `Structs` are can be used to dramatically improve performance in some scenarios.

5.3.3.6 Enumerations

C# supports explicit enumerations of user-defined constants. Code that interacts with enumerations must explicitly use the enumeration elements. Examples of enumerations are red, green, and blue.

5.3.3.7 Delegates

Delegates are a way of supporting generic callbacks within C#. These are similar to function pointers in C++, except they are more like "function references." Delegates can be useful in certain design patterns that invoke a particular method, regardless of the class that implemented it. That is, whereas certain polymorphic behaviors are implemented via inheritance at a class level, delegates support polymorphism at a method signature level.

5.3.3.8 Events

Events are a native semantic in C#. They are constructs that manage references to zero or more delegates that have registered with them. When an object registers an event with another object by passing it a delegate, it essentially provides it with a callback mechanism. Later, when the event is fired, every delegate will be called on each object that registered. This can be a single event, or multiple events. Events are quite useful in advanced design patterns and in GUIs.

5.3.3.9 Deterministic Object Cleanup

C# allows total control over object lifetimes while still supporting a garbage-collection environment. This is accomplished by implementing the System. IDisposable interface. The garbage collector will call the Dispose() method whenever an object is destroyed. Alternatively, objects can call Dispose() themselves to control the lifetime of their referenced objects. Sometimes destroying an object is required to ensure that no resources are being held, such as database connections.

5.3.3.10 Properties

Properties are a technique in C# to simplify access to member fields of a class, while maintaining strict control over this access. Certain fields, such as Salary within an Employee class, for example, might be delicate. Such fields are often marked as Protected or Private. Instead of implementing accessors and mutators for such fields, getSalary() and setSalary(), properties can be used to simplify this syntax.

In the example in Figure 5.30, a property called Salary is defined. To call the property, an object would simply specify employee.Salary. If the value is

```
private double salary;
public Salary

{
    get { if (return salary; }
    set { salary = value; }
}
```

FIGURE 5.30. Defining Properties in C#

```
class Listbox
{
   private object[] items;
   public object this[int element]
   {
      get { return items[element]; }
      set { items[element] = value; }
   }
}
```

FIGURE 5.31. Example of Indexers in C#

being accessed, the "get" method for Salary is automatically called, and while it is being modified, the "set" method is called. Thus, the property appears to be an accessible field of the class, but it is actually a controlled access to a private property.

5.3.3.11 Indexers
Indexers are a special syntax for overloading the [] operator for a class. Figure 5.31 shows an example of indexers in C#.

Given an object list of type ListBox, one could simply refer to list[3] as the fourth element of the private-items field. Again, this simplifies the programming model.

5.4 BUSINESS SERVICES RELATED

5.4.1 XML
XML has evolved into a highly flexible language for describing data. Although XML is extremely powerful and can be used for variety of purposes, its main usage of interest to us is its ability to describe any kind of complex data. The structure of the data being described in an XML document can be defined in a schema definition language called XML Schema that has been adopted by W3C. XML Schema defines the structure of the data in the XML document so that the data can be validated against the schema for correctness. The actual XML document that carries the data conforming to the schema is also referred to as an instance document.

Defining the structure of an XML document has several benefits. First, it allows the developers to express the metadata about the document content. XML itself is a text-based language, so all data that occurs as either attribute values of element values appear as strings.

Figure 5.32 is an example of simple data that describe a bank account. This data structure has only two elements: an accountNumber and a balance. As

```
<account>
  <accountNumber>xyz</accountNumber>
  <balance>12345.67</balance>
</account>
```

FIGURE 5.32. Simple XML Document Fragment

is obvious, both the accountNumber and the balance are string values. A receiving program will have no idea whether to treat the balance as a string, an integer, a float, or a double. The XML Schema fragment shown in Figure 5.33 provides the metadata required to correctly interpret the data in an instance document. For example, this XML schema fragment describes the account having the two elements as accountNumber and balance. Furthermore, it says that the accountNumber is a string and the balance is a double. Each of them is a mandatory element (with min and max occurrences of 1). XML Schema also provides advanced features, such as specializing data structures, by adding elements to them and either restricting them or enhancing them is various ways. Having the constraint system specified so rigorously in an XML Schema document allows parsers to ensure that a received document is a valid document. A validating parser can ensure that the document obeys all the constraints specified in the schema. For example, such a parser will flag an error if the instance document contains an account structure that does not have the balance in its data or has multiple occurrences of it.

There are a couple of other XML-related technologies that are worth mentioning here. The first is *XPath*. XPath defines a mechanism to address parts of an XML document. It provides syntax, using the path notation as in URLs, for navigating through the hierarchy of an XML document. The evaluation of an Xpath expression begins with respect to a context node, which is an XML node, and results in another XML node. By default, the XPath expression navigates in the forward direction, to the child elements. However, a different direction can be specified to navigate backward.

The second important related specification is XML Stylesheet Language (XSL). XSL is is broken down into two parts: XSLT, which is a language to transform

```
<complexType name="account">
   <sequence>
      <element minOccurs="1" maxOccurs="1"
               name="accountNumber" type="string"/>
      <element minOccurr="1" maxOccurs=1
               name="balance" type="double"/>
   </sequence>
</complexType>
```

FIGURE 5.33. XML Schema Fragment

XML documents, and XSL-FO for formatting XML documents. We discuss XSLT here because it is by far the most used specification in the XSL set. XSLT is used to convert a document from one format to another and is most often used either to transform one XML document into another XML document or to transform an XML document to an HTML document. XSLT is based on a hierarchical tree structure of data. XSLT uses XPath expressions to match patterns within an XML document and to apply formatting to those data. XSLT provides syntax for many common operators, such as conditions, copying of document tree fragments, advanced pattern matching, and the ability to access elements within the input XML data in a content source tree.

A major use of XSLT is in application to application integration scenario. As applications are integrated using Web services, the data that are exchanged between them are in the form of XML documents. Very often, although the data elements represent similar concepts, the exact structure of the data varies between applications. For example, two applications being integrated may have the notion of customer with a home address, but one may express the address as one string element whereas the other might represent the address as a separate element with its own subelements. As data are exchanged between these two applications in the form of XML documents, XSLT can be used to automatically transform data from one application to the form expected by the other.

Although it started out as a mechanism that most applications used directly, the use of XML has now shifted to the development tools. Very few application programs now produce and consume XML documents themselves. For example, SOAP uses XML to package application data and exchanges it between peers. WSDL is another technology that uses XML, to describe the interfaces of these services. Now there are tools available in almost all major programming languages that can generate the appropriate data structures in a programming language of choice based on WSDL. With this kind of tool support, a Java program actually will not use XML itself but rather will use the proxy stubs that can be generated from the WSDL. This way, that Java program leverages the familiar and powerful programming model of Java language while taking full benefit of the underlying XML-based technologies.

5.4.2 SOAP

Integration between applications has always been a complex and expensive problem to solve. Various applications use various communication and application-level protocols. To access a service-oriented application, which exposes an API for interacting with it, the problem has always been how to communicate with it. For example, if an application is based on CORBA, then the client is required to have client-side libraries for a ORB implementation, and one also has to deal with interoperability issues. If the service is an EJB-based application, then, again, the client side requires an EJB-compliant client-side infrastructure. Alternatively, the service could be a DCOM-based service, which would limit the accessibility to Windows platforms and also may require expensive client-side infrastructure.

SOAP solves this problem of simple application-to-application integration in an inexpensive and easy manner. HTTP and XML have become ubiquitous technologies. SOAP leverages these two technologies in a very effective manner. However, SOAP is not limited to HTTP. SOAP mappings are easy to develop for SMTP, IIOP, and other messaging protocols such as JMS. If a service supports SOAP, then a client can be written in a very inexpensive manner to invoke methods on that service. SOAP specification is an open and public specification and there are several dozen SOAP implementations. XML has become the desired way of describing data. All the client requires is a client SOAP implementation. There are implementations of SOAP in every programming language. History tells us that no solution lasts an eternity. When CORBA came along, it seemed to be all that was needed. However, although CORBA has been a good choice for integration inside an enterprise, it has been ineffective for computing between business partners. Besides, its scope has continuously increased, making it more and more complex. HTTP has survived the test of time and scalability and SOAP leverages HTTP very well. As we shall see, an important design goal of SOAP has been to support extensibility rather than to specify all present and future requirements. Whereas IIOP has specified how transactions should be propagated, SOAP has deferred that as an extensibility mechanism. This means that, later, when new transaction mechanisms are invented, they can be built on top of SOAP without modifying the core SOAP standard. This is an important design goal which will ensure the longevity of the specification.

SOAP is a protocol that specifies how XML can be used to exchange structured data between two peers. SOAP is a stateless paradigm for exchanging one-way messages. However, it can be used to create more complex message exchange patterns, such as request-response. SOAP does not attempt to address any application-level semantics, such as transaction, security context propagation, or reliable data delivery. Instead, it provides a core set of functionality required to communicate application-specific information in an extensible manner.

The main SOAP construct is a SOAP envelope. A SOAP envelope usually appears inside a transport envelope such as an HTTP header. Figure 5.34 illustrates the structure of a SOAP message. A SOAP envelope consists of an optional header and a body element. When present, the header element appears before the body.

A SOAP header is the main extensibility mechanism that SOAP provides. The elements that appear inside a SOAP header are called SOAP header blocks. A SOAP header is processed by a SOAP processor. The SOAP header anticipates various usages of SOAP protocol and provides various constructs that give hints to the SOAP processor about what to do with a particular header element. For example,

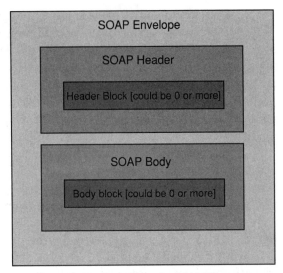

FIGURE 5.34. Structure of a SOAP Message

a SOAP header block may have a Boolean attribute mustUnderstand. If this attribute has the value true, then a receiving SOAP processor must be able to process this header element and, if it cannot, then it should throw an exception. The SOAP block can also be targeted toward specific SOAP processors through the actor attribute. An example of the use of a SOAP header to provide more capabilities might be transaction processing. A set of cooperating applications may include a header block that carries the transaction context. Through use of the mustUnderstand attribute, a SOAP processor can be forced to either properly process the header information of transaction or throw an exception. This means that the semantics of the header blocks have to be understood by the peer SOAP processors. A transactional client, which starts a transaction, has to be able to provide the related transaction context while making the call and a receiving transactional application has to be able to properly that transactional context.

Once all the blocks in a SOAP header have been processed, the SOAP body is processed. The SOAP body carries the application-specific content of the message. By far, most uses of SOAP enable method invocation on a remote service. A SOAP processor may choose various ways of passing this application-specific content of the message to the application itself. For example, the Apache Axis and Sun's JAX-RPC will invoke methods on the target Java classes and pass them the content of the message in the form of parameters to a method. The method name and the parameters are encoded in the SOAP body elements according to well-defined rules. SOAP refers to them as encoding rules. In general, to invoke a remote method, a target method has to be identified and its parameters have to be included in the request as defined by the signatures of the remote method. A response to that method invocation would carry the data returned by the method. SOAP does not provide an IDL, but WSDL (discussed in detail in the next section) serves that role well.

During the course of processing a SOAP message, a SOAP processor may need to generate a fault. A SOAP fault is a SOAP message with a standardized body block. The fault contains a mandatory fault code, a mandatory fault string, and any optional details of the fault. The fault code identifies a fault. The fault string provides a human-readable explanation of the fault. An optional fault actor provides information about the generator of the fault. The optional detail element carries application-specific error information. If the SOAP fault was generated because the contents of the SOAP body could not be processed successfully, then the detail element must be present. It is optional if the fault was generated during processing of the header.

SOAP itself is not about transport. It defines the packaging scheme, encoding rules, and a processing model for header and body elements. To transport messages between peers, it assumes that transport protocols such as HTTP are used. SOAP specification defines the HTTP binding. This binding is not mandatory but it is most useful. When SOAP is used over HTTP, the SOAP envelope appears inside an HTTP message. Transport bindings are not important only for providing a way to manage connections and for sending and receiving data over network connections. Some styles of messaging may also depend upon the transport binding. For example, a synchronous request-response RPC style of interaction requires a request to be made and for the caller to block until a response is received. If this style is implemented over a connectionless network protocol, then the corresponding SOAP implementations would have to use a header to first provide message IDs for correlation purposes. Then, the caller would have to somehow block until a response with the appropriate `messageId` that matches the `messageId` of the request is received before it unblocks. However, when SOAP maps onto HTTP, this becomes very easy to implement without having any additional header entries or without the caller having to block, because HTTP does all of that for you. For this reason, SOAP designers have chosen not to standardize any such header blocks necessary to implement messaging interaction patterns, with the view that they may be specified, on an as-needed basis, by the normative specification of the transport bindings.

5.4.3 Service Description Languages

As Internet-based e-commerce has grown, more and more Web services are being created by companies and are being made available for others to use. However, to make that really happen, the Web services' capabilities have to be described in a standard form so that other computer systems can understand their capabilities. These capabilities of any system, whether it is a Web service, a CORBA system, or a Java program, represent the contract by which the service is bound. Keep in mind, however, that this does not apply to orchestrated services. The orchestrated business services do not provide discrete and atomic services. Their contract is not simply the operations that can be invoked on them, but also a time-variant sequencing of those method invocations. The services and contracts we discuss here apply to basic services that provide discrete and atomic functionality.

Probably, the two earliest description languages were the IDL from OMG, called CORBA IDL, and the IDL from Microsoft, called MIDL. The common characteristic about these early IDLs was that they were not programming languages and could be used only for declaring interfaces. Java language did away with a separate IDL. The EJB platforms utilized Java interfaces to describe the contract of the EJBs. There were two common shortcomings of those IDLs:

1. They were all technology specific. MIDL was specific to Microsoft COM; IDL was specific to the IIOIP protocol. The addressing schemes and the type systems of the target environments were embedded into the definition language. Therefore, it was not possible to use OMG IDL with COM or vice versa, or to use IDL to describe an HTTP-based Web service. It is not possible to express in IDL, the technology-specific details that might be required to invoke a service over SOAP or SMTP or any other protocol. Those details are implicit and are only for IIOP. Since IIOP or DCOM are unsuitable for e-commerce, this made CORBA IDL and MIDL ineffective tools for Web services expression.
2. The description languages were not extensible. It was anticipated that as the corresponding technology matured, new versions of the IDL would reflect the technology changes. Because the type systems were tied to a component model, the type system could not be independently extended. IDL uses OMA's type system and new type systems cannot be expressed in IDL.

IBM and Microsoft jointly developed WSDL and then submitted it to W3C for adoption consideration. Although WSDL has its own shortcomings, it is a giant step forward in providing a technology-independent and extensible description language. The rest of this section discusses WSDL.

WSDL allows clients to create Web services, describe those Web services in WSDL and then register those Web services in some form of business registry, whether it is a public registry or a private one. In either case, the presence of a WSDL document describing those Web services allows others (human or computer) to understand the interfaces supported by those services.

WSDL is technology independent. Its only dependency is on XML Scheme specification. WSDL has two logical sections. The first section describes, in abstract terms, the type systems and the messages to which a service may be able to respond. The second section is specific to technology and adds more concrete details to the abstract sections so that the underlying technology can be used to invoke the service. The technology-specific section is very extensible, and providers of new technologies can offer additional extensibility elements to capture the required details. This ensures that, as the technology changes and new protocols are invented, WSDL will be able to adapt to them without making the standard obsolete.

WSDL reduces the complexity of the applications that use Web services. Without a standard way of describing those Web services, the client has to be programmed to understand a variety of vendor-specific description formats or the applications have to be hard-coded for the particular Web service. This, then, makes it difficult to shop for services, and so, it is difficult to write an application that shops for a certain category of service and then uses it. This has given rise to electronic marketplaces that offer comprehensive facilities to bond consumers and buyers. WSDL reduces the entry bar by allowing the suppliers to describe their services in a standard way, register them in a registry such as UDDI, and be discovered. Of course, this is not enough. To make this dream really come true, specific WSDL templates have to be created for specific industries so that the abstract definitions of all order processing services are similar, to facilitate browsing, searching, and navigating those services. However, it is a giant first step.

A WSDL document describes a Web service. A service definition can be split into multiple files. The other related files can then be imported using the WSDL import command. The outermost element of a WSDL document is always `definitions`. WSDL follows the XML Schema syntax and, in fact, is completely described itself by an XML Schema document. Figure 5.35 illustrates the structure of a WSDL document in block diagram.

A WSDL document contains the definitions in a distinct namespace. The namespace is specified either in the `targetNamespace` part of the `definitions` element or assigned through the `import` statement. Following the XSD rules, all `import` statements should appear as the first elements in the definitions section, before other WSDL constructs appear. The use of `import` allows various elements of service definition to be split into multiple files. A typical split is to provide the `types` definition in one file, the `message` and `portType` definitions in another, and the `binding` and `service` definitions in a third file. Once the other related WSDL or XSD documents have been imported, the remainder of the WSDL constructs can appear. These constructs are described in more detail in the sections that follow.

5.4.3.1 Type System

In this section, new data types are defined using some type system such as XSD. These types are used to describe the messages exchanged. WSDL uses XSD as the intrinsic type system. The XSD type system can be used to provide type definitions

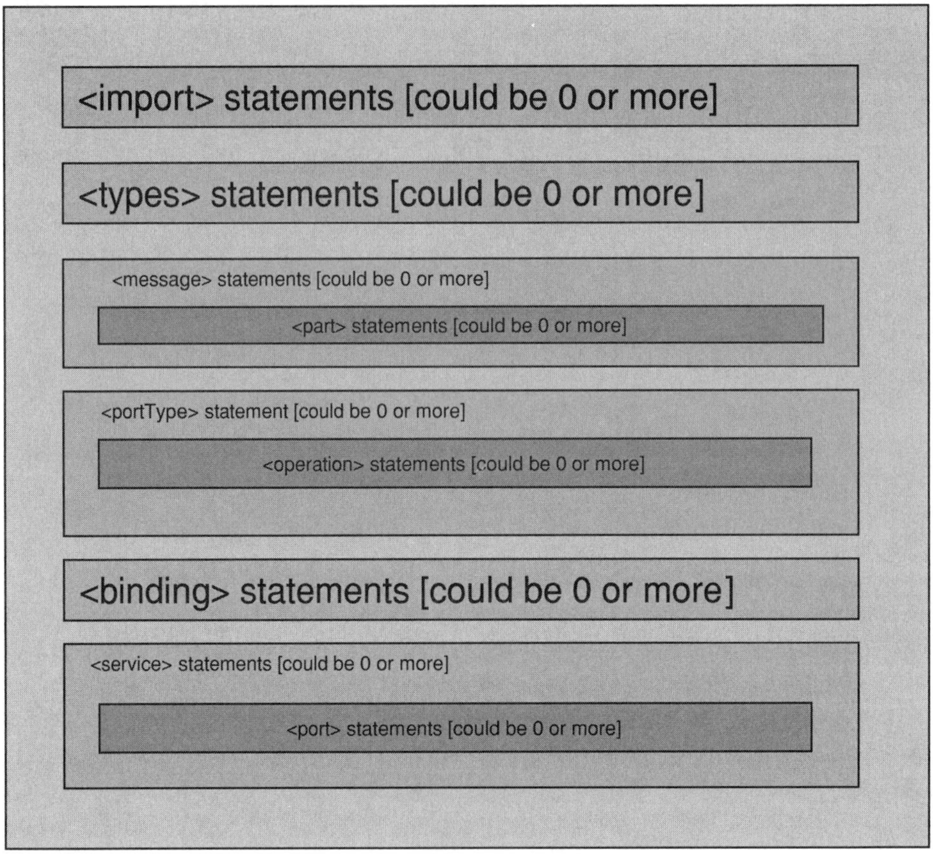

FIGURE 5.35. Block Diagram of WSDL Document

in XML, which would correspond to complex data structures in a programming language such as Java. Figure 5.36 illustrates an address structure that simply contains six strings, representing street number, street name, city, state, zip code, and a phone number.

Notice that the code that appears inside the types section entirely follows XSD syntax. As mentioned earlier, WSDL uses the XSD type system as the canonical type system. The schema element is a standard XML Schema language element that is used as a container to define schema elements.

Since we know that a single type system grammar cannot possibly satisfy the requirements of all present and future systems, WSDL allows new type systems to be described. WSDL allows type systems to be added via extensibility elements under the types element to identify the new type system. The role of this element can be compared to the role of the schema element in the XSD.

```
<types>
   <schema xmlns=http://www.w3.org/2001/XMLSchema
         targetNamespace="http://mynamespace/">
      <complexType name="Address">
         <sequence>
            <element minOccurs="1" maxOccurs="1" name="streetNum" type="string"/>
         <element minOccurs="1" maxOccurs="1" name="streetName" type="string"/>
            <element minOccurs="1" maxOccurs="1" name="city" type="string"/>
         <element minOccurs="1" maxOccurs="1" name="state" type="string"/>
         <element minOccurs="1" maxOccurs="1" name="zipCode" type="string"/>
         <element minOccurs="1" maxOccurs="1" name="phoneNumber" type="string"/>
         </sequence>
      </complexType>
   </schema>
</types>
```

FIGURE 5.36. An Address Type Defined Using XML Schema

The type definition is essentially an abstract definition of application data types. It can be used to define types even when the underlying wire format is not XML. It makes no assumption of how the document will be validated, encoded, or decoded.

5.4.3.2 Messages

When using a service interface, methods are invoked on the service. Most likely, data will be exchanged, whether through input parameters, output parameters, or return values. WSDL allows description of these exchanged data through the message element. A message defines a unit of data that will be exchanged between the client and the service.

A message consists of zero or more logical parts. Parts are defined using either native XML data types or a type defined earlier in the types section of the document. Each part has a part name and a type. Parts define the content of the message in an abstract manner. Later in a WSDL document, a protocol binding describes how the abstract parts of the message may be mapped to the underlying concrete and protocol-specific formats.

Figure 5.37 illustrates a message that has one part that is composed of a person's name and another part that is an address (previously defined).

This assumes that the prefix ns represents the namespace in which the type Address was defined. This message has two parts. The first part is named personName of type XSD:string, and second part is called address of type Address as a previously defined data type.

```
<message name="addAddressIn">
   <part name="personName" type="string"/>
   <part name="address" type="ns:Address"/>
</message>
```

FIGURE 5.37. A Message Declaration in WSDL

5.4.3.3 PortTypes

A portType is a set of abstract operations definitions. A port is really equivalent to an IDL interface or a Java interface. It provides a logical grouping of operations, their input/out parameter declarations, and their fault parameters. Through the message declarations of the operation, its transmission semantics may also be derived. WSDL defines four of these transmission primitives:

1. **One-way**. A message is sent but there is no response message or fault that can be returned from the other side.

2. **Request-response**. The other endpoint receives the request message and then returns the response message.

3. **Solicit-response**. The other endpoint sends a message and then receives a solicited response.

4. **Notification**. A message is received without any outstanding request and no response is sent back to the sender endpoint.

Some of these transmission primitives imply a correlation (e.g., request-response and solicit-response); the correlation is described only by the concrete binding.

Each operation can have an input message, an output message, and a fault message. These messages, of course, come from the message section of the WSDL document. The order and presence of these messages define the transmission primitive.

The presence of only an input message indicates a one-way operation. An input, and an output message and a possible fault message, indicates a request-response. Of course, if the message does not take any parameters, then the input message can be an empty message. An output message, followed by an input message and an optional fault message, indicates a solicit-response primitive and, finally, an operation containing only output message is a notification operation.

Figure 5.38 illustrates a portType that has only one request-response operation, which uses previously defined messages.

In Figure 5.38, the prefix tns represents the namespace in which the addAddressIn and addAddressOut messages were defined.

5.4.3.4 Bindings

So far, all of the WSDL sections described have been abstract in nature. These elements could be safely used to describe the properties of the service contract that were not specific to the underlying technology used to facilitate the interaction between the client and the service. However, for the underlying transport

```
<portType name="MyServicePortType">
   <operation name="addAddress">
      <input message="tns:addAddressIn"/>
      <output message="tns:addAddressOut"/>
   </operation>
</portType>
```

FIGURE **5.38. A PortType Declaration in WSDL**

mechanism to make the invocation, a lot of information, specific to the underlying technology, has to be provided. The binding section in a WSDL document specifies information specific to the binding. One instance of binding corresponds to a portType and makes that abstract definition concrete. In particular, a binding element defines message formats and protocol details for operations and messages in a particular portType.

Binding is an extensible element and it is expected that providers of various underlying transmission protocols would provide the particular extensibility elements. WSDL specification goes ahead and defines the extensibility elements required to define binding to SOAP protocol. We discuss that binding in this section.

For each operation in a portType, the binding section provides protocol-specific binding information. Since a binding can be for only one protocol, there can be multiple bindings for a portType, one for each protocol.

Figure 5.39 illustrates the binding of the MyServicePortType defined earlier in Figure 5.38.

The code segment in this figure illustrates many of the soap-specific details. All the elements prefixed with soap describe the soap-specific information. In

```
<binding name="MyServiceSoapBinding" type="tns:MyServicePortType">
   <soap:binding transport-=http://schemas.xmlsoap.org/soap/http"
      style="rpc"/>
      <operation name="addAddress">
         <soap:operation soapAction="http://mynamespace/addAddress"
            style="rpc"/>
         <input>
            soap:body use="encoded" namespace=http://mynamespace/
               encodingStyle="http://schemas.xmlsoap.org/soap/encoding"/>
         </input>
         <output>
            soap:body use="/>encoded"/> namespace=http://mynamespace/
               encodingStyle="http://schemas.xmlsoap.org/soap/encoding"/>
         </output>
      </operation>
</binding>
```

FIGURE **5.39. Binding Declaration**

```
<service name="MyService">
  <port name="MyServiceSoapPort" binding="tns:MyServiceSoapBinding">
    <soap:address
        location=http://localhost/myservice/MyService.asmx/>
  </port>
</service>
```

FIGURE 5.40. Service Declaration

this sample, the soap prefix points to the namespace of the WSDL/soap binding, which is http://schemas.xmlsoap.org/wsdl/soap/.

5.4.3.5 Services

A service in WSDL is a collection of addressable entities that implement the concrete bindings. Since bindings themselves are not addressable, they only provide information that relates to serialization/deserialization and encoding issues. We also said earlier that a portType can have multiple bindings. WSDL adds another element, port, which defines an endpoint by associating a binding with a URL where the binding can be accessed. A service is then a collection of different ports.

A service can have multiple ports. Most likely, these ports share a portType but employ different bindings to provide alternative means for accessing a service. For example, any .NET-based Web service can be accessed by either SOAP, HTTP-GET, and HTTP-POST. That means, by default, for the same portType, there are three bindings and hence three ports. All three ports are then grouped under one service, hence providing alternatives for accessing the same service.

Figure 5.40 shows the service definition of our example.

Since a port provides a protocol-specific address to a protocol-specific binding, it also uses extensibility elements to provide the address. In the example in Figure 5.40, soap:address is used to provide the URL of the soap-based dispatcher for this service.

5.5 BRIDGES TO LEGACY APPLICATIONS

So far, we have concentrated on platforms and languages. Although they are most useful for building new applications, those platforms do not provide tools to access applications that are built on an entirely different platform. Technology-specific bridges help access the applications that are built on different platforms or to access data from any type of data server. These bridges are very important to BSO because they greatly simplify the process of harmonization of the services that are exposed through them.

Language-independent platforms such as .NET and CORBA are essential to BSO as a source of services from any application that was built using them, regardless of the language. They greatly facilitate harmonization because they expose language-independent metadata that can be harmonized into the homogeneous metadata of the services catalog of BSO.

On the other hand, operating-system-independent platforms such as CORBA and J2EE are the preferred platform for *implementing* services, so that they can be ubiquitous. J2EE application servers are another story. However, all these platforms introduce vendor-specific extension variations to the standards that make implementing BSO in any given container either a permanent strategy or, in trying to support several of them, a maintenance nightmare.

BSO platforms, in turn, need to provide services integration languages (SILs) that are oriented toward integrating services from *any* platform. Although these languages are themselves proprietary, they are syntactically identical to popular languages that are used in current platforms. This avoids the need to reeducate programmers in anything but the specific facilities that pertain to integration, such as added syntax for parsing files, syntax for expressing object transformations and translations, support for associative arrays, and others.

For composition and orchestration to be possible, SILs need to be able to access services that are synthesized in the services catalog and implemented through platforms such as the above or through bridges such as screen scrapers, bridges to data organized into indexed files, bridges to data in legacy hierarchical and network databases, bridges to data in relational databases, and bridges to legacy transaction and application servers.

There are only three ways to noninvasively access services from applications:

1. Through a native API or the API of a messaging service that exposes it (BSO leverages platforms and messaging services to do this);
2. Through the native API into the persistent data store of the application or a standards-based bridge to various implementations of the standard (BSO leverages standards-based bridges to do this);
3. Through a bridge into the data that flow between the application layer and the presentation layer (as a last resort, BSO leverages these bridges if none of the above is available).

5.5.1 Screen Scrapers

In the absence of APIs or when accessible data can be compromised by using bridges to data stores or when those bridges don't exist, the only alternative is to use screen scraping techniques and technologies. Screen scraping technology encapsulates the user interface of an application behind generated classes, effectively converting the user interface screens into an API. Screen scraping is most useful for interacting with applications that provide a user interface as the only means of interacting with them. These screen scrapers are available for the following technologies:

- **Windows.** This leverages the client's interaction with either the server or the Windows operating system. The advantage of the latter is that it can be used independently of the server protocol. An example of leveraging the interaction with the operating system is through screen scrapers provided by AnySoft. Win Runner and Open Connect are other examples of these options for Windows screen scraping. The issue with GUI screen scraping is that, in general, it's positional, and because of the lack of data-related semantics, the approach is error prone. Furthermore, given the high degree of interactivity of GUIs, managing events or exceptions, or even error messages from the back-end, is very difficult.

- **VT220.** There have been many attempts to leverage services of legacy systems written in old DEC or Unix boxes that used character-based terminals (tty). This approach consists of parsing the terminal data stream. Because of the interactive nature of this data stream, the approach is difficult and error prone. Albeit it has been done, and given that these systems usually are not subject to periodic maintenance releases, once the quirks are extirpated from each screen scraping contraption, they work reasonably well.

- **5250 and 3270.** IBM itself has provided HALLAPI interfaces for scraping 3270 and 5250 screens, but there are many others that provide this type of screen scraping. These protocols are not character-at-a-time- or event-based as the two above. They are full-screen protocols, analogous to Web forms in that the labels travel with the useful data. Therefore, these protocols provide semantics for identifying the fields. Open Connect and many others provide very reliable bridges into this type of screen scraper.

One thing that the last two of the above have in common is that they are not adequate for implementing either high-transaction-rate services or mission-critical services. They should be used only as a replacement for purely human interaction. Except in the case of the 3270 and 5250, the act of filling screens by computer at computer time is contrary to the design of the protocols; therefore, the effect of doing so is difficult to forecast and requires much testing.

5.5.2 Bridges to Indexed Files

In the mainframe environment, many large applications still run on ISAM and VSAM. If these applications are transactional and are exposed through CICS or

MQ-Series, they can be accessed through mechanisms available for integrating CICS and MQ-Series. However, when the above isn't an option and the only way is to access the data directly, there are a number of tools that provide SQL-based access to these data sources. For example, Attunity exposes access to ISAM and VSAM files through a JDBC driver. This type of approach is very convenient for BSO, but it usually has a problem: These bridges do not provide a two-phase commit protocol (XLA-type) implementation. IMS can provide access to ISAM and VSAM in a transactional manner, and, the data sources are not transactional, a BSO platform can use compensating transactions to emulate transactionality. It also implements transparent two-phase commits across platforms and data stores when XA-, OTS-, or IMS- type protocols are available, making the orchestrator's job a lot simpler.

5.5.3 Bridges to Databases

Databases have been around for more than three decades. Relational databases have just turned twenty. Before relational databases, we had hierarchical and network-type databases, where the relationships between tables were implemented as physical addresses rather than the logical joins and views of relational database management systems (RDBMSs).

The advantage of RDBMSs was precisely their logical view and the supposedly user-friendly query language that would allow a business person to make queries on demand rather than rely on IT to build the reports that he or she wanted. Although the RDBMS provided very fast and reliable access to flat data, they typically had difficulty dealing with hierarchical data.

Object-oriented databases provided persistence ability for solid-state complex objects rather than just tables, by implementing relational algebra across these objects. Object-oriented databases had all the advantages of relational and network databases but none of their shortcomings. Yet, they were only marginally successful because performance issues were a thing of the past and humans prefer tables to complex structures.

BSO is to the virtual enterprise as RDBMS was to the enterprise – the fundamental automation-enabling solution. Like the RDBMS, it is logical rather than physical, and therefore had a hard time penetrating the IT market initially because of the biases toward a more physical approach (messaging).

BSO platforms need to leverage all of these technologies – hierarchical, network, relational, and object databases alike.

Unfortunately, no standard mechanisms have emerged for accessing less popular database types such as hierarchical, network, and object. However, this is acceptable because the majority of application data reside in relational databases.

There are two main standard access mechanisms for relational databases: JDBC to access relational databases from Java programs and ODBC to access relational databases from Microsoft-based platforms. These two access mechanisms enjoy wide vendor support and there is an astonishing amount of reference and educational material available on them. Using JDBC drivers, BSO platforms can use these databases natively by synthesizing these data sources through means such as introspection.

5.5.4 Bridges to Legacy Transaction or Application Servers

With all the recent progress made in extending the reach of the mainframe applications, IBM has breathed new life in the mainframe. Without doubt, mainframes provide the most scalable and reliable transactional platform that exists today. Mainframes implement a simple, two-tier transaction processing model. This is why CICS, IBM's legendary transaction server is still "alive and kicking" and will stay that way for a long time.

Therefore, given that BSO wants to integrate services from any and every system, it needs to implement a CICS interface. There are a number of providers for bridge between Java and CICS. IBM provides a CICS transaction gateway that allows APIs to access CICS transactions from Java and C++. Microsoft provides Host Server, which allows COM+ components that represent CICS transactions to be built. These COM+ components then can be used from any of the .NET supported languages and can be easily converted into Web services.

There are other bridges to be built. For example, coming from the Java world, a COM bridge is necessary for interoperatation. Some application servers implement such bridges as services. BSO must supply cross-platform and cross-application server harmonization.

5.6 Summary

The technologies presented in this chapter represent an important part of the BSO implementation. We intentionally did not discuss these technologies in detail because, given the scope of this book, we would not have been able to do justice to any of them. Each of these technologies has many books totally dedicated to it. The technology landscape is changing very rapidly. It is entirely possible that, by the time this book gets published, some new technologies will have been invented or the existing technologies will have been enhanced with a lot of new features. We focus more on identifying the requirements for different categories of technologies and then briefly discussing how they meet those requirements. The purpose was to give the reader enough of an overview and touch upon the key capabilities so that the reader can make informed decisions.

Since the interactions between applications are based on open standards, the technologies for individual tasks can be selected on the basis of suitability, available skill sets, and available productivity tools. That is why the emphasis in this book is on the architecture and orchestration concepts. Once understood, suitable technologies can be selected to implement those concepts.

CHAPTER 6

Business Services Aggregation

6.1 INTRODUCTION

Service aggregation is, simply put, service integration. Aggregated services are generally produced by consuming the contracts of multiple services to produce one single unified contract. They represent either functional composition where higher-level business functions are produced by consuming contracts of multiple services at the back end or they simply represent a larger contract that is the sum of its parts. These aggregated services present a contract of their own to their clients and are in turn consumers of the services they are aggregating.

Multiple back-end services are summed up in the contract of an aggregated service to either extend the reach of those back-end services or present a more convenient point of access for the clients. In either case, the motivation is based on technology and convenience. As an example, an enterprise may have various services, all related to one particular business area – say inventory – for its intranet. However, this enterprise decides to outsource its inventory management so that its inventory is visible to its suppliers and they can automatically replenish it as needed. A solution would be to develop a Web service that aggregates all the internal inventory control services and presents an aggregated contract to its business partner to help with the management.

Functional aggregation is more driven by the business need to develop increasingly complex functions and by the need for applications to evolve functionally.

For example, an enterprise system may have a corporate human resources system that carries some employee data and may also have a corporate directory that contains the enterprise demographic data. As new employees are hired and existing employees depart, both systems need to be synchronized. A new service can be developed that presents a single contract to update employee data. In turn, it can perform the relevant operations on the two back-end systems, thus presenting a functionally consolidated view to the clients.

Although the title of this chapter does not reflect service dissemination, it is just as important as the aggregation. Service dissemination is the exact opposite of aggregation. Whereas aggregation involves combining multiple services to present more consolidated services, service dissemination involves providing multiple, componentized services, all interacting with one single monolithic application. The motivations for service dissemination are usually technical. For example, an enterprise may have one big monolithic legacy application. The enterprise knows that it has to extend the reach of the service somehow and also plan for its eventual retirement or migration. To achieve those two objectives, the monolithic service is broken into functionally complete components. Multiple front-end services are then written to match those functional components, each presenting its own contract. With this accomplished, the individual functional components of the back-end service can be migrated to other platforms along independent time lines. The other reason for service dissemination is simply to reduce the complexity of a large application and present more manageable pieces of functionality for consumption.

Both service aggregation and dissemination are classic problems of integration and we examine various technologies and relate to the *Business Services* layer the reference architecture that we presented in Chapter 3, Figure 3.1. Traditionally, application integration has been solved by proprietary integration technologies using asynchronous messaging paradigms and application adapters. We first examine those. Web services provide a compelling low-cost entry into the application-to-application integration domain. We discuss how Web services are used for integration and, more importantly, what are the important technologies that make Web services suitable for this purpose.

6.2 MODES OF COMMUNICATION

Virtually all forms of integration require that a means of communication be established between the suppliers and consumers of business data. In today's complex environment, tightly coupled applications need to be integrated with each other using synchronous communication patterns, whereas loosely coupled applications need to rely on a more disconnected, asynchronous messaging model. The need to integrate applies to both application models equally.

Below, we discuss the two dominant modes of communication between service requestors and service providers.

6.2.1 Remote Procedure Calls (RPCs)

The RPC mode of communication represents the syntax, semantics, and presentation of higher-level subroutine calls. The caller makes the call as if it was a local call. In reality, the function itself is implemented in a remote server. Just like a subroutine call in a local programming language, the procedure being invoked has parameters associated with it and returns the result data through its return type.

Contrary to common belief, the RPC can be made either synchronously or asynchronously. When the RPC is made synchronously, the caller blocks until the remote server is finished processing the request and returns the results. An asynchronous RPC allows the requestor to make the request and then keep on doing its other work. The underlying system makes the request, receives the response, and posts the response somewhere where the requestor can come back and get it later.

The RPC mode of communication is suitable for applications that are tightly coupled. A calling application needs to know a great deal about the providing application in order to prepare the request correctly. The requestor has to know the exact form of the invocation the provider is expecting, the type and order of the parameters, and the returned data. If the requestor provides the information incorrectly, the negative feedback comes back fairly quickly. This also means that the version of the service provider and service requestor has to be in synch. If the service provider later adds an optional parameter to its exposed operation, the requestor has to be modified to incorporate this new optional parameter.

There are definite advantages with this style of communication. RPCs are type-safe and most incompatibilities and inconsistencies can easily be detected during development phases, leading to more robust production applications. The incompatibilities between the expected parameters and the provided parameters are in fact rigorously checked by the RPC system and exceptions are raised to indicate the mismatches. This model suits integration of applications within an enterprise fairly well.

Generally speaking, there are no intermediaries involved between the requestor and the provider. The request flows straight through to the provider and the response does the same coming back to the requestor. This mode of communication also represents client/server mode of communication. The service requestor serves the role of the client and the service provider serves the role of server.

6.2.2 Messaging

Messaging represents the other mode of communication. There are two key characteristics of this communication pattern:

First, messaging systems exchange data in the form of messages or documents. The messages are, of course, created by the requestor, but there is no runtime type checking provided. These messages either conform to a preagreed-upon format or they are self-describing.

The systems that use this style of communication can also be thought of as loosely coupled to each other. If the message contains an attribute that the provider does not need or does not know how to interpret, the interaction does not necessarily fail. The interaction fails only if the message is missing some key pieces of data necessary to fulfill the request. So if, as part of its evolution, the service provider adds some optional new parameter to the request, but an existing service requestor does not provide it, the provider may still be able to fulfill the request by simply using the default values for the missing parameter. Similarly, if the requestor is reusing some messages that have some extra parameters that the provider does not need, it simply ignores them. The important point here is that the underlying system does not perform any checking to make sure that the provided parameters match the expected parameters. That is left for the application to handle. So, when incompatible parameters are received by a provider application, it may either flag that as an error or may respond to the mismatch in a default manner. This allows the service provider and the service requestor to evolve independently of each other.

Second, this mode of communication represents more of a peer-to-peer model. In this mode, the connection is actually established with an intermediary. Requests are then made against the intermediary, which brokers the request and the response between the service requestor and the service provider. The service requestor and the service provider are both clients of the message broker and hence are peers to each other.

These intermediaries are commonly known as the *message brokers*. Message brokers represent a software entity that actually implements the messaging system. So, message brokers can easily be used to encapsulate the functionality of legacy messaging systems such as MQ-Series. Figure 6.1 shows the general architecture of the message broker. The service requestor or the message sender actually establishes the connection with the message broker and sends the message to the message broker. The service provider or the message receiver also establishes the connection with the message broker and registers itself to receive certain messages. The message broker then relays those messages that it receives to the interested receivers. The architecture of the message broker provides several advantages:

- **Disconnected connection model**. The messaging paradigm allows a disconnected model of communication between the communicating peers. Since the

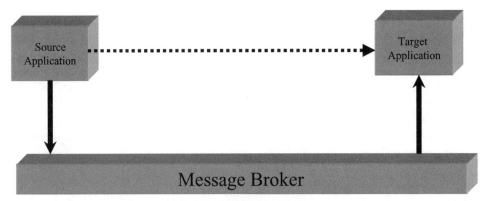

FIGURE 6.1. Message Broker

connection is not established directly between the requestor and the provider, the implementation of the message broker allows for the service provider to connect later and receive the messages that were sent to it.

- **Better connection management**. The message broker presents a hub-and-spoke model of connection among peers, greatly reducing the number of connections that need to be established. Figure 6.2 shows that six direct connections are required between four peers to connect them to each other. This number increases exponentially as the number of peers increase, making it difficult for the whole system to scale up. With the hub-and-spoke model of message brokers, as shown in Figure 6.3, only one connection is required per peer to connect it to the message broker, making the whole system more scalable.

- **Quality of service**. The message broker may provide various levels of quality of service. For example, some message brokers may guarantee reliable message

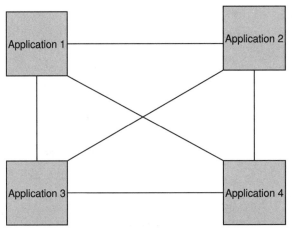

FIGURE 6.2. Direct Connections Between Peers

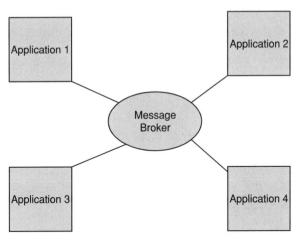

FIGURE **6.3. Hub-and-Spoke Model**

delivery. Once the message sender sends a message to the message broker, the broker may guarantee that the message will be successfully delivered to the receiver, even if the receiver was not connected at that time.

- **Transactionality**. The message broker may implement transactional protocols to actually publish either a batch of messages to the same receiver or multiple messages to multiple receivers in a transactional manner – either all messages get delivered or no messages get delivered.

- **Choice of messaging styles**. The intervention of the message broker opens up possibility for supporting many different styles of messaging. In a simpler style of messaging, the message sender and receiver both have to be connected to the broker for the messages to pass through from the sender to the receiver. Alternatively, the messaging broker might support persisting the messages if the receiver is not connected and allow the receiver to receive those messages when it connects. More sophisticated systems may allow the pull model in addition to the push model. For example, OMG's messaging service allows the pull model where the message receiver from time to time may connect to the message broker and pull any messages for it. Furthermore, the message broker may allow the push model to be mixed with the pull model.

In general, the messaging model provides a very scalable and functionally rich environment between the communicating peers. Next, we describe the two most common styles of messaging.

6.2.2.1 Point-to-Point Messaging
Point-to-point style of messaging follows the notion of a special messaging channel, known as a *queue*, to deliver messages. A queue is generally regarded as a

sequence of messages destined for a single receiver. However, depending on the implementation of the messaging system, it may allow multiple senders to write messages to the same queue.

6.2.2.2 Broadcast Messaging

Broadcast messaging to registered subscribers is commonly known as *publish/ subscribe* messaging systems. In this style of messaging, a single messaging channel is shared among multiple senders and receivers. When the message broker receives a new message, it broadcasts the message to all the registered receivers for that channel. More sophisticated messaging services may allow receivers to specify some sort of criteria that can be used to filter unwanted messages before sending them to a particular receiver.

6.3 MODES OF SHARING DATA

Although the communication layer is an essential element in the technology stack for integration, it does not contribute any semantic support to the integration problem. The effectiveness of the integration system in general then depends upon how data are shared between the peers being integrated.

Figure 6.4 illustrates various levels of integration. The lowest level of integration is the sharing of data directly from the data repositories. This level of sharing of data has the big disadvantage of bypassing any business rules that are used to ensure the integrity of the data. For example, an application may apply several kinds of validation rules on data records before it puts them in its data repository. However, if another application updates this application's data repository directly, then it would have bypassed all the business rules; unless, of course, if the rules themselves are implemented in the data repository itself, thus potentially updating the repository with inconsistent data. Although integration at this level is not preferable, it is still necessary sometimes. There are many older systems that do not expose any kind of API . Those systems were simply designed in a preintegration era and were meant to be closed systems with no regard to integration with other systems. So, the only choice for integrating those systems may be to read or write data directly to their data repositories.

Most of the integration efforts revolve around the application integration. Applications that expose APIs and metadata are quite easy to integrate. SAP is a good example of that. It not only exposes a programming interface but also provides a fairly rich metadata repository. These applications can be integrated by invoking their APIs and passing the properly formatted messages. Invocation of the APIs rather than updating the data repositories allows the application to apply all its business rules, thus preserving the integrity of the data. Furthermore, as new

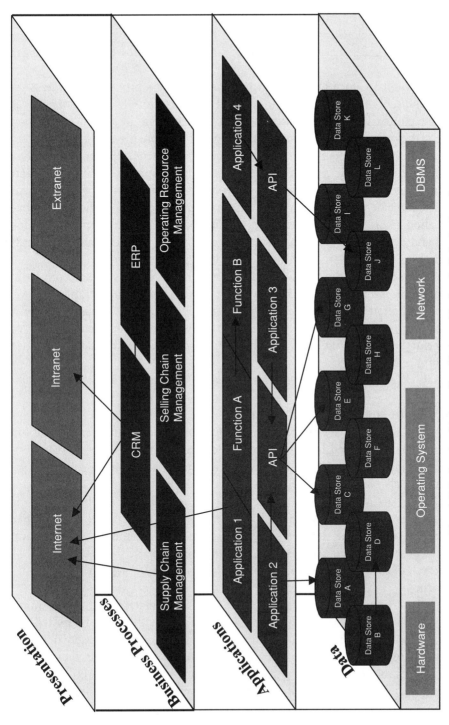

FIGURE 6.4. Levels of Integration (Source: Electronic Data Systems)

versions of the application become available, any changes made to its data formats, internal data representations, or data repository schema changes are transparent to the client applications because it continues to use the exposed APIs .

Systems always work together to implement business processes. Business processes represent the set of steps that need to be taken to fulfill some business goals. These steps usually have an order to them; for example, in an order fulfillment process, the order cannot be sent to manufacturing before the credit has been successfully verified. Business process is the grouping of these steps and their defined sequences and dependencies upon each other. Integration at the business process level deals with automating the steps involved in a business process – *business process automation*. Business process automation delivers the highest value from integration effort because it tends to streamline all the computing and human assets and delivers the entire process in an automated, efficient, and measurable manner.

Integration at both the data level and the application level is focused on sharing the data. This is obvious at the data level, but how so at the application level? Well, the integration mechanisms focus on invoking APIs that provide discrete services as viewed from outside. These APIs are invoked with some set of data and in turn may bring back other sets of data. The focus is still on moving data in or out of that application.

Let us consider some major modes of sharing data among applications:

6.3.1 Point-to-Point Data Movement

In its simplest and most commonly used form, also known as *point-to-point* integration, data are moved from one application into another. Consider the example of a company that invested in a customer relationship management (CRM) system and also has its internal homegrown field dispatch system that is responsible for dispatching the field technician to fix the problem. The field technician also updates this system when he fixes the problem in the field. The company would like to integrate the two systems so that when customers call-in a problem, the customer service representatives can simply update the CRM system. The CRM system can then send the ticket to the homegrown system for technician dispatch.

In point-to-point data movement, when the customer service representative enters a new problem ticket into the CRM, the data will simply be pulled from the CRM system and be put into the dispatcher system. Two separately developed systems hardly every have the same data structures. So, to move data from the CRM system to the dispatcher system, the data may have to undergo some transformation or reformatting. We discuss transformation in detail in the Adapter section.

6.3.2 Data Aggregation

Data aggregation represents the pulling of data from multiple sources and presenting a consolidated or aggregated view of it.

Let us consider a benefits administration system. This benefits administration system may need to get a consolidated view of an employee. This consolidated view includes the employee demographic information, such as address, department, and management chain. This consolidated view of the employee may also contain salary information. Now, assume that the employee's demographic information is kept in a corporate directory system and the payroll information is kept in a SAP Payroll module.

Because the company wants to reduce redundant information, it does not save all the demographic and payroll information in the benefits administration system. So, when an employee wants to either check his/her benefits level or modify them, the benefits administration system invokes the integration layer to get the consolidated view of the employee. The invocation layer retrieves the demographic data from the corporate directory and the payroll data from the payroll system, formats the data according to the predefined rules, and presents the desired view of the data to the benefits administration system.

6.3.3 Data Dissemination

Data dissemination is the opposite of data aggregation. Where the data aggregation is pulling data from multiple sources to present a consolidated view, data dissemination is taking a consolidated view of the data and updating multiple systems with only part of the consolidated view.

Continuing with our previous example of the human resources system, let us assume that the company has a legacy system to enter the data for a new employee. So, when a new employee is hired, the department secretary or the manager uses some sort of terminal-based interface to the legacy system to enter the initial data for the new employee. The legacy system then invokes the integration layer and passes the entered data to it. The integration layer then may use preconfigured rules to update the corporate directory with the available demographic data and the payroll system to update the negotiated salary information.

6.4 ADAPTERS AND TRANSFORMATION FACILITIES

We mentioned an *integration layer* when we were explaining the modes of sharing data. What is this *integration layer*? In traditional style of integration, this integration layer consists of *adapters* and *transformation facilities*. In this section, we discuss them in detail.

6.4.1 Transformation Facilities

Various applications, developed independently of each other, hardly ever conform to the same data definitions. Although a customer record in a CRM system may conceptually represent a customer record in a billing system, it is highly unlikely that the two definitions of customer will be the same. So, as data are moved between applications, the data may have to be transformed from the source form to the target form.

The transformations may be of varying degrees of complexity. Some examples of these transformations are as follows:

- **Semantically equivalent conversions**. The data in one system may be represented as a string in the format mm/dd/yyyy. However, another system may internally use an integer Julian date to represent the same value. The same may apply to other similar fields, such as currency. One system may represent a person's height in feet and inches whereas another may simply use centimeters to represent the height.

- **Aggregated or calculated values**. A billing system may have a detailed invoice, with the unit prices and quantities spelled out for individual components of an order. However, an invoice system may transform the cost of the individual components into a total amount to be billed and then bill it to the relevant credit card.

- **Looked-up values**. Another kind of transformation may actually require that default values or looked-up values of missing data be provided. So, although an order may not have a shipping address because it is the same as the billing address, the shipping system is going to require a shipping address. The transformation layer may retrieve the billing address and create the shipping address from it.

We cannot list all possible kinds of transformations here because there are too many. However, listing a few of the common kinds gives a flavor of what transformations are all about. The exact mechanism for performing transformations may vary from one product to another. Some products may allow you to provide classes written in a programming language such as Java, XSLT, or C#, which can then be dynamically loaded to perform transformations. Others systems may provide some sort of higher level scripting language to perform transformations. Many products also provide user-interface-driven tools to visually specify rules for the required transformations.

6.4.2 Adapters

Whether the sharing is being done at the data level or at the application level, there has to be an intermediate piece of software that can accept requests to do

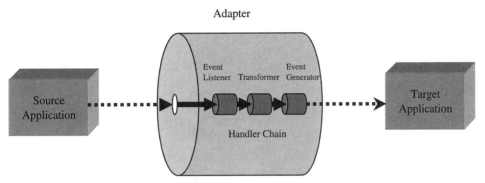

FIGURE 6.5. Logical Model for Adapters

some work, can transform messages using predefined rules, and knows how to invoke either the APIs of the target systems or update their data repositories.

The software entity that is able to accept either asynchronous messages or synchronous RPCs on one end and is able to either deliver asynchronous messages or invoke synchronous APIs of the target applications is known as an adapter. It simple adapts one application for use by another.

Figure 6.5 shows an adapter model. The big container in the middle is the adapter. On one hand, the adapter receives requests from a source application, and on the other hand, it makes requests on the target application. Although there may be many different physical models possible for adapters, this is a conceptual model. Notice that this conceptual model shows transformation taking place inside it. Just by its very nature, the transformation has to take place after the data have been received from the source application and before the data are pushed onto the target application. For this reason, we show transformation inside the adapter container. Other logical elements of adapters are an event listener and an event generator.

An event listener is a software entity that can receive either an asynchronous message or a synchronous RPC. An event generator is a software entity that can either invoke RPCs on a target system or send asynchronous messages to it. Generally speaking, adapters are configured for individual integration scenarios. Many products allow configuration of adapters by dragging and dropping components of the adapter model from component palettes.

The adapter itself can be thought of as a container that provides a pipeline processing model. In this model, an event listener can be the first entity. One or more transformers can be chained together after the listener, and the tail of the pipeline can be carried out by the event generator.

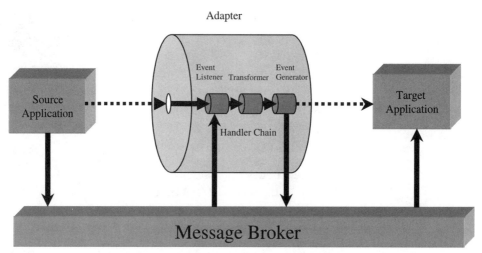

FIGURE 6.6. Integration Broker Architecture

6.5 INTEGRATION BROKERS

An integration broker is not necessarily a software entity, but rather the entire integration package that contains the message broker, adapters, and transformation facilities. Figure 6.6 illustrates the generic architecture of the integration brokers. The burden of communication is handled by the message broker that provides a logical channel of communication between the source and the target applications. However, the physical connections are implemented by the message broker. Furthermore, the source and target applications communicate with each other through the adapter, which acts as the intermediary, providing a pipeline processing model for performing message transformations.

6.6 WEB SERVICES

Integration has always been a difficult problem to solve and the integration brokers have attempted to solve that problem. The amount of success achieved by them is arguable. However, the kinds of problems seen by using the integration brokers are many.

The integration brokers deliver the solution to the integration problem by introducing very complex and proprietary mechanisms. Introduction of proprietary technologies locks the organization into products and makes it difficult for them to maintain their solutions over a period of time. These proprietary solutions also tend to be complex, requiring highly qualified IT professionals to complete an implementation, increasing the cost of not only the initial implementation but its ongoing maintenance as well.

Whereas large organizations with large IT budgets may be able to afford these solutions, they may be beyond what the vast majority of small- to medium-size organizations with smaller IT budgets and staff can afford.

Web services lower the entry barrier for these smaller organizations and bring the solution to their integration problem within reach by relying on open and ubiquitous standards. Because this reliance is on standard technologies, the required tools can be obtained from a large number of competing vendors, and a large number of developers can be found who are knowledgeable in those technologies.

Chapter 5 has already discussed the related Web services technologies and the predominant platforms for Web services. If Web services are used to solve integration problems, then their capabilities have to be compared with the capabilities offered by the integration brokers. In this section, we discuss some of the capabilities that are required from Web services in order to provide a viable platform to aggregate and integrate existing services.

6.6.1 Reliable Message Delivery

Most real-world applications require reliable message delivery. It is important for a requesting application to know that the request it has just issued will be delivered to the target application.

Reliability of message delivery can be ensured either at the application level or the protocol level. Whichever level is responsible for guaranteeing the reliable delivery of messages has to be able to cache the message for possible retransmission and has to implement a protocol of message acknowledgments and retransmissions between peers.

Consider the scenario of an on-line banking application communicating with the back-end banking Web service. The client application issues a request to transfer a sum of money from one account to another. The back-end Web service can perform the transfer of money in a transactional manner once it receives the request. Now, after the client application has sent the request message, the network connection breaks and the client application receives the error. If the message delivery is not reliable, then the client application has no way of knowing whether the network connection broke before the message was successfully received by the back-end Web service or after. If the network connection had broken before the message was actually delivered to the Web service, then the client application would need to retransmit the request again. However, if the network connection broke after the message had been delivered, then there would not be a need to redeliver the message.

Reliable message delivery requires the ability to acknowledge messages, retransmit messages, and detect and eliminate duplicate messages, resulting in

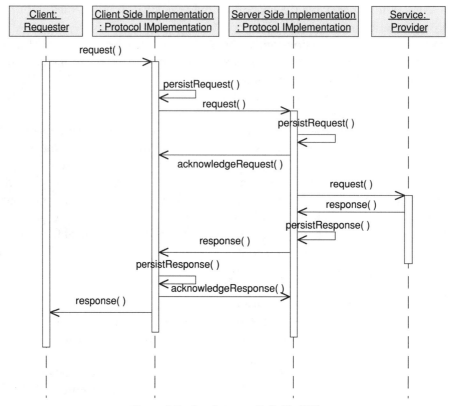

Figure 6.7. Synchronous Reliable RPC

once-and-only-once message delivery semantics. In a system that provides reliable delivery, a receiving application sends an acknowledgment for a message received. If a sender does not receive an acknowledgment within a certain time period, then the sender may retransmit the same message. Since a sender cannot just keep on retrying an unacknowledged message, systems usually have a retry limit, after which they consider the request failed. Reliable messages usually are assigned unique identifiers. The sender may use persistence so that it can retry unacknowledged messages, even if it crashes and comes back up. Alternatively, a sender may only keep an in-memory cache for unacknowledged messages, in which case it would lose all knowledge of the sent messages if it itself crashes. Similarly, a receiver may store the processed messages so that it can detect duplicate messages and not process the same requests twice.

Figure 6.7 illustrates the execution of a reliable synchronous RPC. In this example, the reliability semantics are guaranteed by the underlying implementations of the communication protocol for the Web services between the client side and the server side. The client is not explicitly aware of the details of how reliability is implemented but rather takes it for granted, thus greatly simplifying the client and service implementations. The client makes a request to the remote service. The request is actually received by the client side of the communication protocol (such as reliable Simple Object Access Protocol [SOAP]) implementation. The client-side communication protocol infrastructure first assigns the request a unique identifier and then applies persistence to the request in some form of data store. The persisting of the request is important because, in a distributed environment, things can go wrong. The persistence feature allows the client-side communication protocol infrastructure to retransmit the request if it feels that the request was not successfully received. Anyway, after the request has been persisted, the client-side communication protocol infrastructure starts a timer. The timer is to define the time window under which it expects to receive an acknowledgment of the request. If the acknowledgment is not received within that time window, the client-side communication protocol infrastructure will retransmit the request and will keep on retransmitting until a preconfigured maximum number of attempts has been made. Once that limit is reached, the request is considered undeliverable and the client is informed of the failure through an exception or a fault.

Once the server-side communication protocol infrastructure receives the request, it first uses the unique identifier of the request to make sure that this is not a duplicate request, and then makes the request persistent in its data store. Once the request has been persisted, it sends an acknowledgment message back to the client-side communication protocol infrastructure. Next it dispatches the request to the service implementation and waits for its response. Once the response is received by the server-side communication protocol infrastructure, it follows exactly the same sequence of messages as for the original request, but initiated from the server-side this time.

The above scenario implements acknowledgments per request. This is easy for illustrating the concepts but, of course, not the most optimal way to implement these mechanisms. There are a number of optimization tricks that can be implemented by the communication protocols, such as batching and piggybacking the acknowledgments in requests and responses.

For Web services, reliability can be implemented at many different levels. For example, reliability can achieved at the carrier protocol level. IBM has implemented a reliable version of HTTP, known as HTTPR. This protocol guarantees message delivery on top of HTTP. However, it is not feasible for the infrastructure of the Internet to convert entirely to a new protocol, even if it can provide those benefits. Alternatively, reliability can also be implemented by the XML protocol level. For example, a SOAP provider may implement reliability by defining a series of SOAP headers that must be understood and processed by the processors on both sides.

6.6.2 Business Transaction Protocol

The current distributed transactions are modeled after the two-phase commit protocol (2PC) defined by X/Open group known as XA. This 2PC protocol works very well with tightly coupled systems that need to exhibit the ACID (atomic, consistent, isolated, and durable) properties. These systems have control over the participating resources and rely on a central coordinator to drive the commit protocol. Because these transactions exhibit ACID properties, either everyone involved in the transaction commits or everyone aborts the transaction.

Web services can be tightly coupled as well as loosely coupled. The technology does not restrict Web services to one particular kind of coupling but, rather, equally enables both. Most Web services being used within the enterprise as tightly coupled systems probably need to participate in ACID transactions. However, with Web services, this is not always true. First, Web services may integrate a web of quite diverse and autonomous business partners. In such loosely coupled systems, a central coordinator cannot be relied upon to be there all the time to drive the commit protocol. Each Web service participating in a transaction that spans an extended enterprise may represent independent work flows, with its own set of tightly coupled transactions.

The nature of business relationships that are forged in a federation of systems may be very different from within the enterprise with different rules. Consider a travel reservation system. This system may allow you to book a flight, reserve a hotel, reserve a car, and make a reservation for dinner in your destination city. In a transaction with ACID properties, all of the above four participants would have to agree to commit before the transaction would commit. So, the whole transaction would have to roll back if flight, hotel, and car could be reserved but the dinner reservation could not be made. These kinds of scenarios are common occurrences among the Web services interactions and require application of different rules to make commit or rollback decisions.

The Organization for the Advancement of Structured Information Standards (OASIS) has defined a new transaction protocol, called Business Transaction Protocol (BTP), that is quite suitable for Web services. BTP completely supports the traditional transactions but also extends them to support the above scenario where the all-or-nothing approach might not be appropriate. BTP is an XML-based protocol that can be used over multiple communication protocols. Because of widespread adoption of SOAP for Web services, BTP defines the necessary SOAP bindings required to carry the information about BTP transactions. By design, BTP also supports disconnected systems that might not be available or connected all the time, even when they are participating in a transaction.

In BTP, there are two types of transactions: atomic and cohesive. Atomic transactions are the typical XA-compliant transactions that follow the 2PC protocol. All participating resources vote on the outcome of the transaction. If even a single transaction votes to abort the transaction, the entire transaction aborts. In a Web service, the operations of the Web services being invoked during the transaction are the atoms.

Cohesions are a subset of all the atoms participating in a transaction. In cohesion, the transaction initiator decides whether each atom in a transaction fails or succeeds, even if the atom votes success. The initiator decides on the composition of the cohesion and its outcome by applying business rules. When cohesion begins, atoms are enlisted in the transaction. However, cohesion reduces the choices available, arriving at a single successful outcome at the end.

BTP defines four major actors:

1. **Initiator**: This is a client application that starts a BTP transaction. This application is also the only one that can terminate the transaction and, in case of cohesion, decides the outcome of the cohesion.

2. **Service**: This is a Web service that has one or more transactional operations. After the initiator starts a BTP transaction, it may invoke business operations on one or more services.

3. **Participants**: When a transactional operation is invoked on a Web service, it may enroll one or more participants in the transaction. Participants are capable of responding to *prepare, cancel,* and/or *confirm* commands. The participant is equivalent to an XA resource element that participates in a 2PC protocol.

4. **Coordinator**: The coordinator is responsible for coordinating the outcome of an atom. It tracks a set of participants enrolled in a single atom and instructs them to either prepare, cancel, or confirm.

Figure 6.8 illustrates the relationship between BTP actors. BTP defines only the coordination protocol between the coordinator and the participants and the invocation protocol between the initiator and the service. It does not define protocols between the service and the participants or the initiator and the coordinator. Those interactions are left to the implementer of the BTP protocol and will be handled by specific API implementations.

BTP defines a set of abstract messages and the rules that govern the coordination and participation of different actors. These abstract messages can then be bound to multiple underlying carrier protocols. BTP defines bindings to SOAP and SOAP with attachments.

6.6.3 Security
Web services need tight security because integrating systems and applications over a network can allow access to sensitive information. Although individual

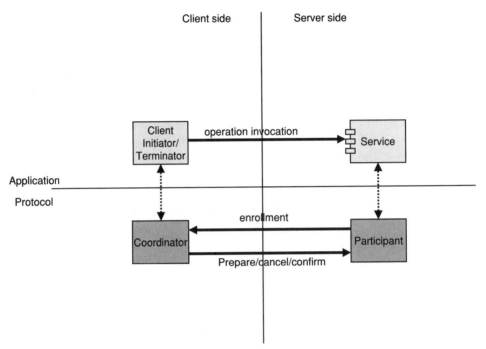

FIGURE 6.8. Relationship Between BTP Actors

technologies required to implement security solutions have been available for a long time, the integrated solutions become complex to implement, and Web services infrastructure is expected to provide those integrated solutions so that the Web services themselves do not become burdened with implementing such solutions. In this section, we discuss the four main capabilities deemed necessary for a baseline support for security in Web services.

In Web services, in addition to authentication and authorization, there are three key security mechanisms: Transport-level security, payload security, and no security (where security is provided by other means such as IPSec). This section mostly concerns itself with the payload security in a manner that is completely independent of a transport protocol.

6.6.3.1 Authentication

Authentication is a process of verifying the identity of an individual or a software entity – known as a *principal*. The evidence required to establish the principal's identity is known as *credentials*. We describe two modes of authentication that are required by Web services.

6.6.3.1.1 Basic authentication. Basic authentication requires the client to identify itself to the server by providing a username and a password. In this case the username provides the identity of the principal and the password provides the credentials. This way of authenticating a user is usually sufficient for most Web services whose users all belong to a trusted domain. Specifically, in Web services domains, basic authentication maps to the basic authentication mechanism supported by HTTP. Using SOAP over HTTP basic authentication mechanism results in the server sending back a response that challenges the client to provide a userid and a password. The client can provide the userid and the password as a base64-encoded string.

This basic authentication mechanism is a nonsecure method for authenticating a client application. It, therefore, assumes that the client is trying to interact with the service provider in a trusted environment as such and that there is no need to encrypt the userid and the password to maintain the client's confidentiality.

6.6.3.1.2 Certificate-based authentication. In this mode of authentication, the client or the server can be authenticated through digital certificates. These certificates provide a set of authentication information and are obtained from trusted third-party sites and establish the credentials of the principal. The information in the certificate itself is authenticated because the certificate itself is digitally signed by the trusted third party, hence making it tamperproof. This discussion is not limited to digital certificates as such and can be used equally well with other authentication mechanisms, such as Kerberos tickets.

To understand certificate-based authentication, one has to understand digital certificates. Although a detailed discussion of digital certificates is out of the scope of this book, we can briefly describe them here. A digital certificate is an electronic document that provides the proof of its owner's (a person or a Web service for which it is issued) identity. These certificates are issues by trusted third parties, called certification authorities (CA). Although there are various kinds of certificates, the most common format of the certificate is defined by X.509v3 certificate and contains information such as the owner's public key. In addition to this, the owner also needs a private key, which is generally provided to the owner separate from the certificate itself. The certificate itself is digitally signed and encrypted by the CA and can be verified and decrypted by using the CA's public key. The private key of the owner is also further encrypted using a simpler user-selected key and is usually stored on that user's machine. The system and services required to generate, manage, and use the digital certificates is called Public Key Infrastructure (PKI).

Applications that use digital certificates themselves become quite complex. Furthermore, the exchange of the key information and its proper management is itself a significant problem that needs to be addressed. So, W3C defines a higher-level service called XML Key Management Service (XKMS). XKMS provides specification for a higher-level service that shields the client applications from the complexities of the underlying PKI. XKMS provides a specification for associating public-private keys with persons or institutions. XKMS provides a tiered model to expose different levels of security-related services instead of providing a single monolithic security service:

1. Tier 0 allows the applications to resolve key information provided as part of the message, without involving a trusted service. In this mode, the signer of a document may provide a reference to the key information that is stored at another location. This information may contain the URI of the remote resource and the type of the resource. The client can invoke the URI to download the resource and, depending on its type, can parse the resource and verify it.
2. Tier 1 allows a trusted service to process the key information. This trusted service can then resolve the key information to public keys. The client can then perform the validation. Tier 1 provides a `Locate` service that resolves the key-related information provided by the signer to a specific credential type. The client can pass the information received from the signer on to the trusted service, which retrieves the credential, parses the credential, and returns a list of name value pairs that contain the name of the key and the actual key value. This service, however, does not validate the credential, leaving that up to the client. This service can act as a gateway to an underlying non-XML-based PKI.
3. Tier 2 allows the trusted third party to provide complete service, including the validation. It essentially extends the Tier 1 service by also validating the credentials, providing additional information such as the validity of the certificate.

For a trusted service to provide support for Tier 1 service, key-related information has to be registered with it. XKMS also provides interfaces to register key information with a trusted service so that that information can be resolved by the trusted service.

The other aspect of authentication is to associate credentials with messages. Since the messages are carried by the underlying protocol, the credentials have to be mapped to appropriate elements in the Web service protocol. There are several specifications that define standard SOAP headers for carrying credential information for a SOAP message. The header can either carry the credentialing information in-line or can carry a URI reference and the type of the credential to be expected in the header. This maps very well to the XKMS specification and the digital signatures because the credential header of the SOAP message could simply carry the `KeyInfo`, as specified by the XML digital signature (XML–DSIG) specification by W3C. In this case, the message receiver can then obtain the actual credential information using one of the three tiered services of the XKMS specification.

6.6.3.2 Message Confidentiality

Message confidentiality deals with keeping the entire message or parts of it confidential by encrypting them. W3C has defined the XML encryption specification to encrypt an entire XML document or parts of it. The granularity of encryption is important because the encryption techniques are quite expensive and encrypting the large messages in their entirety can significantly impact the performance. Most often, there is no need to protect an entire message; only parts of it need to be protected.

Messages are encrypted using many different algorithms. A message recipient not only needs the public key required to decrypt a message but also needs to know the particular encryption algorithm that was used to encrypt the data. This requires some way of exchanging the key information along with the message. The key exchange mechanisms defined by XML signatures specification are applicable for passing the key information.

XML encryption specification defines the XML elements required to pass all the relevant information, and so, no further binding to SOAP messages is required. Having said that, some header entries may need to be defined for encrypted attachments because XML encryption cannot be directly applied to the attachments.

6.6.3.3 Authorization

Authentication deals with the access level of the principal. Once a user has been authenticated and a valid request comes from that user, the receiving service must determine if the requestor should be allowed this request or not. This is an area where, currently, there is no specification that is suitable for Web services. The eXtensible Access Control Markup Language (XACML) deals with policies related to accessing entire XML documents or parts of them. Authorization, as defined here, deals with access to a Web service's functions.

Once a user has been authenticated, authorization does not require any further interaction between the service requestor and the service provider. For this reason, any existing authentication mechanisms will suffice.

The access control list (ACL) model is very tightly coupled and not fully factored. It must synchronize distributed ACL tables over a large distributed environment and does not scale very well.

6.6.3.4 Message Integrity

When a message is exchanged between two parties over the network, it might be important to make sure that the message was sent by the expected party and that the message was not tampered with during flight. This is accomplished by using digital signatures.

When exchanging messages, sometimes the entire message needs to be digitally signed and at other times, only a portion of the message needs to be signed.

Furthermore, different portions of the message may be signed by different entities. Typically, a signer uses a digest algorithm to compute a hash value for the data being signed. This hash value is then encrypted using the signer's private key. This encrypted value is knows as the *signature*. The receiver obtains the hash value by decrypting the *signature* using the signer's public key and then uses the same algorithm to compute the hash value on the signed data. If the two hash values are the same then, first, the receiver is sure that the data were sent by the expected party, because the receiver used that party's public key to decrypt the signature. Second, the receiver is sure that the content was not tampered with because it computed the same hash value.

An integrity solution for Web services should allow for a message or a portion of a message to be signed using XML signatures.

W3C's XML signature (XML-DSIG) specification provides for digitally signing XML messages. There are several specifications that describe somewhat similar mechanisms for applying XML signature specification to SOAP messages.

6.6.3.4.1 XML signatures. A complete discussion of XML signatures is out of scope of this book, but we discuss the salient features of the specification that applies to Web services.

Web services generally support either RPC-style communication, where most of the data are passed as parameters to the operation being invoked, or document-centric computing, where the data are passed as attachments to the operation being invoked. XML signature supports this key requirement by allowing the signatures to envelope the data within the same document or detached signatures over data external to the signature element. In the detached case, the data being signed can be identified either through a URI or a transform.

XML signature actually allows two layers of signing. First, within a single signature tag, several documents or document elements can be signed. Each one is digested and its digest value and the algorithm used are placed within the *Reference* element that represents the data being signed. Then, the whole set of reference elements is signed again. This signature and other relevant information such as the algorithm used are then encrypted. The information related to the public key required to decrypt the above set is also provided.

6.6.3.4.2 SOAP extensions. To use XML signatures with SOAP for Web services, a mechanism has to be defined as SOAP extensions to sign entire or parts of SOAP messages in a consistent manner. There are several specifications that provide slightly similar mechanisms for doing that. In all cases, the XML signature tag is used to provide information about the signed data. A security header is defined to further locate the *signature* tag of the XML signature specification in SOAP header part of the SOAP message.

A typical SOAP extension would allow a `ds:Signature` as defined by XML signature specification in the header part of the SOAP Envelope. Each `ds:Reference` element contained in the signature must correspond to either a resource within the SOAP Envelope (header or body) or an attachment in the SOAP message package. A `mustUnderstand` attribute on that header element may force verification of the signatures found in that header entry.

6.6.4 Performance

Web services allow enterprises to extend the reach of their legacy systems and to easily integrate applications in an inexpensive manner. A lot of these benefits come from leveraging standards such as XML or SOAP over HTTP. HTTP has been very scalable for transporting Web pages from the Web browser clients to and from the back-end servers, and XML has established itself as the key mechanism for describing data.

However, all this flexibility and ease comes at a premium price: performance. HTTP scales very well for human users who have the ability to fetch coffee while certain pages are being downloaded. However, Web services are more about machine-to-machine interaction. A client of a Web service is generally another computer application that happens to be a peer of the service itself but is in a client role for that particular interaction.

As one analyzes performance, it can be generally divided into two components: how much data need to be transported so the underlying transport protocol (such as TCP) can efficiently transport bits, and what kind of processing takes place on either end to process the data received.

A typical Web service client using a Java toolkit for SOAP interacts with a Java-based Web service in the following way:

1. The Java client makes the remote request, passing the Java data structures as the parameters to the remote request.
2. The underlying client implementation of SOAP serializes Java data structures and other invocation information into the XML document that carries the XML message conforming to SOAP specifications.
3. The SOAP message is then packaged with the HTTP header (assuming SOAP over HTTP) and an HTTP `Put` request is made.
4. The Web server on the other side receives the HTTP `Put` request. It then routes the request to the servlet that is processing SOAP. This servlet first deserializes the textual XML document and creates instances of the Java data structures, properly initializing them with the provided data.
5. It next locates the target implementation and invokes the Java operation on that implementation.

6. The implementation processes the request and returns the expected Java data structures as the response.
7. The server SOAP implementation then serializes the Java response data into an XML response document, which is then packaged with an HTTP response header.
8. The client-side SOAP implementation receives the HTTP response and extracts the XML document from it.
9. It performs textual processing on the XML document and creates and initializes the Java response data structures, and passes them back to the Java client.

A typical SOAP-based service is an order of magnitude slower than the same service communicating over remote method invocation (RMI) or the Internet Inter-ORB Protocol (IIOP). That is because those protocols do not have to transform text-based data into language-based structures.

SOAP requires XML data to be transported over HTTP. XML is verbose by nature and increases the size of the data to be transported. If all you need is to transport a byte, you may end up transporting significantly more. This is so because the XML data are tagged by their tag names. However, today's networks are fast and application integration is not performed over dial-up lines. Although sending XML documents back and forth increases the overall load on the network, most networks can handle that load.

The real burden on performance is introduced by the textual processing of XML documents that has to take place on the server side for the incoming request and on the client side for the response. This text processing requires that the document be read line-by-line, character-by-character, and a graph built of the XML elements. Contrary to many who believe that improving SOAP's performance rests on reducing the size of the data to be sent over network, we believe that a real difference can be made only by introducing a binary standard for XML that will allow binary data rather than textual XML documents to be exchanged.

There are two basic ingredients to improving performance of SOAP. The first is to provide a more efficient encapsulation of SOAP messages and the second is to transport XML documents represented in a binary encoding.

6.6.4.1 Better Message Encapsulation

SOAP messages are specified as XML documents. Because XML documents themselves are text documents, there is no way to pass binary data as part of a SOAP document. Additionally, the data being passed as part of a SOAP invocation are the XML string itself; it requires special handling because element values in an XML document cannot contain valid XML.

SOAP solves these two basic problems with its messages by introducing SOAP with attachments. However, SOAP with attachments uses MIME multipart, which itself is associated with significant processing overhead to determine various parts of the message.

The other problem is delimiting SOAP messages. To find the end of a SOAP message, the whole SOAP message has to be processed first. This introduces a significant overhead at the early stages of message processing.

Direct Internet Message Encapsulation (DIME) provides a simple and lightweight format for encapsulating SOAP messages in an efficient manner. DIME actually provides a packing format for general XML documents. More specifically, it provides a format for a DIME message that contains a set of delimited DIME records. Each DIME record contains some payload.

The SOAP message-packing scheme for DIME defines a primary SOAP message, which is the SOAP Envelope and one or more secondary SOAP messages, which are SOAP attachments. The primary and secondary SOAP messages are individual payloads, carried by DIME records.

This enables a DIME processor to easily extract various pieces of a SOAP message and its associated attachments for further processing. DIME is a format used to encode the SOAP messages and its attachments. It is not a protocol binding but rather a property of the transport binding. The DIME message can be carried over TCP or HTTP. When HTTP is used, the DIME message appears as the HTTP entity body.

6.6.4.2 Binary Encoding

Binary encoding for XML reduces the size of the XML documents to be transported by encoding text in binary format and provides for faster processing because, instead of performing character-by-character parsing, a parser can quickly jump from node to node. There are several binary formats for XML documents. For illustrative purpose, we briefly discuss WAP Binary XML (WBXML).

WBXML was developed with the explicit intent of reducing the size of XML to make the most efficient use of the limited bandwidth available to wireless devices without compromising any flexibility of the XML. WBXML defines a set of tokens. The meaning of these tokens depends on the context in which they are used. It defines global tokens, which have the same meaning regardless of where they are used, and application tags, which may take on a different meaning when used for attributes as opposed to elements. WBXML tokenizes an XML document by first converting all markup information and XML syntax into their corresponding tokens. All comments and processing directives intended for the tokenizer parser may also be removed. All other meta information is also removed. All text and character entities are converted to string and entity tokens. There are several SAX parsers available for parsing WBXML documents.

To our knowledge, there are no serious empirical data that quantify the gain in speed and reduction in size achieved by WBXML. However, some other similar open-source projects such a Binary Optimized XML (BOX) have conducted some tests and claim that, for some documents, which have a lot of repetitive data, the reduction in size is up to 85 percent with speed gains of up to 54 percent. If these claims are true, then these are significant differences.

6.7 INTEGRATION BROKERS VERSUS WEB SERVICES

There are many differences between integration brokers and Web services. These differences can be categorized as *technical, economical, and business*. This discussion deals with the technical differences between integration brokers and Web services.

- Integration brokers provide a concrete solution to integration problem, whereas Web services are not an enterprise application integration (EAI) solution but rather a technology that enables EAI. To that extent, Web services may become perfect candidates for integration themselves, which often happens, leading to recursive composition of Web services.

- Integration brokers focus on a data-centric approach and allow for sharing of data in real time. This is typically done by defining a set of data events or messages that encapsulate data to be shared, which can be either generated or consumed by software applications. Using mechanisms such as publish and subscribe, an application can publish a data event or a message and one or more subscribing applications can receive those data in near real time.

- Web services take a service-oriented approach. Instead of defining data events or messages, their focus is more on specifying service interface that represents the aggregation. This service interface or *service contract* can then be implemented by an application, and one or more clients can communicate with this aggregation service through its contract. This allows for real-time sharing of service and all its accompanying business logic, using cheap and standard technologies.

- Since there is no platform neutral-standard for publishing and subscribing to data, integration brokers provide proprietary means of publishing and subscribing to data. Because the integration problem extends beyond the single enterprise and to its business partners, they generally all have to agree on the choice of integration broker to integrate effectively.

- Web services, on the other hand, use the standard and ubiquitous technologies such as XML, HTTP, SOAP, and WSDL among many others. This is quite significant because the HTTP and XML infrastructure exists almost everywhere. No costly modifications are required to the existing IT infrastructures when the integration has to be extended to the business partners. Since the business partners share the same XML- and HTTP-based infrastructure, the integration issue moves away from technology integration to semantic harmonization.

- Simple business processes that need to integrate applications in a nonlinear fashion are hard to build with integration brokers. Such integrations require more sophisticated business-process automation methods, which are not always supported or understood very well. These simple nonlinear application integrations are easier to do in a manner natural to language programmers.

- Web services (using HTTP) work on an intermittent, point-to-point connection model, which is highly resilient. The World Wide Web has proven that model to be highly scalable because the connections can be reestablished transparently if broken without any intervention. If an application issues a SOAP request and the connection breaks, the underlying SOAP implementation or the application itself can try to reconnect and remake the request.

  In contrast, integration brokers provide a hub-and-spoke model, which provides a single point-of-failure and is hard to scale. If the message broker itself crashes, then there are no more choices left for the application. In most cases, the message broker itself has the knowledge of the messaging channels and ensures the delivery of the messages, and thus its crash can be devastating to the overall application. Most integration brokers compensate for that by providing replication architectures (including redundancy and clustering) and support for transaction reliability at significant complexity and cost.

  For example, a company has the machine A as its integration hub. There are numerous clients that use the hub. If the machine goes down, all those clients have to be reconfigured to a different hub. Web services sit behind the Web servers. It is simple enough to configure IP routers that can do hardware/software switching for Web services.

- EAI brokers integrate applications, treating them as single entities. Web services allow companies to break down big applications into smaller, independent logical units and then build wrappers around them.

6.8 INTELLIGENT BUSINESS OBJECTS (IBOs)

We introduced the concept of IBOs in Chapter 1 and discussed them in more detail in the context of the architectural blueprint for BSO in Chapter 3, as well as in the implementation step of the methodology in Chapter 4. Now, we delve into some detail of what IBOs are, how they are constructed, and how they can be serialized into interpretable XML objects (IXOs), which constitute the newest form of intelligent messaging.

```
SapPurchaseOrder = SapOrder.get(OrderNumber)
```

FIGURE 6.9. Usage of a Synthesized Object

We call IBOs intelligent because their main function is to abstract, via generic methods, the interaction with services from applications. These services, in a BSO context, will have been synthesized and harmonized into a homogeneous component catalog. This means that the services used that provided IBO can be delivered via Web services, messaging, RPC, data access, and screen scraping technologies. Because these services are in a homogeneous component catalog, the IBO sees them as simple subroutines that it can use to implement the generic methods that it needs.

We call IBOs business objects, because the idea is to build them at a level of abstraction that can be understood by any business person. Therefore, IBOs should be the likes of Customer, Partner, Supplier, Meeting, Calendar, Person, Inventory Item, Capital Good, Insurance Policy, Bank Account, RFIs, RFQs, Purchase Orders, Inventory Approvals, Invoices, Debit Notes, Credit Notes, Bills of Material, Shipping Manifests, Claims Forms, Quotation Forms, Letters of Credit, Receipts, Sales Orders, Manufacturing Orders, and many others. From the perspective of the data they contain, these objects should provide the closure of all fields in similar objects in underlying applications, services, and back-end systems.

Data aggregation and dissemination were explained earlier in the chapter. They are also among the fundamental objectives of an IBO and we talk about both aspects.

IBOs should be modeled with all business- and system-relevant data. They should be able to pull these data from one or more applications (aggregation) or enable persistence of data in one or more applications (dissemination). The list of applications from which IBOs aggregate data or to which they disseminate data can be modified without any modification to the IBOs themselves.

IBOs then become an abstraction layer that allows the process logic to manipulate process-relevant data and functions instead of using services from applications directly, thus shielding the process model from changes in the infrastructure. This allows for full orchestrations to be reusable across different organizations and infrastructures, and allows change in the services implementation without changing the process logic, and vice versa.

We discussed synthesis in detail in the previous chapters. A synthesis tool from a BSO platform vendor might introspect applications such as SAP and generate synthesized components into a repository. We call that repository a component catalog. For example, synthesis of SAP might result in generation of an `SapOrder` object being generated in the component catalog. This order would have methods such as `get` to retrieve a `SapOrder`. Figure 6.9 shows a typical usage of this object from a process logic perspective.

FIGURE **6.10. Bridge Pattern**

If, later, SAP provides SOAP-based access into its BAPIs, we could instantly resynthesize this component. Therefore, the process that used `SapOrder.get` would not need to change its usage of the component. Most BSO implementations support dynamic binding to catalogued components; therefore, the change would be instantaneous and dynamic.

The problem with the approach in the above example is that, although the order component is independent of the enabling technology, it is not application independent. Furthermore, in all likelihood there would be several processes that use the `SapOrder` component. So, if in the future the company should switch its ERP, chances are that the `Order` class implementation would be different, thus starting a domino effect on all the processes that used the native implementation directly. This is a very common problem in traditional EAI implementations, even if they provide a process layer and process-level objects.

This is actually a classic software design problem and a lot of work has been done in this area. For example, the definitive and pioneering work by Gamma et al. (1995) provided the bridge design pattern that decouples an abstraction from its implementation so that the two can vary independently of each other. Figure 6.10 shows the structure of the suggested bridge pattern.

The IBO layer represents reusable business objects that represent abstract concepts. These abstract concepts are then implemented using the *bridge* design pattern. These objects represent abstract concepts, but they are actually concrete objects in terms of a programming language. So, you have an entire information model that models the generic concepts. These reusable abstract objects are implemented by delegating to the corresponding methods of the synthesized objects.

Figure 6.11 shows an IBO called Order that represents the abstract concept Order. Its implementation might look something like Figure 6.12.

The output of the synthesis process is still the `SapOrder`. However, this synthesized component has been wrapped in the abstract concept that is independent of an application. Now the process using the `Order` object would not change if the ERP system was replaced by PeopleSoft. In that case, the implementation of

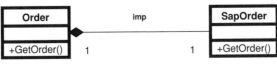

FIGURE **6.11. IBO**

```
PurchaseOrder Order::GetOrder(OrderNumber)
{
    SapPurchaseOrder order = SapOrder.GetOrder(OrderNumber);
    Return new PurchaseOrder(order);
}
```

FIGURE 6.12. Implementation of IBO

the IBO would change from SapOrder to PeopleOrder and the process using the Order would remain unchanged.

Thus, IBOs not only serve as a means to perform data aggregation or data dissemination, but also to provide an abstraction layer that shields the process logic from the underlying service implementation. The synthesized components and the IBOs themselves may be implemented in either a programming language such as Java or in a higher-level scripting language. Their actual implementation may be immaterial. To facilitate easy sharing of IBOs between different implementations of BSO platforms and to make them mobile, we define a format in which IBOs are serialized into XML, resulting in IXOs. These IXOs can then be shared among multiple implementations of BSO or can be shipped to remote customers for usage.

Let us consider a concrete example of IBOs/IXOs by looking at Fuego's implementation. Fuego's implementation of IBOs are called XObjects because the classes are implemented in XML with methods written in Fuego's Component Integration Language (CIL), which has the ability to regard synthesized services as components of a library of the language. Figures 6.13 and 6.14 show an IXO developed using Feugo's component manager.

Figure 6.13 shows an IXO that represents a simple Customer object. Being an object, Customer has data as well as attributes. For the sake of clarity, we have only shown attributes of Customer in Figure 6.13. Figure 6.14 shows methods. Lines 6-33 show all the attributes that this object has, bounded by the tag attributes. Lines 7-13 show an attribute named billingAddress of type BSO.Address. Flags on Line 10 show that this attribute has getter and setter methods and the attribute is a public attribute. Line 11 shows that the setter has the name setBillingAddress and takes a single parameter of type BSO.Address as argument. Similarly, Line 12 shows the signature of the getter method called getBillingAddress. Lines 14-19 show that the Customer object has a public attribute of type string that is called company. Lines 20-26 describe a public attribute of type integer called id. Line 21 shows that this attribute has a default value of 1. Lines 27-32 show a public attribute of type string called name.

Figure 6.14 shows the methods of the Customer object.

Figure 6.14 shows the Customer object to have only one public method, named add, as shown in Lines 7-31. Lines 8-10 provide some general information

```
1.<component        name="Customer"
2. description="BSO Customer"
        ...
3.    signature="Lxobject.BSO.Customer;"
4.    type="xobject"
5.    superclass="XObjectBase">
6.    <attributes>
7.        <object
8.            type="BSO.Address"
9.            name="billingAddress"
10.           flags="in out hassetter hasgetter attribute public"
11.           writeSignature="MsetBillingAddress(Lxobject.BSO.Address;)V"
12.           readSignature="MgetBillingAddress()Lxobject.BSO.Address;">
13.       </object>
14.       <String
15.           name="company"
16.           flags="in out hassetter hasgetter attribute public"
17.           writeSignature="MsetCompany(Ljava.lang.String;)V"
18.           readSignature="MgetCompany()Ljava.lang.String;">
19.       </String>
20.       <Int
21.           defaultValue="1"
22.           name="id"
23.           flags="in out hassetter hasgetter attribute public"
24.           writeSignature="MsetId(Ljava.lang.Long;)V"
25.           readSignature="MgetId()Ljava.lang.Long;">
26.       </Int>
27.       <String
28.           name="name"
29.           flags="in out hassetter hasgetter attribute public"
30.           writeSignature="MsetName(Ljava.lang.String;)V"
31.           readSignature="MgetName()Ljava.lang.String;">
32        </String>
33.   </attributes>
        ...
</component>
```

FIGURE 6.13. Attributes of Customer IXO

about the method, such as the fact that it is a public method and its signatures. Lines 12-15 declare some local variables. Line 12 declares a local variable called billingAddress of type Billing.Address. Similarly, Lines 13-15 declare local variables billingCustomer, bsoCustomer, and crmCustomer of types Billing.Customer, BSO.Customer and CRM.Customer, respectively. Lines 16-30 provide the business logic of the method. Lines 18-21 transfer information from bsoCustomer to billingCustomer. Lines 22-23 store the billingCustomer in the billing system. Similarly, Lines 25-28 initialize the crmCustomer and Line 29 adds the crmCustomer object in the CRM system.

This method can easily be rewritten if either the interface to billing customer, the billing system, the interface for the CRM customer, or the CRM system should change.

```
1.<component       name="Customer"
2. description="BSO Customer"
        ...
3.      signature="Lxobject.BSO.Customer;"
4.      type="xobject"
5.      superclass="XObjectBase">
        <attributes> ... </attributes>
6.      <methods>
7.          <method
8.            name="add"
9.            flags="public"
10.           signature="Madd()V">
11.         add
12.               billingAddress : Billing.Address
13.               billingCustomer : Billing.Customer
14.               bsoCustomer : BSO.Customer
15.               crmCustomer : CRM.Customer
16.         do
17.               // Add customer to billing system
18.               billingCustomer.id = bsoCustomer.id
19.               billingCustomer.company = bsoCustomer.company
20.               Ö
21.               billingCustomer.address = billingAddress
22.               store billingCustomer
23.                   returning bsoCustomer.id
24.               // Add customer to crm system
25.               crmCustomer.id = bsoCustomer.id
26.               crmCustomer.company = bsoCustomer.company
27.               crmCustomer.lastname = bsoCustomer.lastname
28.               crmCustomer.name = bsoCustomer.name

29.               add crmCustomer

30.          end add

31.          </method>
32.      </methods>
33. </component>
```

FIGURE 6.14. Methods of Customer IXO

This abstraction practice is nothing new. It's a simple object-oriented programming approach. What makes it different in BSO is that it is working with components that have been synthesized from different systems (including custom-built Xobjects on the BSO system, as in the case of BSO.Address), a CRM system that implements its API in Java, and a billing system that doesn't implement APIs but is being accessed directly through its RDBMS.

The methods and attributes of an IBO reflect the services that the process needs from that object. The implementation of these methods reflects how these business-level services are composed from existing services from applications and/or people.

```
BSO.Customer bsoCustomer;

// load the EDI document into the ediCustomer class
EDI.Customer ediCustomer = ediCustomer.load

// transform the ediCustomer object into a bsoCustomer object
bsoCustomer <- ediCustomer
```

FIGURE 6.15. Filling an IBO from an EDI Document

This way of designing IBOs is what we referred to as "Composition" in Chapter 2. It composes an add service that updates, in this case, a billing system and a CRM system. In the future, however, it may be doing more or fewer things, depending on the IT strategy of the company.

Composition makes businesses resilient to IT strategy changes (and we all know that technology continually pushes those) and IT strategy resilient to business changes (and we all know that the marketplace continually pushes those).

In the example, the calling processes can then orchestrate services from people in any organization and the services from any applications transparently by just invoking the methods on IBO.

If the customer data are obtained through an EDI document, for example, then the `bsoCustomer` object will be filled through a transformation, as shown in Figure 6.15.

As can be seen in Figure 6.15 above the back-arrow indicates that bsoCustomer should invoke the appropriate object transformation to instantiate itself from an EDI object. This step is completely independent of what the back-end systems are.

If, after instantiating the IBO, the process wants to add it to the back-end systems, it's as easy as invoking `bsoCustomer.add`. This method can be invoked regardless of how the object was instantiated. To illustrate the loosely coupled nature of this construct, we will give another example.

Now, let's suppose that the instantiation of the customer data is going to be done by invoking a human service (soliciting input from a participant using a specific presentation. In this case, we would do something like Figure 6.16.

The input method is invoked without any knowledge of what billing and CRM systems are in the back end and regardless of what the presentation looks like. The

```
input bsoCustomer using
    selectedPresentation = &quot;mainInfo&quot;
    returning selectedButton = selection
```

FIGURE 6.16. Filling an IBO from a Manual Input Through a Presentation

`bsoCustomer.add` method is independent of the services that implement it, and therefore independent of the underlying applications as well as the technologies that expose their services.

This makes this IBO reusable in a variety of processes and makes those processes independent of the underlying infrastructure.

In Chapter 9, we present Visual Business Object, which can add presentation aspects to the IBO.

CHAPTER 7

Metadata and Service Discovery

7.1 INTRODUCTION

As with everything else, we have a very holistic view of metadata and discovery features, looking at the entire reference model described in Chapter 3 and shown in Figure 3.1. In this chapter, we describe all different kinds of metadata that are relevant for a complete orchestration environment. We discuss the role of service discovery facilities and describe what is expected from those facilities.

The role of metadata and service discovery is generally well understood in a service-oriented architecture. Figure 7.1 illustrates the typical publish–discover–bind cycle. A new business service is developed. Its developers publish the service contract in the business registry. The service consumers discover the service from the registry, bind to it, and use the service. In this typical service-oriented architecture, the service contract consists primarily of the service description. This service-level information is generally categorized using some taxonomy scheme. A service consumer either searches the service by name or looks for a service that implements some particular specification.

Although these roles of metadata and service discovery are still true for a complete BSO environment, the metadata for the BSO environment are significantly more complex than what was described above, and service discovery requires some additional capabilities as well.

287

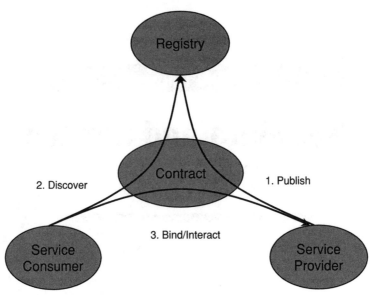

FIGURE 7.1. Publish–Discover–Bind Cycle.

Metadata can actually be split into four broad categories:

1. **Descriptive metadata.** These metadata include service contracts, orchestration definitions, and messages data types.

2. **Rules.** An important part of metadata is various kind of data validation and data transformation rules that have been defined for successfully execute orchestrations.

3. **Access-related data.** While the descriptive metadata are useful for developing applications that will access the services, access-related metadata are used to access services. These service-access data provide the flexibility for the environment to be reconfigured and the implementations to be changed. They also helpful in providing fault tolerance and load balancing in a loosely coupled environment.

4. **Demographic.** Orchestrations rely heavily on user roles and the roles assigned to systems for their participation in an orchestration. Demographic data include these roles as well as security-related information.

In this chapter, we first describe the metadata architecture required for a BSO environment in detail. We then briefly discuss the evolution of metadata and discovery facilities leading to the current state of the technology and then conclude with a description of the comprehensive metadata and discovery facility required for BSO.

7.2 METADATA ARCHITECTURE

A clear understanding of the required metadata is fundamental to successful BSO. A metadata facility should provide a comprehensive information object model and an interface that describes the capabilities and application programmer interfaces (APIs) to the registry service. While the development of a comprehensive information object model is out of the scope of this book, it is important to describe the distinct categories of the metadata to be supported by the information object model. In addition to the categories of the data supported by the information model, the metadata facility has to support some basic capabilities. The general architecture of the metadata facility is captured by Figure 7.2.

The repository described in this picture is a logical repository that is able to store the four categories of metadata mentioned earlier.

7.2.1 Information Model for Meta Repository

As mentioned earlier, there are four basic categories under which all the metadata can be categorized. The relative significance of a metadata category is dependent

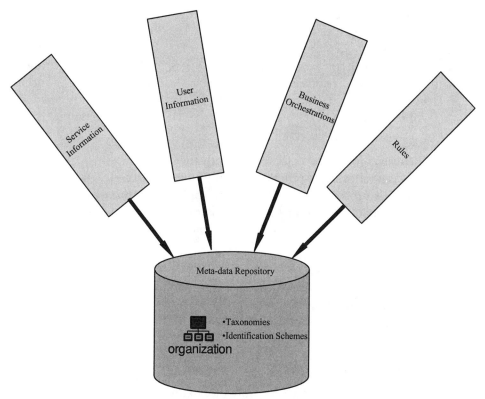

FIGURE 7.2. Metadata Facility Architecture.

upon the solution. For example, an application providing discrete services running in a trusted environment may not need user information. However, an orchestrated business service with work-flow elements may not be able to function without user information.

7.2.1.1 Organizational/User Information

Organization/user information describes the organization structure and provides its demographic data. Directory services are particularly good at organizing and making this kind of information available over the network. The data in this category tend to be hierarchical in nature and contain demographic as well as security information. These data can generally be divided into several subcategories, as described below:

- **Organizational units**. An organization is generally composed of many departments. Each unit may describe a department, a subdepartment, or a group. These organizational units generally serve the purpose of grouping a bunch of users so that roles can be assigned at the unit level. Managing an organization with hundreds of thousands of users can be quite tedious. It is generally acceptable, then, to group the users in these organizational units and manage their attributes, such as roles, at the group level rather than at the individual level. For example, if a finance application needs to be accessed by the finance department and there are a thousand employees in the finance department, then, rather than entering each one of those thousand employees in the access control list of that application, just the finance department can be entered and that will make the application accessible to the whole finance department. The organizational units are hierarchical.

- **Users**. The user-level information is basically the information about an individual. There is no shortcut to providing this information. Of course this basic-level information is probably the most significant piece of information in this category of metadata. Each user belongs to some organizational unit. Generally, access control is not specified at this basic information level.

- **Roles**. Any given user in an organization may fulfill several different roles. A role generally identifies a particular responsibility that a user has in the business scenarios in question. Roles describe the capabilities of the users. Roles sometimes correspond to the title a user holds in an organization but that may not always be the case. For example, an employee in the finance department may hold the title of loan officer. However, this user may sometimes have the role of manager, PowerPoint presentation expert, or loan approver. Roles are used in several different ways. For example, for security purpose, the roles are sometimes used to control access; only those employees that are in the role of a manager may access certain human resources functions. Similarly, there may be many loan officers within the finance department, but only those who are in the role of loan approver may be able to access certain functions within some finance applications. Roles hence describe the areas of responsibilities that an individual has within the organization. Since most service orchestration efforts are aimed at automating the functions performed by individuals, roles play an equally important part in BSO. An orchestration will access these user roles and assign work to their task lists in much the same manner as a human manager or supervisor would.

7.2.1.2 Rules

In a system of orchestrations, the orchestration engine integrates many different applications, exchanging data between them. There are two important rules associated with this data exchange that must be stored as part of the metadata. These rules are not specific to orchestrations per se but are necessary for any system that integrates disparate applications.

- Data validation rules provide logic to validate data. The sophistication of these rules depends on the implementation of the product. Some products may provide predefined validation rules for the data whereas others may even allow some code snippets, in either a proprietary scripting language or a programming language. In either case, the validation rules are specified on input messages expected by the target service.

- In cases in which the system provides predefined validation rules, such as lower and upper ranges of a currency value, the underlying repository will be able to store this information along with the message definition itself. If the validation rules get too complex, the repository should allow the storage of code segments that the engine can execute.

- Data are exchanged between business services, but even conceptually similar data are seldom structured the same way. A customer record in one system may not look entirely like a customer record in another system. For this reason, messages often have to be transformed from one form into another during the exchange. Most BSOs provide very powerful transformation capabilities. The data that describe details of required transformations have to be managed by the environment. A BSO metadata repository should be able to store the transformation rules in code or in some other form.

7.2.1.3 Business Services Information

Earlier in the book, we described different kinds of business services and differentiated between business services that are solo or discrete and composite from those that are orchestrated. This is an important differentiation because the metadata required for the orchestrated services are more complex than the others.

In any case, business services are generally classified according to taxonomies. These taxonomic schemes are discussed in more detail in the next few sections. However, it is important to mention here the classification of these services. This allows for powerful search mechanisms. For example, I can use industry and geography taxonomies to search for order fulfillment services of florists in the southern United States.

Once a service has been located, if it is a discrete service, then more information is required about it to successfully exchange messages with it. Most applications require some sort of handshake. This handshake typically employs exchange of security information. The invoking service must also configure itself for the protocol supported or expected by the target service.

The interface definition of any service is probably the most critical piece of information that is required for successful invocation of methods on the target service. Generally speaking, the interface definition of business services describes the operations supported by the target application, along with the definition of its parameters, its response, and any exceptions raised by the target service's operations. For an orchestrated service, however, this service description must be used in conjunction with the BSO. Whereas the BSO knows the methods that must be invoked, the service description describes what parameters are expected by the target operations. The service description also describes the format of the target operation's parameters.

Finally, the endpoint where the target service can be invoked also needs to be known. This endpoint declaration being part of the metadata is important. Having the endpoint here allows the service to be redirected for planned downtime and load balancing. For example, a service may be listening at a particular URI. However, because the system needs to be taken down for scheduled maintenance, the system administrators may move the service to another system and change the endpoint for that service in the metadata to reflect the move, thus performing maintenance without disrupting the service. The endpoint should be logical and resolved at runtime by a directory service. This way, the changes in the implementation of the service can be transparent to the user.

We introduced intelligent business objects (IBOs) in Chapter 3 and discussed them in detail in Chapter 6. IBOs are the object-oriented, fine-grained, client-side proxies for the course-grained business services. They are an essential part of the business services harmonization process. IBOs completely hide the service usage aspects of the business service and, in fact, present an object-oriented interface to the client. This is a great marriage of the object-oriented concepts with scalability and practicality of the course-grained services. IBOs are essentially XML documents that represent logic about how to interact with the business service through finer-grained application concepts. A BSO metadata repository has to be able to store these objects for later retrieval and usage.

IBOs are not the same as object-oriented technologies such as CORBA or Java objects. IBOs are highly mobile units of data and logic, serialized in XML format that can be shipped around. These objects generally act as intelligent proxies for a remote service that knows how to execute appropriate business rules locally and how to communicate with the remote services that they represent.

7.2.1.4 BSO Definitions

Business processes describe a set of interactions that make up a business function. From an analysis point of view, Unified Modeling Language (UML) has formalized concepts such as use cases and sequence diagrams. During the early stages of understanding a system's requirements, flow of events is defined for how the system will be used. In the process design phase, the focus shifts from how the system will be used to how the work will be performed. During this phase, implementation details are added to the flow. These flow of events, along with all the necessary details, needs to be captured so that a business process orchestration engine can later orchestrate interactions between services on the basis of that flow. Some methodologies, such as UML, allow one to graphically express these flows of events. In any case, there are many flows that are required to describe the requirements of a use case. There is generally one main flow, which describes the sunny-day scenario, and many alternative flows that describe either boundary conditions or exceptions through the system. A business process is the collection of all these paths through the system to fulfill a business use case.

There are several reasons for storing these BSO definitions in a metadata repository. First, these BSOs form the fingerprints of an orchestrated service, and the documentation of what human intervention is required to fulfill the service. A service that implements certain BSO definitions needs to be recognized as such. A BSO involves multiple applications that expose services that they render to the BSOs that they support. However, first these target services need to be discovered before appropriate methods can be invoked from them. An important criterion for this discovery process might be the fact that the target service is needed for the implementation of a BSO. The second equally important need for saving the BSO definition in a metadata repository is so that the BSO can be executed. It is not desirable to store the definition of the BSO in the code that executes it. If the definition is stored in a metadata repository, then it can be changed much easier and can also be shared among multiple applications.

Later in the book, we talk about the BSO definitions in detail, including their desired structure and format, what form they should take in the storage medium, and how they should be exchanged among various tools and among various execution engines. We also talk about synchronizing the BSO interface definitions among various business-to-business (B2B) partners so that they all reference the same versions of the BSO interfaces. This is so that we can change the implementations (loosely coupled) without disrupting the usage of the service.

7.2.2 Capabilities of the Metadata Repository

We have talked about the various elements of the information model that should be supported by a metadata facility. In that discussion, we intentionally left out two extremely important kinds of metadata. That is because it is probably best to discuss those elements as capabilities that the metadata facility should support. Eventually, they have to be part of the information model supported by the facility.

7.2.2.1 Identification Schemes

An identification scheme is usually the primary mechanism for identifying a business. There are several formal schemes in use today, such as Dunn & Bradstreet's D-U-N-S numbers and Global Location Numbers (GLN), U.S. tax identifiers, and European VAT numbers, that uniquely identify an organization.

Identifier schemes are not generally hierarchical in nature. An identifier scheme represents identifier taxonomy, and a specific instance identifier is associated with a single identifier scheme. Metadata facilities should provide predefined identifier schemes for the most popular ones but should also provide an extensible mechanism to create more identifier schemes.

7.2.2.2 Classification Schemes (Taxonomies)

Classification schemes are used to categorize organizations and the services they offer to facilitate searching. A powerful metadata facility can provide sophisticated search mechanisms such as searching for all sporting goods manufacturers (industry classification scheme) in the southwestern United States, among others. Like identifier schemes, there are several well-accepted classification schemes such as the North American Industry Classification System (NAICS), the Universal Standard Products and Services Classification (UNSPC), and ISO 3166. Just as an organization can have multiple identifiers, an organization or its services can also be classified along multiple dimensions.

Although classification schemes are similar to identification schemes, they are different in one significant way. It is important for classification schemes to be hierarchical. For example, an item of the industry taxonomy may be further divided into many subtaxonomies. Figure 7.3 demonstrates the hierarchical nature of classification schemes. It shows a tree-like structure where each node represents a classification. The classification scheme then becomes the whole family of

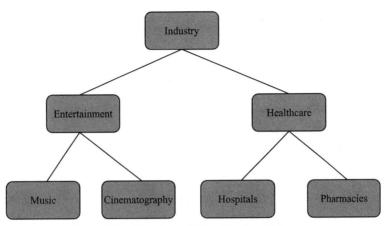

FIGURE **7.3. Structure of Classification Schemes.**

classifications, where every node describes a particular classification. An organization or a service can then be categorized by associating it with a node in the classification scheme. So, for example, a service that is categorized as an industry, which happens to be the root of the industry classification scheme, has the broadest category, as opposed to a movie studio, which is classified as cinematography. Hence the deeper you go into the classification scheme, the more narrowly or precisely you specify its classification.

7.3 DISCOVERY

The ability to discover metadata through search mechanisms is just as important as the ability to store it. The required capabilities can probably be best be describe in relation to the entity who is using the discovery mechanism. We define three different kinds of users of the discovery capability:

7.3.1 Discovery by Humans

The initial focus on registries has been on their usage by humans. They may use the registries to do research on business partners for potential services. Additionally, in a bare-bones environment, the development tools might not be integrated with the discovery mechanisms and the human developers may have to manually download meta information about the target services so that application programs can be written.

A human user will typically browse the registry by performing simple searches based on either taxonomies or a service's technical specifications (technical fingerprints). We consider the taxonomy-based and fingerprint-based searches to be the minimum search capabilities expected from a BSO metadata facility.

7.3.2 Discovery by Development Tools

The use of a BSO metadata facility might be quite similar to the usage by humans. In fact, it is a human developer sitting in front of a development tool. The difference is in how the metadata are used. The developer will probably download the service or orchestration contract and then use some other tools to generate code based on that contract from the development tools. If the development tools support the registry in an integrated manner, then the developer can browse through the registry while in the development tool and select the service to be integrated. The development tool may then interact with the registry to download the service contract and make use of it, such as generating proxies from it.

7.3.3 Discovery by Other Programs

This reflects the most sophisticated use of a registry. There are several different ways that a client program can use the registry and each represents a different level of sophistication.

7.3.3.1 Accessing Service Listening Address

The simplest way for a client program to use the registry is to retrieve the listening address of the service. The service can be better managed if the service listening address is not hard coded. Administrators can move the service around to better manage the upgrades and load balancing and to provide fault tolerance.

In this scenario, the client program stores the unique identifier that represents the service information. The client program provides that unique identifier and gets a single instance of relevant metadata back. It then uses those metadata to bind to the service and access it.

7.3.3.2 Generating Dynamic Proxies

In the simple case described above, the client contains the proxy to the target service. This proxy has all the information about how to create a request message from the parameters provided and how to handle incoming responses. It requires the client to be fully aware of the requirements of the target service.

More sophisticated orchestration engines may be able to actually generate these proxies on-the-fly from the metadata. The client program executes a simple query based on a certain technical fingerprint or taxonomy, retrieves the service contract, uses those metadata to create the service request from the parameters provided, and returns the response. This provides some more flexibility to the orchestration engine because it is no longer dependent on the precompiled proxy stubs.

7.3.3.3 Ad Hoc Queries for Dynamic Participants

This represents the most sophisticated form of querying. Typically, we had programmed very static relationships between the service consumers and the service providers. However, in today's digital economy, this is no longer true. Companies enter into new partnerships and terminate old ones on a much more frequent basis. These partnerships grow by including more services from the same suppliers, or by adding alternative suppliers to the partnerships. Imagine an order fulfillment process of a computer manufacturing company that requires a company to interact with three kinds of service providers: parts supplier, financial services, and shipping services.

In the case of the financial services, the manufacturer may enter into partnerships with both Visa and MasterCard, for example. Later, the manufacturer may also decide to start accepting Discover and American Express. Once the trading partnerships with those new institutions have been finalized, they are registered into the registry. There is an assumption that the business processes supported by all these institutions will be industry-defined standard business processes. In that case, the computer manufacturer can simply retrieve the appropriate entry points to the business partner from the business registry and do electronic binding with them.

In the case of the parts suppliers, the computer manufacturer may have relationships with many of its memory chip suppliers, for example. To increase its supply of memory chips, the computer manufacturer may execute a query against the business registry of preapproved suppliers, predicating the query against certain attributes, to select the appropriate supplier. In the future, more suppliers may be approved to do business with this computer manufacturer and some suppliers may lose their preapproval. Alternatively, this could also be accomplished through a more powerful vertical exchange for memory chips. This exchange may offer more powerful product catalog management facilities and criteria-based product selection. In such a case, the vertical exchange will become member of the partnership network, following the previously defined process, and the manufacturer will perform business with the exchange.

The third external trading partnership is with the providers of the logistic services to ship products. The computer manufacturer may choose to use the partner on the basis of the target destination of the product. For example, it may use one shipping company to ship products to domestic destinations and another to ship products overseas. Again, more shippers can be added to this mix and some may be removed.

All of these cases demonstrate that the target service cannot be hard coded into systems that may need to interact with them. The BSO infrastructure has to support a discovery process that supports e-bonding at runtime. A business registry that supports ad hoc queries facilitates such a dynamic discovery and decision-making process.

7.4 Evolution of Metadata Facilities

Applications have long been storing various kinds of metadata about them. Although the underlying objectives and focus of these facilities have incrementally become more and more sophisticated over time, the basic principle, to provide a level of decoupling between service–consumer and service-provider applications, has remained the same.

7.4.1 Naming Service

The Object Management Group (OMG) popularized the naming service as part of the core services offered by the Object Management Architecture, but then it was also adopted by the Java Architecture. A naming service provides a way to organize services into hierarchical naming contexts. It employs a model, which is actually very similar to file systems, to provide a name-to-object association.

Just as a file system can have directories where each folder or directory can contain subdirectories or files, a naming service can have name contexts (equivalent) to directories and objects (equivalent) to file. When you reach a file in the file system, you get the data associated with the file. In a naming service, when you reach object, you don't get the object itself but rather its object reference. If the object is already active, then this reference is usable right away. If it is not, then the referenced object can be activated at this time.

Naming services are quite useful in their respective component models to organize object references according to application-specific namespaces. In a naming graph, the nodes, which are defined as naming contexts, can have more bindings under them, other contexts, or service bindings. A naming graph represents an earlier form of classification scheme for services. We defined what classification schemes are earlier. The structure of the classification scheme can easily be compared with the structure of a naming graph. A classification node in the classification scheme corresponds to the naming context in the naming graph. The name binding of an object reference is to a naming context what a service being classified is to a classification node. In Figure 7.4, all non-leaf naming contexts, such as Industry, Entertainment, and Retail represent classification nodes and the name bindings represent service objects that are bound in those contexts and represent the services that are being classified.

Although they provide a flexible namespace management mechanism, the name services are, in fact, quite limited:

- **Name services allow only simple context traversals.** The complete path leading to a name binding has to be known ahead of time. There are no search facilities available for object bindings. Clients are expected to navigate naming contexts,

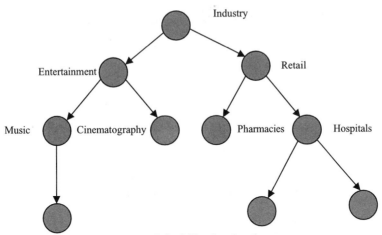

FIGURE 7.4. A Naming Graph.

retrieving lists of names bound to that context, and then further traverse those
bindings.

- **The naming service itself is designed to locate CORBA objects.** The metamodel for naming services is quite simple and does not allow storage of other
  types.

- **Naming services have no concept of taxonomies.** No semantics are associated
  with the name contexts.

7.4.2 Directory Service

Although naming services are useful for locating objects representing remote applications in network environments, they are not helpful in locating other network
resources such as authorized users for those applications. These are critical data
without which business transactions cannot be completed. Furthermore, to locate a resource in the naming service, one has to know the exact path for that
resource. There are no search capabilities supported by the naming services. This
can prove to be quite limiting when trying to select a target application from many
choices.

Directory services overcome some of these limitations:

- Directory services allow storage of all kinds of objects, whether they represent
  applications or users for those applications or just other network resources.
- Directory services allow querying capabilities that can be used to perform powerful searches. For example, a directory service can be queried to retrieve all
  the applications related to order fulfillment.

TABLE 7.1. Standardized Keywords

Keyword	Distinguished Name
CN	common name
L	locality
ST	state or province
O	organization
OU	organization unit
C	country
STREET	street address

A directory is quite like a database, although with significant differences. Databases provide powerful ad-hoc search and comprehensive transaction capabilities. In contrast, directory services store more descriptive, attribute-based information. Directories also tend to be more read-optimized and hence provide faster querying capabilities and look-ups of a high volume of data but relatively slow updates.

The biggest use of directory services, such as those that are based on X.500 Directory Service Standard, is for managing demographic data about an organization's employees. They accomplish this by mapping an organization's topology into the directory schema.

We previously described the kind of metadata that are essential for orchestrated business services. In addition to providing the user and role information to facilitate task-based workflows, these data are also essential in providing general application-level security.

The discussion of directory services has become synonymous with the Lightweight Directory Access Protocol (LDAP). LDAP was initially designed to provide access to X.500 directories without incurring its resource requirements and overhead.

Objects in LDAP are defined as a set of attributes. Each object has a *distinguished name* (DN) that is used as the primary key for the object. The DN uniquely identifies the object. Each attribute itself has a type and one or more values. A DN is made up of mnemonic keywords such as "cn" for common name or "o" for organization. Table 7.1 lists some of the keywords used to construct a DN. These keywords can also be used for types.

A DN is constructed by concatenating its name with those of its ancestors. Figure 7.5 shows an example DN. In this example, the DN for Waqar Sadiq would be "CN=Waqar Sadiq, OU=EIT, O=EDS,C=US" while the DN for Felix Racca would be "CN=Felix Racca, OU=EVP, O=Fuego, C=US".

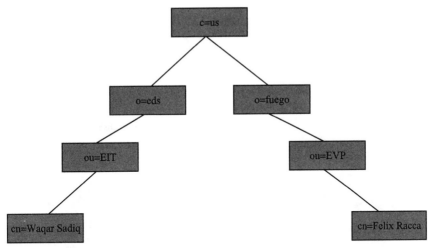

FIGURE **7.5. An Example of an LDAP Directory Tree.**

7.4.3 OMG's Trader Service

Experience with the naming service quickly revealed that being able to list services by name was not enough and that there was a need to provide a more sophisticated mechanism for searching. Specifically, the services need to be discovered on the basis of a set of properties. The trader service allows dynamic discovery and late binding of services.

Applications advertise their capabilities by providing a set of properties that qualify the service offering. Once the service offering has been advertised with the trader, the clients can discover the service by executing a query against the trader service itself. Figure 7.6 describes the well-accepted publish-discover-interact cycle that the trader service follows.

You can see the similarity between the service discovery cycle described in Figure 7.6 and the one described in Figure 7.1. Except for the "service contract," the two are essentially the same. This is further proof of evolution of the discovery mechanism and of new registry mechanisms learning and building upon the past ones.

A service provider publishes a *service offer* with the trader service. This *service offer* comprises a service type name, a reference to the CORBA object that implements the service offering, and a set of zero or more properties that represent the behavioral and other aspects of the service that are not captured by its interface. The clients use a service type name and a query language to select the service they need. OMG defines a *Standard Constraint Language* for the clients to form a query. This query is then executed by the trader service. The result set of the query may

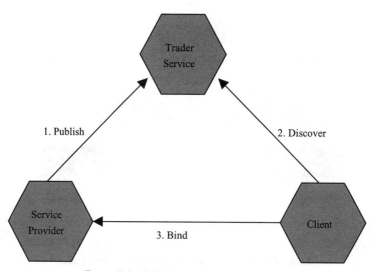

FIGURE 7.6. Publish–Discover–Bind Cycle.

be one or more service offerings. It is then up to the client to sort out the results and select from the result set.

OMG expected a large number of services to be published with the trader service. Scalability was a concern because it had proven to be a problem with the a Naming service. The trader service therefore has a federated architecture, in which various trading services are linked to each other, each making its set of published offerings available to the others. As more and more traders are linked to each other, a larger number of traders become reachable. These linked traders form a directed graph. This is then known as the *trading graph*. Clients can use various policies to limit the scope of the query when the trader service executes it.

The trader service has many important concepts that show up in the modern-day registries. However, it also suffered from some deficiencies:

- It is specific to CORBA object references. Hence it can only be used to publish a CORBA object.
- It provides a set of properties over which a query can be predicated. However, it does not provide a formal way of specifying a schema that can be rigorously checked. For example, a rigorous schema would have allowed all shipping services to always provide a set of properties that can be used for querying by the shipping client. This facilitates industry-standard schemas.
- It does not provide ways of creating classification schemes. The classification concept is loosely incorporated in the properties, but it is not formally recognized.

7.5 BUSINESS REGISTRY

We have talked about evolution of metadata facilities. The metadata lineage is much longer than what we have discussed in the preceding section. However, what we have talked about are the relevant standards and facilities that have developed so far to support a service-oriented architecture that is suitable for process orchestration. Registries that are specifically designed from the ground up to store metadata about business services are called *business registries*. These *business registries* have the following characteristics:

- They should be able to support the information model for metadata discussed in Section 7.2.1.
- They support methods for defining identification schemes.
- They support flexible classification schemes.
- They provide various methods for retrieving metadata. These methods are not limited to browsing and drilling down but may also support flexible queries.
- They support XML-based protocols for client access. The client-side access can be specified either by describing a set of SOAP-based messages or a WSDL or by defining a language-based (such as Java) API for the clients to use. A SOAP-based API is preferable because it is language neutral and a client can use a variety of tools to format the messages and execute its queries.

With these capabilities in mind, let us discuss some of the more dominant registry-related specifications and discuss how they can be used to facilitate BSO.

7.5.1 Universal Description, Discovery, and Integration (UDDI)

UDDI is a specification for Web-based registries that allows service providers to publish information about their Web services so that the users of those services can discover and use them. The published information about the Web services can be either nontechnical, such as business addresses or human contact information, or technical, such as what standards are supported by the services.

Various companies, approved by the UDDI consortium, build and run instances of compliant registries, known as *operator sites*. These operator sites participate in the public network of UDDI registries and make up a logically centralized but physically distributed service with multiple root nodes that replicate data with each other. Hence any service information entered into one of the operator sites is visible to the users of other operator sites, given the latency of the replication frequency. Information that is published in the UDDI registry is available to anyone

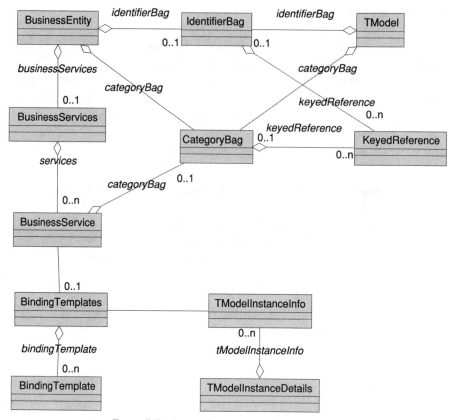

FIGURE 7.7. Core Information Model for UDDI.

with the ability to access the UDDI operator sites. No authentication is required and no security is performed for querying the registry.

7.5.1.1 Information Model for UDDI

UDDI defines a core information model with five core concepts in it. Each of the five concepts maps to specific data structures in the information model. Figure 7.7 shows the simplified UDDI core information model described in UML. The specification itself defines the information model in the form of an XML Schema document.

7.5.1.1.1 TModel. The most important and overloaded concept in UDDI is a TModel. In the registry, TModels provide a reference system based on abstractions. Since TModel takes the form of keyed metadata, you can store many different kinds of data in it. Although there are many ways for using a TModel, the UDDI consortium has formalized only some usages.

TModels can be used to represent identifier schemes. UDDI has identified two common identifier types and TModels for those types are a core part of UDDI registries. These are Dun & Bradstreet D-U-N-S numbers and Thomas Register supplier IDs. Other identifier schemes may be created, such as US tax codes and European VAT codes.

The other important use of TModel is to specify taxonomies. Similarly to identification schemes, UDDI has identified four taxonomies and made them a core part of UDDI registries. These are the NAICS, UNSPSC, and ISO 3166 (the international standard for geographical regions, including codes for countries and their first-level administrative subdivisions). Another taxonomy, named "Other Taxonomy," is for general-purpose classification schemes. New classification schemes can be created. For example, an organization may have its own taxonomies to classify its business services according to their functional characteristics.

TModels are also used to mark the technical fingerprints of business services. For example, a TModel may exist for a particular RosettaNet PIP. A business service that implements that PIP may be marked with that TModel. UDDI formally recognizes technical specifications in XML and WSDL.

7.5.1.1.2 BusinessEntity. All data published in UDDI are owned by one organization or another. An organization is represented by BusinessEntity. BusinessEntity then serves as the overall container for the information published by that organization. TModel is the only exception where data are owned by an authorized user but not by the organization. When a BusinessEntity is removed, all information owned by the BusinessEntity is also removed.

A BusinessEntity has one or more identifiers and categories. This is important because UDDI search mechanisms for BusinessEntity are predicated over identifier and categorization schemes.

The BusinessEntity serves as the container for all the services offered by that organization.

7.5.1.1.3 BusinessService. Each instance of a BusinessService represents a specific service offering. A BusinessService is contained in a BusinessEntity. BusinessService instances can be categorized using one of the predefined categorization schemes or the ones created specially by the organization.

7.5.1.1.4 BindingTemplate. A BusinessService in UDDI does not carry much useful information. In fact, it is a mere container for BindingTemplates. BindingTemplates contain two important pieces of information: First, they contain the technical fingerprints of a service. This is accomplished by having the BindingTemplate contain one or more instances of TModels, each representing a fingerprint. Second, they contain information required to access that particular instance at runtime. For example, in the case of a Web service, the BindingTemplate will contain the URI for accessing the service.

7.5.1.1.5 PublicAssertion. UDDI recognizes that sometimes large organizations may not be represented by a single BusinessEntity. For example, General Motors is a large organization and has multiple autonomous units such as Buick and Pontiac. Similarly, a marketplace may register itself as a BusinessEntity. However, it is still important to preserve the individual identity of the participant organizations in the marketplace. PublicAssertion allows publishing assertions about these business relationships.

7.5.1.2 Access Interfaces for UDDI

UDDI API is specified in terms of SOAP messages. These messages are grouped in two families, one for searching the registry and the other for publishing to the registry.

7.5.1.2.1 Inquiry. The inquiry API is used to search the registry and is further broken down into two groups. The first group of API, beginning with `find_xxxx`, usually takes a criterion and returns some summary-level information. This information is generally suitable for display or further selection. The search criterion itself is not a declarative criterion as in SQL or OQL. Rather, it is specified through a set of category schemes, identifier schemes, or TModels. This criterion can be further refined by specifying a set of qualifiers to further constraint or override the behavior of the queries.

The second group of inquiry API contains the messages that generally take a unique identifier and return the data structure identifier by that unique key.

Inquiry APIs do not require any kind of authentication. The user does not need to provide a userID or a password or does not even need to be registered in the registry in any way. All data published to the registry are visible to anyone else who has the ability to access the registry.

7.5.1.2.2 Publication. Publication requires the user to be authenticated. Publication APIs require HTTPS for secure communication. For the most part, publication APIs are split between adding information and deleting information. UDDI does not really provide separate APIs for creating new items or updating existing items. The behavior of the functions is dependent upon the contents of data. For example, while saving a new BusinessEntity, if the business key is empty, then a new BusinessEntity will be created in the registry. However, if the BusinessEntity key is not blank, then an attempt will be made to update an existing BusinessEntity. The operation requested upon a data structure actually acts upon its content as well. For example, if a business entity is provided to save_business and the BusinessEntity provided has several BusinessServices, then all the BusinessServices will be saved as well. If the set of BusinessServices does not contain a service that was previously part of the set, then saving the BusinessEntity will, in effect, delete that BusinessService.

APIs in the other group specifically delete the data structures in the registry. These APIs typically require just the unique key being for the data structure. Again, the action is performed on the contained types as well. So, if an organization has several business services registry, deleting the organization also deletes all of its services.

7.5.1.2.3 Authentication. As mentioned earlier, authentication in UDDI is required for publishing to the registry. UDDI does not specify any authentication mechanism. It only requires that all publication messages be sent over a secure connection and that each publishing API take a parameter that represents an authentication token. The rest is up to the registry implementer.

Typically, a user registers himself/herself with a registry operator. This registration generally means getting a userID and a password for that registry implementation. UserIDs and passwords are not replicated across the other UDDI nodes. So, registering a user in one UDDI operator does not allow that user to publish at other UDDI nodes. However, their published data are replicated across nodes.

Because the communication with the registry is required to take place over a secure connection, the user may need to obtain the servers' client digital certificate, which contains its public key, before he or she can even authenticate himself or herself to the registry. Authentication is performed by the registry by sending it a special message called get_authToken. This method takes a userID and a password and provides an authentication token back to the client. The client then includes that authentication with every publish-API call that it makes.

7.5.1.3 Usage Patterns
UDDI specification anticipates three usage patterns:

1. **Browse.** In this usage pattern, a user explores data by starting out with some broad, high-level information. This usually results in large sets of information, which can then be drilled down into. This pattern is typically used to display the initial results of a search in some visual form so that one or more items can be selected for more detail. For example, you might want to display all the services registered by an organization. The result set typically includes the

most essential information, such as object keys, necessary to drill down further. UDDI supports this pattern by `find_xxxxx` calls in its query API.

2. **Drill down.** In this usage pattern, the user already has the key information and can use it to drill down further and retrieve more specific information. This results in the detailed information about the object being sought. UDDI supports this pattern by `get_xxxxx` calls in its query API.

3. **Invocation.** This pattern allows the application to use remote Web services. UDDI supports a binding template data type that contains the location information about the registered Web services. An expectation is that programs can, at runtime, obtain the binding template for a service that conforms to a specific technical specification. Since the binding template provides the access URI for a Web service, the service can then be invoked.

7.5.1.4 UDDI for BSO

There are several issues that challenge the suitability of UDDI as the appropriate repository for BSO:

- The information model of UDDI is not extendible. This is a problem because, as we discussed earlier in this chapter, the metamodel requirements of BSO are, in fact, quite extensive. Since UDDI cannot allow additional information to be stored, a BSO platform may have to provide other registries to supplement UDDI. For example, most organizations have business and technical owners for different services. When using a private UDDI registry, these organizations would like to store these business and technical owners as contacts for individual service instances. Since UDDI does not allow contact information to be stored at the service level, the organization will have to use a supplemental registry to store that extra information.
- Most organizations are not interested in publishing their service information to the world. In UDDI, when you publish information, it is visible to everybody on the planet who has access to the UDDI registry. This will seriously affect the usefulness of public UDDI nodes.
- BSO requires execution of tasks and activities. In many cases, this involves business applications that perform discrete tasks. These business services are easily described by their WSDL document. There is a little bit of confusion between the nature of a *binding template* and a *WSDL* document. The binding template provides a point where the service can be accessed. However, a WSDL document also has a section devoted to describing the service and this section includes the access point for the service. A better approach is to standardize the WSDL document. The WSDL document can be downloaded from the Web server and will always provide the correct location of the service.

- The query patterns supported by UDDI are fairly basic but BSO requires something more powerful. An important characteristic of B2B relationships is that they are no longer static. A B2B relationship should be viewed as a collection of business partners. This collection shrinks and grows as business demand and competitive pressures change. BSO has to select a partner with whom to do business for a particular activity. This involves issuing an ad-hoc query over that set of partners and then downloading its WSDL to use its interface. UDDI does not support ad-hoc query.

7.5.2 ebXML Registry & Repository

The role of the ebXML Registry & Repository service is to provide persistent storage for a wide range of submitted content. This submitted content may be XML schema and documents, process descriptions, UML models, business profiles, and so on.

The ebXML Registry & Repository service defines a flexible information model. This information model defines a tree-like structure, elements of which are called classification nodes, to define taxonomies. It also defines an object model to describe the metadata. This model supports objects that are stored in the repository (e.g., a DTD or a process description) as well as objects that are stored externally (e.g., a business entity's homepage).

The information model is encapsulated by the registry interfaces:

- **Registration service.** This allows parties to register themselves as clients of the ebXML Registry Services.

- **Object management service.** This allows registered parties to submit content and manage the life cycle of any submitted content.

- **Query management service.** This allows clients to query the registry service for the content. Such queries are supported by a flexible classification scheme within the metamodel that allows for browse, drill down, navigation, and ad-hoc queries.

7.6 CLIENT-SIDE APIs

There are various *business registry* standards today. These standards will continue to evolve and new standards will continue to be formed. This creates a tremendous burden for the clients that use these business registries. A client written to a business registry becomes dependent on that registry's information model and its APIs. As registry standards continue to evolve, the clients may want to migrate to a different registry that has better functionality. There are several hurdles to

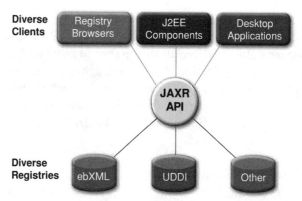

FIGURE 7.8. JAXR Model (Source: JAXR Specification).

doing that. First, the programmers have to understand the information model of the target registry. These information models tend to be fairly complex and comprehension of them requires a certain level of experience with registry internals and fundamental concepts. Second, once the information model has been understood, the programmers have to rewrite the client code to access the new registry. This could be a significant project in itself. Using a different registry may involve learning a different communication protocol. For example, UDDI uses SOAP messages to interact with a client whereas ebXML Registry & Repository uses ebXML Transport & Routing Protocol.

Java Community Process's JSR 93 – Java API for XML Registries (JAXR) – has pioneered the idea for a client-side API for registries that defines its own information model and then maps that information model to a multitude of business registries. This is a very powerful API that not only provides a consistent access method for business registries, which are very different from each other in capabilities, but can also provide additional capabilities that may not be offered by the underlying business registry.

Figure 7.8 illustrates the JAXR model that allows Java-based clients to access different kinds of underlying registries.

7.6.1 JAXR Information Model

The key to JAXR providing consistent access to potentially quite different registries is having its own information model. This allows the specification to keep a consistent client-programming model as the underlying registries evolve.

The JAXR information model is essentially based on ebXML's information model with some extensions borrowed from UDDI. It defines a normative binding to the ebXML information model and the UDDI data structure specification. As shown

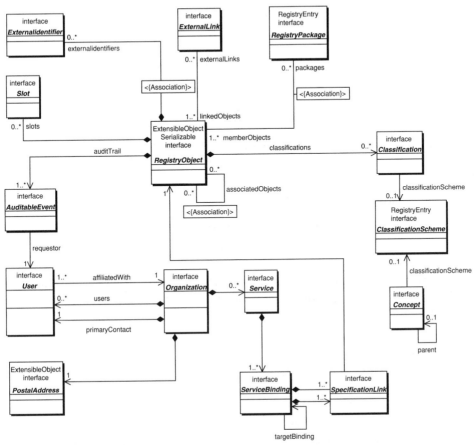

FIGURE 7.9. JAXR's Unified Information Model (Source: JAXR Specification).

in Figure 7.9, it is sort of a unified information model from the dominant registry specifications.

This is a fairly extensible information model that allows a reasonable mapping to the two dominant registry specifications with ease. The most significant characteristic of JAXR's information model is that it truly is a metamodel that can be used to store any kind of data. These data can be either organizational information, service definitions, or business process definitions. This information model can store it all.

7.6.2 JAXR Architecture

JAXR has been designed from the ground up to support multiple registry specifications. Figure 7.10 shows the JAXR information model. JAXR registry service interfaces are client-side APIs. In its current design, the JAXR client and the

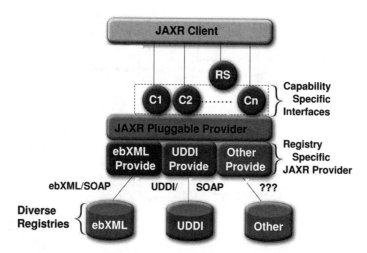

FIGURE **7.10. JAXR Architecture (Source: JAXR Specification).**

JAXR provider are expected to execute in the same Java virtual machine, and the only distributed interactions occur between the JAXR provider and the registry provider.

7.6.3 JAXR Client Interface

JAXR has been designed to support various patterns of communications. Regardless of the nature of the underlying registry, JAXR Client Interface provides synchronous or asynchronous communication with the underlying registry. For registries that are essentially asynchronous in nature, such as ebXML Registry & Repository, the JAXR Client Interface simulates synchronous communication by waiting under the covers for the response to come before returning to the caller. For asynchronous communication to registries that are essentially synchronous in nature, such as UDDI, it returns before making the actual call and then provides the results asynchronously.

An important task that the JAXR Client Interface performs is managing the underlying connection to one or more registry providers.

7.6.4 Capability Profiles

The underlying registries that JAXR strives to encapsulate provide very different levels of capabilities. For example, UDDI provides high-level focused business APIs that make querying easy but a bit more constrained, whereas ebXML Registry & Repository exposes low-level generic APIs that are significantly more powerful. Instead of taking the "least common denominator" approach, which would have significantly restricted the usefulness of JAXR, it has taken a capability-based approach.

JAXR categorizes its API by two capability profiles:

- **Level 0**. Support for Level 0 profile is required by all JAXR providers. These are the most basic methods and are considered necessary for basic function of the registry.
- **Level 1**. Support for Level 1 is not mandatory. The Level 1 profile includes methods that make the registry more useful by giving it additional control over the underlying registry's metamodel.

Each method in the JAXR API is assigned a capability level. This assignment is really at the documentation level and there is no enforcement of that at runtime. The capability assignment is done at the method level only.

A JAXR client may be written to use either Level 0 or Level 1 methods in a portable manner.

7.6.5 Pluggable Provider

As is evident from the architecture and the discussion so far, JAXR has been designed to support multiple registry specifications. The JAXR pluggable provider supplies a single abstraction for all registry-specific providers. It is not an abstract interface that is implemented by the registry-specific providers. The registry-specific providers plug into the pluggable provider. The pluggable provider receives the client requests and delegates them to the registry-specific provider, which then interacts with the underlying registry.

7.6.6 Value-Added Services

Because JAXR provides its own information model, it can afford to provide some other services that the underlying registry may not be able to provide. Since most of these value-added services are provided in effect to overcome the deficiencies of UDDI, they are discussed in comparison to UDDI.

7.6.6.1 Taxonomy Browsing

In UDDI, a tModel is used to define either taxonomy, an identifier namespace, or a technical fingerprint. It is, in fact, a unique pointer with no real semantic value. This overloaded use of tModel allows UDDI to accomplish many different objectives while keeping the core UDDI data types to a bare minimum. Unfortunately, it has a negative effect. Identifiers, taxonomies, and fingerprints are fundamentally different things. Identifiers are used for identifying a namespace and tend to be flat namespaces. There is generally no requirement to identify these namespaces as such. Taxonomies, on the other hand, can be represented by fairly complex hierarchical data structures. Furthermore, there are many situations in which a browsing application needs to get a list of available taxonomy schemes. Finally, technical fingerprints really have no special requirements at all. They are just unique pointers, which may also have a specification document associated with them.

JAXR represents all three concepts discussed above with first-class objects in the information model. `ExternalIdentifier` represents indentifiers, `ClassificationScheme` and `Classification` represent taxonomies, and, finally, `SpecificationLink` represents a technical fingerprint.

JAXR allows retrieval of all available taxonomies so that an application may traverse them looking for a suitable one. This can be important when a list of available taxonomies has to be presented to the user for selection.

7.6.6.2 Internal and External Taxonomies

In UDDI, taxonomies are defined by tModel. Since tModels are simply pointers or unique markers, there is no structure to them and thus it simply is not possible to define a complex hierarchical structure using them. JAXR allows two kinds of taxonomies. The simplest form is called `ExternalTaxonomy`. In external taxonomy, a classification simply points to a unique value. In the case of UDDI, this can be the unique key of the tModel. However, if a user wishes to have a more complex taxonomy, then the other option available is to have an `InternalTaxonomy`. In internal taxonomy, the registry knows the structure of the taxonomy scheme, which can be hierarchical. An internal classification scheme uses a node from the classification scheme.

7.7 A Suitable Metadata Registry for BSO

We have defined the metamodel required to support BSO. We have also examined several of underlying registry and directory specifications. Although various registries offer features required by BSO, no single registry specification or directory service meets the current requirements.

LDAP has the ability to store any kind of content and organizational demographic data. In fact, it is the preferred means for storing organizational demographic data in the industry. However, LDAP is blind to the notions of business services. It does not give first-class status to the identification and classification schemes that are essential for the business services. It also does not expose a crisply defined API for business service discovery. This API, although not essential, certainly goes a long way toward easy understanding and effective usage of a business registry.

UDDI is defined more for the human user who sits in front of the browser and navigates through the registry. The metamodel of the registry is constrained to store only prespecified data. Anything else can be referred to only through the URIs while the actual content is outside the control of the registry itself. This does not lend itself very well to the highly optimized registry required by BSO. Additionally, UDDI does not allow any way to store organizational demographic data that are so essential to completing workflow-related tasks in a BSO. UDDI also does not provide any mechanism to perform ad-hoc queries. This limits the use of UDDI in situations in which a query has to be performed to select a target business service, from a set of multiple services, to perform an activity.

The ebXML Registry & Repository probably has the broadest support for the BSO requirements. This is not by chance. As a consortium, ebXML defined many different specifications, such as a business process definition, and a fundamental objective of the registry and repository specification was to support all the other specifications. The issue with ebXML is that it does not share. All the data have to be in ebXML registry. This poses a problem for the organizations that already store their demographic data in directory services such as LDAP.

JAXR has promoted some very powerful concepts. The unified information model of JAXR provides a uniform model that can be mapped to any underlying business registry. However, JAXR suffers from some of its own weaknesses. First, JAXR is language dependent. This is because it is a specification born out of Java Community Process. However, it is a shame not to share that kind of specification with other programming environments. Second, JAXR is a client-side API. While more efficient, this makes sharing its implementation among multiple programming environments impossible. Third, JAXR cannot map its information model among multiple underlying registries. This makes it impossible for JAXR to unify multiple data sources into one information model.

Since JAXR comes closest to supporting the requirements of BSO, the BSO metadata registry should be based on JAXR. However, we propose the following extensions to JAXR for its use with BSO:

7.7.1 Registry Consolidation

As we have realized in this chapter, there are many different sources of metadata needed for BSO. Many organizations already have some of these data, which they use for other purposes. A good example of this is the demographic data of an enterprise. Most enterprises already have their organizational and user information in LDAP servers. It is unreasonable to expect that they will duplicate these data into another registry. Duplication of these data in multiple registries will significantly increase the cost of maintaining these data and keeping them synchronized.

JAXR has done an admirable job of consolidating the various information models of business registries. However, the current version of JAXR still treats a single registry instance as the source for its data. We believe that the BSO registry should allow consolidation of not just the information models, but also the consolidation of multiple data sources. This, of course, could be accomplished by a flexible and configurable deployment mechanism.

By mapping the elements of the information model to various data sources, the BSO suite has one comprehensive API to get all the metadata it needs. This greatly simplifies the programming and data management tasks. For example, one could configure a metadata registry to interact with LDAP for managing the user information and for other things such as auditable events and to interact with UDDI for other elements. Once this mapping has been done, metadata API will automatically know which registry-specific provider to use for which information model elements.

7.7.2 Metadata API in the Form of a Model

BSO is completely model driven. The user develops the model of his or her orchestration. This model is rigorous and is able to generate a significant amount of execution code. It is fitting for the BSO metadata registry to be model driven also.

The BSO metadata registry should be specified in terms of a rigorously defined UML profile. Once this is defined, various implementations of the registry can provide standard language bindings for many different languages, such as Java, or vendors' proprietary languages such as Fuego's CIL, to access the registries. This also leaves the vendors with enough flexibility to provide either a client-side API that maps to the model or a shared service deployed in the BSO environment.

CHAPTER 8

Business Services Orchestration Language (BSOL)

8.1 INTRODUCTION

So far, we have spent a great deal of time in covering the reference architecture for business services orchestration, and defining the necessary methodology and the underlying technologies that make it possible to orchestrate business services. The actual development process for coming up with orchestration sequences is covered in the methodology section. Additionally, methods and processes, such as the Unified Process from Rational, are also a great source for going through the modeling process. This chapter devotes itself to the key concepts that need to be modeled. We talk about the necessary components of a BSO, which need to be visually rendered through a BSO notation and need to be captured by a BSO specification language (BSOL).

BSOL captures the protocol that the collaborating systems need to follow in order to interact with each other in a meaningful business manner. In a typical BSO scenario, there are many business services. These services have their public interfaces, which may have been captured by a specification language such as Web Service Description Language (WSDL). The orchestration of these services is all about how these services interact with each other in a state-full manner, typically in long-running business transactions. A buyer may send a purchase order to a seller. The seller may take several days to fulfill the order and then send an invoice back to the buyer. Although the buyer and seller services have their interfaces, the protocol defines the order in which those interface operations can be invoked. For example, the seller cannot invoice the buyer before the buyer sends the purchase order. Capturing this business protocol is the key goal of BSOL.

BSOL is significant in many ways. First, it forms the technical fingerprint of the BSO. A notation used to capture the model visually is strictly a visual rendering of the specification, and the same specification could be rendered using many different notations. A standard specification mechanism serves as the main means of interoperability between different BSO engines. Various BSO engines may utilize the same specification and perform different roles as captured in the BSO. If the BSO processes are registered in the BSO metadata registry, the BSO language will be the prime candidate for the technical fingerprint.

A BSO separates the external protocol specification from the internal implementation of the protocol. Once this protocol is captured in the specification, various BSO engines can consume these specifications and interact collaboratively with each other. Since XML has emerged as the meta language of choice to express information, it is desirable to express BSOL in XML. This way, BSOL can be constrained and validated through an XML Schema. Different BSO engines can utilize various XML tools to parse BSOL and interpret it in ways specific to their tools.

There are many XML-based BSOLs that exist today. The most notable ones are ebXML Business Process Specification Schema by OASIS, Business Process Modeling Language (BPML) by BPMI, Web Services Flow Language (WSFL) by IBM, XLANG by Microsoft, and Web Services Conversation Language (WSCL) by HP. We will not discuss any of these specifications in any amount of detail because all are public specifications and we do not have the time and space here to do justice to even a single one of them. Each has its innovative features and, in some instances, areas that require further development. Our intention in this chapter is not to invent yet another BSOL but to discuss the required features that any BSOL should be able to capture.

Any specification for BSOs has to be able to express these concepts in such a way that they can be interpreted by service orchestration tools and runtime engines. Throughout this discussion, we present XML Schema code to demonstrate how the concepts should be represented. This XML Schema code is not meant to provide a new specification.

One important point is that any specification should leverage any existing relevant specifications. To that extent, we believe that WSDL is very relevant to a BSO specification language. WSDL describes the behavior of a business service. This behavior can really be the public contract of a service, the messages that can be sent to this service and to which it will respond to, or they could be private behavior, the methods the Web service will execute in order to invoke methods on other Web services. WSDL captures this really well. A BSOL complements WSDL. Where WSDL describes the behavior of a business service, BSOL defines the business protocol that must be followed, the legal and time-dependent ordering of messages that can be invoked to accomplish an overall business process. This is an important distinction and a good opportunity for developing standards by leveraging other standards.

8.2 FUNDAMENTAL CONCEPTS

In this section, we discuss the fundamental concepts for service orchestration in details.

8.2.1 Abstract Concepts

In BSO, there are many concepts that can easily be defined abstractly. These abstract concepts need not contain any implementation detail. Later, we add the details required for various implementations in a concrete protocol section. This pattern is being lifted from WSDL. WSDL also defines `types`, `messages`, and `portTypes` in an abstract manner and later adds the detail required to make those abstract definitions more concrete.

8.2.1.1 Message Definitions

First and foremost, processes have to communicate with each other and this is done by exchanging messages with each other. These messages may be composed of primitive types or more complex types. WSDL already defines the mechanism for using XML Schema definitions (XSD) to define user types. It also allows composing messages from parts comprising the built-in or user-defined types. We do not see anything different for the messages for BSOL. In fact, the purpose of defining these messages is precisely the same as the purpose of WSDL messages. Hence, we expect that the user types and messages and portTypes will be defined completely in WSDL.

8.2.1.2 Roles

BSOL is all about how business services can be orchestrated to achieve a business objective. This requires business services to interact with each other in a way where each business service assumes a role that defines the context of its participation. As an example, consider how a simple order fulfillment process would take place in a simple enterprise application integration (EAI) scenario. This order fulfillment process will require various internal departments to work together in order to successfully finish the process. When the order is received, a request may be sent to the warehouse to check inventory, and to finance to verify credit. Once that is accomplished, the order may be accepted and sent to manufacturing. After the product has been manufactured, inspection may be asked to inspect the product. After the inspection has been finished, finance may be requested to send the invoice and shipping may be requested to ship the product. There are various internal departments involved in this process and there will be various systems and individuals representing these departments. These are termed *roles*.

The above discussion was mostly from an EAI perspective. However, this business process will also involve multiple business partners. For example, it is very likely that the company does not maintain a very large inventory of parts because it has integrated its part suppliers in its supply chain so that parts can be ordered when needed. Furthermore, the company may also use some other clearinghouses to verify credit and invoicing. Furthermore, the company may also use some outside shipping agencies for shipping its finished products to its customers. So, when this same process is viewed from a business-to-business (B2B)

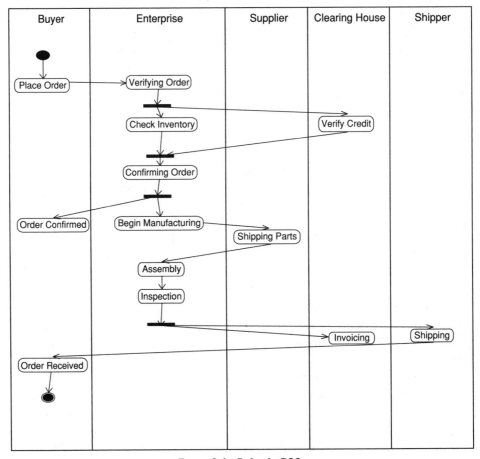

FIGURE 8.1. Roles in BSO.

```
<complexType name="roleType">
   <attribute name="name" type="NCName" use="required"/>
   <attribute name="type" type="NCName"
        use="required"/>
</comlexType>
```

FIGURE 8.2. Schema for Role Definition.

persepctive, the roles change to represent the business partners, such as `sup-plier`, `financial_partner`, and `shipping_agency`. This is fine because the roles represent the context of interaction, which changes from EAI to B2B.

For visual representation, Unified Modeling Language (UML) provides the swim-lane metaphor, which is able to express the context quite nicely. Figure 8.1 uses these metaphors to illustrate the roles played by different entities. This figure mostly shows the view of the business process as seen in an extended enterprise context, showing the roles that different business partners play in executing the business process.

The sum of messages flowing in a role may be viewed as the contract of that role as seen by the other participants. The role itself may present a business service, with its contract captured in the WSDL. Internally, the implementation of this contract may execute one or more private processes in order to fulfill it. The roles are hence represented by business services interfacing themselves and have a `type` associated with them, which may map to the WSDL `portType`. Having declared this `type` then defines the legal methods that may be invoked on that role. Note that this defines the interface of the business process. This is not to say that this is a Web service and these methods can necessarily be invoked on it from outside. We consider that issue later in this chapter. For now, let us just say that this serves to define the `type` of the business service.

Figure 8.2 provides a possible XML Schema segment for defining roles. The type of the role is defined in terms of a WSDL portType. This is, of course, very useful because theoretically, WSDL is not limited to Web services. Figure 8.3 illustrates a possible example of using this schema segment.

For each role, there is a WSDL file that describes its types, messages, and `portTypes` that completely define the contract of that business partner. This type is logically separate from the `serviceProviderType` that is used to describe a Web service that provides concrete operations that can be invoked to implement activities.

```
<role name="financial_partner"

type="finance:ClearingHouseInterfaceProcess"/>
```

FIGURE 8.3. Role Declaration of Financial Business Partner.

```
<complexType name="activityType">
   <sequence>
      <element name="action" type="bso:actionType"
         minOccurs="1" maxOccurs="unbounded"/>
      <element name="exceptionHandler"
         type="bso:exceptionHandlerType"
                  minOccurs="0" maxOccurs="1"/>
      <element name="timer" type="bso:timerType"
                  minOccurs="0" maxOccurs="1"/>
   </sequence>
</complexType>

<complexType name="roleType">
   <sequence>
      <element name="serviceProvider"
         type="bso:serviceProviderType"
         minOccurs="0" maxOccurs="unbounded"/>
      <element name="activity" type="bso:activityType"
         minOccurs="0" maxOccurs="unbounded"/>
      <element name="decision" type="bso:decisionType"
         minOccurs="0" maxOccurs="unbounded"/>
   </sequence>
   <attribute name="name" type="NCName" use="required"/>
   <attribute name="type" type="NCName" use="required"/>
</complexType>

<element name="role" type="roleType"/>
```

FIGURE 8.4. Specification of Activities.

8.2.1.3 Activities

Activity is one of the most fundamental concepts in BSOL. A business process is the sequential execution of activities and the flow of messages between activities. Activities consume and produce messages. They consume messages that flow into them and may in turn produce one or more messages. An activity represents one or more actions performed by the system and takes some time to complete. An activity may itself represent or start a complex process to be completed. Figure 8.1 illustrated a simple business process. This business process representation shows messages flowing between activities within a role and across to other roles.

Activities are performed by roles and the sum of all activities performed by a role constitutes its interface. This interface is described in WSDL and the operations in the WSDL `portTypes` represent these activities. This defines the `type` of the role.

Figure 8.4 illustrates the specification of activities. Activities are declared inside a role, and are performed by a WSDL operation invoked on the portType specified as the `roleType`. Figure 8.5 explains this by using a more concrete example.

Activities have to be implemented also. The implementation of the activities involves doing one or more action. These actions involve either invoking methods

```
<role name="OrderFulfillmentRole"
        type="OrderFulfillmentProcessPortType">
    <serviceProvider name="ofsService"
        type="ofs:OrderFulfillmentServiceSoap"/>
<!-- This activity is implemented by a local script -->
    <activity name="AcceptOrder">
        <action>
            <implementor scriptName="AcceptOrderScript"/>
        </action>
        <exceptionHandler>
            <implementor
                scriptName="genericExceptionHandler">
            </implementor>
        </exceptionHandler>
    </activity>

<!-- This activity is implemented by the web service of
provider ofsService -->
    <activity name="GetPartsToOrder">
        <action>
            <implementor provider="ofsService"
                operation="GetPartsToOrder">
            </implementor>
            <compensator provider="ofsService"
                operation="UndoGetPartsToOrder">
            </compensator>
        </action>
    </activity>
</role>
```

FIGURE 8.5. Activities Declaration of Financial Business Partner.

on a remote Web service, executing a local script, or sending a work item to a workflow manager. Other implementations will probably allow other mechanisms also, such as publishing messages to a Java Messaging Service (JMS) channel, but we are going to limit ourselves to these three mechanisms only. We keep on emphasizing the interface type of the role itself, which includes all its activities and the implementations of those activities. There is no Web service in the physical sense that implements the roles defined here. The Web service is in fact the business process instance itself. In a normal Web service, you would write the code to implement the operations of the Web service. For a role defined here, you configure, using the implementation-provided tools, to give the process instance enough intelligence to transform the messages and invoke operations on a remote Web service that probably provides some discrete services.

Figure 8.5 illustrates two activities of the role. The first activity is Accept-Order. This activity is implemented by a local script. There can be many different scripting languages. Additionally, some implementations may allow Java or some other code to be executed. In any case, this is local code that is executed. In the case of a scripting language, the BSO engine will provide the environment for the script to be executed and in case of the programming language code, the environment may either allow compiled code to be dynamically loaded and executed or may require language code and may itself perform the compilation and execution. In either case, it is implementation dependent. What may be expected from BSOL here would be the necessary information to locate the code and any transformations necessary before arguments are passed on to the local code.

The second activity is `GetPartsToOrder`. This is an example of an activity that is implemented by invoking an operation `GetPartsToOrder` on service provider `ofsService`. BSOL requires the service providers, who provide the Web services that have operations used to implement activities, to be declared up-front in the role. Those service providers help with the implementation of the role. In the case of the remote Web service methods, there are many implementation details that are required also, which are all presented later in this chapter.

8.2.1.4 Transitions
When an activity has been completed, the BSO engine selects the next activity that needs to be executed. The edge that leads the path from one activity to another is called a transition. Multiple transitions may lead out of an activity, depending on corresponding conditions being met. The BSO engine selects the next activity to execute by first getting the set of all transitions leading out of an activity and then checking the firing conditions on all transitions. The transition whose firing condition evaluates to true will then be selected and that in turn will lead to the activity to be executed next.

The condition can be specified by evaluating either the parameters of the input message of the source activity or the instance variables or both. Instance variables are discussed in detail later in this chapter. For now, we can just think of instance variables as a set of variables that are for the particular instance of the business process and are available to all the activities of the business process.

Since our desire is to leverage the existing standards wherever possible, we would like to use XQuery as the language to specify conditions.

Figure 8.6 shows the XML Schema to specify transitions. Activities and transitions form the activity graph, which captures the flow of messages and the legal navigation paths that make up the BSO. A condition is, of course, optional if the source activity has only one transition that has that activity as its source. However, if there are multiple transitions with the same source activity, then conditions must be specified.

8.2.1.5 Timeouts and Exceptions
There are two special conditions that should be specified. This is a desired feature but not mandatory. In real life, many transitions are time dependent or have a due time period. In our example scenario, we have an activity called `Begin`

```
<complexType name="transitionType">
   <attribute name="name" type="xsd:string" use="required"/>
   <attribute name="source" type="NCName" use="required"/>
   <attribute name="target" type="NCName" use="required"/>
   <attribute name="condition" type="xsd:string"/>
</complexType>

<complexType name="transitionsType">
   <sequence>
      <element name="transition" type="transitionType"
         minOccurs="0" maxOccurs="unbounded"/>
   </sequence>
</complexType>

<element name="transitions" type="transitionsType"/>
```

FIGURE 8.6. Specification for Transitions.

`Manufacturing`. In that activity, we may send the message to the supplier to place an order for more parts and wait for its acknowledgment. However, the contractual requirements may state that the supplier will acknowledge the order in two hours. This is an example of an activity with a due time period. A timeout facility on the activity allows activities to time out after the specified time period has elapsed. The timeout of the activity may result in some other actions being taken. These actions may involve either some local scripting code to be invoked or an operation on the `portType` implementing the `roleType` to be invoked, an exception to be generated, or the activity to be escalated to a higher role.

Exception is another deviation from the normal execution of the activity. An exception could simply be a system exception, such as target Web service not being accessible or the messaging service being unavailable. It could also be a timeout-driven exception or a user exception generated by the target Web service being invoked. In either case, the generation of an exception may require that an alternative path be taken by the system.

8.2.1.6 Orchestration (Abstract Process)

Orchestration is a business process. Syntactically, an orchestration is called a set of activities and the transitions connecting them in a manner meaningful to business. Orchestration represents a complete unit of functionality that can be packaged and executed. It describes either a business process or a subprocess.

An orchestration needs to have several things defined in it. The orchestration is the sequencing of the previously defined activities in such a way that it results in a flow of control. A BSO engine creates an instance of the orchestration and manages the lifecycle of that instance. Orchestration defines all the parameters required to manage the flow of control and this instance.

```
<complexType name="processType">
    <sequence>
        <element name="transition" type="transitionType"
            minOccurs="0" maxOccurs="unbounded"/>
        </element>
    </sequence>
</complexType>
```

FIGURE 8.7. Process Specification.

Collectively, the transitions defined here form a directed graph of activities.

We have previously talked about an abstract concept and a concrete implementable manifestation of the abstract concept. We represent the abstract concept by keyword process and the concrete version of that with orchestration.

An orchestration adds all the details that are needed to make the abstract concepts concrete. These details are described in later sections in detail. In any case, the orchestration is actually executed by the BSO engine and not the process. Figure 8.7 illustrates a sample schema for specifying an abstract process as a sequence of transitions. The transitions, activities, and roles would have been previously defined.

Figure 8.8 provides a sample schema for an orchestration. An orchestration has an input and an output. If the orchestration represents a straight-through process, then the orchestration represents the input required by the first activity and the output represents the output of the last activity.

Input/output are described in greater detail in a later section. Also note that the orchestration includes instance variables. Instance variables of the process instance are no different than the instance variables of a Java object. They get created when the instance itself is created, and the action code for any of the activities can either reference them or set their values. Instance variables are also discussed later in the chapter.

```
<complexType name="orchestration">
    <attribute name="input" type="bso:parmType" use="optional"/>
    <attribute name="output" type="bso:parmType" use="optional"/>
    <sequence>
        <element name="instanceVariable" type="bso:instanceVariableType"
            minOccurs="0" maxOccurs="unbounded" />
    </sequence>
    <attribute name="name" type="xsd:string" use="required"/>
    <attribute name="type" type="QName" use="required"/>
</complexType>
```

FIGURE 8.8. Specifying Orchestrations.

8.2.1.7 *Human Intervention*

When we think of automating business processes, we often think of how humans perform a particular job and then automate those steps. Process refinements occur during the analysis of how the job is performed manually. This is done in Phase 2 – Analyze and Design – of the methodology described in Chapter 4. In any case, the motivation behind the automation of processes is to replace humans, making the whole process timelier, more efficient, less error prone, and less expensive.

However, for many jobs, humans simply cannot be replaced. For example, in our scenario of an order fulfillment process, once the component has been manufactured, it has to be inspected. Unless it is inspected, the process really cannot move forward. It is important for the process to allow exits to human intervention.

Human intervention is typically performed through task lists and policies dictating how jobs can be removed from those tasks. For example, the department policy may dictate that anyone out of a pool of inspectors can take ownership of the inspection and perform that task. In that case, the whole pool of inspectors may share a task list. As the product is manufactured, its specification may be placed in the inspection task list with the relevant information. Once an inspector takes ownership of a product inspection, he marks the task busy and it is removed from the task list or is marked as "being worked on." When the inspector finishes the task, he or she marks the task done. At this point, the process may resume from the point where it had been suspended and go on to the next activity.

8.2.2 Implementation

The abstract concepts of a process are devoid of any particular implementation knowledge. However, different BSOs may take different approaches to execution of the process and hence may require specific kinds of details. For example, a particular BSO implementation may support synchronous as well as asynchronous message exchange.

In this section, we discuss how the abstract concepts may be made concrete by adding implementation-level details to the abstract processes.

8.2.2.1 *BSO Process Input/Output*

A process generally starts from an external stimulus or from a regular timed event such as an insurance renewal. This usually happens when an external entity sends a message to the BSO engine. The input message to the very first activity can be considered the initiating message that triggers the process. Similarly, a process may have an output type that is the output of the process when it terminates. The input and output of the process orchestration can be defined in terms of WSDL messages.

An activity is typically executed by invoking a method on a Web service. That method may itself encapsulate an entire business process that runs to its completion before returning. When we normally invoke Web service methods, we provide an input message and receive an output message. If the Web service method actually implements an encapsulated process, then the message that would be provided to the Web service method becomes the input to this business process, and the output of that business process maps to the output message of the Web service method. This way, the business process itself can be implemented as a Web service method and still allow the BSO engine to prepare the input for the downstream activity. We talk more about this capability later in this chapter when we discuss recursive composition.

A message received by the activity that represents a business process may not be the same as the message expected by the first activity of that business process. Similarly, the message produced by the last activity of the business process may not be the same as the message produced by the activity representing the business process. Hence, it should be possible to apply some transformation logic to the received messages to produce the expected messages. In fact, the need for this transformation logic applies just as well to messages expected and produced by all activities and is discussed in detail later.

8.2.2.2 Instance Variables

Business processes have a life cycle with a well-defined starting state and an ending state. When a new business process is started, the BSO engine creates an instance of the business process. The lifecycle of this business process instance is independent of the lifecycles of the physical operating-system processes in which it executes. The operating system processes may be stopped and restarted and the business process can be re-created to its current state. During the life of this business process instance, activities are executed and states are transitioned from one to another. This business process instance maintains the state of the process itself.

The business process instance hence has some implicit instance variables that it needs in order to maintain its identity and state. Perhaps the most important one of these implicit variables is the business process identifier, which uniquely identifies the business process instance and is essential in directing the incoming messages to the correct instance of the business processes.

In addition to these implicit instance variables, the application may also need some user-defined instance variables. As messages flow from one activity to another, sometimes there is loss of information. For example, when a purchase order is received, it may have a lot of data about the user, his or her financial information, and shipping information. Most downstream activities may not require all that information. However, toward the end, this information may be needed again for the purpose of invoicing and shipping. The instance variables allow one to save information that may be needed for activities but is not otherwise available in the messages produced by the previous activity. The process instance *persists* this information along with the other implicit variables in some form of persistent storage, and they are always available for the application code to use.

8.2.2.3 Activity Implementation

In the definition of the abstract sections of the BSOL, we defined all the activities. When the BSOL identifies an activity, it is in fact identifying the code that needs to be executed next. An activity represents the work to be performed, to consume the input message, and produce the output message. Often, the messages are just for the purpose of triggering the activity, but the activity nevertheless performs the work.

An activity has to be implemented. However, there are some exceptions to that condition. We define some predefined activities, such as start activity, end activity, split activity, and join activity, that do not have an executable code associated with them. Their purpose is more to manage the flow of control.

When an activity finishes, the control normally returns to the BSO engine. The engine then selects the next activity to be executed and transitions to it, passing the output of the previous activity to this activity as input. More often that not, the output of the previous activity does not match the expected input of the selected activity. As explained earlier, the expected message often has to be created using the output message of the previous activity, some of the instance variables, and maybe some other formatting. In either case, as the messages are mapped, they may need to be transformed. It is important to be able to specify these message transformations.

In Fuego this only happens when you call a subprocess. Within a process, what flows are the instance variables (objects), thus not needing the context switches described above.

Figure 8.9 shows a sample message transformation. A transformation can take input from multiple messages, including instance variables. It can do simple assignment or the user can provide some code that can be executed to do the transformation. The exact mechanism of the how transformation are performed may be dependent on the implementation.

User-defined activities can be implemented in several different ways. First, an implementation may provide some form of scripting language to provide the code that contains the logic. It is not important to know which scripting language because that is implementation dependent. However, it may be that this scripting language or some other segment of code that is executed in-line, right in the same operating-system process as that of the business process instance. In this case, execution of that activity logic has to be facilitated by the process instance. For example, Fuego's business process management (BPM) provides Component Integration Language (CIL), which may be used to write activity implementation

```
<complexType name="mapType">
   <attribute name="source" type="NCName" use="required"/>
   <attribute name="target" type="an XPath statement"
      use="required"/>
   <attribute name="action"
      type="bso:transformationActionTypeEnum" use="optional"/>
</complexType>

<complexType name="messageTransformationType">
   <element name="output" type="QName" minOccues="1"
      maxOccurs="1"/>
      <sequence>
         <element name="input" type="string" minOccurs="0"
            maxOccurs="1">
            <sequence>
               <element name="map" type="bso:mapType"
                  minOccurs="0" maxOccurs="1"/>
            </sequence>
            <attribute name="message" type="QName"
                use="required"/>
         </element>
      </sequence>
   <attribute name="name" type="string"/>
</complexType>
```

FIGURE 8.9. Sample Message Transformation.

code. Others may provide similar scripting languages, and some implementations may provide compiled Java code for the activity implementation.

The other most likely possibility for the implementation of the activity is by mapping it to the operation of a port. Earlier, in describing roles, we mentioned that the roles are represented by the business services themselves. In fact, the definition of activities within the role also contains the name of the operation that implements it. In the concrete section on defining an activity's implementation, some other detail on the implementation may be required. For example, if the method on the Web service is an asynchronous message with a separate response coming later, the BSO engine may have to wait for that asynchronous response before considering this activity completed. Details like this can be specified here. This kind of information generally will not be available in a WSDL document.

As discussed previously, an activity may also utilize human services. In this case the control may need to be transferred to task lists in a work portal and the process may have to be paused until the tasks in the work portal are completed and control is transferred back to the business process instance.

8.2.3 Miscellaneous

There are many other miscellaneous concepts for business process orchestration that need to be mentioned here.

```
<wsdl:import
    namespace=http://bso.samples.OrderFulfillment/
location="file:///D:/Samples/wsdl/OrderFulfillmentService.bsol
"/>
```

FIGURE 8.10. Import Another File.

8.2.3.1 Start and End Activities

So far, the representation of the BSO that we have been discussing is semantically equivalent to UML's activity graphs. As explained earlier, when an activity finishes, the flow of control passes immediately to the next activity. The transitions, from one activity to another, then, are not triggered by an external event per se but rather are a consequence of the previous activity finishing up. However, the flow of control has to start at some point and there has to be an exit point somewhere also.

A start activity is an implicit activity and defines a beginning point. Business processes also have to have a start activity. There is no action associated with this activity; it is just used to mark the beginning of the process. When the business process starts, the process engine can use this activity as the start marker and look for the user-defined activities that are preceded by this start activity.

The end activity is the same way. When the end activity is reached, the business process instance reaches the end of its lifecycle.

8.2.3.2 Code Organization

We talked about abstract aspects of BSOL and concrete concepts. Sometimes, it is useful to organize different sections of the specification in separate files for better readability and also to facilitate multiple concrete bindings of the same concepts to many different implementations.

In Figure 8.10, the `wsdl:import` statement can be used to accomplish that very easily. In the figure, the file, specified by its location, is imported in this definition and is associated with the namespace specified by its value.

8.2.3.3 Startup/Creation

How does the life of a business process instance begin? A business process has to be started externally and this can happen in many different ways. A process instance can be created as a result of an explicit user action, initiated through a work portal. Alternatively, the instance can be created through an application program that uses the lifecycle API provided by the BPM implementation. Also, if the business process is packaged as a Web service, then it can be started as a result of invocations being made on the Web service.

In any case, some application-specific initialization code may need to be provided to accept the input message and initialize from it the instance variables and the input message of the first activity.

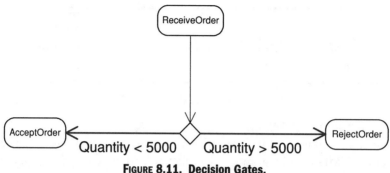

FIGURE 8.11. Decision Gates.

8.2.3.4 Conditions

There are many cases in which some conditional logic has to be applied. For example, often when an activity is completed, there may be more than one possible activity candidate for execution. The selection may be dependent on the some conditions being true.

Figure 8.11 illustrates a simple condition branch. In this figure, once the order has been received, the order quantity is checked. If the quantity is <5000, then the order is accepted. However, if the quantity is >5000, then the order is rejected.

Usually, the decision can be made on the basis of the contents of the output message of the activity just completed and/or the instance variables. However, different implementations may provide different mechanism for actually making decisions. Most existing BSO languages, such as WSFL, use XPath statements to specify condition code.

8.2.3.5 Splits and Joins

Many situations require two or more parallel paths of execution. For example, Figure 8.12 describes a simplified order-acceptance business process. In this example, an order is received. Once the order has been received, there are two activities that can be performed in parallel to each other. There is really no linear dependency between them. So, the credit verification and inventory check can proceed independently of each of other.

A split marks the beginning of parallel paths. It is quite different from a decision gate because, in a decision gate, only one activity that meets the criteria is selected for execution; and it may be considered an error if more than one activity meets the criteria. When a BSO engine encounters a split, it selects all the activities leaving the split and may start parallel threads for their execution.

A join is the other end of split. Joins are also sometimes referred to as *sync points* because they provide an opportunity to synchronize between parallel threads of process flow. When a BSO engine encounters a join, it waits. The activity preceding the join is not selected for execution until all activities leading to the join have been completed successfully.

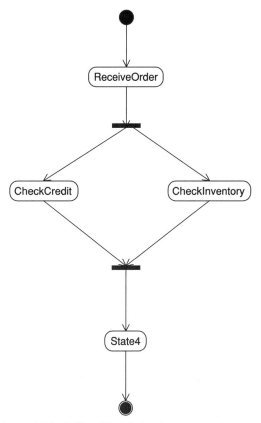

FIGURE **8.12. A Simplified Order Acceptance Process.**

8.2.3.6 *Timers*

Many business activities need to be completed in a certain amount of time. There is often a need to start a timer when a business activity is entered. Then, if the business activity is not finished before the timer pops, some alternative action may be taken.

The actions performed when the timer goes off may be all of the legal actions that can be performed when an activity is entered. So, in a sense, timers are equivalent to activities themselves. However, their execution is conditional. For example, when a timer goes off, possible legal actions could be the execution of one or more operations on some remote business services, the execution of a local script, or simply a transition back into same activity or mark that the activity is complete, causing the engine to select the next activity for execution. So, in a way, timer is a specialized form of an activity and any activity can contain zero or one timer.

Timers can be relative or absolute. Relative timers are generally relative to the start time of the activity itself and are defined as a certain elapsed time from activity start. Absolute timers specify an actual date. The state of a timer is part of the state of the activity itself. Since the business process instance state is always persisted and kept up-to-date, timers have to be persisted in the database also.

8.2.3.7 Exception Handling

Many different kinds of exceptions can occur during the execution of an activity. Exceptions can happen in two ways. The first is a system error. Examples of those errors may be things such as the target Web service not being available or the inability to perform message transformations. The other source of exception may be the asynchronous receipt of an exception business signal, which is described later in this chapter. This is a predefined business signal that a failure has occurred. All other situations are not considered exceptions and their handling has to be part of the process definition itself.

In a transactional system, the most likely outcome of an exception flow would be the rolling back of the current active transaction. This would be an implicit action that the system will perform. In addition to this action, the user may specify some other processing, such as execution of a local script or invocation of one or more methods on some remote service.

8.2.3.8 Compensating Transactions

When an activity is executed, it may perform various actions. From the purpose of the BSO, those actions may be atomic. An implied action here is also the state management of the process instance itself.

When the process instance enters an activity, the engine will invoke the actions specified for that activity. Once all such actions have been taken, the BSO also updates the state of the process instance itself in its persistence storage. This ensures that if any instance variables were modified in the execution of the activity, then they are also saved.

Bad things can happen at any time. If distributed transactions are supported and the end applications that are target of action do support distributed transactions, then there is no problem because the transaction can be rolled back. However, this does not work if the target application is not transactional, which is often the case. A compensating transaction executes an application function that is the inverse of the function performed earlier.

For example, a local script may implement the order confirmation activity in Figure 8.1. The script in that activity may precharge the user's credit card for the order amount and decrement the part count in the inventory. Then, if after precharging the user's credit card, for some reason it is unable to decrement the parts count in the inventory, the transaction will have to be rolled back. A compensating transaction is simply an alternative action specified for the activity that will be taken if the transaction has to be rolled back. In this case, an alternative local script or a Web service method may be provided which will functionally roll the transaction back, which, in this case, will be to credit the user's credit card with the amount charged.

The specification of compensating transactions is the same as the specification of the actual action for the activity. The only difference is that it is invoked in case of failure and the BSO engine may not attach any special semantics to it.

8.3 ADVANCED FEATURES

In this section, we discuss some of the advanced features that are not essential to BSO but are highly desirable.

8.3.1 Parameterization

It is important for BSOs to be parameterized. This allows implementations of BSO to be reused by providing different parameters. We discuss two important areas where parameterization is useful for BSOs.

8.3.1.1 Parametric Subprocesses

Often, a subprocess implementation may differ depending on variables such as the organization that executes it, the organizational unit that executes it, or others. When the input and output objects in the process being invoked are identical, it is very convenient to be able to invoke the different implementations implicitly according to the value of the parameters.

As an example, let's suppose that a certain company has divisions in the United States, Brazil, Mexico, and Argentina. In the United States, bookkeeping is done in SAP, in Brazil using Oracle Financial, in Mexico using Quick Books, and in Argentina using a local ERP system. In this case, the implementation of the subprocess that updates these systems, for intracompany transactions, will differ from organizational unit to organizational unit. The intracompany transaction will be sent from one division to any other division in the form of an IBO that will be the same for all divisions.

The treatment of the IBO will be different from division to division. Each country has its own taxes, may need to print the transactions in the local language for internal records, may have different approval processes, and, as we said earlier, may update different bookkeeping modules. Not only may the treatment differ, but the evolution of the processes may be totally asynchronous.

Because of the above reasons, hiding the implementation behind the process name and its input and output arguments as well as a parameter that determines which implementation needs to be used greatly improves flexibility and maintainability of the overall system. Parameterization of these subprocesses allows each of the implementations to vary at its own rhythm without affecting the whole.

Parametric subprocesses combined with the ability to maintain different versions of the same process variant running simultaneously allow for seamless execution in an environment of continuous change.

IBOs, as we will see in detail in Chapter 9, isolate the process logic from changes in the back-end systems. Parametric subprocesses isolate orchestrations that invoke them from the idiosyncrasy of their implementations.

8.3.1.2 Parametric Roles

In many real-world scenarios, the people that belong to a role are assigned at runtime rather than at design time or admin time. For example, in a project management process, the project team may be different, depending on the project. So, if the process has the roles of

- project manager,
- analyst,
- programmer,
- QA,
- user,

then, for a given project, the selected team could be described as

- Project manager(project)
- Analyst(project)
- Programmer(project)
- QA(project)
- User(project).

This allows the creation of processes where the participants in a role are dynamic according to a parameter, in this case the project name.

Another example would be in a support team, where companies usually work with shifts, and so the parametric role would be: support engineers.

It is easily inferred from these examples that BSOLs that don't support parametric roles may be inadequate to model this type of process.

8.3.2 Composibility

As business processes are defined, they themselves become services. Composibility refers to the ability to package the business processes themselves so that they appear to be services.

8.3.2.1 Business Process Representation as a Service

As mentioned, a business process itself is a service. This service, like any other service, can be invoked through a variety of mechanisms. For example, an order entry business process may be invoked through a Web portal. A front-end application may prompt the Web user for the necessary information and then invoke the business process with that information. The business process may then take over and take the order to fulfillment.

It should be possible to invoke the business process through a variety of mechanisms. Perhaps one of the most important mechanisms will be invocation as a Web service. A business process packaged as a Web service would allow itself to be invoked through a SOAP message that corresponds to its input message sent to its service port. Most often, a business process will expose a life-cycle method that creates an instance of the business process, executes the initialization code to initialize its instance variables, and perhaps perform the initial transformation to create a message compatible with the expected input of the first activity.

The other possibility is for the business process to be packaged as a CORBA service. Other possibilities are Enterprise Java Beans or as a JMS client. The actual choices may be dependent on the BSO implementation and cannot be discussed in detail here.

If the business process is exposed as a Web service, what should be its interface? There are two choices here. First, we discussed earlier that a role is implemented by a portType, possibly implemented by a Web service. If this business process is packaged as a Web service, should this portType become its public interface or should the public interface of the business process only comprise the lifecycle methods that are used to control its execution? The answer is probably "both," depending on the situation.

Some processes are designed as straight-through processes. Once invoked, they will run to completion. These processes generally will not interact with the entity that started them and only return when finished. To an external software entity, invoking such a process is no different than invoking a synchronous or an asynchronous request/response method. For example, let's say that the activity is checking the inventory. The process for checking the inventory requires looking up the inventory and, if the part is in enough quantity, then reserving it. If the part supply is too small, it needs to be ordered from the part supplier. However, this whole is a subprocess that needs to be processed straight through and returned only when it has finished. This process itself could be defined separately of any invoking process. This results in smaller and more reusable business processes, which can be invoked synchronously or asynchronously. These processes only have to expose a lifecycle method, an input message, and an output message to start the process.

On the other hand, there are some business processes that are conversational in nature. These processes just don't provide discrete services as a business process but rather themselves are significant service orchestration. For example, the parts order subprocess that we described earlier interacts with the order system of the supplier. However, the two need to interact with each other in a conversational manner in order to accomplish the task at hand. This will always be the case if one of the roles modeled in a business process is implemented by a separate Web service. In that case, the business process has to have its portType, which implements its activities, exposed as Web service methods. This complicates the interaction because now the implementation has to support the business methods as well as the lifecycle methods. Furthermore, the portType interface provides the interfaces but the legal order of invocations cannot be inferred from the portType alone. The BSO definition is required in addition to ensure the correct flow of interactions. In this method, each activity of the role would represent either a straight-through process or a discrete service.

8.3.2.2 Recursive Composition

In the preceding section, we talked about business processes being represented as Web services. This section deals with building business processes that in turn use other business processes.

As discussed earlier, business processes have activities that are selected for execution by the process engine, based on different conditions being met. Activities have to be implemented. The activities in a role may be implemented by one or more Web services. Recursive composition allows business processes to be created by utilizing other previously created business processes.

Business process analysis often requires defining common business processes, which are then reused over and over. The analysis process requires decomposing the processes to various degrees and then building upon them. Hence, one or more activities that make up a business processes may themselves represent those finer-grained business processes.

A business process engine should not really care whether the implementation of an activity is a separate business process itself or not. It should invoke the relevant mapped methods in a manner consistent with its capabilities and should just be able to get the expected result back.

8.3.2.3 Nested Processes

When activities in a business process are themselves represented by other business processes, those business processes may be known as nested business processes or subprocesses. There are many ways that a subprocess may be invoked, for example, in a manner very similar to a remote procedure call (RPC). The invoking process invokes the subprocess, waits for it to finish, and then returns its result. Alternatively, the invoking process may fire and forget. In this case, the activity may be considered to be completed as soon as the subprocess has been successfully started. The started subprocess will execute in parallel to the invoking process, completely independent of its lifecycle. Yet another way of starting the business process would be asynchronously, but mimicking a synchronous invocation. The starting process would start the subprocess asynchronously and then pause in that activity until an expected reply arrives back asynchronously. Only then might the BSO engine proceed further and mark this activity done.

8.3.3 Dynamic Participants

In the simple case, all participants in a process orchestration are known in advance. However, the relationships between business partners tend to be more dynamic in nature.

Consider the example of Figure 8.1. Assume that the roles of supplier, financial clearinghouse and shipper are all business partners and the business partners provide systems that follow the required business protocol (a WSDL and BSOL schedule). This way, the systems can be integrated. However, the nature of partnerships is more complicated than the simple case that this previously represented. Let us assume that there are multiple suppliers that have entered into partnership with this manufacturer. They all provide services that implement the same BSOL schedules so that the manufacturer can bind with any one of them. But the question is, which one? Maybe the manufacturer wants to select the most appropriate partner at runtime on the basis of certain criteria (e.g., shortest delivery time). The business process engine has to allow dynamic selection of the Web service to interact with it at runtime. The underlying business registry plays an important role in that and is discussed in significant detail in a later section.

The criteria could be based on many things. The manufacturer may use one clearinghouse for MasterCard and another to verify Visa. Again, this is a query that will be performed at runtime by the lookup engine, based on user-defined criteria. Also, in the case of shipper, the manufacturer may use one shipper for domestic deliveries and another for overseas deliveries.

Additionally, these partnerships may grow or shrink, and so, no assumptions can be made about them. The manufacturer may constantly be entering into more business partnerships and some business partners may elect not do business with each other and hence drop out of partnerships. A business registry will keep the partnerships current and the BSO engine should use the look-up agent to select the partner with whom to interact.

Since this really deals with the implementation of an activity, the look-up engine has to be used by the BSO engine while executing an activity. When a BSO engine selects an activity for execution, it first checks to see how this activity is implemented. If the activity is implemented by a local script, then there is no need to look up anything. However, if the implementation is really done by a Web service, then the BSO engine uses the look-up agent to retrieve the bindings for that service. If there is a criterion for the locator, then it executes that criterion; otherwise a simple look-up is performed.

However, this dynamism implies that the target services have to be invoked without any prior stubs. The easiest means of executing a Web service is through the proxy stubs that have been previously generated through some build-time tools using the WSDL. However, that implies that the stubs have been previously generated and have been linked in or loaded into the BSO engine. In case of dynamic participants, it is not always realistic that the appropriate stubs can be provided to the engine at the time of invocation. The BSO engine therefore has to select the target Web service at runtime, build a proxy for it runtime, and invoke methods through that dynamic proxy rather than through stubs. This is know as dynamic invocation and renders a lot of flexibility to the process orchestration engine.

8.3.4 BSO Management

Manageability is an important part of service-oriented architectures. Services – businesses process or otherwise – have to be started and stopped. The bottlenecks have to be identified, and loads have to be balanced. Most importantly, the business process itself has to be monitored not only with a system focus but also with a business focus.

8.3.4.1 Life Cycle

A business process instance has to be started through some external command. This external command may be executed from through a variety of means, such as a Web portal or an application that uses the business process API to start it. In either case, the business process that has been packaged as a service has to expose some lifecycle methods that allow that kind of control from an external application.

Following are some of the possible lifecycle methods that have to be provided by the business process engine to control the execution of a business process instance:

- **Call.** This operation invokes the business process in a synchronous manner. The operation starts the business process and does not return until the process has finished.

- **Spawn.** This operation starts the business process but does not wait for it to finish. Rather, the activity is marked complete as soon as the business process is started successfully.

- **CallAsynch.** This operation starts a business process asynchronously, as in Spawn, but then goes into a mode where it waits for an asynchronous reply to come in. Only after that reply comes in is the activity marked complete and that asynchronous reply becomes the output of that activity.

- **Suspend.** This operation suspends a running business process instance.

- **Resume.** This operation resumes a previously suspended process instance.

- **Terminate.** This operation terminates a business process.

- **Inquire.** This gets the status of a business process instance.

8.3.4.2 Interprocess Synchronization

Managing time and synchronization on a global scale is germane to orchestration. Enterprise-systems-savvy readers will easily recognize the headaches that synchronization produces in almost every enterprise system. For example, simply ensuring that a third-party invoice is associated with the accepted delivery of the goods before paying it has been a major issue for every ERP system. The reason for this headache is that sometimes the invoice arrives before the goods are accepted and sometimes things happen the other way around. Therefore, associating the acceptance to an existing invoice may not be possible at a given point in time.

It's also clear that, in a global setting, there are calendar rules that differ by city, time zone, holidays, and working hours, which may clearly determine constraints on or advantages of doing things at one site or another. In these situations, two working hours may differ substantially in the net result they can provide from one place to another at a given moment.

In process-centric approaches both the invoice and the acceptance of the goods are associated with a process instance; therefore, ensuring that a process instance has all of the necessary elements to be able to proceed to the next step is natural to the model. Advanced BSO systems provide the semantics to explicitly model these situations. These semantics need to include the following:

- **Synchronous subprocess calls.** The calling process waits for the termination of the instance that it creates in the subprocess.

- **Asynchronous subprocess calls.** The calling process continues to the next activity as soon as it has called the subprocess.

- **Process termination wait.** This activity waits for the termination of a previous asynchronous process call. The combination of this and the above allow the calling process to perform a number of activities before synchronizing with the end of the asynchronous call. Where there is only an asynchronous call without any termination wait in a process is like a split or a fire-and-forget situation.

- **Process notification**. Any process may need to notify another process of an event to synchronize with it.

- **Process notification wait**. Any process may need to be listening for events from other processes or applications to synchronize with them.

These advanced semantics allow for processes to perform complex and long transactions in a perfectly synchronized way.

For example, let's suppose that, in a purchasing orchestration, we have the following activities:

1. Invoke asynchronous subprocess by sending a PO.
2. Prepare warehouse for delivery.
3. Wait for shipping manifest of the goods.
4. Accept adequate goods; if finished continue, otherwise go to 2.
5. Notify acceptance of goods.
6. Reserve funds.
7. Wait termination of the subprocess bearing the invoice.
8. Pay invoice.

These activities clearly illustrate how the calling process makes optimal use of time, ensuring the correct synchronization of steps in the transaction. Between each touch point between the parent process and the called subprocess, the parent is free to perform other productive activities, but it will not continue beyond the points of synchronization.

8.3.4.3 Interruption Handling

Advanced BSOL must also support at least three different types of preemptive process interruptions.

Preemptive process interruptions are those that take priority over the process in controlling the interrupted instance. The three types are:

1. interruptions thrown by invoked services or the process engine itself – for example, out of memory, connection failed, instance timeout;
2. interruptions due to notifications from external systems or processes – for example, system failure in plant, bank holiday declared in Argentina, name change in a partner company;
3. interruptions produced manually by a supervisor – for example, a customer asks to increment an order 10 percent, a supervisor wants to expedite a certain transaction, a CEO wants to freeze all transactions with a given company.

Robust interruption handling must support recursive nesting. If, for example, a process throws an interruption due to the lack of availability of an entry in a translation table and – as this interruption is being handled – the underlying database gets disconnected and the system throws another interruption, the process engine needs to maintain the state of all interruptions to be able to resume at the point of each interruption as the issues are resolved.

It is impossible to overstress the importance of this feature. One of the main reasons that process models are often unsuccessful is because they attempt to reflect 100 percent of the cases within the mainstream process logic. This is impossible.

It's important to be able to design and implement processes for Pareto's law: Build the 20 percent of the rules that support 80 percent of the cases and implement the remaining 20 percent as interruptions or exceptions. Having nested interruption-handling capability helps ensure the consistency of the overall system.

8.3.4.4 Process Monitoring

Business processes provide essential and often mission-critical business services. The optimal execution of business processes is important not only to improve the efficiency of the organization but also for legal purposes such as meeting service-line agreements.

Monitoring is often associated with monitoring system-level data such as the number of threads and server uptime. Although those data are very critical for the system managers to keep the systems going, they are Greek to the business managers. The business managers need to see the data about the performance of the business-level activities. Because the business processes generally represent the business steps required to fulfill business obligations, monitoring the performance of the activities would usually make the most difficult-to-please business managers smile.

Let us consider an example. In Figure of 8.1, we described a business process in which we placed order with a supplier for parts. The activity is completed only when the part order has been accepted. Assume that the supplier is contractually obligated to accept the order within 15 minutes. This means that, if the activity took longer than 15 minutes to complete, it would most probably mean that the supplier was not meeting its legal obligations.

The business managers should define the granularity of the monitoring because the activity-level monitoring may not be enough for all managers. For example, a process owner will be very interested in performance of each individual activity. However, recall dynamic participants from our previous discussions. A manager overseeing a relationship with a particular business partner will be more interested in the performance of only those activities that interact with particular target services. At the same time, a manager responsible for the manufacturing process is interested in the overall performance of the parts ordering activity as a whole because it affects his manufacturing schedule.

The problem of monitoring can actually be broken down into various parts. First, the BSO engine has to provide necessary instrumentation to capture the metrics. It may capture these metrics at the finest level of granularity based on method calls, keeping track of not just synchronous calls but also of asynchronous request/reply invocations. Once these fine-grained data have been collected, they can be aggregated and transformed according to different monitoring policies. A digital dashboard can then be used to configure the particular view that an individual user might wish to see. The BSO should then allow the user to define the kind of aggregation or transformation to be performed on that service in order to view it properly. Of course, these metric data have to be persisted also because they may actually have legal significance.

8.4 PREDEFINED SIGNALS

In RPC-style computing, when a remote method is invoked, the invoking application waits for the method invocation to finish. When the invocation returns, the return results are available on the call stack.

However, in most interenterprise systems belonging to the business partners use asynchronous messaging. Most of these systems follow interaction protocols such as RosettaNet, where a request is dispatched to a remote business service asynchronously. The business service performs initial validation of the request and then accepts it for processing. The acceptance of the request is acknowledged by sending an asynchronous acknowledgment signal back. Later, within the contracted time period, the remote business service processes the result and sends the response message. In this scenario, the first signal did not have any business semantics or data with it. Its sole purpose was to communicate an acknowledgment event between the two services.

The following signals can be predefined:

- **Receipt acknowledgment.** This signal acknowledges the receipt of a business request. In the business sense, this signal accomplishes two objectives. First, it informs the sender that the request has been received. Second, it provides an indisputable proof of having received the request – nonrepudiation of the message receipt.

- **Acceptance acknowledgment.** Similar in nature to receipt acknowledgment, this signal communicates the acceptance of the request. The exact syntax of the event could depend on the specific application. Generally speaking, it means that the request has been validated and processing of the request will now begin.

- **Exception signal.** This signal communicates an error condition.

8.5 WORKFLOW

An automated business process usually automates business activities by orchestrating the work performed by various business applications. Most of the time, this is done with a view toward removing the human intervention involved in fulfilling the business process. After all, in the absence of such a business process, the humans would interact with various systems and accomplish the task.

However, this is not always desirable and, in some cases, is simply impossible. Sometimes you want to retain the "control" and "authorization" responsibilities in the hands of human "thinking devices." For example, if an assembled product has to be inspected by a person, then the business process has to support that. Workflow is distinguished here from the normal automated business process, as an automated business process that allows human intervention in executing the business process.

We introduce some essential concepts that are related to workflow.

8.5.1 Task Lists

Most workflow systems work by creating task lists. Task lists are created and work items are placed on the task lists. This is sort of the way humans perform work also.

Humans assume various roles in an organization and the tasks that they can/should perform depend upon what roles they have. For example, an inspector may have the role of an inspector in an order fulfillment process. The same person may also have the role of a supervisor in a human resources system. In the end, it is his or her role in a particular business process that determines what part he or she plays.

There are various kinds of tasks. Some may be *exclusive tasks*. In exclusive tasks, a person holds a role. Only that person may perform that task and no one can substitute for that person, unless properly authorized. For example, John Doe may be the only person in the corporation to make press releases. The task to make a new press release shows up in his task list and cannot be performed by another. Some are *shared tasks*. In shared tasks, the task may be performed by anyone in the group. For example, there may be five inspectors in a group. Any inspector who is not busy may inspect the next available product. When one of the inspectors starts working on a task from a shared list, that task is removed from the shared list and placed in his personal task list.

Tasks may also have due dates associated with them and there may be an escalation process associated with them. For example, an inspector may be required to inspect a product within eight hours. If the task remains on the task list for more than eight hours, then a supervisor may be alerted.

8.5.2 Work Portal

In workflow systems, humans interact with the BSO software. This interaction may involve many things. A human may actually be able to invoke a business process, thus creating a new process instance. A human may look at tasks in his/her task list.

A work portal provides the interface to the process for human interaction with. It provides all visual metaphors for all the interactions. Examples of some of the activities are as follows:

- A human may be able to start instances of business processes. A customer service representative may be able to take orders for a product over the phone and then start an instance of the order fulfillment business process through the work portal.
- Human parties involved in a business process may use the work portal to perform their tasks in the business process.
- A supervisor/administrative may be able to search for the status of business processes to see where individual business processes are.
- Business managers may use the portal to check the performance of the business processes to identify the bottlenecks in them.

8.6 SUMMARY

As mentioned earlier, many XML-based languages have been developed as part of various industry efforts. Additionally, there are many BSO products that have developed their own proprietary XML-based process definition languages. The fundamental concepts that these languages have to be able to express and understand are pretty much the same. However, they do differ in the advanced features that they support.

Developers actually never write the BSOL themselves. The language is really meant to be produced and consumed by process modeling and process execution engines. So, why do we need to have standard BSOL. Actually, the real need for standard BSOL is so that BSO models can be exchanged by different BSO engines. Having a standard BSOL allows developers to combine the best modeling tools with the best execution engines or even have multiple execution engines configured and working together to execute business processes.

CHAPTER 9

Integrating Human Services

9.1 INTRODUCTION

An objective of business services orchestration (BSO) is to remove or minimize human intervention that is not justified by business considerations. This is driven by the motivation to reduce swivel-chair operation, thereby reducing latency between activities, and to minimize errors. However, human intervention is sometimes extremely necessary. For example, let us consider a scenario in which a procurement request is entered into the system. Because of legal ramifications and internal policies, a human has to approve and digitally sign the request. Because we view everything in the service-oriented architecture as a first-class service, we view human participation as a service that is provided by people, similar to the service provided by a software application.

BSO sees human participation in a process as a service. This view of human services is germane to true BSO. It's not capricious. The reason for this level of abstraction is that the ultimate goal of any BSO implementation is to replace routine, repeatable services from people with services from applications that automate them. When human participation in a process is treated by the process as a service invocation, it becomes transparent to the process whether the service is from a human or from an application. In fact, it is always from a human through an application anyway.

The standard application component of a BSO suite that is used to invoke services from people is the work portal. In some cases the nature of the service being invoked requires other presentations that are more specific to what the person needs to do. These presentations can be regarded as extensions to the work portal.

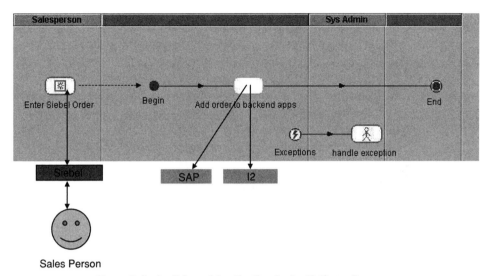

FIGURE **9.1. An External Application Instantiating a Process.**

In BSO, services from people can also (often) be *explicitly* invoked from existing applications within a process context. This makes the orchestration aware that a certain human activity has been performed, as opposed to the service having invoked implicitly as traditional integration does. This type of functionality is illustrated in Figure 9.1.

As can be seen above, the salesperson will have an entry in his or her work portal that invokes a Siebel function that allows the salesperson to enter an order. When the salesperson indicates that the service is complete, a process is instantiated that proceeds to automatically put the order in SAP and I2. In that same process the system administrator is called upon to manage exceptions, such as a disconnected database management system or the lack of an entry in a translation table.

The advantage of having this explicit invocation capability is that the orchestration engine then "knows" when a certain transaction has been initiated by a person. There is no need to resort to adding triggers in database or to initiate interval-based polling into an API to know if something has been added, changed, or deleted.

Something similar happens when it's possible to invoke a function from an external application within the process, as in Figure 9.2.

In this case the process waits for a message that indicates that the invoice has been created in SAP. The invoice is automatically put into Siebel and then the process invokes a Siebel component that allows the salesperson to approve the invoice. The approved invoice then goes into SAP and I2. As can easily be seen,

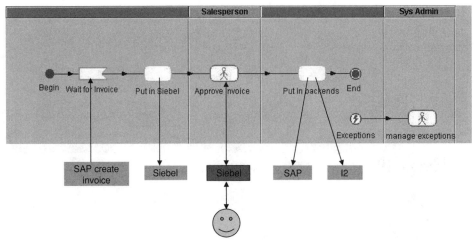

FIGURE 9.2. Invoking a Human Service from Within a Process.

this capability of intermingling human services within a process solves one of the greatest nightmares of integration: the ability to synchronize events from different sources (people and systems).

Obviously, in the case in which the granularity of the underlying system makes it impossible for the process to invoke a single function such as those depicted above, it becomes necessary to create what we have called work portal extensions or visual business objects (VBOs), which were introduced in Chapter 3. We will go into more detail on these objects further on in this chapter. If Siebel did not allow access to the invoice approval function independently, then the process in Figure 9.2 would look more like the one depicted in Figure 9.3.

Figure 9.3 illustrates how the process is simplified by using a VBO, and how the process plus the VBO are independent of the back-end systems, meaning that if they change, there would be no change in the process or the VBO.

Most of the time, customers want to make the orchestrations back-end independent or to simplify the user interface to the back-end systems. However, customers often prefer to build a more complicated, hardwired construct to avoid having to retrain users in the new interfaces. BSO can handle both situations at a much higher level of abstraction. Current integration approaches, on the other hand, are forced to build interval-based polling mechanisms into the databases of the underlying systems or create triggers that spawn events to trigger work to be done by the system. Obviously, if it's the only acceptable way to do things (which up until now has never happened), BSO, too, can easily set up polling mechanisms and passive listeners and do the same thing that current approaches are *forced to do*.

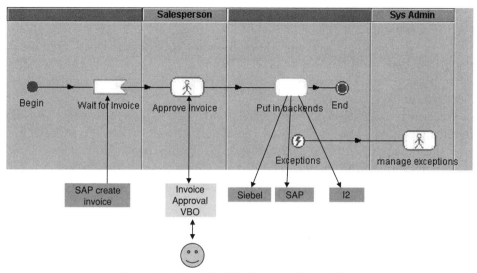

FIGURE 9.3. Front-End Applications Using VBOs.

9.2 THE "PARTITURE" OR WORK PORTAL

Partiture, in French, means the booklet that holds the pentagrams with the keys and notes that a specific member of the orchestra needs to play. The work portal is similar to a partiture because it holds the specific processes, activities, and work instances that prompt a human participant to deliver adequate services according to the roles he or she was assigned.

The difference between a work portal and an information portal (or the so-called enterprise portals) is that the work portal dynamically prompts the participant for the work that he or she needs to perform according to the rules of the orchestrations and the status of the instances thereof. Although work portals also present a menu of optional functions that the participant may perform, its main function is to invoke work from the participant on the things that need to be done at that specific moment.

Enterprise portals can be seen as dynamic windows to the *information* that a person needs to see and a static menu of the *functions* that that person may perform according to the user type or group. On the other hand, a work portal is a window into the current instances of work that a person needs to perform according to his or her roles in the company's orchestrations. These work lists or "to-do" lists change every moment as they are processed and transition from one activity to another. As the person clicks on one or more to-do items, the orchestration engine brings up the corresponding application or work portal extension that may be needed to fulfill the service being invoked.

The work portal behaves more like an e-mail application than a traditional portal. The only substantial difference is that in a work portal, once the work is done, it automatically disappears, whereas in e-mail, the person using it needs to delete the entry.

Precisely because of this similarity, we would like to extend the concept of work portal to include e-mail systems as a possible implementation. We will discuss why this is important in the next two sections in this chapter. In any case, be it a work portal native to the BSO platform suite or an e-mail application, it must have the following characteristics to be useful as the interface to services from people:

- They must be sensitive to the participant's roles, presenting only those items of work that correspond to them.
- For convenience, there should be only be one work portal that centralizes all of the work instances from every process (cross-platform and cross-applications) in a single place.
- Their work lists must be dynamic, adding instances in real time as they are ready for the services to be performed by the user who receives them.
- They must be able to interact with their extensions and/or applications so that the participant does not need to manually invoke the corresponding functions.
- They must have information on the history of the instance so that the participant knows what has happened to it before it reaches his or her in-box.
- They must be configurable to the language and preferences of the participant by the participant.
- They must support attachments, preferably using MIME encoding to facilitate the invocation of the appropriate applications.
- They must provide search capabilities for a participant with the adequate privileges to be able to find an instance in whatever process or activity it occurs.
- They must provide, at a bare minimum, a description of the item, the time and date when it arrived into the in-box, its priority, and if it's available to be processed or blocked by another participant.

BSO is usually structured around activities where each activity performs several tasks. So, it is natural then that the human participation in a BSO also is modeled as tasks. This is similar to the way we work anyway. We generally have our list of things to do that define the work that we perform during the day. Task lists are electronic to-do lists that engage the humans in the process. There are some important characteristics of task lists that need to be understood:

- Tasks are usually associated with a role in the BSO. For example, in Figures 9.2 and 9.3, the task to approve an invoice is with the role `Salesperson`.
- Generally, tasks are shared with all different people in a particular role. When one person among a group of people in the same role takes responsibility for a task, it is removed from the shared list. For example, there is a group of customer support representatives and there is a call queue. When one customer support representative becomes available and takes a call from the queue, that call is then removed from that queue. However, there are situations in which tasks need to be performed by a specified number of people. For example, to ensure better quality and to avoid oversights, a parts manufacturer may require at least two inspectors to inspect each part. In this case, when the first inspector starts inspecting the part, that part may still be available for others to inspect.
- In addition to the shared-task lists, there are also individual-task lists. Tasks may require some time to complete. When an individual takes responsibility for a task, it becomes part of that person's private task list. The private task lists can be modified only by that person or a designated supervisor with proper authority. However, while a task is in an individual's private task list, it may still be visible, with appropriate status, in the shared-task list so that others can see its status.
- Many times, there is an escalation process also. This is sometimes to ensure that the work is not stopped for any reason. For example, if an employee calls in sick, and this person was working on some critical tasks, the supervisor may be able to either release them back to the shared-task list for reassignment or reassign the tasks to specific individuals.
- Tasks may have due dates associated with them. This may not always be necessary but sometimes it is needed. Due dates are especially useful when service level agreements (SLA) requirements mandate some turnaround time for a task.
- Associated with the due date may be an escalation process for tasks. If a task is not completed by its due date, an alert may be sent to the designated supervisor, who may either remind the individual to complete task or reassign it to someone else.

Work portals are similar to the work-list handlers of workflow products. The greatest difference is that most work-list handlers tend to be engine-centric, whereas work portals are connectionless and Web-centric. Work portals suppose that they are working with a federation of clusters of process engines and have no knowledge of the physical engines that are providing the work lists. Work portals are only aware of the user. The cluster of process engines is usually managed by the cluster manager, which can always map requests to the physical engine in the cluster based on the userID. This characteristic makes work portals easy to implement as linearly scalable and fault tolerant.

There are many advantages to imagining orchestrations as functioning exclusively on-line, but in the real world, things are not that simple. Processes often need services from people who are in situations where they cannot be on-line. People also often prefer to work off-line and ship work in batches. An example of this would be a salesperson who is calling on a customer and entering data into a "call report form." This salesperson will probably deem it unacceptable to ask the customer for an Internet connection and will probably perfect the content of the form on the airplane during the return trip.

Therefore, services from people, as well as services from applications, need to be able to accessible on-line or off-line.

9.2.1 On-Line

On-line work portals are those that are continuously connected to the back-end process engines. These portals are typically used in an environment where connections to the process engines are constantly available and the amount of data that is required to perform the activities is high.

On-line work portals can be implemented as thin clients or as Web applications. The advantages of thin clients are the following:

- They can be used as proxies for client-side applications that need to be integrated.
- They allow for more sophisticated implementations of work portal extensions.
- They usually perform better.
- They can be a vehicle for callbacks to the process engines.

The advantages of Web applications are:

- They don't need installation or maintenance.
- They work off of the application (Web browser) that people use most after their e-mail client.
- They easily support a variety of media.
- They require less user training.

In any case, on-line work portals are the only ones that support a workable single-queue-per-role algorithm.

A single queue per role works exactly like check-in at the airport. There is a single queue and the next available representative calls the first person in the queue. This algorithm has proven to be more efficient than creating a queue for each available representative and expecting intelligent customers to balance them. The reason it works better is because nobody can predict in an attendant-specific queue whether a certain person is going to have a complicated check-in, creating greater wait time for everyone in it. A single queue balances itself out across all the available attendants, obtaining the minimum average wait time for everyone.

In an on-line work portal, everyone in a role sees all the instances available to that role. As any given participant starts processing any instance, it ceases to be available for the rest. Many times, this algorithm alone produces enough productivity gain to justify a BSO project.

As we said before, on-line work portals work with virtual connections with a cluster of process engines rather than a physical and dedicated connection to a process engine. This approach is highly scalable and adequate for Web-based work portals. The most important reason for this type of approach is that it allows implementation of totally transparent failover capabilities. Since the work portal is connected to a cluster through virtual connections, if an engine ceases to function, the work portal can receive its information from any other available engine in the cluster.

These on-line work portals can also reconfigure themselves on-the-fly for any language and portal style, depending on parameters that are determined by the user. This capability in itself makes work portals and their extensions very valuable front ends for more rigid applications.

9.2.2 Off-Line

Off-line work portals are not always connected to the back-end process engines. They usually have the ability to connect to the back-end engines, retrieve their work items, and then disconnect. The user can then work in the portal while it is disconnected. As the user completes his or her work, the work is queued. Next time, when the portal is connected to the back-end engine, the queued work is sent over to the engine.

The ideal off-line work portal is an e-mail client. Granted, during the time it pops the server or sends messages it needs to be on-line. If using IMAP it needs to be on-line more than if using POP. Web-based e-mail needs to be on-line to be usable. Therefore, ubiquitous e-mail clients – using a POP protocol – are the ideal off-line work portal. People can connect during the time it takes to download the mail, disconnect, work off-line and when finished, connect again when possible, and in minutes send the work that was done off-line back to the orchestration. For the work to be performed off-line, the work portal extensions also need to be able to work off-line, therefore these extensions cannot be implemented as Web pages.

As we will see in the next section, off-line work portals are a key to incorporating human services from small-sized companies that do not have an expensive IT infrastructure. They also allow people to do their work even when they do not have the ability to connect to the network, for example, in an airplane.

Some examples of who might need to work off-line are:

- small businesses with dial-up connections,
- field engineers or salespeople,
- freelance professionals,
- anyone who uses a PDA or a cellular telephone for organizing work,
- logistics workers,
- warehouse workers,
- retail tellers.

To provide enough coverage for the BSO paradigm to be able to sustain those services from people is a part of any orchestration, and so, off-line service management capabilities are a must.

9.3 WORK PORTAL EXTENSIONS OR PRESENTATION COMPONENTS

Work portals can usually prompt a participant for simple inputs. When the amount of data to be entered goes beyond simple and flat inputs, Web portal extensions or presentation components are needed. These presentation components are what we call VBOs.

In most cases VBOs are used to provide a form that allows the participant to provide values for intelligent business objects (IBOs) or is used to display their content. This is why, in general, VBOs use IBOs as data sources and/or targets. Hence, a VBO can be thought of as an extension to IBO, which adds a visual interface to the IBO. Figure 9.4 shows how IBO and the VBO are related to each other. Since a VBO is an extension to an IBO, it can be serialized into an interpretable XML object (IXO), as described in detail in Chapter 6. IXOs are further discussed in the next section.

Any given IBO can have an infinite number of associated VBOs. They may be different for different roles, or different activities of the same role, according to the client device that will host them, depending on the business-rule-related restrictions or validations to be performed, etc. The number of presentations possible

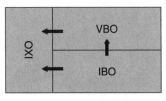

FIGURE 9.4. IBO/VBO/IXO.

```
<presentation
     id="mainInfo"
     reference="Customer"
     width="413" height="181">
     <table border="false"
          cellpadding="2"
          cellspacing="2">
          <row>
               <cell hexpand="3"
                    vexpand="1"
                    fontface="BOLD"
                    fontsize="16"
                    alignment="left"
                    valignment="center">
                    <label id="customerLabel">

                         <value>
                              Customer information

                         </value>
                    </label>
               </cell>
          </row>
          <row>
               <cell hexpand="1"
                    vexpand="1"
                    fontface="BOLD"
                    fontsize="0"
                    alignment="left"
                    valignment="center">
                    <label id="idLabel">

                         <value>
                              ID:

                         </value>
                    </label>
               </cell>
          ............
```

FIGURE **9.5. Implementation of a Presentation in XML.**

for the same data set is very large. For example, an IBO that contains a pick-list
can be shown as a pick-list, a bill of materials, a shipping manifest, and others.
At the same time, there may be a presentation that is read-only, another that doesn't
show certain fields or blocks them from editing, and yet another that allows full
privileges to the user. Simultaneously, there may be forms for a Nextel handset, a
Palm Pilot, a PC, or Linux PDA.

Figure 9.5 shows a possible XML implementation of these presentations. This
implementation is the standard presentation format for Fuego's Xobjects, which
were summarily discussed in Chapter 6. The figure represents the XML implementation of one of the possible presentations for bsoCustomer objects.

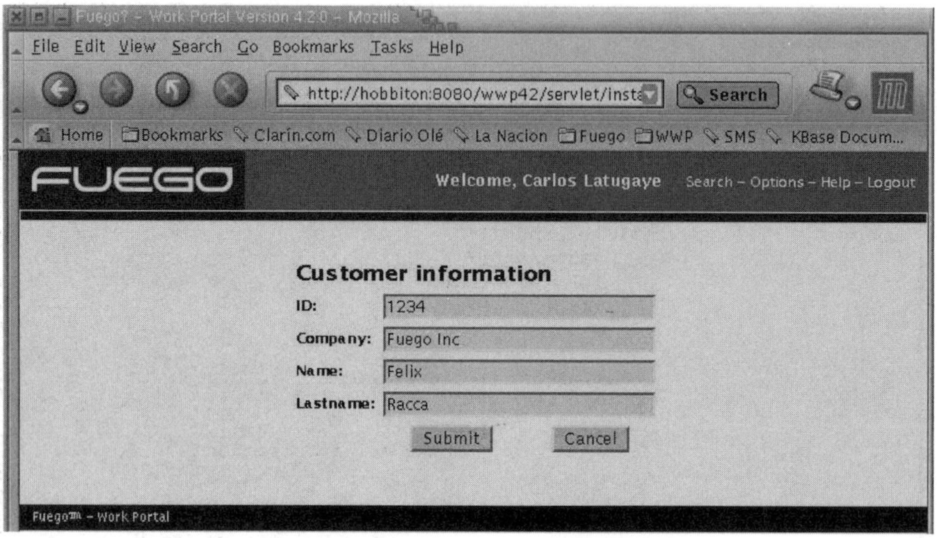

FIGURE 9.6. Rendering of a VBO in Swing.

In this implementation, the frame in the output device is seen as a table that can support rows of a certain width and cells within those rows. Each cell can be a visible label, a graphical object, a widget, or a value.

The objective of these lightweight presentations is to be able to input complex data structures through a representation that is compatible with HTML and at the same time usable by lightweight client-side plug-ins. In Figure 9.6, we show a rendering of one of these presentations in Java's Swing graphical user interface.

Fuego's Xobjects are context sensitive, meaning that if the host of the presentation is a Web-based work portal, it will display the presentation in HTML. If it is a thin client, the work portal will display it as Swing; if it is a remote plug-in, it will also be displayed as Swing.

This capability makes it very easy for developers to create VBOs that are independent of the client in which they will be rendered.

Figure 9.5 shows that a VBO, such as Fuego's Xobject presentations, can deliver a reasonable interface through an extremely lightweight implementation.

9.4 IXOs

Kip Martin from the Metagroup illustrated one of the most important problems that e-business solutions need to solve to become viable.

> Beyond enabling large Tier 1 suppliers to participate in supply-side e-business solutions, the more significant challenge will be enabling electronic interactions with small and

medium-sized enterprises (SMEs). For many Global 2000 organizations, SMEs may represent only 20% of total enterprise spend, but can account for 80% of buying transactions. Buying organizations have a range of options for enabling electronic interaction with suppliers, with the more complex and technically sophisticated techniques becoming increasingly viable for SMEs through 2007.

Traditional B2B integration options are unviable because of their cost and complexity.

Web-based forms interfaces are costly because they require the buyer to dimension the Web infrastructure for a large number of users. On the small supplier side, this approach becomes impractical because of the following reasons:

- Extracting data from or putting data into Web pages automatically requires Web-scraping mechanisms that are neither easy to use nor reliable.
- Users need to be on-line to operate manually or automatically.
- Users, if they work with more than one customer, need to remember the user name and password of each Web site with which they will interact and undertake swivel-chair operations.
- To make it easier to participate in a process, users need to be notified by e-mail that there's a new document on a certain Web site (typically done by providing a link to it). Anyone who has utilized this method knows that it is cumbersome and slow.
- If there is any internal process, for example, escalation, to a supervisor, it becomes even more cumbersome

Web Services will, without any doubt, be an adequate alternative for the more sophisticated of the mid-sized enterprises. Small suppliers that are equipped with a desktop computer and a dial-up Internet connection, but don't have the IT infrastructure required to be able to integrate Web services to their systems (if they happen to have any) will not benefit from this approach.

To address the need to integrate these small enterprises, the ultimate idea is to produce IXOs.

IXOs are interpreted by a generic plug-in on the client side. This means that the object class need not be known by the recipient before receiving the object. In essence the class definition is self-contained in the object, allowing the recipient to avoid downloading a DTD or an XML Schema and the parser to be able to understand the data content of the object.

Furthermore, an IXO contains not only data but also executable methods IBOs, and one or more presentation VBOs (forms to be able to interact with the object). Therefore, an IXO can be delivered to a user through any valid XML transport mechanism, for example, e-mail, XML/SOAP, FTP, or any messaging system.

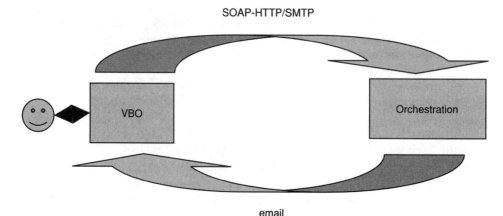

SOAP-HTTP/SMTP

email

FIGURE 9.7. Usage of VBO.

Once the IXO is resident on the recipient's machine, it can be executed by the user or the process that received it. IXOs could have different methods for execution in different ways:

- `RunPresentation` presents the VBO and allows the user to fill it in or view it.
- `Print` allows the user to obtain a hard copy of the form.
- `Open` allows a bridge to interact with the object as if it were a component or an API (e.g., a COM to Java bridge would allow a Visual Basic programmer to see the IXO as a COM component).
- `Submit` offers the IXO to the next recipient in the IXO's path of recipients (list of e-mail addresses).
- `RunTransformation`, although a risky capability and not provided by any IXOs today, may be a required feature in the future. It allows the IXO to run a prebuilt transformation that would either instantiate it or persist it from or to an existing system.

In the simple case where the user runs the presentation, he or she can press the submit button (which runs the submit method) when finished, and the IXO will route itself to wherever it should go according to its internal rules (typically back to the sender). The object also knows how to bring up other IXOs and modify or delete them.

Figure 9.7 shows one scenario that describes the usage of VBO. In this scenario, the orchestration sends the VBO in IXO form to the remote user as an attachment to an e-mail. When the user receives this e-mail, he detaches the attachment from the e-mail and double clicks on the attachment. This opens the interpreter for the IXO. As the IXO is turned into a VBO, the user interface specified in the VBO is re-created. The user interacts with the user interface (probably form-based) and hits the send button. This can send an SOAP message back to the BSO. This message SOAP can be sent either through an HTTP connection or over a simple mail transfer protocol (SMTP) connection.

9.4.1 An Imaginary Usage Example

Let us now further explain the interaction of VBOs by considering an imaginary, but almost real, example of John Parker.

John Parker has a family business that molds and cooks ceramics for spark-plug manufacturers. He receives orders from the manufacturers, returns a delivery plan, and, upon acceptance of the delivery plan, he proceeds to package and ship the ceramics according to it. For shipping, he uses UPS and FedEx and he buys packaging material from several different companies. After an order is fulfilled, he proceeds to calculate and fax an invoice to each manufacturer according to their purchasing rules.

John Parker has two PCs. In one, he runs Quick Books. The other one he uses for e-mail and Web browsing over a dialup connection.

One of the major spark-plug manufacturers once asked John to adopt their standard EDI strategy for receiving orders, responding with delivery plans, and sending invoices. Parker calculated the cost of setting up an EDI facility and determined that the investment and recurring costs of such an investment would put him out of business.

Another major spark-plug manufacturer shortly thereafter asked John to put in a spoke of a well-known B2B hub-and-spoke suite. Analyzing the license and maintenance cost plus the cost of developing the applications that would allow him to visualize and respond to the specific messages that he received, plus the fact that the first spark-plug provider had asked him for a different setup, John seriously thought that this e-business craze was going to put him out of business. He started making plans on how to resist this avalanche of irrational requests. He started talking to his peers and competitors about creating a common front against these potential impositions from the big companies.

Finally, John was approached by Web services mongers. They told him all about the benefits of exposing his offerings through Web services so that he would only have to do this once and all the customers, suppliers, and partners would use his exposed Web services. He got real excited until he realized that his infrastructure was lacking: he would have to upgrade to broadband, put in a firewall, install and maintain a Web server, manage security, and develop or buy the applications that support the Web services as well as develop and publish the Web services themselves.

IXOs are a solution for John. BSO platforms are expected to provide free plug-ins that can interpret IXOs and render them in either a browser or in some other application environment.

The spark-plug manufacturer approached John and told him to go to their Website, download the plug-in for his Outlook Express or Outlook e-mail systems and he will start receiving executable orders by e-mail. The orders actually arrive in the form of IXOs as e-mail attachments. When John double clicks on the attachments, the plug-in is executed that instantiates the VBO and renders it. All John has to do is fill in the forms that appear and submit them. It doesn't matter if he works on-line or off-line! With the order, they will send him a delivery form that he needs to fill in and an invoice calculator that automatically takes the data from the fulfilled orders, creates an invoice, allows him to print it, and, once approved by him is submitted for payment. The submit logic can either format a SOAP message over SMTP and put it in John's outbox or, if an Internet connection is already open, send a SOAP request over HTTP.

This requires no change in John's current infrastructure, no programming, and no maintenance. The best thing about this solution is that it's his customers, partners, and providers that can offer it to him without any extra cost for them and with a huge productivity benefit for their businesses.

John is now receiving a dynamic order management system by e-mail that caters to the requirements of the spark-plug manufacturers. As other spark-plug manufacturers catch on, they too start sending their forms to John, therefore receiving consistent data according to the needs of their processes. John has had to do nothing and is much more productive. John is happy and so are his customers.

As UPS and FedEx catch on to the idea, they send their shipping manifests by e-mail to John. John keeps these manifests in a folder and uses them every time he requires a delivery. John hits the print method to print the manifest for his records and the IXO manifest is sent to UPS and FedEx by e-mail so they don't need to enter the data by keyboard. John doesn't need to type it on a typewriter. Furthermore, they send him an invoice at the end of each month that John approves. John can authorize direct debits within the same form and submit it back to them, whereupon they proceed to send the debit authorization automatically to John's bank. UPS and FedEx have seen their productivity increase substantially.

The spark-plug manufacturer works with 200 small companies that supply it with parts and consumables. It used to send the orders by fax and receive paper delivery plans and invoices. Sometimes they were unreadable; sometimes the people who typed them into the system made mistakes. The manufacturer now has an order object, a delivery plan object, and a third-party invoice object that it maintains and that are common for all their 200 small companies. It's BSO environment that receives these orders, checks for security, acts as a soft firewall, and puts them into its back-end systems without any human intervention and without any data transformation maps. The spark-plug manufacturer has reduced its order-to-billing cycle by 50 percent, errors by 30 percent, and administrative costs by two dollars per transaction. It had invested in BSO to help integrate its back-end systems and got a free bonus.

A similar, but much more impressive story can be repeated for UPS and FedEx. John has now fulfilled his dream: he has bought a new boat.

9.4.2 IXOs from the Process Perspective

In the above example, there's a clear advantage to IXOs being able to work off-line as well as very clear scalability benefits. The spark-plug manufacturers don't have to create a huge, load-balanced Web server farm to support reasonable response time for their partners. IXOs, as explained earlier, are the ultimate peer-to-peer solution for process enactment. They require no maintenance on behalf of the users or the creators.

> IXOs are VBOs that use an XML representation of an IBO with methods implemented as executable scripts that are interpreted by the IXO plug-in.

Figures 9.8, 9.9, and 9.10 illustrate the power of combining the parametric subprocess capabilities of BSO with EDI, Web Services, and IXOs, covering the complete spectrum of the business community of a company.

In Figure 9.8, the n-split node forks into as many threads as suppliers to whom we decided to send the RFQ in the "select suppliers" activity. The way parametric subprocesses work is that, according to a parameter (e.g., the supplier organization ID), a different implementation of the subprocess will be called. These different implementations of the same subprocess are called variations. There are only three variations: EDI, Web Services, and IXOs in these examples. In Figure 9.8, we show how a subprocess that deals with IXOs would look. There's an activity that serializes and sends the IXO to the recipient company by e-mail and waits to receive a corresponding return e-mail. When that e-mail is back, the activity returns to the calling process.

In Figure 9.9, the subprocess will invoke a Web service using SOAP on the suppliers that offer them; the payload is the RFQ. In this case, we suppose that it goes into a sales orchestration at the supplier side. This sales orchestration does what it has to do and, when finished, invokes a Web Service from the subprocess, which notifies the wait node with a response to the RFQ.

It's not self-evident from the figure, but there needs to be a transformation between the format of the RFQ object that the sender uses and RFQ that is exposed by the Web service supplied by the receiver. The same thing needs to happen when the receiver invokes the Web service supplied by the sender. In the example, we have implemented these services as asynchronous because of the latency that we suppose will exist between receipt of the RFQ and issuance of the response.

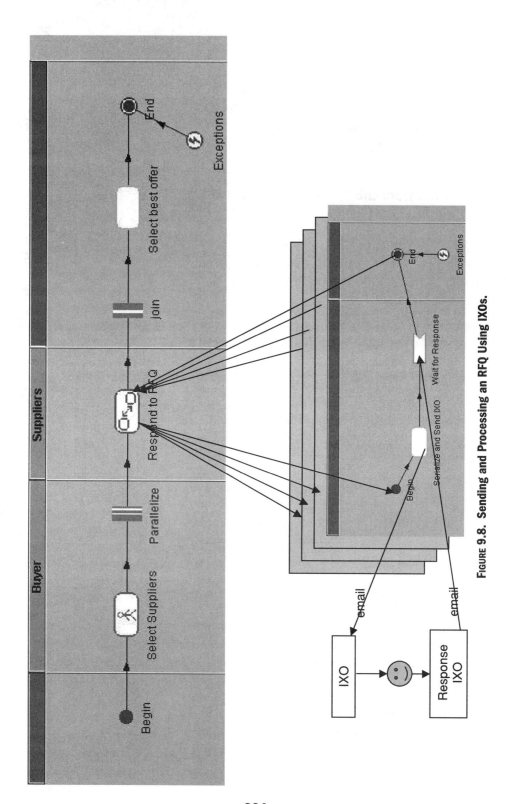

FIGURE 9.8. Sending and Processing an RFQ Using IXOs.

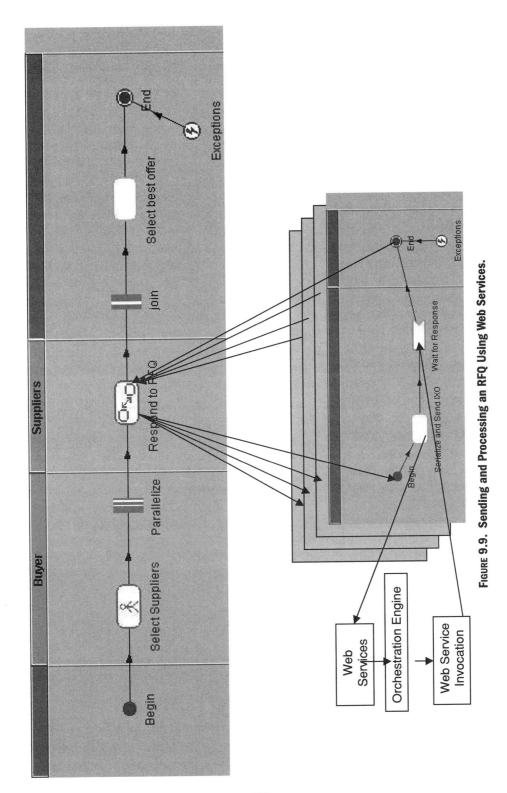

FIGURE 9.9. **Sending and Processing an RFQ Using Web Services.**

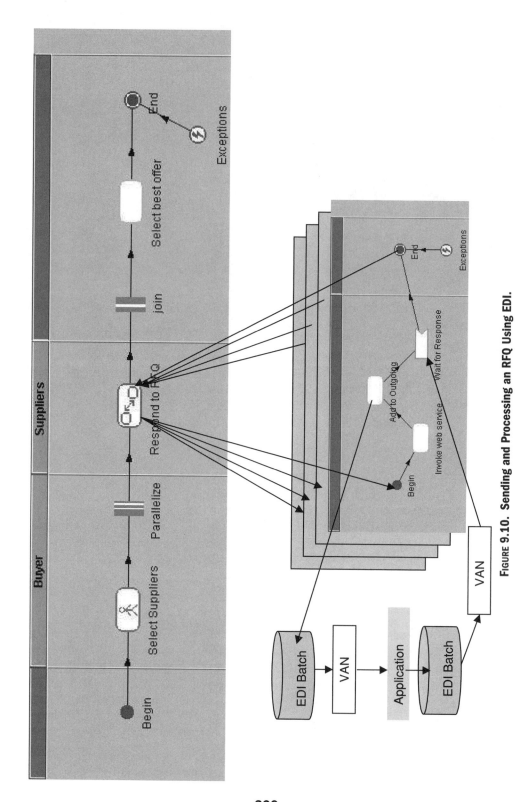

FIGURE 9.10. Sending and Processing an RFQ Using EDI.

In Figure 9.10, we illustrate an EDI subprocess implementation. Without any doubt, it is the most complicated of the three. The sender adds the RFQ to an outgoing batch, and then the batch is sent to the VAN. The VAN then routes the appropriate messages to the receiving application on the receiving side. The application creates an outgoing batch, the batch is then sent to the VAN, and the VAN routes the response appropriately. In both cases, there needs to be a transformation from internal to EDI and from EDI to internal on the receiving end, from internal to EDI on the receiving end, and then from EDI to internal on the original sender's end.

Index